U.S. MERCENARIES
AND THE
CONDOR LEGION

Titles in the Series

Airpower Reborn: The Strategic Concepts of John Warden and John Boyd

The Bridge to Airpower: Logistics Support for Royal Flying Corps Operations on the Western Front, 1914–18

Airpower Applied: U.S., NATO, and Israeli Combat Experience

The Origins of American Strategic Bombing Theory

Beyond the Beach: The Allied Air War against France

"The Man Who Took the Rap": Sir Robert Brooke-Popham and the Fall of Singapore

Flight Risk: The Coalition's Air Advisory Mission in Afghanistan, 2005–2015

Winning Armageddon: Curtis LeMay and Strategic Air Command, 1948–1957

Rear Admiral Herbert V. Wiley: A Career in Airships and Battleships

From Kites to Cold War: The Evolution of Manned Airborne Reconnaissance

Airpower over Gallipoli, 1915–1916

Selling Schweinfurt: Targeting, Assessment, and Marketing in the Air Campaign against German Industry

Airpower in the War against ISIS

To Rule the Skies: General Thomas S. Power and the Rise of Strategic Air Command in the Cold War

Rise of the War Machines: The Birth of Precision Bombing in World War II

At the Dawn of Airpower: The U.S. Army, Navy, and Marine Corps' Approach to the Military Airplane, 1907–1917

The Birth of British Airpower: Hugh Trenchard, World War I, and the Royal Air Force

The History of Military Aviation
Paul J. Springer, editor

This series is designed to explore previously ignored facets of the history of airpower. It includes a wide variety of disciplinary approaches, scholarly perspectives, and argumentative styles. Its fundamental goal is to analyze the past, present, and potential future utility of airpower and to enhance our understanding of the changing roles played by aerial assets in the formulation and execution of national military strategies. It encompasses the incredibly diverse roles played by airpower, which include but are not limited to efforts to achieve air superiority; strategic attack; intelligence, surveillance, and reconnaissance missions; airlift operations; close-air support; and more. Of course, airpower does not exist in a vacuum. There are myriad terrestrial support operations required to make airpower functional, and examinations of these missions is also a goal of this series.

In less than a century, airpower developed from flights measured in minutes to the ability to circumnavigate the globe without landing. Airpower has become the military tool of choice for rapid responses to enemy activity, the primary deterrent to aggression by peer competitors, and a key enabler to military missions on the land and sea. This series provides an opportunity to examine many of the key issues associated with its usage in the past and present, and to influence its development for the future.

U.S. MERCENARIES AND THE CONDOR LEGION

AIRPOWER IN THE SPANISH CIVIL WAR

CHRISTOPHER G. MARQUIS

NAVAL INSTITUTE PRESS
Annapolis, Maryland

Naval Institute Press
291 Wood Road
Annapolis, MD 21402

© 2025 by Christopher G. Marquis
All rights reserved. No part of this book may be reproduced or utilized in any form or by any means, electronic or mechanical, including photocopying and recording, or by any information storage and retrieval system, without permission in writing from the publisher.

The Scripture quotations contained herein are from the *New Revised Standard Version Bible*, copyright © 1989, by the Division of Christian Education of the National Council of the Churches of Christ in the U.S.A. Used by permission. All rights reserved.

Library of Congress Cataloging-in-Publication Data

Names: Marquis, Christopher G., author
Title: U.S. mercenaries and the Condor Legion : airpower in the Spanish Civil War / Christopher G. Marquis.
Description: Annapolis, Maryland : Naval Institute Press, [2025] | Series: The history of military aviation | Includes bibliographical references and index.
Identifiers: LCCN 2025026223 (print) | LCCN 2025026224 (ebook) | ISBN 9781682479735 hardback | ISBN 9781682479759 ebook
Subjects: LCSH: Germany. Luftwaffe. Legión Cóndor | Air power—History—20th century | Mercenary troops—Spain—History—20th century | Spain—History—Civil War, 1936–1939—Aerial operations | Spain—History—Civil War, 1936–1939—Participation, American
Classification: LCC DP269.4 .M36 2025 (print) | LCC DP269.4 (ebook)
LC record available at https://lccn.loc.gov/2025026223
LC ebook record available at https://lccn.loc.gov/2025026224

♾ Print editions meet the requirements of ANSI/NISO z39.48–1992 (Permanence of Paper).
Printed in the United States of America.

9 8 7 6 5 4 3 2 1

Maps created by Chris Robinson.

CONTENTS

List of Illustrations ix
Preface xi
Acknowledgments xiii

Introduction 1
Chapter 1. Airpower 3
Chapter 2. Sorties 27
Chapter 3. Airlift 51
Chapter 4. Counterair 76
Chapter 5. Interdiction 102
Chapter 6. Close Air Support 126
Chapter 7. Aerial Bombing 151
Chapter 8. Aircraft Technology 178
Chapter 9. Air Superiority 204
Chapter 10. After-Action Report 227

Notes 253
Bibliography 289
Index 303

ILLUSTRATIONS

PHOTOGRAPHS

1. First flight	7
2. Billy Mitchell's court-martial	17
3. Townsend Griffiss' West Point photo	31
4. Junkers Ju 52	60
5. Francisco Franco at Emilio Mola's funeral	133
6. Junkers Ju 87 "Stuka"	161
7. Bebe Daniels and Henry H. Arnold	215
8. Madrid flyover, 1939	228
9. Albert Baumler, 1943	245

MAPS

1. Nationalist-Republican Territory, July 1936	49
2. Nationalist-Republican Territory, March 1937	100
3. Nationalist-Republican Territory, January 1938	159
4. Nationalist-Republican Territory, July 1938	176
5. Nationalist-Republican Territory, March 1939	225

TABLES

1. Pursuit aircraft employed in Spain, 1936	73
2. Bomber aircraft employed in Spain, 1936	75
3. Naval aircraft employed in Spain during the civil war	187
4. Bomber aircraft employed in Spain, 1937–39	190
5. Pursuit and attack aircraft employed in Spain, 1937–39	193

PREFACE

Generally speaking, this book is about the Spanish Civil War. More specifically, it is about air operations during the Spanish Civil War. In particular, it is about American observations of air operations during the Spanish Civil War. It is thus structured with Chapters 1 and 10 placing the conflict in the context of the early development of American airpower, from the first flight of the Wright Brothers to the build-up of the U.S. Army Air Forces on the eve of the ambush on Pearl Harbor.

Chapters 2 through 4 tell the narrative of the Spanish Civil War from the attempted Nationalist coup in July 1936 to the Battle of Guadalajara in March 1937. Chapter 5 breaks the narrative to discuss the role of American pilots in the service of the Spanish Republican government, partially adapted from a paper I had written while at Auburn University. Chapters 6 and 7 resume the narrative of the war, from the Northern Campaign to the March to the Sea, in April 1938. Chapter 8 addresses the development of aerial technology during the war, mostly adapted from work conducted at Auburn. Chapter 9 concludes the narrative of the war, with the fall of Barcelona, Madrid, and Valencia.

Chapter 10, along with covering the development of U.S. airpower before the nation's entry into the Second World War, also considers lessons from the conflict and the fates of several of the characters. One character featured prominently in this work is Townsend Griffiss, an American pilot and military attaché, after whom Griffiss Air Force Base in Rome, New York, was named. His fate is a fitting conclusion to this history.

ACKNOWLEDGMENTS

I extend my gratitude to the following people for assistance with this project:

P. J. Springer, Department of Airpower, Air Command and Staff College (ACSC), Maxwell Air Force Base, Alabama, for his advice and guidance on my research and for his support in the publishing of my work.

Robert Mahoney, former Chair of the Department of Joint Warfighting, ACSC, for his mentorship and support.

Joel Bius, historian, for his encouragement and ready insight into the art of historical scholarship.

James Cortada, historian, for being willing to speak to me at length, and to offer advice, guidance, and insight on writing about the Spanish Civil War.

Other colleagues from my time at ACSC, who provided assistance and encouragement: Trevor Albertson, James Campbell, Michael Grumelli, James Forsyth, Charles Kamps, Robert Kerr, John Minney, Brian Price, John Terino, and Heather Venable.

Staff of the Air Force Historical Research Agency, who were helpful in the collection of primary source material at that location: Archangelo "Archie" DiFante, Maranda Gilmore, Daniel Haulman, Tammy Horton, and Forrest Marion.

Alexandria Aldridge, Air University Library, for her assistance with my research in the library's archives.

Sylvia Naylor and Rutha M. Beamon from the National Archives, College Park, Maryland, for their assistance in my research at that facility.

George Fuller, from the National Archives, St. Louis, Missouri, for his assistance in retrieving the records of Townsend Griffiss.

Christopher Robinson for the development of the maps found in this work.

Chris Brooks of the Abraham Lincoln Brigade Archives, and Sebastiaan Faber of Oberlin College, for reading copies of the original submission of my manuscript and offering their constructive recommendations.

Stephanie Attia Evans, for her in-depth and excellent copyediting of my manuscript.

From the Naval Institute Press:

Paul Merzlak, former Editorial Director, for taking on my project.

Pat Carlin, Senior Acquisitions Editor, for guiding me through the submittal and revisions of my manuscript.

Adam Kane, Director, for his leadership in the marketing and publishing of the book.

Ashley Baird, Senior Production Editor, for seeing the book through the final stages of production.

Elena Pelton, Publishing Assistant, for her efforts in marketing my book.

All other Naval Institute Press employees who contributed to the publication of this work.

My family:

My parents, Sydney and Jackie Marquis, and my in-laws, Ted and Joy Hill, for their unflagging support through the long years it took to complete this work.

My sons, Peter, Luke, Paul, and Matthew; and my daughter, Mary Joy, for their patience and love during the years of my studies, research, and writing.

My beautiful wife, Jenny, the love of my life. Throughout our marriage—and particularly during these past few years in which I have retired from the Air Force, started a new career in the aerospace industry, and written this book—she has been my rock. She has done a miraculous job raising and teaching our loving but spirited children and making our home a happy sanctuary from the stresses of life. Words cannot express my gratitude to her.

INTRODUCTION

Everything is very simple in War, but the simplest thing is difficult.
—CARL VON CLAUSEWITZ, ON WAR

This book makes four key assertions:
1. Airpower was a critical component in the Nationalist victory over the Republicans in the Spanish Civil War.
2. American observers, particularly military attachés located in Spain, drew conclusions regarding the use of airpower that would be relevant in the Second World War and beyond, even to the present time.
3. American airpower leaders, though they publicly dismissed or ignored these lessons, would subsequently adopt many of them.
4. The Spanish Civil War neither proved nor disproved the theory of strategic bombing, the dominant airpower theory of the time.

The four assertions above lead to the ultimate conclusion of this work: the Spanish Civil War proved airpower's importance as an independent force, even when it was not tethered to ground forces or let loose for strategic bombing. Its contributions came in many forms across a spectrum of functions, such as airlift, counterair, reconnaissance, and interdiction.

INTRODUCTION

July 17, 2026, will mark the ninetieth anniversary of the start of the Spanish Civil War, yet an examination of its history is still relevant to warfighters and military planners today. This history examines how relatively new technologies can be incorporated into military strategy. It also studies how lessons are learned, and it considers whether they are actually the correct lessons to learn. It is told from an American perspective. It is hoped that this book may serve as a source of information and contemplation for military professionals and all those interested in studying how wars are won.

CHAPTER 1

AIRPOWER

Proficimus More Irretenti

—MOTTO, AIR CORPS TACTICAL SCHOOL

ADVENT OF FLIGHT IN AMERICA

Human flight is arguably the most anticipated invention in history, dating back at least to the Greek tale of Daedalus and Icarus escaping from King Minos's tower with wings of feather and wax. Modernity, instead of suppressing this passion as a quaint fancy of antiquity, illuminated the possibilities of human endeavor. Man, far from forgetting his dream of flight, became intent on bringing it to fruition. He could traverse the oceans in steamships, he could cross the continents in locomotives, he could communicate long distances through telegraph wires, he could build canals and bridges and tunnels, he could raise towers and flatten mountains, but he still could not fly. By the eve of the twentieth century, practical human flight seemed at last to be within reach, and many of the sharpest intellects of the Western world sought to make the dream a reality.

In America, the most heralded of the modern Daedalians was the Smithsonian Institution's professor Samuel P. Langley (1834–1906). In 1891, he published *Experiments in Aerodynamics*, which offered hope and credibility to those who believed in the practicality of flight. In 1896, he accomplished several successful experiments with two unmanned aircraft, the *Aerodrome No. 5* and *Aerodrome No. 6*, each of which flew for several thousand feet when launched by catapult from a houseboat on the Potomac River. Intrigued by such exhibitions, the U.S. War Department furnished him with a $50,000 contract to develop a piloted aircraft.[1] Another $20,000 was provided from private sources, including Alexander Graham Bell and Langley himself. The product of Langley's work, the *Great Aerodrome*, was a tragic and humiliating failure. In two widely publicized experiments, on October 7 and December 8, 1903, the aircraft, with pilot Charles Manly at the controls, plunged into the cold waters of the Potomac, failing to attain flight beyond the momentum of the catapult launch.[2]

Yet, while newspapermen and their readers were shaking their heads in disparagement at the foolishness of flight, two brothers from the American heartland, working discretely but intently, were preparing to accomplish a great leap for humanity. The setting and manner of the conduct of their tests, so consequential to the course of world history yet so unassumingly performed, were precisely suited to the character of the inventors themselves. Wilbur Wright (1867–1912) and Orville Wright (1871–1948) were, respectively, the third and fourth sons of Milton Wright, a bishop of the United Brethren Church. The elder Wright fostered learning in his household, but did not exert prejudice toward a particular field of study, nor did he show much concern for formal education. Neither Wilbur nor Orville received a high school diploma, yet both were industrious multidisciplinary autodidacts. When Orville, the more enterprising of the two, acquired a bicycle in 1892, the new vehicle was so intriguing as to inspire the brothers to open a bicycle shop in Dayton in December of that year.[3] In the following years, while reading of the glider experiments of a German engineer, Otto Lilienthal (1848–96), both brothers developed an interest in flying.[4]

While other experimenters were working on ways to get into the air, Lilienthal was more concerned about what to do once in the air. Experience was what was needed, and between 1891 and 1896, he performed thousands of experiments with gliders of his own design. "Can any sport be more exciting than flying?" he exhorted the readers of *Scientific American* in March 1896. "Strength and adroitness, courage and decision, can nowhere gain such triumphs as these gigantic bounds into the air."[5] But the source of the thrill was the inherent risk, and a scarce four-and-a-half months after writing these words, Lilienthal crashed his glider and died.

Yet his tragedy inspired the Wrights to take up aeronautics. "My own active interest in aeronautical problems dates back to the death of Lilienthal in 1896," Wilbur told the Society of Western Engineers in 1901.[6] The Wrights appreciated Lilienthal's hands-on, trial-and-error approach to invention. It reflected the Wrights' own appreciation of experimentation, which Wilbur compared to riding an untamed horse: One may get on and learn to ride through multiple efforts, or one may study the horse from afar, and then draw up a plan for riding him. In Wilbur's words, "The latter system is the safest; but the former, on the whole, turns out the larger proportion of good riders."[7]

Also similar to Lilienthal, the Wrights realized that the key problem with flying was the ability to control the vehicle once in the air. They thus conceived of the idea of *wing-warping*, or the bending of the wings to offset disparities in pressure on either side. In 1899, Wilbur commenced experiments of this concept with a homemade kite, using handheld wires to bend the wings accordingly. The results were encouraging enough for the brothers to pursue their studies further.[8]

The brothers first arrived at Kitty Hawk on the Outer Banks of North Carolina in September 1900. They would return to the coast annually for the next three years, though their bicycle shop back in Dayton, Ohio, would require their attention at least part of the year. Through methodical research and experimentation, they would address the most pressing problems in turn. For instance, when they suspected that Lilienthal's table of air pressures against differently angled planes was erroneous, they constructed their own six-foot long wooden wind tunnel back at their Dayton shop to record new data.[9] When they installed a two-finned tail onto their glider, they experienced a phenomenon later known as "tail-spinning," in which the surfaces of the tails, rather than balancing the pressure on the wings, would intensify it and cause the machine to spin out of control. The brothers compensated for this hazard by making the tails controllable with the same device used for wing-warping—thus reducing the chance of pilot error—and by replacing the twin configuration with a single rudder.[10] Unable to find an existing engine suitable to their requirements, they set about designing their own. For the actual construction of the motor, their mechanic Charlie Taylor produced a 152-pound, 4-cylinder, 12 horsepower (hp) gasoline engine, which they positioned on the craft next to the pilot's right leg.[11] The brothers then turned to the issue of the propellers. Originally assuming that maritime engineering would provide sufficient information to apply to air travel, they found that the subject among shipbuilders was one of guesswork rather than hard science. As with wing curvature, the brothers were obliged to devise their own calculations; they ultimately decided to install two rear-facing propellers, synchronized in their counter-rotation motions by means of sprockets and chains similar to what one finds on the gear of a bicycle. The design of their flyer, which would successfully accomplish the first flight at Kitty Hawk, was thus complete.[12]

On December 17, 1903, Orville and Wilbur Wright conducted the first powered, sustained, controlled, heavier-than-air flight from the sandy dune of Kill Devil Hill. At about 10:35 that morning, with a cold late autumn wind blowing at speeds between 24 and 27 miles per hour (mph), their machine, a wooden and fabric biplane with a 40-foot wingspan positioned on a wheeled-plank on a 60-foot wooden monorail track, was pushed forward by two propellers powered by a 12 hp gasoline engine. On board was Orville, lying prone on the lower wing. Beside the craft was Wilbur, holding onto the right lower wing while keeping pace with the vehicle. When the craft had advanced two-thirds of the way down the track, it lifted, and Wilbur released his grip. Not exceeding ten feet of altitude, Orville steered the aircraft along the downward slope of the hill. After a voyage of 12 seconds and 120 feet, he landed smoothly.[13] The brevity of the exhibition understated its significance, as later established by the brothers: "The first flight lasted only 12 seconds, a flight very modest compared with that of birds, but it was, nevertheless, the first in the history of the world in which a machine carrying a man had raised itself by its own power into the air in free flight, had sailed forward on a level course without reduction of speed, and had finally landed without being wrecked."[14] The brothers made three more successful tests that day, two with Wilbur and one with Orville, each exceeding the previous flight's duration and length. After the fourth round, a strong wind flipped the flyer over, taking with it one of the local spectators who became entangled in its wires and fabric while attempting to hold it steady. He was not seriously hurt, but the craft was sufficiently damaged to end the trials for the year.[15]

By the end of 1904, the brothers had managed to make flights of over twenty miles. Yet their unsolicited offers to the U.S. War Department went unheeded. It was not until 1907, when President Theodore Roosevelt became aware of the Wrights' work, that he encouraged the Army to work with them. To the resulting solicitation, the Wrights made an offer to build and provide one aircraft capable of reaching 40 mph, with payment of $100,000 pending a successful trial. To this, the Ordnance Board balked. The $100,000 amount exceeded their authorization

Photo 1. On December 17, 1903, the Wright Brothers made history with the first successful flight at Kitty Hawk, North Carolina. *U.S. Air Force*

without congressional approval. Further negotiations proved fruitless and suggested a lack of seriousness on the part of the government. Fortunately, that same year, 1st Lt. Frank Lahm, whom the brothers had previously met in Paris, assumed an assignment at the Signal Corps. He convinced his organization to issue its own solicitation for a flying machine. If there were ever a time for a sole source, or "no bid," contract, it would have been in 1907 for the procurement of an aircraft from the Wright brothers. Yet, to avoid the extra bureaucratic hassle of justifying a sole source acquisition, the Signal Corps issued the solicitation open to all offerors able to provide a deposit equivalent to 10 percent of their asking price. To the chagrin of the contracting officers, they received three qualifying offers, the most expensive of which belonged to the Wright brothers. Fortunately, when the Signal Corps offered contracts to all three, the two low bidders revealed their unseriousness and bowed out. At long last, on February 8, 1908, the Wright brothers commenced work with the U.S. government.[16]

September 3, 1908, was the scheduled date for an exhibition of the new Flyer. Although some initial delays and the evident nervousness of Orville led to the increasing skepticism of the "doubting Thomases" among the spectators, at 6 p.m. the aircraft began racing down the track, pulled by the falling weight of a derrick positioned behind the vehicle. At first, the craft's separation from the ground was barely discernible, but it steadily climbed to about thirty feet and, to the amazement of all witnesses, circled the field.[17] The *New York Times* report testified to the collective reaction: "It was a magical moment, and the spell of it fired the spectators with a common impulse. That impulse was to shout and shout; every one did while the great machine circled with an evenness and a quick response that was amazing, and darted across the lower end of the drill grounds."[18] In less than a week, thousands of spectators were crowding the grounds to witness Orville fly laps in the sky for over an hour at heights of up to 150 feet and at speeds of over 40 mph. On September 6, Lahm accompanied Orville on a short flight of six minutes, witnessed by the Secretaries of War and the Navy. The American military now had a practical aircraft.[19]

EARLY AMERICAN MILITARY AVIATION

As the death of Lilienthal had shown, the thrill of flight carried with it the risk of injury or death. Gravity had been defied but not defeated. On September 17, 1908, while Orville Wright was continuing his exhibitions for the Army, one of the propellers of his Flyer broke loose. The craft fell seventy-five feet and crashed. Orville suffered a broken leg and broken ribs. His passenger, Lt. Thomas Selfridge, was not so fortunate, and died soon afterward. His death marked the first American aircraft fatality.[20]

Yet this calamity did not signal the end of the American aviation program. Neither America nor any other nation could turn back from the opportunities offered by flight now that they were attainable. The best one could do was to mitigate risks through familiarity. To this end, flying schools were established to train pilots on the Army's new vehicles. The Wrights, similarly undeterred by misfortune, established one such school in Montgomery, Alabama.[21] In January 1911, Glenn Curtiss opened a training school in San Diego, California. In July of that year, the Army itself established an Aviation School at College Park, Maryland.[22] As training increased, the military utility of these new vehicles became manifest. In 1910, Eugene Ely became the first aviator to take off from a ship.[23] The following year, an airman at College Park fired a machine gun from his craft.[24] Lt. Myron Crissy became the first airman to drop a live bomb (in a test environment) near San Francisco; although it was an Italian, Giulio Gavotti, who was the first to drop a bomb in a combat environment on November 1, 1911, in Libya.[25]

Within a few years, bombs were falling on European soil, as that continent's Great Powers descended in 1914 into the destruction and slaughter of a general war. The young technology of flight became a familiar sight over the front, a reassurance to friends and a frightful menace to foes. It was soon evident that European aviation had surpassed the American variety. Dutch engineer Anthony Fokker had mastered the art of synchronization and was able to build aircraft with machine guns capable of firing through the propeller without damaging it. The German Gotha G.IV aircraft could wield a payload of 1,000 pounds of bombs, and starting in the spring of 1916, it began to wreak havoc on the British homeland in a way that the ominous but unwieldy Zeppelin dirigibles were unable to do.[26]

Yet the United States maintained a strict neutrality and allowed its military aviation arm to languish in a state of feeble immaturity. Issues more domestic pressed upon the minds of the nation's leaders, particularly as the election of 1916 approached. On March 9, 1916, rebel bandit Francisco "Pancho" Villa crossed the border from Mexico and raided the town of Columbus, New Mexico. American blood was shed, and President Woodrow Wilson ordered Villa's capture. Brig. Gen. John J. Pershing led his Punitive Expedition into Mexico, accompanied by the First Aero Squadron, under the command of Capt. Benjamin Foulois (1879–1967).[27] The first significant combat mission for American flyers did not attain the level of grandeur one would have hoped. As summed up in a history from the Air Force Historical Research Agency, "The deployment turned out to be a fiasco, and nothing much was achieved beyond the ferrying of Pershing's Christmas cards back to the United States for posting."[28] The American pilots were restricted by the limitations of their machines; their 90 hp Curtiss JN-3s had trouble scaling the heights of the Sierra Madres. As a silver lining, the obvious shortcomings of airpower were compensated for by the passage of the National Defense Act in June 1916, making appropriations for 148 officers, up from the previous 60. This was followed two months later by a special appropriation of $13,000,000 for active duty and National Guard aviation.[29]

On April 6, 1917, the United States declared war on Germany, following that nation's provocative commitment to unrestricted submarine warfare. Into the maelstrom of European air warfare came the Americans. Apart from the members of the volunteer Lafayette Escadrille, who had served with the French before America's formal entry into the war, the air forces of the United States lacked the experience and equipment of both their friends and their foes. The nation's political and military leaders realized that if the United States was to have a material impact on the war in its own right, it needed to produce aircraft and pilots on a large scale. In imitation of a Canadian program that had developed pilots with admirable results, the United States established a system of three progressive and increasingly exclusive stages: ground training, primary training, and advanced training. The final stage would be conducted in Europe, where the trainees could receive instruction from veterans flying the latest models. The program turned out 1,600 pilots by war's end.[30]

The Joint Army-Navy Technical Board, meeting in May 1917 and including the now-Major Benjamin Foulois, set a production goal of 4,500 aircraft by the summer of 1918, inspiring Congress to appropriate $640 million to bring it about. A total of 7,000 aircraft were produced by the end of the war, with 1,200 making it to France before the armistice. Most of these were British-designed DeHavilland DH-4s.[31] However, the key American contribution to aerial technology in the Great War was not an airframe but rather the Liberty Engine, designed by Jesse Vincent and Elbert J. Hall in six days in the late spring of 1917. About 15,000 such engines were produced by war's end, most of them a powerful 12-cylinder design.[32] Yet the dream of American pilots flying American aircraft in the war remained unrealized. Instead, Americans relied upon mostly French-designed products, such as Nieuport 11s and Spad XIIIs for pursuit missions, and Breguet XIVs for bombardments.[33]

Nevertheless, in September 1918, it was an American who had the privilege of leading a massive, combined force in a major battle, when Col. William "Billy" Mitchell was given tactical control of almost 1,500 Allied aircraft in the successful St. Mihiel offensive. The power exerted by concentrated air assets made a lasting impression on Mitchell's views of aviation. By war's end, it was clear that American capabilities were advancing at a rapid pace, and the record of the Air Service, formed in 1918, was respectable: Suffering about 1,200 casualties (nearly evenly divided between combat and noncombat losses) and the loss of 290 aircraft, the Air Service destroyed 776 enemy aircraft, greater than a 2.5-to-1 ratio.[34]

The end of the war brought about renewed interest among the flying community to test its limits. Undoubtedly, the most daring, spectacular feat during these postwar years, and the greatest peacetime event in American aviation since the Wright brothers' first flight at Kitty Hawk, was Charles Lindbergh's solo, nonstop transatlantic flight from

New York to Paris, on May 20–21, 1927. Similar to the Wright brothers, Lindbergh (1902–74) was a Midwesterner with a keen interest in mechanics but little in the way of academic accomplishment, having failed out of the University of Wisconsin. His father was a Republican congressman of independent, perhaps eccentric, political views. The young Lindbergh fostered an interest in flying and trained in the Army Air Service. Returning to private life, he worked as an airmail pilot (a daring profession), often flying between St. Louis and Chicago. It was in this capacity that he learned of a contest for the Orteig Prize, one of many such contests to test the latest capabilities in flight. He convinced sponsors to support his endeavor, and purchased an aircraft built specifically for such a trial—a lightweight (1,930 pounds) high-winged Ryan monoplane, christened *The Spirit of St. Louis*.[35]

It was nighttime in Paris on May 21, when Lindbergh's small, silver-colored aircraft appeared in the sky above Paris and alighted at Le Bourget Airfield. Before the pilot could climb down from the plane, he was seized and held aloft by a crowd that had broken through barriers and rushed to celebrate his amazing accomplishment. This was merely a fraction of the more than 100,000 people who had come to the field to welcome the American. Before the French multitude could affectionately tear the hero to pieces, two French pilots managed to rescue him. He was brought to the American embassy and hosted by Ambassador Myron Herrick. Reporters swarmed the residence, and Lindbergh gamely spoke with them for a few minutes before Herrick ushered them out to allow his guest some much-needed rest.[36] In a statement to the press, William P. MacCracken Jr., assistant secretary of Commerce, succinctly placed the event in perspective, from an American point-of-view, declaring, "The glory of the first flight from New York to Paris should do much to impress the people of this country with the success of our own aeronautical enterprise."[37]

American ingenuity and hard work had once again conquered the elements. The opportunities offered by aviation technology seemed limitless. Within military circles, planners and theorists were considering ways to harness this power in anticipation of the next war.

AIRPOWER THEORISTS IN THE INTERWAR PERIOD

The period from the 1920s through the 1930s was a fruitful time for the development of airpower theory. The fact that several ideas produced during these years were far removed from the observations and experiences of the Great War was remarkable, but understandable. For in that war, aircraft played a supporting role and were most appreciated for those missions that directly assisted the ground forces. However, flight, though not yet fifteen years old, had developed at an extraordinary pace between 1914 and 1918. It stood to reason that the technology would continue to advance before the next major conflict. Further, the carnage of that war, much of it brought on by outdated ground tactics executed along a lengthy, static Western Front, sickened military professionals for its waste and ineffectiveness. Could airpower provide the key to avoid another such calamity?

Many thought it could, yet airpower advocates were pushing against institutional inertia. Of the Great Powers, only Britain had an independent air force by the end of the war. Airpower theorists thus tended to adopt one of two approaches to incorporating their chosen platform into the strategy of future wars. The first of these argued airpower was capable of achieving victory on its own through strategic bombing. The second approach placed skepticism on the effectiveness of strategic bombing and instead stressed the importance of other types of airpower missions, such as air superiority, close air support, interdiction, or defensive counterair. Representatives of the strategic bombing group included British general Hugh Trenchard, Italian general Giulio Douhet, and American general Billy Mitchell; while the advocates of other types of airpower missions were represented by British general John Slessor, Italian general Amedeo Mecozzi, and American major Claire Chennault. The more recognizable names in the former category reflect their dominant influence over airpower thinking in the interwar years.

Hugh Trenchard (1873–1956) had briefly served as the first chief of the Air Staff of the newly minted Royal Air Force (RAF) in 1918. However, within weeks, problems with his civilian counterpart caused him to resign from that position and take over the Independent Force in

France for the duration of the war.[38] While it was a nominal demotion, it was also an opportunity for Trenchard to escape an ugly bureaucratic situation for an operational command more suitable to his character. That character was one of offensive aggression, almost regardless of the cost. Though the idea of strategic bombing was by now recognized as an aspirational exercise of airpower, the exigency of the German Spring Offensive and the limited range and payload capabilities of Allied aircraft made such a campaign unattainable. Rather, Trenchard concentrated on close air support, the interdiction of forces, and strikes at infrastructural and transportation targets in the short to medium range of the front.[39] After the war, however, Trenchard was once again made chief of the Air Staff, working with the far-sighted Winston Churchill, who had been appointed minister of War and Air. Trenchard would thrive in this position, and he helped solidify the RAF's existence as an individual service.[40]

Trenchard's general approach to airpower stressed the offensive, and he saw the enemy's *will* as the true target. He estimated the psychological impact of bombing as being twenty times the value of its physical impact. In 1921, he managed to convince the chiefs of the Army and Navy to sportingly agree to a parochial cease-fire for a year so that he could find his footing as head of the young RAF without having to fend off interagency attacks. He used this time to oversee the production of the first doctrinal publication for the RAF: "Operations," which stressed the importance of air superiority and morale factors in warfare. In 1923, he gave his public endorsement to strategic bombing theory with his Buxton Speech, in which he spoke of the impact of bombing on the enemy's morale. In 1928, the RAF produced AP 1300, the "Royal Air Force War Manual," which prioritized strategic bombing over the attainment of air superiority. It listed "vital centres" as appealing targets, meaning those areas that served as transportation or communication nodes, or key infrastructural objects. However, while it targeted civilian *morale*, it did not specifically endorse attacks on civilians, per se.[41] This somewhat paradoxical approach remained as a cornerstone of British airpower doctrine up to the second year of the Second World War.[42]

The desire to avoid a repeat of the stalemate of the Great War made theorists and political leaders alike more receptive to ideas that, while seemingly extreme and untested, offered a swifter path to peace. Such was the thinking of the great Italian airpower theorist Giulio Douhet (1869–1930). Douhet joined the young Italian army as an artillery officer in 1892. As soon as he learned of the advent of flight, he became an early advocate on airpower's behalf. By the time Italy entered the Great War on the Allied side, Douhet had already commanded an aviation battalion. He was assigned to division staff and promoted to colonel. He had strong opinions and was uncompromising in his criticism of what he saw as wasteful and ineffective measures. He did this publicly enough and harshly enough that he was court-martialed in 1916 and sentenced to a year in prison. Unrepentant, he served his time and returned to service in 1917. He retired from the army in 1918, and his conviction was overturned in 1920. Thus vindicated, he was promoted to brigadier general but decided to remain retired. In 1921, his famous *Command of the Air* (*Il domino dell'area*) was published. He died in 1930 and was thus unable to see his theories put to the test in real-world situations.[43]

While British doctrinal writers were circumspect about the consequences of strategic bombing, Douhet was blunt. This uncompromising approach made for a simple, straightforward, and, perhaps ironically, compelling argument: "A man who is fighting a life-and-death fight—as all wars are nowadays—has the right to use any means to keep his life. War means cannot be classified as human and inhuman. War will always be inhuman, and the means which are used in it cannot be classified as acceptable or not acceptable according to their efficacy, potentiality, or harmfulness to the enemy."[44]

Like Trenchard, Douhet viewed aerial warfare as purely offensive. Defensive counterair was inefficient and ineffective. As new models of aircraft increased their radius of action, they could attack an increasing number of targets. Since it was impossible to tell where exactly an aircraft was headed except through continuous visual confirmation—in these years before radar—how could one properly defend against an aerial attack except to position aircraft on the ready at every potential target? Antiaircraft weapons were inaccurate, and the cost of arming every possible target with such a weapon was similarly prohibitive.[45] The enemy air force should be destroyed, but this should be done by striking their aircraft on the ground at their airfields. Air assets should not be dispersed, but massed for offensive action.[46] So applied, these measures would provide one's force with *command of the air*, defined by Douhet as "that state of affairs in which we find ourselves able to fly in the face of an enemy who is unable to do likewise."[47]

Once this command of the air is established, then the bombing campaign could commence to bring about a breaking of the enemy's will.[48] Targets of bombardment would include "peacetime industrial and commercial establishments; important buildings, private and public; transportation arteries and centers; and certain designated areas of civilian population as well."[49] Under such an onslaught, the enemy's people would lose faith in their cause. The government would be obliged to sue for peace, since "the time would soon come when, to put an end to horror and suffering, the people themselves, driven by the instinct of self-preservation, would rise up and demand an end to the war—this before their army and navy had time to mobilize at all!"[50]

While Trenchard and Douhet were advocating for an investment in an air force that could respond to a close or neighboring enemy, William "Billy" Mitchell (1879–1936) had the more difficult challenge of championing the idea of an independent air force for a nation still out of the range of aircraft from potential adversaries. Like Douhet, he embraced the possibilities of flight early in his career and became only more certain of them with time. He was present when Orville Wright made his first successful demonstration of his Flyer at Fort Myer, Virginia, in September 1908, and he later took flying lessons from Orville himself.[51] On April 10, 1917, four days after the American entry into the Great War, Mitchell arrived in Paris to study Allied aviation. He sought out and spoke with Trenchard, who significantly influenced his thinking on the use of airpower.[52] In 1918, Mitchell served as commander of the Zone of Advance and then transferred to leadership positions within I Corps and later First Army.[53] In that capacity, Mitchell directed air operations for the St. Mihiel Offensive and the Meuse-Argonne Campaign. The ability to direct hundreds of aircraft on a single mission, which he did on October 9, 1918, when ordering 200 bombers and 100 pursuits to interdict German troops, revealed to him the potential of concentrated airpower.[54]

By the end of the war, Mitchell was a brigadier general and assigned as assistant chief of the Army Air Service, first serving under Maj. Gen. Charles Menoher and then under Maj. Gen. Mason Patrick. He used his position to agitate for an independent air force, which he now believed was essential to national defense. He antagonized the Navy into agreeing to a series of bombing tests, culminating in the sinking of the captured German battleship *Ostfriesland* on July 21, 1921. His agitations endeared him no more to his superiors than they did to Navy brass. In March 1925, he was reduced to colonel and transferred to the VIII Corps Area in San Antonio. This failed to quiet him, and when he publicly blamed political and military leaders for a couple of aerial mishaps in September 1925, including the fatal crash of the airship *Shenandoah*, he was court-martialed and convicted. He was suspended for five years and resigned from the military on February 1, 1926.[55]

Photo 2. William "Billy" Mitchell's devotion to the cause of airpower led to his open criticism of political and military leadership, resulting in a career-ending but legend-making court-martial. *U.S. Air Force*

Mitchell's views of airpower were best encapsulated in his book *Winged Defense: The Development and Possibilities of Modern Air Power* (1925). Writing for a wider audience beyond military circles, he employed lines of argument designed to resonate with a public wary of future European entanglements and inclined to focus on domestic affairs. He established the urgency of the situation by highlighting the increasing ranges of aircraft, which would soon negate the expanse of oceans as barriers to attack. He stressed the emerging dominance of aircraft over more traditional forms of warfare, claiming, "Neither armies nor navies can exist unless the air is controlled over them," and, "Nothing can stop the attack of aircraft except other aircraft."[56] To a pre–New Deal public, traditionally wary of major government investments, he also made an argument on economic grounds, stating that aircraft were more affordable than ships, to the tune of 1,000 aircraft for one battleship. The dual civilian and military roles of aircraft meant that a single plane could prove useful in peacetime and in war.[57] Like Douhet, he was dismissive of static defenses such as antiaircraft artillery, though he believed, unlike Douhet, that an enemy air force could be defeated in the air.[58] He argued that an air force, not the Navy or Army, should be responsible for coastal defense.[59]

The extent to which Douhet influenced Mitchell's thinking is unknown. Douhet's *Command of the Air* was not widely available in an English translation until 1942, but Mitchell had met with Douhet after the Great War.[60] His views of strategic bombing seemed to echo those of the Italian general:

> To gain a lasting victory in war, the hostile nation's power to make war must be destroyed—this means the manufactories, the means of communication, the food products, even the farms, the fuel and oil and the places where people live and carry on their daily lives. Not only must these things be rendered incapable of supplying armed forces but the people's desire to renew the combat at a later date must be discouraged.... Aircraft operating in the heart of an enemy's country will accomplish this object in an incredibly short space of time, once control of the air has been obtained and the months and even years of

contest of ground armies with a loss of millions of lives will be eliminated in the future.[61]

An independent air force was thus an economical way to defend the American homeland and to swiftly defeat an enemy nation.

Such strategic bombing theories, while popular within the airpower community, were not unanimously embraced. Among the skeptics were John C. Slessor (1897–1979), a British combat pilot who had been a subordinate of Trenchard's. In spite of his admiration for his senior officer, Slessor's views on the use of airpower, articulated in his book *Air Power and Armies* (1936), differed significantly from those of his former superior. As he stated bluntly, "No attitude could be more vain or irritating in its effects than to claim that the next great war—if and when it comes—will be decided in the air, and in the air alone."[62]

Slessor's beliefs on the proper use of airpower were shaped by his knowledge of the unique capabilities of aircraft that made them distinct from surface forces, namely their flexibility in switching objectives and their ability to maneuver without lines of supply.[63] According to Slessor, air forces should be constantly focused not on *command of the air* but on *air superiority*, which he defined as, "a state of moral, physical, and material superiority which enables its possessor to conduct operations against an enemy and at the same time deprive the enemy of the ability to interfere effectively by the use of his own air forces."[64] This was a more modest and transient condition than what Douhet sought.[65] For Douhet, command of the air was a necessary condition in order to conduct strategic bombing on targets that would break the will of the population. For Slessor, air superiority enabled aircraft to assault lines of communication. Such attacks would make it difficult for the enemy to resupply and reinforce its armies. The massive armies and lines of trenches of the Great War would be relics of the past.[66] Slessor did not overtly reject his former commander's advocacy for morale bombing, but he stressed the use of airpower in ways in which the effects were more immediately recognizable, such as targeted attacks on the modes of production and supply.[67]

While Slessor was circumspect in his criticisms of Trenchard, Italian officer Amedeo Mecozzi (1892–1971) was quite open with his disagreements with Douhet. Mecozzi had enlisted in the Italian army as an engineer, but he became a pilot soon after Italy's entry into the World War. By Armistice Day (November 11, 1918), he was an ace with six victories and the recipient of the War Cross. After the war, he served as a test pilot, then as now a position reserved for flyers of the highest quality and confidence. By 1937, he was a brigadier general of the Regia Aeronautica and commander of an assault group.[68]

Mecozzi's public criticism of Douhet began soon after the Great War, even before the publication of *Command of the Air*. Unlike Douhet, he believed in the practicality of defensive airpower, the importance of close air support to surface forces, and the transient nature of air superiority or command of the air. He ultimately took aim at Douhet's prioritization of strategic bombing. This was a wasteful, ineffective use of airpower, Mecozzi maintained. Bombers were vulnerable to interception, and their ability to strike targets from high altitudes was unreliable. He also (ultimately) concluded that it was unethical to target population centers. To Mecozzi, the primary mission to which aircraft were best suited—and most useful to the national war effort—was to interdict enemy ground forces behind the front lines. He accordingly supported the development of ground attack (or "assault") aircraft.[69]

Perhaps the most famous strategic bombing skeptic within the American airpower community was Claire L. Chennault (1893–1958). A native of Louisiana, in 1917 he was commissioned into the infantry through the ninety-day officer training school program. He then transitioned into the Aviation Section of the Signal Corps to become a pilot, although the war ended before he earned his wings. Nevertheless, his career prospered over the next decade. He commanded a pursuit squadron at Luke Field in Hawaii, where he took the initiative to establish a ground-based observation system and airborne patrols. The combat exercises he organized and performed were impressive, and he even wrote a manual on fighter tactics. For the purposes of public relations, he was hand-picked to fly for an Army Air Corps demonstration team. He was then assigned to the Air Corps Tactical School, first as a student and then as a faculty member. It was here where he developed his theory on airpower, thanks to his personal experiences and his observation of exercises.[70]

Much of Chennault's early views were summarized in his work, *The Role of Defensive Pursuit* (1933). He started the work by paying homage to the mantra of the time. He echoed the beliefs of strategic bombing theorists when he stated that the "will to resist of a people can be destroyed most effectively by destroying their means of resistance,"[71] and conceded, "The ability of a nation to wage war can be impaired if not wholly destroyed by an enemy who is able to employ, without opposition, a vast number of bombardment airplanes" against key targets.[72] However, having dispensed with such formalities, he proceeded to reject the notion of the invincible bomber. Douhet and others had been influenced by the difficulty of pursuit aircraft to intercept bombers during the First World War, but Chennault attributed this primarily to a lack of timely information regarding the approach of bombers. He believed a combination of airborne and ground-based observations could provide sufficient information to allow a defense against attack.[73] He made much of the results of exercises held between Fort Knox, Kentucky, and Patterson Field, Ohio, in May 1933. In these maneuvers, the defending "Red" forces at Fort Knox were able to continuously track the bombing "Blue" forces from Patterson due to a lack of Blue pursuit aircraft to chase away Red observation aircraft, a vulnerability Chennault highlighted. During one phase, when Red was restricted only to ground-based observation, its defending pursuits were still able to intercept an entire Blue formation.[74] Over the course of the exercises, eighteen Blue formations were intercepted during the daytime, and one was intercepted at night.[75] Influenced by such results, Chennault recommended the establishment of a "mobile intelligence system" and a four-squadron "Air Defense Information Group" under control of the air force.[76]

Characteristically for airpower theorists, he developed a combative style of argumentation that ultimately proved his undoing. In 1934, in his appearance before the Howell Commission on aviation, he openly criticized the Army brass for its failure to properly conduct exercises.

His subsequent removal from the list of attendees to the prestigious Command and General Staff College indicated his days in the Army were numbered. He retired in 1937 and soon left for China to visit Chiang Kai-shek and his air forces.[77]

THE U.S. ARMY AIR CORPS

Mitchell's conviction and suspension would at first appear to have struck a critical blow to the cause of an independent air force. Yet by the time of his resignation in February 1926, measures were underway to grant military aviation greater autonomy within, albeit not formal independence from, the U.S. Army. In September 1925, a couple of weeks after Mitchell leveled a charge of negligence against President Calvin Coolidge's administration, the president commissioned hearings by a board chaired by his friend, investment banker Dwight Morrow, for the purposes of examining the state of military aviation. In December, the Morrow Board submitted its findings and recommended the formation of an Army Air Corps, along with the creation of an Assistant Secretary for Air in the War Department. Congress subsequently codified these changes in the Air Corps Act of 1926.[78]

This new status gave military aviation greater leverage in budgetary matters. Between 1926 and 1936, the direct appropriations made to the Air Service, or Air Corps, tripled, from $14.9 million to $45.4 million. This represented not only an absolute increase in funding but an increase in the share of the Army's total appropriations, from 5.7 percent to 13.3 percent.[79] Personnel during this same time almost doubled, from 9,674 to 17,233.[80] The standing of American military aviation could scarcely have done better had it been made an independent force; yet these concessions, far from satiating the ambitions of airpower advocates, merely whetted their appetites for greater autonomy and prominence in war planning.

The Air Corps Tactical School (ACTS) led the way in advocating for both a strategic bombing initiative and an independent air force. Originally established after the Great War as the Air Service School at Langley Field in Virginia, it became the Air Service Tactical School in 1922 and, finally, ACTS in 1926. Although it had initially embraced a strategy that focused on air superiority and coordination with ground forces, by the time it assumed its identity as ACTS, it had definitely shifted toward a strategic bombing doctrine, albeit with an emphasis on industrial centers and infrastructure nodes rather than on terror bombing.[81] Maj. Gen. James E. Fechet, who became chief of the Air Corps on December 14, 1927, looked to ACTS to foster the intellectual support for this doctrine. A training exercise in Ohio held in May 1929 seemed to confirm that bombers could have second- and third-order effects in halting enemy ground forces by attacking lines of communication and even command systems far from the front lines. Douhet's belief in the inability to effectively intercept bombers seemed to hold. Years before the British politician Stanley Baldwin made the expression infamous, the Air Corps had embraced the idea, "The bomber will always get through."[82] In 1931, ACTS moved from Virginia to Maxwell Field in Montgomery, Alabama, where the Wright brothers had once established a training school.[83] Its tradition endures to this day, and one can find instructors at the Air Command and Staff College bearing the heritage badge of ACTS on their right sleeve.

The concept of a swift victory through strategic aerial bombardment, in spite of its appeal, had a discernible weakness. As historian Timothy Moy observed, "The primary difficulty, of course, was that the Air Corps' conception was, as of the early 1930s, technically impossible."[84] The theory called for bombers with the range, payload, speed, and precision to carry out an effective mission. Such aircraft were currently absent from the Air Corps inventory. The introduction of the Martin B-10 in 1932 seemed to augur the coming of a technological solution. The B-10 was an all-metal monoplane with retractable landing gear, powered by two Wright Cyclone R-1820 engines producing 1,550 hp. Its maximum speed could top 200 mph, with a range of 1,200 miles, and a metric ton payload. Its four-man crew could defend itself with three .30-caliber machine guns, one of which was mounted to a rotating turret. The issue of precision appeared to find resolution in the development of a bombsight designed and built by Carl L. Norden, which he had demonstrated for the Navy (and Army observers) the previous October. So impressive were the results that the Army sought a contract with Norden but was precluded from doing so by the Navy contract. The Army Air Corps was thus reduced to the indignity of purchasing this vital piece of equipment through its sister (and rival) service.[85] This uneasy arrangement lasted until 1936, when the Air Corps, weary of going hat-in-hand to the Navy, started to purchase S-1 bombsights in large numbers from Norden's competitor, Sperry. This freed the Air Corps from having to work through the Navy, though the new sights were of inferior quality to Norden's.[86]

Nevertheless, aviation technology seemed to be moving in the direction anticipated by strategic bombing advocates. The results of West Coast exercises in 1933, contra to the Fort Knox exercises cited by Chennault, supported the premise that pursuits could not stop the latest bombers. This encouraged further development. A solicitation released in June 1934 called for a bomber with a 2,000-pound payload, a 1,020-mile radius of action, and a maximum speed of 250 mph. Under the conditions of the solicitation, the winner of this competition was the two-engine Douglas XB-18. However, Major General Foulois, now chief of the Air Corps, and the other Air Corps leaders had their eye on Boeing's submission: the four-engine B-17 "Flying Fortress." In 1936, the Air Corps contracted directly with Boeing for a limited quantity of B-17s to ensure the total price did not exceed the threshold for competition requirements.[87]

In 1934, the Air Corps faced a crisis, costly in lives and resources that could have been calamitous to its reputation and autonomy but that ultimately worked to its institutional benefit. On February 9, President Franklin Delano Roosevelt canceled all existing air mail contracts with commercial airlines. The previous autumn, a committee chaired by Alabama senator Hugo Black had found that great irregularities occurred with the original selection of contractors during a previous administration. Black learned that former Postmaster General Walter Folger Brown had engaged in seemingly unethical, preferential practices, resulting in awards to bidders who did not offer the best value to the government. The air mail contracts were highly lucrative, and such a scandal was sure to outrage a public still mired in the Great Depression. In one audacious example, representatives of Transcontinental and

Western Airlines (TWA) had apparently bribed a potential competitor to *not* bid on the air mail solicitation.[88]

Beginning February 19, 1934, Army Air Corps pilots assumed the mission of delivering the mail. However, almost immediately calamity struck the effort. The winter was the worst time of year for pilots inexperienced in bad weather and night flying to assume responsibility over long-distance mail runs. Within the first week, six airmen were killed in mishaps (though, technically, three were killed in the days before the air mail mission commenced).[89] A total of twelve would be killed by late May, when operations were permanently halted. There were a total of 66 crashes, and a delivery rate of 66 percent. The pilots were brave and determined, and they delivered 400 tons of mail.[90] However, the program was considered a failure by the public, and the administration was harshly criticized. Among the critics was Charles Lindbergh, an employee and stockholder of TWA and still a revered public figure.[91] In an open letter sent the day after the cancellation of the contracts, he argued that Roosevelt's action "condemn[ed] the largest portion of our commercial aviation without just trial," and that his policy would "unnecessarily and greatly damage all American aviation."[92] Results seemed to confirm these sentiments. New contracts were issued, and commercial services recommenced on May 8, 1935.[93]

As with the 1916 Mexican Expedition, which resulted in increased congressional investment in airpower because of, rather than in spite of, its lack of success, the air mail controversy led to an examination of the status of military aviation and a determination generally agreeable to airpower leaders. A board chaired by former secretary of war Newton Baker (and including Foulois) endorsed the idea of the establishment of a General Headquarters, Air Force (GHQAF) to assume operational control of American-based combat aircraft while the Air Corps would maintain administrative control. The Baker Board also called for increased procurement of aircraft, training with instruments and night flying, and an increase in annual pilot hours. Roosevelt approved of the board's conclusions, and on March 1, 1935, the GHQAF was activated at Langley Field, Virginia, with Brig. Gen. Frank Andrews assuming command.[94] Foulois called the establishment of the new organization "the most important and forward looking single step ever taken to secure a military air unit of adequate striking power to insure to the United States a proper defense in the air."[95]

The idea was not unanimously embraced. A young officer included on the Baker Board, James "Jimmy" Doolittle, issued a minority report, requesting an independent budget for the Air Corps, along with its own promotion system. At a subsequent commission chaired by journalist Clark Howell, junior officers testified on the potential of strategic bombing and the need for an independent air force. The atmosphere was admirably open and encouraging to honest input—though, as indicated above, Captain Chennault paid a price for his bold assertions. Billy Mitchell also testified before the Howell Commission and criticized as insufficient the establishment of a GHQAF.[96]

Mitchell remained true to his convictions to the end. His obituary in the *New York Times* would describe him as the "stormy petrel of American aviation." He was the "prophetic and vitriolic critic" of aviation policy, who had correctly foreseen the increased speed of aircraft to 250 mph and the ability of aircraft to cross the Pacific Ocean. Mitchell, like Douhet, would not live to see his beliefs on strategic bombing tested in the laboratory of war. His death by "coronary occlusion" came on February 19, 1936, a little over thirty-two years after the first flight at Kitty Hawk, ten years after his resignation from the military, two years to the day after the beginning of the Army Air Mail flights, and five months before the start of the Spanish Civil War.[97]

CHAPTER 2

SORTIES

Marc Antony: Cry 'Havoc,' and let slip the dogs of war.
—SHAKESPEARE, *JULIUS CAESAR*

SILENCE FROM SPAIN, JULY 18, 1936

At the height of a hot summer, in the midst of the Great Depression, American thoughts were riveted on domestic matters. A casual reader of the July 18, 1936, late city edition of the *New York Times*, might have overlooked or merely glanced at a two-column report, below-the-fold on page one: "Telephone Service with Spain Shut Off; Gibraltar Hears of Revolt in Cartagena." On the afternoon and evening of July 17, there had been no phone service between Paris and Spain; nor was there service between Lisbon and Spain. In London, a Reuters correspondent reported that at 3:35 a.m. on July 18, "a cryptic message from Spain" announced: "There have been incidents at Cuenca, about ninety miles southeast of Madrid." From Madrid, the Associated Press reported that "strict censorship" was being enforced on telephone calls and that Manuel Azaña (1880–1940), the president of Spain, had left his presidential house the night before and moved into the National Palace.[1] These reports understated the seriousness of the situation. In fact, civil war had swept through Spain like an inferno.

One man who may have been able to report on the situation was neither a newspaper correspondent nor a foreign secretary but a career infantry officer stationed at the embassy in Madrid, Col. Stephen O. Fuqua (1874–1943). Fuqua was born in Baton Rouge, Louisiana, the son of a former Confederate army colonel who had died a year after the boy's birth. In 1893, Fuqua matriculated at the United States Military Academy at West Point, New York, but left in 1894, completing his college education at Louisiana State University. In 1898, he joined the volunteer infantry and served in the Spanish-American War in Cuba and later the Philippines. In 1901, as a result of this service, he received a commission into the regular army as a second lieutenant. He would go on to serve another two tours in the Philippines, one in 1905 and another in 1908.[2]

During this time, Fuqua earned a reputation for both bravery and compassion. *Time* magazine later highlighted a couple of episodes from his service that illustrated the virtues of his character: "In the Philippines his men were once demoralized by peppery fire while fording a stream. Drawing them up beneath a sheltering hill, Lieut. Fuqua drilled them in the rudimentary manual of arms until their nerves were steadied. Again, plunging through Philippine underbrush, he found an orphan Filipino being flogged by his uncle. The Lieutenant bought the boy for 30 pesos ($17), gave him freedom, education, employed him as personal servant."[3]

Fuqua graduated from the Infantry-Cavalry School in 1907, with honors, and from the Army Staff College in 1908. Like many officers in the U.S. military of the early twentieth century, his career proceeded in fits and starts; by America's entry into the First World War, he was still a captain—sixteen years after his commissioning. Yet war brought advancement, and he was promoted to major and assigned to the 37th Division as assistant chief of staff, and then to the 28th Division, where he rose to the position of acting chief of staff. On October 30, 1918, he was breveted to colonel (which nine-and-a-half years later would finally be made permanent). By then, he had been appointed to the operations section of the First Army staff. In such capacities, he was involved in some of the most important American battles of the war.[4] As noted in his citation for the Army Distinguished Service Medal: "Colonel Fuqua was responsible for and supervised the movements incident to the concentration of troops for the St. Mihiel and Meuse-Argonne offensives of the 1st Army, which involved many thousands of men and was accomplished with the greatest success."[5]

In March 1929, the new administration of President Herbert Hoover appointed Colonel Fuqua to the office of Chief of Infantry, a position that carried with it the rank of major general. This sudden turn of fortune met with criticism in some circles, for Fuqua was leapfrogging over more senior officers (he was 165th on a list of colonels). His path to his initial commissioning was also a source of concern. As the *New York Times* reported at the time, "Another point which irks army officialdom is that Colonel Fuqua is not a graduate of West Point."[6] The objections of Army officialdom notwithstanding, the Senate approved the nomination in May 1929.[7]

The question whether to base promotions on merit or seniority has been a recurring one throughout military history. The idea of a hero rising from the ranks to lead his fellow soldiers in triumph has a romantic appeal, and there are sufficient historical examples to grant such an idea feasibility. Yet military merit is ultimately a subjective determination, one that is hard to gauge in a peacetime force, as was the case in 1929. Seniority is certainly an objective criterion, but too rigid an adherence to it renders the military a uniformed bureaucracy, with longevity serving as a surrogate for other, more martial, virtues. Perhaps there is some ideal mix between seniority and merit that would suffice, but even the best system is imperfect, and there will always be justifiable grievances by those left unsatisfied with their station.

In any event, Army officialdom was evidently no worse for wear by the time Fuqua had completed his tour as Commander of Infantry and had resumed his permanent rank of colonel. That same year, 1933, his son, also named Stephen, graduated from West Point.[8] Such personal triumphs would have served as fitting conclusions to any career, but the elder Fuqua must have felt he was good for one more assignment. On October 1, 1933, at age fifty-eight, he arrived at the embassy in Madrid to serve as military attaché to Spain.[9]

Military attachés were an elite group of officers who, like ambassadors, were sent abroad to represent their nation in foreign lands friendly to the United States, though their role was more one of observation and information gathering than of active diplomacy. In this capacity, they were answerable to the Military Intelligence Division of the War Department. The men selected for such an assignment tended to be officers of distinctly high quality, for the tasking was usually a stepping stone in an ascendant career or a reward for previously distinguished service. The attachés were briefed on their duties but were not formally trained as to what exactly they should do. Their ability to improvise was thus a key skill for the job. As Army compensations were often insufficient to meet the cost of living and socializing as befit a dignitary in a foreign land, attachés usually also had to be independently wealthy.[10]

Fuqua adjusted well to this new assignment. He retained a youthful desire to explore new locations and have new adventures. The U.S. ambassador to Spain, Claude Bowers (1878–1958), later recalled when he and Fuqua took a trip to southern Spain, prior to the civil war: "Though a serious-minded soldier, Fuqua was always as gay and eager as a boy on these excursions, witty jovial, adjustable. The professional habit of years had made him a slave of the map, and out it would come with every change of scenery, and along with it, from some mysterious hiding place, would appear a book with full information about every village we touched."[11] Such interest and resourcefulness made him a suitable military attaché. He was the ideal type of man to have on location in time of crisis. Certainly, he would have been able to accurately convey what was transpiring in Spain on July 18, 1936.

In July 1936 there was another officer in Europe who, though located in Paris and not in Madrid, was poised to play a significant role in the acquisition and dissemination of information coming from Spain to the U.S. War Department during the next couple of years. This was Capt. Townsend Griffiss (1900–42) who, since September 1935, had served as assistant military attaché for air for France, Spain, and Belgium.[12]

Griffiss had been born into a wealthy family; his mother was the granddaughter of Cicero J. Hamlin of Buffalo, New York, a horse breeder and founder of the Buffalo Grape Sugar Company.[13] Griffiss attended

Photo 3. Townsend Griffiss as a cadet at the United States Military Academy. This photo appeared in *The Howitzer* (West Point Yearbook) in 1923. *United States Military Academy Library Digital Collection*

West Point, graduating in 1922 and joining the Air Service as a fighter pilot. In the 1920s, he spent three years at Wheeler and Luke Fields in Hawaii, where he served under Maj. George S. Patton on the Army's polo team. Though he remained a lieutenant for almost thirteen years before his promotion to captain in 1935, Griffiss's career seemed to consist of a string of successful assignments. Following his service in Hawaii, he was assigned as commandant of cadets first at March Field, California, and then at Randolph Field, Texas. He then served as commander at Bolling Field in Washington, D.C., before joining the office of the Assistant Secretary of War in 1934.[14]

The access this position provided, along with Griffiss's own talents and demeanor—an appealing joie de vivre—secured him his assignment as assistant military attaché for air working out of the Paris embassy. It was a distinctive and, one may assume, much sought-after tasking. According to the U.S. War Department's adjutant general's report from April 1936, there were only five such postings at the time, the others being held by Lt. Col. Martin Scanlon in London, Maj. Samuel V. Constant in Peking, Capt. Theodore Koenig in Berlin, and Capt. Thomas White in Rome.[15] The War Department had made a wise decision in selecting Griffiss to report on the developments in the areas under his purview, for he had already proved himself to be a skillful writer. In 1930, he published a travel book on Hawaii, appropriately named *When You Go to Hawaii, You Will Need This Guide to the Islands*, with information collected through research and from his own experiences during his assignment there. The book was an impressive 344 pages in length, with a wealth of information on local history, advice for tourists, and even insight into current military practice and doctrine. The following passage is typical of the tone of the book: "Wheeler Field is twenty-three miles from Waikiki, and it takes about an hour to drive there by motor. Flying activities start promptly at eight-thirty and continue throughout the morning on week-days except on Wednesdays and Saturdays, which are devoted to maintenance and inspection of equipment. So the earlier the start, the better, if we would arrive at Haleiwa in time for luncheon. And do not forget the bathing-suits and towels."[16]

As assistant military attaché in France, the quality of Griffiss's work brought him attention from the highest levels in the military. In November 1936, Maj. Gen. Oscar Westover, chief of the Air Corps, called Griffiss's annual report on aviation in France, "the best single report on foreign aviation in any country which I have seen."[17]

Events were soon to bring Griffiss to residency in Spain, where he would utilize his skills of observation in an environment of open warfare.

THE FAILED COUP

The kingdom of Spain, which had once ruled an ocean and laid claim to a hemisphere, had long since descended into second-tier status among European powers. The empire came to a definite end after the disastrous Spanish-American War in 1898. The monarchy came to an abrupt termination on April 14, 1931, when King Alfonso XIII, in the face of popular discontent, abandoned his throne and fled the country.[18] This could have led to an orderly transition into a more democratic society; but for reasons beyond the purview of this history, the political climate of Spain rendered moderation impractical and compromise unattainable.[19]

Three governments held power during the Second Republic in barely more than five years before the outbreak of the civil war. The first of these, 1931–33, a Republican-Socialist coalition, was led by President Niceto Alcalá Zamora (1877–1949) and served as a time of social and economic reform. This period was punctuated by an attempted coup by Major General José Sanjurjo (1872–1936), commander of the Carabineros—the militarized border police. The insurgency was ill-planned, and Sanjurjo received little support and had no success outside of Seville, which fell in a few days.[20] The second government, 1933–35, which was a partnership of Radical Republicans (by then a misnomer for center-right Republicans) and conservatives, undid many of the reforms of the previous government. This administration was also beset with uprisings, this time by separatists in Catalonia and workers in Asturias. The former were quickly subdued after some violence and the arrest of the leaders, among them Luis Companys (1883–1940), the self-declared president of Catalonia.[21] The latter were brutally suppressed in an operation orchestrated by the young Major General Francisco Franco (1892–1975) that featured the deployment of members of the Foreign Legion as well as troops from the Moroccan units, the Regulares.[22] The elections of February 1936 presented another reversal of fortunes.

Left Republicans, Socialists, Communists, and even Anarchists joined together in the Popular Front coalition and captured a ruling majority in the Cortes, the Spanish Parliament.[23] The forces of the Left celebrated by avenging themselves on their political and social rivals. According to historian Hugh Thomas, "Day after day, the tension was maintained by news of a murder here, an attempted lynching there, a church, nunnery or newspaper office burned down in a provincial capital."[24]

An example of the shifting sands of law enforcement in the country was evident in the spring of 1936, when General Eduardo López Ochoa was removed from command of the Third Inspectorship of the Army and criminally charged for his actions in crushing the 1934 workers' rebellion in Asturias. He had been awarded the Cross of San Fernando by the previous (conservative) government for the very same actions but now found himself regarded as a felon. Such alternating standards of justice, wrote Colonel Fuqua at the time, "must necessarily prove detrimental to the morale of the army, particularly at this rather grave moment in the readjustment of the new government."[25]

Conservative politicians and military officers began to meet privately to discuss possible courses of action. Sanjurjo's failed coup had been instructive to them. He had expected his own troops to follow him in his uprising against the Republican-Socialist government, but they overwhelmingly remained loyal to the government. A general lack of support had isolated him and doomed his program.[26] If a new plot were to succeed, the conspirators needed to coordinate their efforts. This would mean the near-simultaneous seizure of the major cities: Madrid, Barcelona, Seville, and Valencia. The effort needed to be comprehensive and not restricted to the military brass but instead open to all sympathetic (i.e., non-Leftist) parties and individuals. The transition of power would be ensured by General Sanjurjo, currently in exile in Portugal, who was standing by to take over once the government was overthrown.[27]

As the political situation intensified, the plan became more feasible to the conspirators and the need for action more evident. If an erstwhile hero like Ochoa could fall, any senior military officer was at risk. Through the spring and early summer of 1936, the conspirators made their preparations and waited for the right moment to strike.

The kindling was set to start the fire of rebellion. All that was needed was a spark.

On the evening of July 12, 1936, Lieutenant José Castillo of the Assault Guards (the left-leaning militarized urban police) was murdered outside of his home in Madrid by unknown assassins. In response, a group of his fellow Assault Guardsmen received warrants to arrest well-known members of the Falange (the Spanish Fascist party). Instead, they arrested and shot José Calvo Sotelo, a leading monarchist and former minister to General Miguel Primo de Rivera during his dictatorship in the 1920s.[28]

Colonel Fuqua reported to Washington that the situation was highly incendiary. Calvo Sotelo had been a well-respected politician, and no fascist. His death signaled to conservatives that their lives were not protected by the government. The murder, under the appearance of state sanction, might "seriously affect the stability of the present governing regime and even that of the Republican State."[29] Fuqua would later observe that it was this murder that caused the leaders of the coup to act.[30]

Consequently, General Emilio Mola, the conspirators' lead planner, set July 18, at 5 a.m., as the date and time for the coup. It seemed like that might even be too late, as Spain appeared on the brink of implosion. On July 14, four people were killed in riots at the twin funerals of Castillo and Calvo Sotelo, both unwisely held in the East Cemetery of Madrid. On July 15, at a committee meeting of party representatives, monarchist and conservative leaders announced their boycott of the Cortes. Faced with this escalating crisis, the delegates of the remaining parties adjourned, agreeing to convene the Cortes on July 21.[31]

Events obliged the conspirators to act prematurely. On the morning of July 17, in the small North African city of Melilla, rebellious officers had gathered to discuss their plans for the uprising. The local military commander, General Manuel Romerales Quinto, in spite of being—in the words of Hugh Thomas—"the fattest of Spain's four hundred generals, and one of the easiest fooled,"[32] was nonetheless loyal to the government. When he learned from an informant that some of his subordinate officers were plotting rebellion, he dispatched his security forces to arrest the participants. The rebel officers realized the danger they were in and took action. With the assistance of the Foreign Legion, they forced the surrender of the police sent to arrest them. They then arrested (and later executed) Romerales and declared martial law in the city. Word of their success spread, and soon garrisons throughout Spanish Morocco, and then on the Spanish Peninsula itself, rose in support.[33]

Details of the success or failure of the coup in various parts of Spain and Morocco are well documented in general histories of the struggle.[34] For our purposes, it is sufficient to report that by the end of July, the rebels had captured Galicia and Leon in the northwest, Navarre and much of Old Castile in the north, and much of Andalusia minus Málaga and the coast in the south. Beyond the Peninsula, they controlled Mallorca and Ibiza in the Balearics as well as the Canary Islands and Spanish Morocco. However, that was the extent of the initial successes of the rebellion. The Spanish government retained power in Madrid, and the key cities of Barcelona and Valencia remained loyal. The government still controlled Aragon, the Mediterranean coast from Málaga to the French border, much of Estremadura to the border with Portugal, New Castile (although Colonel José Moscardó declared for the rebellion and took refuge with his forces in the Alcazar of Toledo), most of Basque territory and Asturias in the north (notwithstanding Oviedo, where Colonel Antonio Aranda had declared for the rebellion), and Minorca in the Balearics.

The Spanish government made a concerted effort to dismiss the threat posed by the uprising. It stemmed the flow of information by restricting phone service, thus explaining the silence from Spain on the eighteenth of the month. Foreign reporters were obliged to use the telegraph at government offices, where, according to one report in the *New York Times*, "after preliminary examination of their messages the censor stands by their side to prevent any departure from the authorized text."[35] Further, the Spanish government issued statements downplaying the magnitude of the uprising: "Enemies of the state are still indulging in spreading false news, but the loyalty of all the forces to the government in Spain is general. Only in Morocco are there still parts of our army that are showing a hostile attitude toward the republic."[36]

Sudden changes in the administration proved these assurances to be false. Within the first twenty-four hours of the coup, both Prime Minister Santiago Casares Quiroga and his successor Diego Martínez Barrio resigned, leaving the minister of the navy, the able and underappreciated José Giral, to take up the effort to control the rapidly deteriorating situation.[37]

Further, the rupture in the Spanish armed forces was much deeper than the official government accounts suggested. By July 1936, the army on the Peninsula had consisted of about 110,000 troops. Between one-quarter and one-third of these were on leave at the time of the coup and thus did not immediately join one side or the other. Of those on duty, about 26,000 joined the rebels while 33,000 remained loyal to the government. Of the 60,000 militarized police forces (Assault Guards, Civil Guards, Carabineros), the division was similar: about 27,000 to the rebels and 33,000 to the government. The rebels could also rely on about 30,000 troops in the Army of Africa, consisting of legionnaires and Moroccan Regulares, though these were still mostly in Morocco at the end of July. In numbers, the government held a slight edge in manpower on the Peninsula among professional soldiers.[38]

In addition to these troops, militia forces on the right and left arose in arms. On the right, the militiamen of the Carlists (conservative Catholic monarchists), who were called Requetés, numbered about 8,400 in July 1936.[39] The Falange (Fascists) could supply about 8,700 willing fighters.[40] These numbers would swell once the fighting commenced.[41] However, these were initially dwarfed by the multitudes who flowed to the government's cause. Hugh Thomas estimated that, of the 20,000 Catalan troops sent to the Aragon front in July, 18,000 of them were militia.[42] From Madrid, Colonel Fuqua reported that by early August there were perhaps 25,000 armed citizens in that city alone. Though ostensibly on the side of the government, this organic force was largely undisciplined and autonomous. Fuqua feared that it could become a "menace to society when withdrawn from the front lines."[43]

The government also retained control of most of the navy. As minister of the navy before the war, a wary Giral made certain to place loyal radio operators on board the ships.[44] This move reaped immediate benefits at the onset of hostilities. News of the coup reached the enlisted radio operators first, while their monarchist officers were left in the dark. Officers of the destroyers *Almirante Valdés* and *Sánchez Barcaiztegui* were thus surprised by their own crews and overpowered. Similar battles were waged on many of the other warships, almost always resulting in a victory for the enlisted crewmen.[45] As a result, after the initial coup, the government still possessed control of the battleship *Jaime I*, the cruisers *Libertad*, *Miguel de Cervantes*, and *Méndez Núñez*, twelve of the thirteen destroyers, twelve of the fourteen submarines (as well as four others under construction at Cartagena), and a majority of the smaller military vessels. In addition, the Basques possessed two destroyers of their own, along with more than thirty smaller vessels. The rebels were able to take possession only of the cruisers *Almírante Cervera* and *Navarra*, the destroyer *El Valasco*, and some smaller vessels, along with those ships docked at El Ferrol in Galicia for repair or construction: the battleship *España*, the unfinished cruisers *Canarias* and *Baleares*, and five unfinished destroyers.[46] By holding onto the majority of the navy, the Republicans had an opportunity to block the transport of the Army of Africa across the Straits of Gibraltar, and thus maintain a majority among the troops on the Peninsula. This they sought to do, though the removal of officers from many of the vessels severely degraded the navy's effectiveness.[47]

In the division of the air forces (which were composed of both the Aviación Militar and the Aeronáutica Naval) the government held a nearly two-to-one advantage in military aircraft (130 to 73) and almost all of the naval aircraft (87 to 5). It also held most of the postal aircraft, civil aircraft, and privately owned aircraft. At the time of the coup, the Spanish air assets formed a small and heterogeneous force, with Breguet XIX bombers and Nieuport Ni-H 52 fighters constituting the majority of their combat land-based aircraft, and Savoia-Marchetti SM.62s and Dornier Wals ("Whales") their most numerous of the naval aircraft. There were about 500 pilots prior to the rupture. As many as 300 were reported as missing from the government rolls after the first week of the fighting. When the dust settled from the initial excitement, about 150 pilots were available for service to the Madrid government, while about

90 joined with the rebels.[48] Thus, on land, air, and sea, the government could boast superior numbers, while the rebels found their forces geographically divided into three areas, on the perilous edge of defeat.

Among their setbacks, the rebels suffered two significant losses that threatened their nascent undertaking with an early demise. On July 19, fresh from the seizure of Mallorca in the Balearics, where he had been military commander, General Manuel Goded (1882–1936) flew to Barcelona, expecting to arrive to a hero's welcome; from there, he had planned to join with Mola and march on the capital. Instead, he was met with a hostile city, saturated with leftist elements armed to the teeth. He surrendered to the overwhelming force and was later executed.[49] Then, on July 20, it was revealed that General Sanjurjo, the presumptive head of the military junta set to assume power in Spain, was dead. While taking off from a remote airfield in Portugal, his plane, a DeHavilland Puss Moth, had struck the tree tops and crashed in a fireball into a stone wall. The pilot survived, but Sanjurjo, the only passenger, was killed instantly.[50]

The rebels were now faced with a crisis of leadership. The coup had failed, for though significant territory had been lost, the government remained intact and in control of the capital. Spain was now poised to serve as the setting for a civil war. Who would lead the rebels, or the Nationalists, as they would come to be known? American ambassador Claude Bowers, witnessing these events from the border with France, later summarized the situation, "Calvo Sotelo—Sanjurjo—Goded—three of the very strongest men among the conspirators—all dead or doomed within four days. And General Franco—where was he?"[51]

FLIGHT OF THE DRAGON RAPIDE

The flight that brought Major General Francisco Franco Bahamonde to Tetuán, Morocco, while perhaps not the first air mission of the war, could be classified as the first air mission with strategic consequences. The man who would become the leader of the Nationalist cause and long-term dictator of Spain arrived at the center ring of the Spanish Civil War aboard a small British passenger aircraft.

On July 9, eight days before the coup, a pair of conservative journalists, one Spanish and one English, met for lunch at a restaurant on the

Strand in London. The Spaniard, Luis Bolín (1897–1969), of the monarchist newspaper *ABC*, was on a unique assignment for his publisher, the Marqués de Luca de Tena, and financed for that purpose by Spanish businessman Juan March. Bolín was to charter a passenger aircraft and retain the services of a pilot for a confidential mission. He had readily secured a De Havilland Dragon Rapide, piloted by Captain William Henry Cecil Bebb. Having completed the first part of his task, what Bolín now needed were passengers to serve as vacationers, so as to give the trip an air of legitimacy and plausible deniability. The English journalist with whom he was lunching, Douglas Jerrold, recommended that a friend of his, Major Hugh Pollard (1887–1966), serve as the cover for the endeavor. When asked by Jerrold to fill such a role, Pollard readily agreed. So, on July 11, at Croydon Airfield, Pollard, accompanied by his nineteen year-old daughter Diana, Diana's friend Dorothy Watson, and Bolín, boarded the aircraft and, with Bebb in the cockpit, took off from England for Las Palmas.[52] Far from being a credulous, disinterested English gentlemen, as he may have first appeared, Pollard was, according to Graham D. Macklin of the British National Archives in Kew, a veteran of British intelligence with "experience of wars and revolutions in Mexico, Morocco, and Ireland, where he had served as a police adviser in Dublin Castle during the 'stormy days' of the Black and Tans in the early 1920s."[53] His politics were decidedly rightist; he was a strong Roman Catholic and anti-Communist. As Macklin notes, although Pollard "feigned a 'gentleman's distaste' for politics," he would later describe "his precise political stance as 'extreme right.'"[54]

The aircraft Bebb and his passengers flew to the Canary Islands was a De Havilland DH.89, designated the Dragon Rapide, described by British historian Gerald Howson as "one of the most famous and longest-enduring piston-engined airliners ever built."[55] Dragon Rapides were not new to Spanish skies. The Spanish postal service Líneas Aéreas Postales Españolas (LAPE) had acquired one model in 1934, and the Aviación Militar followed suit with the acquisition of three in January 1936. It was a two-engined, 400 horsepower (hp) biplane, capable of carrying up to nine people, including the pilot. It could fly at 16,000 feet, with a cruising speed of 132 miles per hour (mph) and a range of

520 miles.⁵⁶ Bolín had thus selected a suitable, reliable aircraft for his mission. It departed Croydon on July 11 and arrived at its destination three days later.⁵⁷

In these tense days leading up to the final rupture of Spain, the conspirators, keeping their communications to a minimum, often worked at cross-purposes or with some redundancy. On the morning of July 15, at Las Palmas, General Luis Orgaz had summoned the local Lufthansa representative Otto Bertram to a discrete meeting at a doctor's office. Orgaz requested, in somewhat insistent tones, that he had a need for one of Lufthansa's aircraft for some purpose he was not yet able to disclose. Bertram, suspecting a political motive behind the request, declined to accommodate the general, insisting that he had no such authority to grant use of the aircraft other than for company business.⁵⁸

On July 17, while the first blows of rebellion were being struck in Melilla, Franco, then forty-three years old, was in Las Palmas in the Canary Islands for the funeral of General Amadeo Balmes. Balmes had shot himself during target practice on his firing range, in what historian Raymond Proctor described as a "very strange accident for a professional soldier." This apparent accident and incredible coincidence allowed Franco an opportunity to leave his station at Tenerife and arrive at Las Palmas, where transportation had been secured to fly him to Morocco.⁵⁹

Franco, who had served as chief of staff for the conservative government, had been assigned to the Canary Islands by the new leftist government in the futile hope of removing him from national influence.⁶⁰ Born in Galicia, Franco came from a naval family but had spent his entire professional life in the army. He was a devout Catholic whose worldview must have been heavily influenced by his pious mother, who had died of pneumonia on a pilgrimage to Rome in 1934. He was also likely negatively influenced by his civil servant father, a Freemason and political liberal, from whom he was estranged. He had developed an early skepticism of politicians, as a result of the humiliation of the Spanish-American War, and a pugnacious spirit at the Academia Militar de Infantería in the Alcazar of Toledo, where he would strike back fiercely at schoolyard bullies.⁶¹

By the time of the coup, Franco may have been the most famous Spanish officer in the army. He was combat-tested and personally brave, having been wounded in the stomach while battling tribesmen in Morocco.[62] His martial ardor was an aberration by interwar standards. As Hugh Thomas remarked in his history of the Spanish Civil War, "Franco always was known as a cruel disciplinarian. He had a reputation for bravery and for good luck under fire: he rode white horses in battle."[63] In 1920, together with the intense and eccentric Colonel José Millán Astray, Franco had established the Spanish Foreign Legion.[64] He claimed to have planned, and definitely did participate in, the Alhucemas landing that led to the ultimate victory in the Rif War.[65] He had not joined in Sanjurjo's coup attempt in 1932, but he was instrumental in crushing the workers' revolt in Asturias in 1934, which made him immediately suspect in the minds of the left.[66] When the Popular Front took over the government, they assigned Franco to a remote command in the Canaries, where he presumably could not cause much trouble.[67] When not in combat, Franco's defining characteristic was his discretion, which took on the guise of aloofness. He was thus uncommitted to the coup until Calvo Sotelo's murder convinced him of the urgency of the situation.[68]

On July 18, Franco learned of the uprising. He went to the military headquarters in Las Palmas, declared himself for the rebellion, and issued a proclamation. "Blind faith in our triumph," he announced, "Long live Spain with honor!" He then boarded the Dragon Rapide, which took off for Morocco.[69] By the time he reached Tetuán on July 19, the protectorate was firmly in rebel hands. General Gómez Morato, the military commander of Morocco, had been informed of the uprising by Prime Minister Casares Quiroga. He had decided to survey the situation for himself and flew to Melilla, where he was promptly arrested. Franco's cousin, Major Ricardo de la Puente Bahamonde, declared his loyalty to the government and tried to hold the Sania Ramel Airfield, but he too was defeated and apprehended.[70] In the initial confusion of the situation, rumors had spread that Franco had been arrested. His appearance in Morocco at the head of the rebel troops invalidated such tales.[71] Franco recognized the importance of the flight that brought him decidedly and ultimately decisively into the war. He later expressed his gratitude to Major Pollard and the others who had taken the Dragon Rapide from England to the Canary Islands by awarding them the Knights Cross of the Imperial Order of the Yoke and the Arrows.[72]

A few days after Franco was retrieved from the Canary Islands and brought into the midst of the insurgency, the American government sought to retrieve one of its own from the war. At the time of the uprising on July 17–18, Ambassador Claude Bowers had been vacationing with his family in Fuenterrabia, near the French border. Rumors had spread that Bowers was missing, perhaps abducted by communists. In fact, Bowers was at liberty and well, and had been kept apprised of the situation throughout Spain by the San Sebastián embassy.[73] Nevertheless, on July 24, Capt. Townsend Griffiss of the Paris embassy was dispatched to locate the ambassador and satisfy the concerns of the U.S. government.[74]

The next day, from Hendaye in the South of France, Griffiss was taken under escort across the border to the Popular Front office in Irun for processing. While Griffiss was thus detained, he was surprised when Ambassador Bowers arrived to greet him.[75] Bowers had been unaware of Griffiss's mission to find him, though earlier in that day he had been informed by the State Department in Washington that the newspapers were reporting he had "disappeared." Bowers had been in Irun to seek the release of a couple of Americans who had been apprehended by local authorities.[76] He was remarkably unconcerned about his personal safety. As a historian, he knew that such military *pronunciamientos* had been fairly routine occurrences over the past century: "For so it had always been in Spain. A thousand soldiers would march from barracks to the Cortes and turn out the deputies, and, in former times, the citizen, leaning against a building in the sun, would turn, with a yawn, to his companion with the comment that they seemed to have another boss. But that was before Spain had awakened from her long sleep."[77]

Griffiss, reassured of Bowers's well-being, returned to France. But the next day he learned that the rebels were within a mile of San Sebastián.[78] The following day, he again came to Fuenterrabia, this time to insist the ambassador and his family relocate to France at once. Griffiss was accompanied by Hallet Johnson of the embassy in San Sebastián and Eddie Flynn, a New York politician and friend of Bowers's. Griffiss informed Bowers that the insurgents and loyalists were separated only by the mountain range.[79] As Bowers contemplated his predicament, Flynn drove the point home, gravely telling the ambassador, "If anything should happen, and they had to send marines in to get you out, and some were killed, you would never forgive yourself."[80] That settled the matter, and Bowers reluctantly consented to depart Spain. He and his family took up residence in the Gold Hotel in Saint Jean-de-Luz on the French side of the border.[81]

As it turned out, the small stretch of land linking Basque country to France would be the site of some of the earliest fighting of the Civil War in which aircraft played a prominent role. However, despite their proximity and seemingly imminent success, the Nationalists would not take San Sebastián until mid-September.[82]

EARLY AIRPOWER ACTIVITY, JULY 1936

It may be possible to date the origin of Spanish airpower to February 1909, when King Alfonso XIII, while visiting Pau, France, took a seat on the Wright Flyer while listening to Wilbur Wright explain its mechanics. The king would have cherished the opportunity to go aloft in the aircraft, but he had promised his queen and government that he would take no such risk.[83] (The concerns were not unfounded. That same year, Antonio Fernández became the first Spanish aviator and would perish while flying his self-designed biplane from France to Spain.) In the year 1911, Spain purchased its first military aircraft, and soon pilots were being trained at Cuatro Vientos Airfield west of Madrid. Among these first trainees was Alfredo Kindelán, who would later command Franco's air force. By 1913, there were sufficient aircraft and pilots to dispatch to Africa to battle the activities of the tenacious Rif tribesmen.[84] Although Spain maintained its neutrality during the First World War, the Hispano-Suiza company developed a highly popular aircraft engine, nearly 50,000 of which were produced in France and elsewhere throughout the war. Production of Spanish-designed aircraft never fully matured, however, since the end of the war and the importation of surplus aircraft from the former belligerents precluded any need to develop a native aircraft industry.[85]

Perhaps the most famous event in Spanish aviation history before the civil war came on February 10, 1926, when Major Ramón Franco (the younger brother of Francisco), Captain Ruiz de Alda, and Sergeant Pablo Rada landed their Dornier Wal, the *Plus Ultra*, in Buenos Aires, completing a 6,420-mile, 60-hour east–west flight across the South Atlantic: a historic first.[86] It is remarkable that two brothers from a family of the minor gentry, Ramón and Francisco Franco, could independently rise to such national prominence in different fields. Also remarkable is how they differed politically in the years before the civil war. Ramón Franco's politics tended leftward, and he would eventually rise up against the military dictatorship of General Miguel Primo de Rivera in 1929.[87] This earned him the favor of the Republican government. At the time of the coup in 1936, he was a military attaché in Washington, D.C. However, the ties of family would ultimately triumph over political differences. In September 1936, he would return to Spain and reconcile with his brother, who secured for him the position of air commander of the Balearics.[88]

In the 1930s, there was no independent Spanish Air Force. Rather, as with the United States, airpower assets were divided between the army and the navy. Some efforts were made to provide comprehensive airpower leadership. A decree issued on July 14, 1934, placed administrative authority of army (military), navy, and civil aircraft in the hands of the newly created position of director general of aeronautics, which was to carry with it the rank of major general in the Spanish Army. Originally, the director general was placed under the direct supervision of the prime minister; however, a decree of October 4, 1935, delegated the supervisory responsibility to the War Department instead. It appears that there was some trend toward establishing an independent air force, when the Popular Front government moved the aviation portfolio to the newly established Ministry of Air. However, the political crisis of 1936, which culminated in the civil war, postponed the enactment of such plans.[89] During the administration of the conservative government (1933–36), War Minister José María Gil Robles attempted to carry out a modernization of the air forces. However, of the 249 aircraft he ordered from foreign nations, only three were delivered by the time of the civil war, these being militarized models of the De Havilland DH.89 Dragon Rapide.[90] As Captain Griffiss later observed, "In July 1936 Spain in the Air was in no position to engage in warfare either with a foreign power or to combat a revolution within its own boundaries."[91]

On July 18, 1936, once it became clear that the coup was widespread and involved many of the highest-ranking officers in the military, the government attempted to find out who remained loyal. The director general of Aeronautics, General Miguel Núñez de Prado, was dispatched to Saragossa to confer with his colleague General Miguel Cabanellas. As it turned out, Cabanellas had joined the insurgency. He had the credulous and dutiful Núñez de Prado arrested and later executed, eliminating at the onset of the conflict the leadership of the government's air arm.[92]

When the dust had settled following the initial uprising, the government found itself in control of the Number 11 Group at Getafe Airfield, south of Madrid, consisting of three squadrons of Nieuport Ni-H 52 fighters; the Number 31 Group, also at Getafe, consisting of Breguet XIX bombers; and the Number 13 Group at Prat Airfield, near Barcelona, containing a single squadron of Nieuports. There was a seaplane group of Dornier Wals at Los Alcázares, on the coast near Murcia, and an assortment of independent squadrons throughout the government zone. The government navy retained most of the seaplanes, thanks to a swift reversal of an uprising at San Javier air-sea base by troops from nearby Los Alcázares. The rebels (later Nationalists) held the bases of three of the Breguet Groups: Number 21 at Leon, Number 22 at Seville, and Number 23 at Logroño, although two squadrons of these groups had been transferred to Madrid before the coup and thus remained in government hands. The rebels also controlled Breguet Group Number 1 in Africa. However, they were short of Nieuports and thus outnumbered in fighters. Only eleven seaplanes, five Savoia-Marchetti SM.62s at Marin and six damaged Dornier Wals in Cádiz, were taken by the rebels. These, and an assortment of other land-based aircraft and seaplanes, along with appropriated civil aircraft and private light-craft, made up the respective belligerent air forces of Spain in July 1936.[93]

At this point, the war in the air could hardly be called an experiment in state-of-the-art equipment. The aircraft designs for the Nieuport Ni-H 52s, Breguet XIXs, Savoia-Marchetti SM.62s, Vickers Vildebeests, and Dornier Wals all dated back to the 1920s. However, the war was a display of Spanish craftsmanship, for the French-designed Nieuport Ni-H 52s and Breguet XIXs and the British-designed Vickers Vildebeests were all manufactured in Spain—the Nieuports at the Hispano-Suiza Sección de Aviación in Guadalajara, and the Breguets and Vildebeests at the Construcciones Aeronáutica S.A. (CASA) factory at Getafe, near Madrid.[94] In addition, several of the German-Italian-designed Dornier Wals were manufactured at the CASA factory at Puntales, near Cádiz.[95]

The CASA-Breguets, introduced in 1923, were light bombers of a sesquiplane-design (*sesquiplanes* are biplanes in which the top wing is significantly larger than the lower wing). They were constructed of metal frames with fabric covering. They possessed a single Hispano-Suiza 12-cylinder V-shaped engine capable of producing 500 hp, enabling the aircraft to reach speeds of 143 mph, with a ceiling of almost 20,700 feet and a range of nearly 500 miles. For comparison, the British Hawker Hart, introduced in 1928, produced 525 hp and could fly at 184 mph, with a ceiling over 21,300 feet, albeit with a range of 470 miles. The Breguet was equipped with up to four Vickers 7.7-mm machine guns and could carry 880 pounds of bombs, as compared to the Hawker Hart's three 7.7-mm machine guns and 520 pounds of bombs.[96]

The Hispano-Nieuport Ni-H 52s were licensed to be built in Spain in 1928 and were first fielded in 1931.[97] They were sesquiplane fighters of primarily metal composition. Like the Breguets, they were powered by 500 hp, 12-cylinder Hispano-Suiza V-engines. They could reach speeds of 140 mph and had a ceiling of almost 27,000 feet. They were armed with two Vickers 7.7-mm machine guns. By the time of the civil war, the Nieuport's capabilities were lagging behind those of fighters of more recent designs. For instance, the American Boeing P-12E could fly at 189 mph, the Curtiss P-6E Hawk at 198 mph, and the German Heinkel He 51 at 205 mph. The Nieuport's maneuverability did not favorably impress Frank Tinker, an American pilot who flew for the Republican government. He found it to be extremely difficult to handle and was relieved to still be alive after a bouncy landing. As he recalled, he was astonished that he "had found a worse plane than the Breguet."[98]

The CASA-Vickers Vildebeests were first produced in 1929. These metal-framed biplanes were covered in fabric and could be equipped with either floats or wheels, depending on where one wished to land them. They were each powered by a Hispano-Suiza liquid-cooled engine, which generated 600 hp and allowed for a maximum speed of 137 mph, a ceiling of almost 14,300 feet, and a range of almost 750 miles. They were armed with a Vickers gun on the port side of the fuselage and had a Lewis gun mounted to a ring around the observer's seat. They had a 1,000-pound payload, which could consist of either bombs or a single 18-inch torpedo. These were capable aircraft but few in number. Only twenty-five had been produced in Spain, the final one delivered to San Javier in April 1936.[99]

The Dornier Wals, the most famous of which was the *Plus Ultra*, mentioned above as the craft with which Ramón Franco had traversed the Atlantic, were originally designed in 1922. Starting in the late 1920s, three types of this aircraft were produced in Spain, those of the military, naval, and passenger varieties; the key difference among the three was the type of engine used in each. They were monoplanes of the *parasol* style, meaning the wing was suspended above the fuselage; and the naval variety were *flying boats*, meaning they had no landing gear and touched down on the water with their fuselage. Their two engines were located on the parasol wing, one facing forward, the other backward; together they were capable of producing a total of between 900 hp (for the military variety) and 1,200 hp (for the naval variety).[100] They were large and slow, reaching speeds of only 112 mph and a ceiling of 16,400 feet, but they had a wingspan of 73 feet, 10 inches; a length of 56 feet, 7 inches; a loaded weight of 12,680 pounds; and a payload capacity of 1,500 pounds. It therefore could deliver a hefty blow, so long as the skies were uncontested, or when sufficient escort protection was available.

According to Spanish historian Jesús Salas Larrazábal, the first claimed aerial victory of the war came from Republican Captain Manuel Cascon, flying a Nieuport out of Getafe on July 20, 1936.[101] Soon, aircraft were taking part in combat across the Peninsula. In Madrid, rebel

General Joaquín Fanjul (1880–1936) was injured in a bombing at the Montaña barracks. The next day, the commander of a relief force, General García de la Herrán, was killed by aircraft fire, and the relief attempt aborted. On July 22, rebels marching toward Madrid were halted in the Somosierra Pass in part because of the harassment from the skies by aircraft from the nearby bases at Getafe and Cuatro Vientos. To the west, at Guadaramma Pass, rebel forces were almost driven back after two of their leaders were killed by attacks from the air.[102] On July 25, over the Strait of Gibraltar, insurgent pilot Miguel Guerrero shot down a Dornier Wal flying out of Málaga. By the end of the month, he would vanquish two more Republican aircraft, both Vickers Vildebeests, over Andalusia. Government forces struck back when a Douglas DC-2 shot down an insurgent fighter over Córdoba on July 31.[103]

Map 1. Nationalist-Republican Territory, July 1936

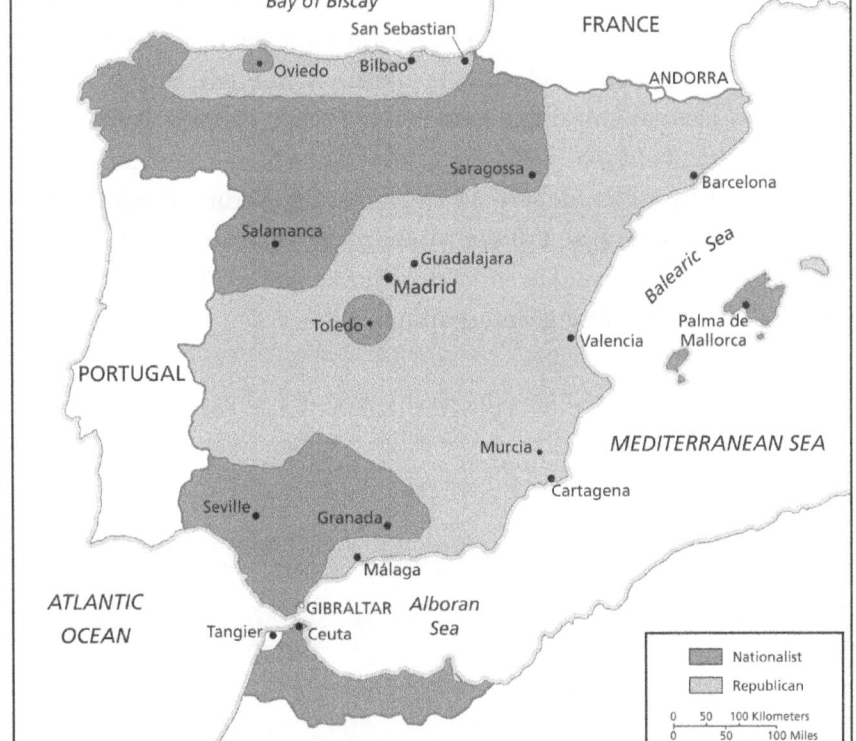

Operations to establish dominance over the airspace of the southern part of the Peninsula were important, because the insurgents were struggling with the thorny question of transporting the Army of Africa across the Strait of Gibraltar in the face of a hostile navy in the Mediterranean. As seen above, if the insurgents could join their African forces to those already on the Peninsula, where they were currently inferior in number, they could tip the balance of power in their favor. If they could not cross by sea, that left the air. Within a day of Franco's arrival in Morocco, a small, heterogeneous mix of aircraft began transporting legionnaires and Regulares across the Strait to Seville. This transport force was originally composed of three Fokker F.VIIbs, two Dornier Wals, one Douglas DC-2, and one Fokker F.VIIa.[104] The capacity of this ad hoc air bridge was limited, for the Wals could carry twelve passengers each, the Fokkers eight each, and the Douglas fourteen, for a total of seventy passengers per trip.[105]

It was soon clear that outside assistance would be needed to support this effort. Franco turned his gaze from the Peninsula eastward, to possible like-minded benefactors in Germany and Italy. By July 21, Luis Bolín was in Rome making a personal appeal to dictator Benito Mussolini on behalf of Franco. A couple days later, a Spanish officer and two German businessmen departed Las Palmas for Berlin, with the intention of asking for support directly from Chancellor Adolf Hitler.[106] The needs of airpower would in short order draw intervention from abroad and make the Civil War an international affair.

CHAPTER 3

AIRLIFT

Wherever the corpse is, there the vultures will gather.

—MATTHEW 24:28 (NRSV)

FRENCH AND ITALIAN INTERVENTION

The decisions made by the leaders in Spain and throughout Europe during the months of August, September, and October 1936 would ultimately prove decisive in the outcome of the civil war in Spain. During those months, Hitler's Germany and Mussolini's Italy would enter the war on the side of the Nationalists; the Western democracies, after an initial show of support by France, would opt for neutrality; the desperate Republic would begin to lean upon the broken reed of Stalin's Soviet Union; and Franco would consolidate his support and unite the Nationalists under his personal and indisputable command. Remarkably, all these events would be linked closely, if not directly, to the use of airpower in the war: it would be with aircraft that the Germans, Italians, and French would first become significantly involved in the conflict; it would be Russian aircraft, more so than their tanks or advisers, that would establish that nation's credibility as an effective ally to the Republic; and it would be with aircraft that Franco would transport his Army of Africa to the Peninsula, tipping the scales of the conflict to the advantage of the Nationalists.

Very early in the war, American officials had firsthand knowledge of foreign intervention in the conflict. On July 24, 1936, Capt. Townsend Griffiss, on his mission to locate Ambassador Claude Bowers, arrived at the airport in Bayonne, France. There he learned that the airdrome was closed, and that the Air Meet scheduled for July 26 had been postponed. However, on July 25, the French authorities announced that the Air Meet was back on as scheduled, and that the Armée de l'Aire would participate.[1] As Griffiss recorded,

> That afternoon, 7 Potez-25, 4 Potez-54, 1 LeO-20, 1 Potez-29 hospital, 1 Bloch-81 hospital, and 5 Morane Saulnier-225 acrobatic pursuit planes landed at Bayonne Airport. The Potez-25 were from Pau, the Potez-54 from Toulouse, and the pursuit from Etampes. It was not until the 28th that all but two Potez-25 took off for their home stations. The two remaining observation type planes were armed with front and rear machine guns and were equipped with bomb-racks.[2]

The local press had declared that the government was taking precautions to guard the French-Spanish border, therefore requiring patrols of armed aircraft. When Griffiss arrived in Perpignon, France, on July 29, he observed six military aircraft circling the field and then returning north. He asked an official if they always turned back, to which the official replied in the negative. The day before, six planes had continued flying south, toward Spain.[3]

In August, Colonel Fuqua confirmed French support for the Spanish government, estimating in a telegram that the Republicans had received twenty-five French aircraft.[4] However, this support was limited and conditional. Many of the aircraft the French shipped to Spain lacked armaments; this was done in order to avoid the prohibition on weapons and equipment. Upon their arrival, the aircraft were equipped with inferior weapons they were not designed to use. However, some even lacked mountings for armaments.[5]

Such unsatisfactory deliveries were the result of the indecisiveness of the administration of Léon Blum (1872–1950), who had been elected as premier of France on the Popular Front ticket in June 1936. The astute José Giral, upon taking over as the Spanish prime minister after the resignation of his predecessors, had appealed to Blum for assistance. Blum was willing to support a fellow Popular Front leader and, together with Air Minister Pierre Cot (1895–1977), Blum set in motion a system to deliver matériel to the Republic. However, within the week, on a visit to England, Blum found himself subtly encouraged to adopt a noninterventionist stand. Upon returning to France, he decided that France would allow only commercial or private support to the Spanish Republic. Yet, in contrast to his superior's public malleability, the tenacious Cot continued to employ certain devices to transfer aircraft to Spain without arousing suspicion.[6] This explains the lack of armaments on several of the aircraft and the discretion exercised by authorities in transferring these aircraft to Spain, as witnessed by Griffiss at Perpignan. Finally, on August 8, 1936, France agreed to the Non-Intervention Treaty, thus completely ending all open support for the Republic.

However, in the early months of the war, French support helped to prop up the Spanish Air Force. Griffiss estimated that by November 1936, Paris had dispatched seventy-eight aircraft to the Republic.[7] Numbers vary on the quantities and types of aircraft sent to Spain, but it appears that the Potez 54 bomber class and the Dewoitine 371/372 fighters were most prominent among France's contributions. Several of these aircraft were flown by the famed España squadron, commanded by French novelist André Malraux (1901–76), who had arrived in Madrid on July 31. His pilots were well-paid volunteers and he, though no pilot, flew aboard Potez 54s on missions.[8]

At the time of the outbreak of the Spanish Civil War, the Potez 54 was considered the cornerstone of the Armée de l'Aire's bomber force. It was built to impress, and its design strikes one as the embodiment of the flying fortress. It was a twin-engine monoplane with a tall fuselage and large windows. It had two gun turrets—one in the nose, one dorsal—encased within windowed enclosures that historian Gerald Howson accurately describes as "birdcage like" in appearance, along with a ventral gun position, and a 2,205-pound bombload. It possessed radio communication and night-flying equipment, new and rare capabilities for that time.[9] Both models, the Potez 540 and

542, could reach maximum speeds of about 190 mph. The Potez 542 model (with two 720 hp engines, as opposed to the 690 hp engines on the Potez 540) had a higher cruising speed, though the 540 boasted a superior ceiling of 33,000 feet (compared to the 542's ceiling of 28,000 feet); the 542 also had a range of nearly 750 miles (compared to the 540's range of 620 miles.)

The Dewoitine 371 and Dewoitine 372 were essentially the same aircraft, their key distinction being the armaments for which each was specifically designed, a distinction that was negated when they were shipped unarmed to Spain. Introduced in 1934, they were metal monoplane fighters with fabric-covered wings, capable of reaching speeds of about 240 mph, thus topping most contemporary competitors. They also had a high rate of climb, reaching 16,400 feet in just 5 minutes, 33 seconds.[10] It was for this reason, along with the aircraft's maneuverability, that Griffiss—writing the following February—would rank the Dewoitine 371 as the second-best fighter in the war up to that time, next to the Russian I-16.[11]

While the Republicans may have been the first to invite foreign intervention into the war, this was merely because it took less time for Giral to telephone Blum than for the Nationalists' representatives to fly to Berlin or Rome. On July 21, Luis Bolín, the procurer of the Dragon Rapide that had conveyed Franco from the Canary Islands to Morocco, arrived in Rome at Franco's behest to request assistance from the Italian dictator Benito Mussolini (1883–1944).[12] Mussolini, Il Duce, was soon convinced of the value of intervention in Spain. A Nationalist victory would enhance Italy's power vis-à-vis France, which would then be bordered on three sides by right-wing governments. Fresh from victory in Ethiopia, another triumphant adventure could place Italian military prowess beyond dispute.[13] These were all considerations in favor of intervention. However, still conscientious of international opinion, Mussolini's government used discretion in the early days of the war. On July 30, when twelve Savoia-Marchetti SM.81 bombers set out from Sardinia for Morocco, their Italian markings were removed or covered.[14]

The SM.81s were tri-motor bomber-transports, each with five-man crews. They were equipped with three gun turrets: a dorsal, a waist, and a ventral turret, each turret featuring twin 7.7-mm Breda-SAFAT machine guns. In addition, they had .303 Lewis guns on either side of the fuselage, and they carried 2,205 pounds of bombs. They boasted of a maximum speed of 211 mph, a range of 932 miles, and a ceiling of almost 23,000 feet—though Howson reasonably suspects that the claimed speed estimates were exaggerated.[15]

It was not until the arrival of the Fiat CR.32 fighters that the war finally had its first truly impressive aircraft. Ironically, these were biplanes at a time when more aircraft were appearing with the more streamlined, monoplane design. The Fiats, known in Spain as "Chirris," had been introduced in 1933. They were fabric-covered metal-framed aircraft of a sesquiplane wing design. With a mere 592 hp engine, they could achieve 220 mph, with a range of 485 miles and a ceiling of 25,264 feet. They were armed with 7.7-mm Breda-SAFAT machine guns and 220 pounds of bombs.

The first shipment of Fiats arrived in Spain on August 14, 1936. When they were ready for service, they were incorporated into the Italian expeditionary air force, the Aviación del Tercio, under Colonel Ruggero Bonomi (1898–1980). The Aviación, in turn, operated with the consent and under the control of the Nationalists, in the person of General Alfredo Kindelán (1879–1962), Franco's air commander. Within a week of their arrival, the Fiats were in combat, shooting down a Nieuport Ni-H 52 above Córdoba. It was soon clear that the Chirris were well-suited for combat in Spain. Pilots found them easy to fly; Spanish Capt. Joaquin García Morato (1904–39), after a mere eighty-five minutes of training on the aircraft, was leading combat missions in the plane. They were also easy to repair and able to incorporate parts from wrecked aircraft.[16] Spanish historian Jesús Salas Larrazábal, maintained they were superior to both the French Dewoitine 371s and the German Heinkel He 51s, stating they were "the best fighters in Spain until the Ratas arrived," the Ratas (Rats), a name for the Russian I-16 fighters, also known as the Moscas (Flies), which would not commence operations in Spain until November 1936.[17]

As if to stress this point, on August 27, above Granada, a Fiat brought down a Dewoitine. Italian and French aircraft were now engaging each other in the skies above Spain, and the performance of the Fiats seemed to defy their anachronistic biplane design and modest statistics.[18] Yet, it would be months before the direct intervention of the Italians became evident. In late November 1936, the American military attaché in Rome, Maj. Norman Fiske, reported that he suspected Italian aviation assistance to be "quite considerable," but he provided no details.[19]

THE AIRLIFT

The mission to airlift Nationalist troops from Africa to the Peninsula was arguably the most significant air operation of the Spanish Civil War. It was that mission that brought the German Luftwaffe into the conflict, allowing it to both test its capabilities and intimidate its Great Power competitors, all while seeking to establish a friendly, and perhaps dutiful, regime in Madrid.

As we saw in the previous chapter, the Nationalists had once before attempted to coax German cooperation for their cause, when, on July 15, 1936, General Orgaz unsuccessfully sought to acquire use of a Lufthansa airliner from the local representative in Las Palmas for the purposes of taxiing Franco to Morocco. After the rebellion broke out in Morocco, the Nationalists once again sought out Lufthansa's support. However, this time they did not ask, they simply took. On July 18, Captain Alfred Henke, piloting a Junkers Ju 52/3m D-APOK, was ordered to land at Villa Cisneros. He was later allowed to continue to Las Palmas, but there his aircraft was impounded for Orgaz's use. This sensitive situation was resolved when Franco met with Henke in Tetuán, Morocco, and made a personal request for a diplomatic favor. Franco asked the pilot to transport two resident Germans sympathetic to his cause, Johannes Bernhardt and Adolf Langenheim, and one Spanish officer, Captain Francisco Arranz Monasterio, to Germany to meet with German dictator Adolf Hitler (1889–1945) as his representatives. This Henke consented to do, and on July 24, his aircraft with its three passengers touched down at Gatow, near Berlin.[20]

The meeting between the men and Hitler in Bayreuth on the night of July 25–26 is a notorious example of Hitler's ability to bend the course of international politics to his will. Initially, the Führer was unwilling to become embroiled in a civil war and annoyed at being asked to do so. His ministers reinforced his opposition to intervention, believing it risked a direct confrontation with Great Britain and France, which Germany was still unprepared to contemplate. Yet, over the course of the next several hours, Hitler shifted his opinion, becoming convinced more through his own open contemplations than by any arguments put forth by Franco's delegates. By the end of the night, the delegates had secured Hitler's pledge of support.[21]

The program that brought Germany into the Spanish Civil War was given the Wagnerian title of Unternehmen Feuerzauber (Operation Magic Fire). German intervention was to take a noncombatant form. Transport aircraft were to be supplied to taxi troops from Morocco to Spain. Those planes that were piloted by Germans could fire only in self-defense. Front corporations were to be established to smuggle aircraft to Spain and to process the payments. These became known as Compañía Hispano-Marroquí de Transportes (HISMA), the Spanish/Moroccan-based business that would import German equipment; and Rohstoffe und Waren Einkaufsgesellschaft (ROWAK), the German-based company that would import Spanish raw materials. To consolidate these efforts, the Germans organized their operations under a newly established headquarters staff, based in Germany and known as Special Staff W, under the command of General der Flieger Helmuth Wilberg (1880–1941).[22]

The first responsibility of Wilberg and his staff was to get equipment and men to Morocco and Spain quickly but discretely. Even before Special Staff W could organize its first detachment of men and matériel, Henke and his delegation had flown out of Germany and arrived in Tetuán on July 28. Once his craft was refueled and prepped, Henke flew on to Tablada Airfield near Seville with a contingent of troops. Thus Henke, reluctantly recruited into Nationalist service, was the first German to operate the airlift across the Strait of Gibraltar.[23] On July 29, the first of a squadron of ten Junkers Ju 52s took off from Stuttgart for Morocco, led by Captain Rudolph Freiherr von Moreau. Unlike Henke's Lufthansa aircraft, these Junkers were specifically built for military use. However, they received civilian registrations, and their gun ports were covered with metal sheets. Despite these precautions, when one flew off course and landed in Republican territory, it was impounded by the government and later used as evidence of German intervention.[24]

On July 31, General der Flieger Erhard Milch addressed a gathering of ninety-five volunteers in Döberitz, Germany. He let them know that their assignment was to serve solely in the role of air transport, and they were not to engage in combat except in self-defense. These volunteers, who were given the nondescript name of the Tourist Group Union (Reisegesellschaft Union), were then conveyed to Hamburg, where they boarded the steamship *Usaramo*. Their leader, Major Alexander von Scheele, accompanied the volunteers to the point of embarkation. Also on board were crates containing ten unassembled Junkers Ju 52 bomber/transports and six unassembled Heinkel He 51 fighters, along with armaments and other equipment.[25]

The *Usaramo* arrived at Cádiz harbor on the night of August 5. It entered the port with dimmed lights, unseen and unhindered by the Republican Navy. The troops and equipment were forwarded to Tablada, where the aircraft were assembled. In the meantime, the remainder of the Ju 52s that had flown from Germany had arrived in theater. By the second week of August, the initial German force was in place and the airlift was fully operational. Of the Ju 52s sent to Spain, one was captured when it landed in Republican territory, and nine (of those shipped over on the *Usaramo*) were handed over to Spanish pilots and formed into bomber squadrons (*escuadrillas*). This left eleven Ju 52s (one of those shipped on the *Usaramo*, the nine remaining of those flown directly from Germany, and Henke's aircraft) to conduct the lion's share of the airlift.[26]

As discussed in chapter 2, the arrival of the Germans was not the beginning of the airlift. Initially, Franco had a small air contingent with which he commenced the transportation of troops across the Strait of Gibraltar on July 20.[27] It is not certain how many troops were actually carried by these initial (Nationalist) aircraft. The contingencies of war often caused the planes to be tasked to other missions; and once the Germans began to arrive, the Spanish yielded the transportation responsibilities to them.[28] According to historian Raymond Proctor (citing German records), from July 28 to August 4, as the Germans arrived and began operations, they transported 1,207 troops to the mainland. Between August 5 and August 12, when regular routes were established, the number of troops transported was estimated at 1,282.[29] The Nationalists managed a single sea convoy of troops on August 5, bringing some 3,000 soldiers with arms and matériel to the Peninsula under the protection of Nationalist and Italian air cover, but this was done at great risk and required a heavy concentration of forces to challenge the Republican blockade of the Strait.[30] Under such conditions, an established air bridge seemed the logical choice to distribute the risk and resources of the transport mission going forward.

It was thus that the Junkers Ju 52 became the workhorse in bringing Franco's army across the Strait of Gibraltar. Starting with his work in the Great War, aircraft engineer Hugo Junkers distinguished himself with his all-metal designs, often featuring the aluminum alloy duralumin.[31] The Ju 52 carried on this tradition. It was originally built in 1930 but had undergone a number of alterations in the half-dozen years before its first appearance in war. The latest version was a duralumin-covered monoplane with three 660 hp BMW 132 radial engines. The military version of the aircraft was meant as an auxiliary to the Dornier Do 11 and 23, but it became instead the lead bomber-transport in the German inventory. It was operated by a five-man crew and could be equipped with two 7.9-mm MG-15 machine guns and up to 2,205 pounds of bombs.[32] In terms of self-defense, the Ju 52 was deficient in ways that would soon reveal themselves. Its maximum speed was 180 mph. It therefore could comfortably outpace the pursuits it would encounter early in the war, such as the Nieuport Ni-H 52s (140 mph). However, once the Russians entered the conflict, the Ju 52s found themselves facing the much faster I-15s (216 mph) and I-16s (282 mph). In addition to its relative slowness, it was ill-equipped to shoot its way out of a conflict. As Griffiss observed the following spring, "The bomber [Ju 52] has two gunners one aft on top and the other aft underneath and any other attack approach exposes the attacker to machine gun fire. The forward part is unprotected and just above the heads of the pilot and bomber is the exposed reserve gasoline tank."[33] Even so, these vulnerabilities would become manifest only in November, after the Germans had completed

CHAPTER 3

Photo 4. German Junkers Ju 52s similar to this one at the National Museum of the United States Air Force were the key vehicles employed to carry Franco's Army of Africa to the Spanish Peninsula at the start of the Civil War. *U.S. Air Force*

the airlift. As transport aircraft, the Ju 52s more than delivered on their promise. Upon arriving in Tetuán, the Germans removed the furnishings from their aircraft and found they could fit thirty-five passengers inside, more than doubling the plane's normal capacity. The thirty-fifth passenger would not be very comfortable, but he would fit.[34]

The aircraft assigned to provide escort to the Ju 52s were the Heinkel He 51s. These were first produced in 1933 under the pretense of use by a German sports-flying club because the remilitarization of German flight was not yet an acknowledged fact.[35] Like the Fiat CR.32s, they were metal-framed, fabric-covered biplanes with a 550 hp engine; they were capable of reaching speeds of 205 mph, and had a range of 342 miles and a ceiling of 25,493 feet. Their speed and range were thus inferior to those of their Italian counterparts (220 mph, and 485-mile range), although their ceiling was slightly higher than that of the Fiat (25,264 feet). The Dewoitine 371 also bested the He 51 in speed and range (239 mph and 516 miles, respectively). All this put the Heinkel's abilities in doubt and made it clear that the Germans required a more suitable fighter.

Nevertheless, once fully operational, the airlift progressed with marked efficiency. The throughput for the balance of August was particularly impressive. Between August 5 and August 23, a total of 4,800 troops and 22 tons of matériel had been transported. By the end of the month, the totals were 6,100 troops and 25.5 tons.[36]

Although the Germans were supposed to have avoided combat, it was inevitable that they were soon drawn into hostilities. As early as August 13, German-piloted Ju 52s had bombed the battleship *Jaime I* in the Bay of Malaga. It was therefore largely a formality when Hitler, on August 28, 1936, authorized German pilots to engage in combat in Spain.[37] A mere four days prior, Germany had signed the Non-Intervention Agreement, declaring its support to keep foreign influence out of the Spanish Civil War.[38]

Still, the airlift remained the key mission of the Germans, and throughout the next six weeks, Ju 52s hauled the Army of Africa, both men and equipment, to Spain. By October 11, the unofficial end of the mission, 13,000 men had been flown to Spain from Morocco by the Germans. This amounted to about 173 troops delivered per day. The airlift also transported 298 tons of matériel, or about 4 tons per day.[39] This was arguably the first strategic airlift in history, strategic not so much due to the magnitude of the shipment (though it did far exceed any previous effort) or the distance involved but rather due to the effects that it brought about, effects that would not have occurred had the majority of the Army of Africa remained in Morocco until regular sea transport could have been secured. We will see the impact of this force in the following section.

Unfortunately, it would be some time before American observers were aware of the airlift, and what information they received was inaccurate. Almost eleven months after the start of the war, on June 8, 1937, Maj. Edward Raley of the Information Division of the Office of the Chief of the Air Corps (OCAC) recorded news from a report by the military attaché in Paris: "Franco used for the transport of troops from Morocco to Spain, the Savoia-Marchetti, Caproni & Junkers planes. By reducing the petrol tanks, space was obtained to carry men, arms & ammunition & in this way several battalions were transported."[40]

The report made the error, common at this point, of confusing Savoia-Marchetti SM.81s for Capronis. In Ethiopia, when SM.81s were airlifting supplies to advancing troops, reports had similarly confused the aircraft for Capronis.[41] No Capronis were involved with the Ethiopian airlift, nor were they involved with the Moroccan-Spanish airlift. Further, involvement of even SM.81s in the airlift is unclear, and likely minimal because they were not dispatched for that purpose as were the Ju 52s.

Major Raley was also in correspondence, the following October—a year after the completion of the airlift—with Maj. E. O. Sawyer Jr., an inactive reservist who had served in the Military Intelligence Division (MID) and who now resided in Berkeley, California. Sawyer himself had somehow been in communication with Lieutenant Enrique Bolín, the brother of Luis, procurer of Franco's Dragon Rapide and his emissary to Mussolini. Sawyer passed on Enrique's statement verbatim:

> By this time the revolt had gained publicity in Spain and General Queipo de Llano had taken and was holding Seville with less than 200 men. Franco sent these planes [the Italian SM.81s] at once with all speed to support General [Queipo] de Llano.
>
> Franco's plan was to send his men across the Strait on available sea transports, but there was an uprising of the crews on Spanish warships, who killed their officers and prevented for a time sea traffic by Franco. He, however, had been able to send one or two small steamers each carrying a few hundred men, across the Strait before the revolt occurred. He had four transport planes each with a capacity of 30 men plus pilot and mechanic. He put these in service at once, making two round trips a day, and in the course of two months transported his army of 18,000 men to Spain.[42]

Enrique's account had a few inconsistencies from what is now known about the airlift. One is the implication that the airlift was completed entirely by the "four transport planes" that had been in Franco's possession at the start of the war. Another inconsistency is the statement that 18,000 troops were transported to the mainland by the airlift, while making no mention of the August 5 sea convoy or explaining how the armaments and equipment of these troops were also transferred. Sawyer expressed his belief that matériel must have been sent over during "night trips by fishing trawlers" and via "other planes and aid extended by Italy," but no mention is made of German support. Sawyer also stated that Enrique and a fellow officer "were flown from Morocco to Spain as the 33rd and 34th occupants of one of these planes nearly a month after the outbreak of hostilities," and he added, "These transports were Spanish planes."[43] As stated above, the Junkers Ju 52s had capacity for thirty-five passengers when fully stripped, while each of the other aircraft involved in the airlift—the Dornier Wals, the Douglas DC-2, and the Fokker F.VIIa and VIIb—had a much smaller capacity. It is apparent that Enrique Bolín was being reticent regarding the involvement of Germans in the Spanish Civil War.

As it was early in the war and the U.S. government had no formal contact with the Nationalist leadership, it is no surprise, then, that it lacked contemporary awareness of the airlift, let alone the precise details of it. However, even the Spanish Republican government appears to have been unaware of the magnitude of the operation. This would explain how the Nationalists were able to launch a surprise offensive from Seville northward and eastward, that threatened to capture the Spanish capital and to end the war by November.

NATIONALIST ADVANCES, AUGUST–OCTOBER 1936

As early as August 3, there were sufficient numbers of Army of Africa troops on the Peninsula to allow Franco's subordinates to lead a breakout offensive north of the perimeter around Seville, within which the Nationalists had been held since Queipo de Llano's seizure of that city. Colonel Juan Yagüe assumed command of these forces and captured Mérida on August 10. Four days later, the Nationalists seized Badajoz on the border with Portugal. Yagüe's columns then turned eastward toward Madrid, reaching Navalmoral de la Mata on August 23. In the north, General Emilio Mola's troops occupied Tolosa and began to shell San Sebastián, engaging Basque troops near Irun.[44]

Attempts by the Republican government to recapture the initiative failed. In Andalusia, a government advance on Córdoba was halted on

August 20. An amphibious invasion of Mallorca was similarly checked and forced to withdraw on September 4. These defeats were sufficient to discredit Giral's command, and on the same day as the retreat from Mallorca, his government fell and was replaced by a leftist administration under the leadership of old-guard socialist Francisco Largo Caballero (1869–1946). It was a tragic fall for Giral, whose early decisions in arming the militias and securing the loyalty of the ships' crews may have saved what was left of the Republic in July. His left liberal politics generated initial support from France and over time may have secured more sympathy from England, as well. But events were driving the two sides in Spain to the poles of political extremism, and Largo Caballero better represented the intensity of feeling for the cause of Republican Spain. This change of administration also indicated that a government victory, should it come, would not result in a status quo ante bellum but in a much more socialistic composition of Spanish society.

In the meantime, Colonel Fuqua, with military efficiency, was busy transforming the U.S. embassy into an "information center." Fuqua left no stone unturned in his effort to support the intelligence-gathering mission of his post. His preparations are paraphrased as follows:

1. A radio room for receiving and intercepting transmissions from both local and international sources.
2. A map room containing maps of the nation and capital with details on infrastructure and the movement and location of troops.
3. Contacts through all of the major governmental and commercial sources of information in the capital, both pro-government and pro-Nationalist as well as foreign ambassadors and American staffers at the telephone company.
4. An intelligence section established under a former American reserve officer named Samuel Rily Williams, charged with organizing unofficial means of information-gathering and funded through an "Extraordinary Personal Expense Fund."[45]

To this last point of unofficial information channels, Fuqua discovered that his fellow Americans in the press corps provided a wealth of information. As he recorded, "The American newspaper men in Madrid are more intelligent, better paid and far more on the alert than those of any other nation."[46] These included Edward Knoblaugh, whom we will meet later.

Even so, American officials had little firsthand knowledge of the air battles being waged throughout Spain. One of the few early reports came on the last day of August, courtesy of an agent of the Office of Naval Intelligence (ONI); the report recounted a Nationalist attack on Irun from three days prior. Each side was represented by three aircraft, which did not engage one another but instead focused on performing reconnaissance or on bombing ground targets. The agent was unimpressed, reporting, "The aircraft activities witnessed at Irun were, as far as could be learned, completely futile. A dive-bombing attack by one or more planes on Fort San Marcial or a horizontal bombing attack by a formation of several planes on the same objective, would have had a decisive effect in favor of the Rebels."[47] As for their reconnaissance capabilities, "These observation flights could not have been of much value, since neither side had field radio communications with its planes, and the Rebel planes [were] based 60 kilometers away from Irun at Pampl[o]na, while the Red planes [were] based 25 Kms. away, at San Sebastián airport."[48] According to the report, the aircraft could have been better employed assisting the battleship *España*'s bombardment of Fort Guadeloupe on August 27, which—due to lack of spotting—was completely ineffective. The correspondent could not definitively identify the types of aircraft, but he assumed the Republican aircraft were French-built Potez 25s. He guessed that the Nationalist aircraft consisted of a Breda bomber, a "Morane-type monoplane pursuit," and an unidentifiable sesquiplane.[49]

The use of airpower began to increase in frequency and variety throughout August 1936. The Nationalist DC-2, diverted from its airlift activities by the promised arrival of the German Junkers, conducted raids on Badajoz as early as August 4. With the arrival of the Junkers, the Spanish began to use them in their attacks on the city. A week later, these aircraft were joined by Nationalist-flown Breguets operating from Mérida.[50] Meanwhile, above Antequera in Andalusia, Captain García

Morato achieved his first victory when he shot down a Vickers Vildebeest.[51] On August 18, at the same location he shot down a Potez 54 while flying a Heinkel He 51. The same day, another Spanish Nationalist pilot, Julio Salvador, also flying a Heinkel, destroyed a Nieuport and Breguet above Mérida.[52] On August 20, a Fiat shot down a Nieuport above Córdoba but was itself brought down when it collided with a Breguet. A week later, a Fiat defeated a Dewoitine near Granada. But perhaps the crowning achievement of Fiats in the month of August came on the twenty-eighth, when they aided in the defense of Mallorca against Republican forces, destroying two docked seaplanes and shooting down a third, in which the commander of the invading force, Capt. Alberto Bayo, was flying as a passenger. The pilot was killed, and Bayo had to take over the controls of the crippled aircraft. It crashed, but he survived.[53]

August 3 had marked the first air attack on Madrid, although Nationalist troops were still far from threatening the city by land.[54] After the fall of Mérida and Badajoz, as Yagüe's columns started their eastward advances, the attacks became more frequent. The Nationalists bombed Getafe Airfield to the south of the capital on August 23. They struck nearby Cuatro Vientos airport on August 25. This was followed by the commencement of more continuous bombing of Madrid two days later. The War Ministry was struck by the end of the month.[55]

In the face of these aggressions, the Republicans appeared to lack a coherent airpower doctrine. France's support had temporarily relieved the question of aircraft. What were needed were trained pilots and planners. To this end, on August 20, a pilot school commenced operations at Alcalá.[56] Meanwhile, at the government-level, the portfolios of Marine and Air came under the ministry of socialist Indalecio Prieto (1883–1962). Prieto was a fifty-three-year-old former newspaper editor from Bilbao. He had served in the Spanish government since his election to the Cortes in 1918. Although appointed by fellow-socialist Largo Caballero, he was as much a rival as a colleague to the prime minister. He seemed to be a thoughtful and hardworking man, caught up in an ever-deteriorating situation. Historian Hugh Thomas, writing of Prieto's character during his service in the Second Republic, notes,

"Prieto was the outstanding figure who knew what was the right course, even if he was too mercurial to pursue it."[57] One of Prieto's first acts as Air Minister was to place the Republican air forces under the command of Ignacio Hidalgo de Cisneros, one of the few upper-class Spaniards who supported the Republican cause.

In September, the Nationalists made progress on all fronts. On September 4, they captured both Irun and Fuenterrabia, which Ambassador Bowers had made his vacation home before being convinced to relocate to France.[58] On September 13, San Sebastián fell, and the northern Republican sector of Basque Country and Asturias became geographically isolated from France. In Andalusia, on September 16, General José Varela captured Ronda.[59] While not strategically important in and of itself, this victory carried a moral significance. Apparently, at the outbreak of the war, a mob had rounded up all suspected fascists, beaten them, and then thrown them to their deaths in a ravine that ran through the town. Ernest Hemingway would later portray a vivid, fictionalized version of these events in his novel *For Whom the Bell Tolls* (1940). In the meantime, Yagüe's troops continued their march toward Madrid. On September 20, they reached Santa Olalla; the next day, Maqueda; and the day after that, Torrijos, thus bringing the Nationalists within sixty miles of Madrid.[60]

It was at this point that Franco made the consequential decision to divert the Army of Africa southeastward toward Toledo—to relieve the Nationalists besieged there within the walls of the Alcazar—rather than allowing them to continue northeastward toward the capital. This order apparently so rankled Yagüe that he was replaced by Varela. Yet Franco's decision stood since on September 21 he had been elected Generalissimo at a meeting of the Nationalist junta in Salamanca. He had no serious rivals for this position, for Sanjurjo and Goded were dead, Cabanellas and Queipo de Llano were suspected of Republican tendencies, and Mola's standing was diminished by the initial failure of the coup, which he had largely planned. Franco's power vis-à-vis the other generals derived from the fact that he led an army of fierce Moroccan and Legionnaire troops, who could repel Republican forces and seize territory. He benefited not only from the transportation of these troops to the mainland but also from the terms by which this assistance was provided. Both the Germans and the Italians had pledged their support not to the Nationalist cause generally but to Franco specifically.⁶¹ Whatever the reasons, Franco's rise united the Nationalists under a single leader, giving them an advantage over their Republican foes, for unity of command was, and is, a key element of effective warfighting.⁶² His order for the rescue of the Alcazar was not long in execution, for despite the Republican militia's attempts to storm the fortress or destroy its walls with mines, the garrison held on until it was relieved on September 27.

The Nationalist advances were aided by their growing aerial dominance. On September 11, above El Real de San Vicente, near Toledo, Nationalists fighters destroyed seven government aircraft, including a Nieuport Ni-H 52 shot down by a Fiat flown by Captain García Morato.⁶³ A raid led by Capt. Ángel Salas Larrazábal at Jaen in Andalusia damaged eleven aircraft and destroyed another.⁶⁴ But the Republicans were not without aerial victories that month. On September 12, above Sierra de Guadarrama, antiaircraft fire shot down a Nationalist Nieuport.⁶⁵ On September 25 near Toledo, for the first time a Junkers Ju 52 was shot down, although the pilot of this doomed aircraft was a Spanish Nationalist, not a German.⁶⁶

Yet these were insufficient to counter the growing Nationalist threat, and October proved to be even more perilous for the Republic than September had been. Franco consolidated his civil as well as his military power by becoming the Caudillo on the calends of the month. The Army of Africa, swollen by the thousands of men airlifted by the air bridge, began to set its sights once again on Madrid. On October 6, it resumed its march, pushing through Torrijos.⁶⁷ Illescas, northeast of Toledo, fell on October 15. On October 20, the Republican militias, showing some residual resolve after their retreat from Toledo, countered and surrounded the town, but three days later this assault was broken.⁶⁸ In combat between Esquivias and Seseña, Italian tankettes made their first appearance. On October 24, Varela drove back the Republican militia and occupied Seseña.⁶⁹ The Caudillo's soldiers were within twenty miles of Madrid. Before the month was out, the capital was subject to continuous bombing.

As the fate of the southern sector of the Republic grew dim, those in the northern sector looked to their own defense. On October 7, Basque representatives met at Guernica, an ancient town soon to achieve worldwide fame, and there elected José Antonio Aguirre (1904–60) as their president.[70] This achieved a centuries-long desire for political autonomy by the northern provinces, yet it came at a time of great risk and uncertainty. To guard against the same menace that was marching on Madrid, the Basques began construction of the "Iron Ring" around Bilbao. This consisted of a series of fortifications and barbed wire, not unlike the Maginot Line under construction on France's border with Germany.[71]

Meanwhile, in the main Republican sector, Largo Caballero's administration was making decisions that would set its course for the remainder of the war. On October 15, the Popular Army was established as a replacement for both the Republican Army, which had been torn asunder by civil war, and the militias, which were too uncoordinated, undisciplined, and uncontrollable to effectively support the government.[72] Largo Caballero, understandably suspicious of the professional military leadership and cognizant of the need for a free state to maintain civilian control of the armed forces, assumed the role of commander-in-chief. By the end of the month, men between the ages of twenty and forty were subject to conscription.[73] President Azaña, his duty fulfilled with the formation of a new government, relocated to Barcelona and was scarcely noticed and hardly missed throughout the increasingly polarizing political atmosphere of Madrid.[74]

It was in October that one may have noticed strange comings and goings in the Republic's southern sector. On October 4, the Russian ship *Campeche* appeared at the port city of Cartagena. Eight days later, the *Komosomol* arrived. That in turn was followed three days later by the *Stari Bolshevik*.[75] What business, one may have wondered, did Stalin's regime have with the Republic? The Nationalists took notice of these visitations with great alarm, and from October 18 to 20, SM.81s and Ju 52s attacked the port and the city itself.[76] On October 25, Nationalist aircraft attacked the ships, directly damaging one.[77] Meanwhile, the first contingent of 500 members of a force referring to itself as the International Brigades arrived in Republican Spain.[78]

The Germans, their mission fulfilled with the conclusion of the airlift, faced a dilemma. Should they return to their homeland, having fulfilled Hitler's promise to Franco to deliver the Army of Africa to the Peninsula, or should they stay and help bring to fruition the final victory of their Spanish ally? This question was resolved in favor of the latter, and on October 30, the German air detachment assumed the title of Condor Legion, with General Hugo von Sperrle (1885–1953) commanding. Franco now had two reliable patrons, Germany and Italy, to provide his swiftly advancing forces with air cover. The Republic, its capital prostrate before the Nationalist menace, braced itself for a final stand.

Yet something unexpected occurred at this time, insufficient in itself to halt the Nationalist advance, but a harbinger of a new development in the war. On October 27, unidentified bomber aircraft attacked the airfields near Seville. Salamanca and other locations were attacked in a similar matter.[79] Where did these aircraft come from? Who was flying them? What consequences did they portend for the course of the war? Within a week, it would soon become clear to the Nationalists and their German and Italian allies that there was a new enemy in the skies. The Russians had arrived and had cast their lot with the Republic.

RUSSIAN INTERVENTION

Stalin's support for the Republic was more gradually decided and more grudgingly offered than Mussolini's and Hitler's support for the cause of the Nationalists. On July 21, at a secretariat-level meeting in Moscow, Stalin expressed sympathy for the Spanish government. He favored the shipment of food to the Republic, along with subtler means of support and influence, but he stopped short of directly supporting the war effort.[80] On August 3, the Communist International (Comintern) publicly announced its support for the Republic.[81] However, there was still no direct Russian involvement; and on August 23, Stalin gave his consent to the Non-Intervention Agreement, forbidding the exportation of war materials. This did not lessen Russian interest in the fate of the Republic, as indicated by the dispatch of formal Russian representatives to Spain. Soviet consul-general Vladimir Antonov-Ovssenko

(1844–1937) came to Barcelona on August 25, and Ambassador Marcel Rosenberg arrived with his staff in Madrid two days later.[82]

However, in September, as the situation rapidly swung to the favor of the Nationalists with the support of their German and Italian patrons, and as the Western democracies withdrew into aloofness from the plight of the Republican government in Madrid, Stalin decided to act. The Soviet counterpart to the German Special Section W, known as Operation X, stood up and commenced the organization of aid to the Republic. It was commanded by Semon P. Uritsky, the head of the GRU, the Russian military intelligence organization.[83] In the meantime, the Comintern put out calls for volunteers throughout the world to come to fight in Spain. The products of this appeal were the International Brigades, the first of which arrived just as the Nationalists came within striking distance of Madrid.

Meanwhile, the Spanish Republican government, unaware of these favorable developments, concerned itself with a pressing dilemma. The fate of the gold reserves held in Madrid banks, numbering over 1.6 billion pesetas, or $546 million in 1936 U.S. dollars, caused much anxiety.[84] Should they need to evacuate the capital, the gold could fall into the hands of the Nationalists. In July and August, the Giral administration had shipped almost nine-and-a-half tons of gold to Paris, but the French government's declaration of neutrality seemed to place doubt upon their willingness to keep Republican property secure.[85] Treasury Minister Juan Negrín (1892–1956), perhaps influenced by Soviet economic adviser Artur Stashevsky, conceived of the idea to transfer the reserves to Russia.[86] On September 16, the gold reserves were transferred to the port city of Cartagena on the Mediterranean. On October 14, Largo Caballero, accepting his minister's advice, proposed to the Soviets the idea of shipping the gold to Russia.[87] On the night of October 26, under threat of enemy air strikes, four ships left Cartagena for the Soviet Union, bearing more than half of Republican Spain's gold reserves.[88] There apparently had been some understanding that the Russians would use the treasury as an account against which to debit the expense of their material support to the Republicans, but they ultimately did so at an exchange rate disproportionately advantageous to the Russians when compared with the worldwide rate.[89] When speaking of the high price of Russian matériel, Republican Air Minister Prieto told Associated Press correspondent H. Edward Knoblaugh, "All this is expensive but we've got a $700,000,000 gold reserve—the fourth largest in the world—and we'll spend it all rather than let it fall into the enemy's hands."[90] And so, just as fleets of galleons had once crossed the Atlantic, bearing the treasures of the fallen empires of the Americas to the monarchs of Spain, ships traveling through the Mediterranean now transported the gold of the collapsing Spanish Republic to the coffers of the Soviet Empire, never to return.

Yet the Soviet Union, broken reed that it was, provided substantial aid to the Republic in this dark period.[91] On the October 4, Soviet arms had started to arrive in Spain. Men, firearms, tanks, and aircraft came to the support of the flailing government forces. These included T-26 Soviet tanks, weighing 10.5–11.5 tons and armed with 45-mm cannons, which would soon prove more than a match for the 3.3-ton Italian Ansaldo tankettes with their fixed machine guns.[92] More importantly, these arms shipments also included Russian aircraft, including twenty-four I-15 Chato (Snub nose) biplane fighters, thirty-one I-16 Mosca (Fly) monoplane fighters, and thirty-one two-engine Tupolev SB-2 Katiuska bombers.[93] Their arrival was fortuitous for the Republic. As the first aircraft were being unloaded, the small, heterogeneous, and aging Aviación Militar was approaching its endpoint. According to a later report by Griffiss, by October 30, the Spanish government's military aircraft inventory (not including the Russian equipment that had just recently arrived) had been reduced to eighty-nine aircraft with the legacy Nieuport Ni-H 52s and Breguet XIXs accounting for almost half of the still serviceable vehicles. The Republic also had ninety-two navy aircraft, but these were hardly suitable for combat against the Nationalists' land-based fighters.[94] The Russian aircraft arrived just in time to provide air cover in the skies above the beleaguered capital and to bring the fight into enemy airspace.

The introduction of Chatos and Moscas soon impressed friend and foe alike. Both aircraft were the products of the mind of the brilliant Russian engineer Nikolai Polikarpov of the Soviet Central Design Bureau

(TsKB). Polikarpov had developed the fighters in 1933 as complements to one another in aerial combat. The I-15's mission was to destroy enemy fighters, clearing the way for the I-16s to strike down their bombers. Together they formed a lethal combination against the enemy air force.[95]

Table 1. Pursuit aircraft employed in Spain, 1936

Designation	Name	Year introduced	Nation	Mission	Horsepower (total)	Max speed (mph)	Ceiling (ft)	Range (miles)
Hispano Nieuport-Delage Ni-H 52		1931	France (Spain)	Fighter	500	140	26,904	249
Heinkel He 51		1933	Germany	Fighter	550	205	25,493	342
Fiat CR.32	Chirri	1933	Italy	Fighter	592	220	25,264	485
Polikarpov I-15	Chato	1934	Russia	Fighter	480	216	30,185	298
Loire 46 C1		1934	France	Fighter	930	255	34,450	466
Polikarpov I-16 Type 5	Mosca	1935	Russia	Fighter	710	282	30,448	510

The I-15 was a single-seat biplane, with fabric-covered wooden wings and a metal fuselage. It was propeller driven with a 480 hp Gnome-Rhône radial engine, enabling it to reach speeds of 216 mph, with a 30,185-foot ceiling and a 298-mile range. This was later replaced by a 700 hp M-25 Wright Cyclone radial engine, which raised its maximum speed to 228 mph, its ceiling to over 32,000 feet, and its range to 317 miles. The I-15's armaments primarily consisted of four 7.62-mm machine guns ringing the fuselage.

The I-15 held a superficial resemblance to American designs. When American pilot Frank Tinker, a Navy veteran, had an opportunity to fly it, he readily took to the plane, which reminded him of the Boeing F4B that he had flown in the U.S. Navy.[96] The Nationalists referred to the craft as the "Curtiss," due to its resemblance to the Curtiss F9C Sparrowhawk or Hawk II. However, historian Gerald Howson defends the originality of Polikarpov's design, and dismisses the disparagement of Russian aircraft engineering, stating, "Although it is now common knowledge that the I-15 owed nothing to any of these fighters, the story that the Russians were too backward to design their own aircraft made good propaganda."[97]

There was no disparaging the I-16. This low-wing monoplane, equipped with a 710 hp M-25 Wright Cyclone engine at the beginning of the war, was able to reach speeds of 282 mph, far outpacing its rival fighters, the Italian Fiat CR.32 (220 mph) and the Heinkel He 51 (205 mph). Both the Nationalists' key bombers, the Savoia-Marchetti SM.81 (211 mph) and the slow-moving Junkers Ju 52 (180 mph) were easy prey. The Mosca also had an impressive range, 510 miles, thus making it fast and far-reaching. While it boasted of only two machine guns for its armaments, along with about 440 pounds of bombs, these were rapid-fire weapons, each capable of discharging 1,800 rounds in a minute. This was lethal, particularly when the Mosca dove on its victims at speeds reaching 360 mph.[98] Griffiss later observed that the I-16 and other Russian aircraft were impressive for their simplicity and for the reliability of their motors. "Instruments are Russian and are limited to the necessities of flight," he observed. "All waste motion has been done away with and the ease of assembly and maintenance have been stressed."[99] However, there was one vulnerability: the large fuel tanks, covered only by the plywood skin of the fuselage, were liable to ignite under enemy fire.[100]

Apart from seeking out enemy bombers to destroy, the I-15 and I-16 were charged with escorting their own Russian bombers. These were the Tupolev SB-2 Katiuska, which first appeared in 1934. It was a metal-framed aircraft with a semi-monocoque covering, powered by two 830 hp engines with the capacity to reach speeds of 263 mph, a ceiling of over 31,300 feet, and a range of just over 900 miles. It defended itself with four 7.62-mm machine guns, two in the nose turret, one in the rear turret, and one ventral; but it could carry only a light load of 1,100 pounds of bombs. Albert Baumler, an American pilot who, like Frank Tinker, had flown for the Spanish government during the war, later provided information to Major Raley of the Intelligence Section of the OCAC. They discussed the Katiuska at some length, which Baumler acknowledged had a superficial resemblance to the Martin B-10 bomber, though the Katiuska's design was more streamlined. As Baumler wrote, "This ship had excellent climb, and was quite maneuverable. Its construction was sturdy, and it seemed to be the best of all the Russian ships sent to Spain."[101] The Martin B-10, introduced a couple of years before the Katiuska, was inferior to the Russian craft in speed (210 mph to 263 mph) and ceiling (24,400 feet to 31,300 feet), but superior to it in range (1,200 miles to 900 miles) and bomb payload (2,200 pounds to 1,100 pounds). They were thus, apart from their appearances, two different aircraft suitable for different missions.

Table 2. Bomber aircraft employed in Spain, 1936

Designation	Name	Year introduced	Nation	Mission	Horsepower (total)	Max speed (mph)	Ceiling (ft)	Range (miles)	Bomb load (lbs)
CASA-Breguet XIX		1923	France (Spain)	Bomber, light	500	143	20,670	497	880
Junkers Ju 52/3m	Tante Ju (Auntie Ju)	1930	Germany	Bomber/transport	1,980	180	18,046	552	2,205
Savoia-Marchetti SM.81	Pipistrello (Bat)	1934	Italy	Bomber, medium	1,950	211	22,967	932	2,205
Potez 540		1934	France	Bomber, medium	1,380	193	32,810	746	2,205
Tupolev SB-2	Katiuska	1934	Russia	Bomber, light	1,660	263	31,366	901	1,103

The Republic now found itself the beneficiary of, and thus the partner to, a pariah nation run by a brutal, paranoid dictator. It would slowly dawn on the more conscientious leaders of the Spanish government that they were viewed as a junior partner, engaged in a proxy war between Great Powers with extreme and expansionist agendas. In the meantime, both sides could now wield some of the most advanced flying machines in the world, and Spain would be the setting for experiments in modern aerial warfare. The vultures had arrived and were circling above the dying prey.

CHAPTER 4

COUNTERAIR

The flying fortress died in Spain.
—TOWNSEND GRIFFISS

THE GOVERNMENT FLEES TO THE COAST

Russian intervention on behalf of the Republic, as beneficial and welcome as it may have been to the government, was insufficient to halt the Nationalists' advance on Madrid. By November 1936, it became evident that the capital would soon be under direct assault. The Nationalist general Emilio Mola boasted of a "Fifth Column" of secret supporters who would rise to welcome their liberators, and he promised to soon sip coffee at a café in the middle of the city. Outwardly, the government exuded confidence and encouraged the Madrileños to make a brave stand. A public announcement called the people to arms: "It is now or never. If you prove yourself cowards your men will be killed, your wives and daughters ravished. The government is here to guide you and keep you from this fate. It will never desert you in your hour of need. Always remember that."[1]

Within days, the citizens received a different message through the newspapers: "Yes, it is true the government has left. International complications which would arise should the government remain and be captured prompted it to go to Valencia where it can best look after the nation's interests. Even though Madrid should fall the war is not lost. The government in Valencia will be able to carry on until we have wiped out the last of the *canalla*."[2]

On November 6, Prime Minister Largo Caballero had announced to his subordinates his decision to leave Madrid. Two days earlier, on November 4, the Nationalists had seized Getafe Airfield, and the capital could expect heavy bombardment preceding a ground assault by the legionnaires and Moroccans of the Army of Africa any day. A single key road ran from Madrid eastward to the Mediterranean. Rather than remaining until all routes of escape were cut off, the administration opted to retreat to the coast to organize further resistance.

General José Asensio, the Republican undersecretary for war, summoned General José Miaja, the commander of the Madrid forces, and General Sebastián Pozas, the commander of the Army of the Center, and solemnly handed each a sealed envelope containing their orders. They were to remain in Madrid and open their envelopes the following morning. Asensio then took his leave to join the rest of the government ministers in their retreat to safety on the coast. Miaja and Pozas dutifully obeyed Asensio's instructions, but only until he was out of sight. Then they immediately tore open the seals and read the contents of their letters. It was fortunate they did so. With typical government efficiency, they had each been issued the other's orders. After sorting out that discrepancy, Pozas learned that he was to relocate his headquarters to Tarancón about fifty miles to the southeast. Miaja was to remain in the capital and bear responsibility for the defense of Madrid. His orders were to establish a junta, with himself at its head, and stop the Nationalists from seizing the capital. To Miaja, this was like a death sentence. Few expected Madrid to hold out for more than a week.[3]

General José Miaja (1878–1958) seemed an unlikely champion of the Republican cause. He was a career military man, approaching sixty and anticipating retirement when the civil war ignited. Prior to the war, his politics tended toward the conservative side, and he had been a member of the rightist Unión Militar Española (UME), along with Franco and Mola. He seemed to have remained loyal to the Republic more out of inertia and a sense for self-preservation than from any deep-seated commitment to the government. However, when roused to action, Miaja proved a competent and resourceful commander. He came to terms with the communists and included their representatives in his junta. They in turn propagandized on his behalf, turning him into something of a folk hero. Volunteers from Spain and abroad migrated toward the capital to contribute to its defense. Thus fortified under a united command, Madrid stood like an anvil, prepared to face the numerous Nationalist hammer strikes.[4]

In the meantime, the U.S. State Department, not wishing for its representatives to be caught between belligerents, directed its embassy staff to relocate with the Republican government to Valencia. The War Department in turn ordered Col. Stephen Fuqua to accompany the embassy in this move.[5] Fuqua was reluctant to do so and made his objections known to Ambassador Claude Bowers, who was still stationed in France. Bowers relayed these concerns to Secretary of State Cordell Hull: "I think Fuqua feels professionally humiliated at being refused permission to witness battle for Madrid. My suggestion implied no status as representative of the State Department. I would not ask him to remain but he asks it and evidently has no fear. Am surprised that War Department does not want a military observer at the probable battle."[6]

Bowers's message made its rounds, obliging Col. F. H. Lincoln, assistant chief of staff for G-2 (Intelligence), to defend the orders in a memorandum to his superior. In short, he argued that Fuqua's role as military attaché should not (officially) encompass that of military observer:

> By memorandum of October 1, 1936, approved by the Deputy Chief of Staff on October 3, this Division recommended that the present orders of Colonel Fuqua (to remain with the American Embassy as long as it functions on Spanish soil; and, if the Embassy is closed in Spain, to proceed at the first favorable opportunity to Lisbon, Portugal, and open his office there) be not changed. This recommendation was made on the ground that the presence of an American officer with either side in a civil war might easily give rise to embarrassing incidents, without compensating advantages.[7]

This information was passed to John Morgan, head of the Western European Division of the State Department, who in turn passed it on to Bowers.[8]

Thus Fuqua, the career infantryman, was required to leave Madrid on the eve of the battle for that city. Edward Knoblaugh, an American correspondent for the Associated Press, had high praise for the colonel, whom he viewed as a natural leader. Fuqua was "beloved by Spaniards and Americans alike for his fearlessness and cool-headedness, his energy and organization ability, and his Louisiana chivalry."[9] Further, "Although Secretary Eric Wendelin was in acting charge, it was Col. Fuqua's seasoned experience as a veteran of many wars which was principally responsible for the smooth running of the embassy during those nerve-wracking days before it was officially closed."[10] In spite of his evident disappointment, Fuqua was a dutiful soldier and followed his orders.

Interestingly, by the time the embassy had relocated to Valencia, the first Battle of Madrid had already been fought. The assault itself, originally planned for November 7, was postponed by General José Varela (1891–1951), the Nationalist commander. This one-day delay had fateful repercussions, as Republican soldiers found his orders on the corpse of a Nationalist officer. This opportune discovery allowed the defenders to concentrate their forces on their right flank in the Casa de Campo, the focus of the Nationalist attack.[11] Overall, the forces of the Nationalists and Republicans were about equal at 40,000 each, though Republican reinforcements from the XI and XII International Brigades and Anarchists under the command of Buenaventura Durruti (1896–1936) added several thousand more to the defender's strength at key moments in the battle.[12] As before, the Nationalists were relying on discipline and experience to overcome Republican fervor. This had worked well in the war of maneuver in Andalusia and Estremadura, but now, the high stakes and urban atmosphere had filled the defenders with a mighty resolve.

The Río Manzanares bordered Madrid on the west, and this proved to be a key to the defense. Repeated attempts to cross the river were repulsed, and it was not until November 19 that Legionnaires and Moroccan Regulares forced their way into the University City in the

Madrid outskirts, on the defender's right flank.[13] Door-to-door urban fighting was new for these seasoned veterans of northwest Africa, and the defenders took advantage of their unique experience in this environment. For instance, at the Clinical Hospital, elevators were booby-trapped with bombs, waiting for unsuspecting intruders. The expected collapse of defenses did not materialize, and Franco was obliged to call a halt to the assault on November 23. The surprising Republican victory was costly, as each side suffered around 10,000 casualties. Among the losses was Durruti, shot dead under circumstances that remain unclear.[14]

Above the fierce, close-action fighting in the city, Nationalist and Republican aircraft were engaged in the heaviest aerial combat since the Great War. Two dozen fighters waged a battle on November 5, the day after the Nationalists had seized the Getafe Airfield. Captains Joaquín García Morato and Ángel Salas Larrazábal were among the Nationalist pilots involved in this engagement, and they each accounted for the destruction of an I-15 during the fighting, the only permanent losses from the battle.[15] The next day, two I-15s, one Fiat CR.32, and one Junkers Ju 52 were destroyed. At about this time, the Italian commander Colonel Ruggero Bonomi forbid his fighters from engaging in combat when they were fewer in number than their opponents.[16] This order was swiftly violated. On November 13, fourteen Fiats engaged eighteen Republican aircraft: thirteen I-15s and five Katiuskas. The Fiat pilots shot down two I-15s and damaged four Katiuskas at the cost of one Fiat. The pilot of one of these Katiuskas parachuted safely from his aircraft, but upon reaching the ground, he was set upon by a mob who mistook him for a German and beat him so severely that he died soon after. Following this event, Miaja prohibited attacks on parachutists.[17] During the battle, a German Heinkel He 51 squadron intervened, much to its detriment. The squadron commander, Lieutenant Kraft Eberhard, crashed and died with a bullet wound to his heart. Another pilot, Lieutenant Oskar Henrici, was also shot through the heart, though he somehow managed to land safely before dying.[18] There were additional air battles on November 16, 17, and 19, featuring the monoplane I-16 Moscas. Dozens of aircraft were involved, but actual results were hard to determine since the Nationalists and Republicans tended to report more favorable versions of events for themselves.[19]

The last week of the battle featured a determined bombing campaign by the Nationalists. About four dozen bombers were utilized for this mission, flying primarily at night due to the increasing counterair capabilities of the Republicans. Between November 14 and November 22, these bombings caused more than 1,000 civilian casualties and damaged 303 buildings.[20] Since both Junkers Ju 52s and Savoia-Marchetti SM.81s had payloads of 2,205 pounds, they could potentially drop a total of 100,000 to 110,000 pounds of bombs per sortie. Yet this was insufficient to overwhelm a city that had swelled from one million to 1.5 million people during the early months of the war.[21] According to Knoblaugh, before the bombing operation, Franco had announced a safe zone within the city that would be spared from the bombing. It was anticipated that this would be used to house women and children and other noncombatants. Instead, the defenders took advantage of Franco's uncharacteristic naivete and moved their barracks and armory into the safe zone.[22]

Regardless, neither enemy troops nor enemy bombs were sufficient to break the will of the defenders, and by the end of November, against all expectations, the city of Madrid remained defiant and unconquered.

MADRID UNDER ASSAULT

As it became clear that Madrid was not on the verge of collapse, belligerents and onlookers alike considered the likelihood that the war might continue for months or even years more. The early battles featuring German, Italian, and Russian technology suggested to other national governments that the struggle could provide important lessons on modern industrial warfare. As Lt. Col. O. S. Wood, a G-2 executive officer, wrote to the American military attaché in London: "The conflict has now reached a stage of acute interest for all first class military powers in that the capabilities of certain post-war developments in aircraft, weapons and armored vehicles are undergoing the practical test of war."[23]

Military attachés throughout Europe were to collect information on the conflict in earnest. Every "appropriate opportunity" was to be taken to find out through official channels what was happening in Spain.[24]

Meanwhile, having failed to take the capital, the Nationalists underwent reorganization. Reluctantly, Franco agreed to the establishment of a separate Italian command. This would become known as the Corpo Truppe Volontarie (CTV), commanded by General Mario Roatta (1887–1968), an intelligence officer who had previously served as the liaison with Germany to coordinate intervention in Spain.[25] Similarly, by the end of December, most Italian air assets and pilots were consolidated under the Aviazione Legionaria. Italian airpower had been impressive in the war, thus far, and the new distinction, placing them on an even status as the Germans' Condor Legion, was well deserved. Up to that point, Italian fighter aircraft, flown by both Italians and Spaniards as part of the Aviación del Tercio Extranjero, had earned 131 credited victories in aerial combat. Four Fiat pilots had already achieved ace status, the foremost being the Spaniard García Morato, with eleven victories, followed by the Italians Adriano Mantelli, Bruno Montegnacco, and Giuseppe Cenni, with nine, seven, and six victories, respectively.[26]

Conversely, the Germans were facing a crisis. The Luftwaffe's introduction to aerial warfare had not gone as planned. During the fighting in Madrid, they were obliged to withdraw their increasingly disappointing Heinkel He 51s from escort duties, leaving greater responsibility to the willing Fiat pilots.[27] How was the Luftwaffe to engage in modern warfare when their premier fighter had proven insufficient in combat? In seeming response to this question, a new officer arrived who would feature prominently in the history of the Luftwaffe. This was Colonel Wolfram von Richthofen (1895–1945), who had come to command the experimental aircraft section of the Condor Legion.[28] He was the cousin of the legendary Red Baron, Manfred von Richthofen. Like his more famous cousin, Wolfram was both a baron and a veteran pilot of the Great War. He had also served as a cavalry officer, and his experience with both land and air operations had given him a unique perspective on the coordination of the two forces to a common end, a concept now known as *joint operations*. He was influential in Germany's aerial rearmament following the prohibitions on flight imposed by the Versailles Treaty.[29] He was thus an ideal candidate to help lead the Luftwaffe in its first war. He earned a reputation for being a stern, confident commander, very different from his superior in Spain, the bon vivant General Hugo von Sperrle. As biographer James S. Corum writes, "If von Richthofen was not liked much by his men and staff, he was certainly respected. No one who served with him would ever describe him as being other than coldly rational."[30]

November 29, the day of Richthofen's arrival, coincided with the commencement of the Nationalist Corunna Road offensive. This phase of the operation was actually a series of assaults, lasting roughly a month-and-a-half, attempting to outflank the Republicans on their right by pushing north and northeast of the city. The first Nationalist advance was engaged and checked by a force under the command of the Romanian Moishe Stern (known in Spain as "Kléber"), a member of the Soviet GRU and former commander of the XI International Brigade. Following this setback, the Nationalists paused, regrouped, and formed the Madrid Reinforced Division under Brigadier General Orgaz, the staff officer who had attempted to secure Franco's flight from the Canary Islands the previous July. General Varela assumed command of one of the brigades of this division, consisting of 10,000 men and 52 guns. On December 16, he launched a new offensive against Kléber's 12,000-man force. By December 19, he had advanced eleven miles from Villaviciosa de Odón to Boadilla, creating a salient in the Republican lines but unable to exploit this gain.[31]

The Republican Air Force had taken the offensive in the skies, introducing a new Russian platform to the struggle. The R-5 Resantes (Skimming), similar to the I-15 Chatos and I-16 Moscas before them, were designed by the Russian engineer Nikolai Polikarpov. First produced in 1928, they were classified as reconnaissance-bombers, though they would fall into the category now known as "attack" aircraft, or those aircraft designed for strafing and bombing ground forces. They were biplanes of mostly wooden construction, powered by a 680 hp engine, with a maximum speed of 158 mph, a ceiling of 21,327 feet, and a range of 684 miles. The original models sent to Spain were armed with two machine guns, one on the port side of the fuselage, and one on the observer's cockpit, along with an 800-pound bomb payload.[32] The Resantes first appeared in combat in Spain on December 2, when eighteen of them attacked the airdrome at Talavera, west of Madrid. One Savoia-Marchetti SM.81 was destroyed, and two others were damaged on the ground. One of the Resantes was lost due to anti-aircraft fire. The Nationalists claimed to have shot down three more with their Fiats. This is possible, because the Resantes were slow, lumbering aircraft compared to the Italian fighters.[33] Nevertheless, two days later, the Resantes struck again, this time farther west, at Navalmoral. Six Ju-52s were damaged on the ground.[34]

Back at the capital, the Madrileños had a respite through Christmas and New Year's Day, but on January 3, 1937, the attack resumed on an 8.5-mile front, with three Nationalist columns wheeling clockwise toward the Corunna Road that linked Madrid to the Atlantic coast at El Ferrol. The attackers had armor with them and drove the discouraged and undersupplied defenders back. The XI and XII International Brigades were thrown into the breach, but the fighting was fierce.[35] On January 6, the Thaelmann Battalion was dispatched to Las Rosas, about thirty-five miles up the road from Madrid, and ordered to hold that position. The next day, when the order came to advance, it was met with the response, "Impossible. The Thaelmann Battalion has been destroyed."[36]

Miaja had appealed to the Largo Caballero administration for additional ammunition, but had been rebuffed.[37] Ultimately, the day was saved by his ability, through the use of interior lines, to swiftly send reinforcements to the vulnerable points on the front. A mixed brigade and two International Brigades were transferred to the area, along with the Russian tank corps, now under command of General Dmitri Pavlov. The Nationalist advance ground to a halt on January 8, having captured eight miles of the Corunna Road, with the easternmost point at Aravaca, about ten miles from the Río Manzanares. A counterattack by the Republicans failed to make headway due to the poor coordination between the Russian armor and the Spanish and International infantry. Fighting continued until January 16, when the Nationalists stabilized their lines and neither side could make further advancements.[38] Most estimates of the battle place the casualties at 15,000 each, though historian E. R. Hooton believes this to be exaggerated and estimates the Nationalist losses at 1,500 and the Republican losses at 6,775.[39]

The fighting had generated a flurry of activity by the military attachés, who capitalized on reports and interviews from those who had witnessed these events. Of particular interest was the impact of the Nationalist bombing on the capital. By now, Capt. Townsend Griffiss was stationed in Valencia with Colonel Fuqua, and the two had returned to visit Madrid since their arrival on the Mediterranean coast. Fuqua forwarded to the Military Intelligence Division an air raid map showing the locations on Nationalist bombing strikes. He noted that on January 4, a Nationalist mission had flown over the vicinity of the embassy, and that a building housing refugees belonging to the Chilean government had been bombed, killing a woman and wounding others. Yet there was no widespread destruction or terror, nor was there a revolt against the Republican government by a distraught public demanding peace at any price, as airpower theorist Giulio Douhet had anticipated. According to Fuqua, "It is apparent that the results of the bombing from November 1st to December 22d are not what might be expected from modern bombardment activities."[40]

Other correspondents elaborated on Fuqua's conclusion. From Paris, American Lt. Sumner Waite forwarded a translation of a report by the G-2 assistant chief of staff of the French Army. The report asked, "Why is it that two months later Madrid is still offering resistance? The answer is this: The 'intimidation bluff' practiced by the nationalists failed while the 'resistance bluff' of the government succeeded."[41] Waite offered his own commentary: "Evidently Franco put too much dependance on his aviation during his first days before Madrid. The Reds refused to be scared. It becomes increasingly evident that while aviation may to a large extent help prepare the way, the effect is fugitive and as soon as the bombers have passed the defenders come out of their holes. To move forward, take and hold positions, the pressure must be constant."[42]

Waite's senior in Paris, Lt. Col. Horace Fuller, reinforced these views in his report on a conversation with the local German military attaché. According to this source, aerial bombardment was not as effective as anticipated, being "too transitory" in its nature and uncoordinated with military movements on the ground.[43]

Similarly, Lt. Col. Raymond Lee, the American military attaché for Britain, passed on information "from an unbiased source in London enjoying unusual facilities for obtaining reliable information," describing how the people of Madrid had adjusted to the bombings.[44] Lee conveyed this observation from his source: "One of the remarkable features of the war so far has been the amount of punishment the inhabitants of Madrid have taken from bombardment. Most military critics have hitherto assumed that continual bombardment of a civil population would completely disorganize the community life, but this has not proven true in Madrid."[45] This divergence from Douhetian theory would need to be explained.

Frustrated by their failure to take Madrid, the Nationalists turned their attention temporarily to the south, making use of the ground forces of their allies. By now there were 17,000 Italians troops in Spain, for whom the costs of maintenance were being shared by the Spanish and the Italians. (By contrast, the 7,000 German troops on Spanish soil were fully financed by the German government.)[46] Although the Italian presence was something of a burden to Franco, he suppressed his resentment and agreed to their terms of support. As a gesture of confidence and goodwill, he invited them to take part in (and take credit for) the seemingly easy conquest of Málaga, located on the Mediterranean in a narrow salient of the otherwise Nationalist-dominated region of Andalusia.[47]

The assault came in two main prongs, one from the west by the Spanish Nationalists, led by the Bourbon Duke of Seville, and one from the north by a mechanized column of Italians, led by General Roatta. The Italians numbered about 10,000, and the Nationalists another 2,000 or 3,000. On January 17, Marbella in the southwest fell to the Nationalists. The Spanish Republican commander appealed to Valencia for support, but as with Miaja in Madrid, he was rebuffed. Against the moderately sized and divided enemy force, 12,000 Republican defenders should have been able to put up substantial resistance by exploiting their interior lines and utilizing the obstacles characteristic of an urban environment, as their brethren were doing in Madrid. But there were only 8,000 rifles available to these troops, thus a third were unarmed, and morale was minimal. The final attack commenced on February 3, and by February 8, the Italian-Nationalist force was in control of the city at the cost of a few hundred casualties.[48]

Air operations had been limited in the region before the battle. The Condor Legion had struck port facilities in Málaga in early January, but otherwise their participation was light.[49] The Italians attempted sorties late in the month, but poor weather resulted in accidents and the loss of four Fiats. Republican appeals for air support received a response little better than their appeals for munitions and rifles. The only available aircraft reinforcements were a fighter and five bombers, stationed in San Javier, about 260 miles away. In spite of these limited assets, the sole significant air engagement of the battle, on February 3, appears to have been a Republican victory, with five I-15s engaging three Nationalist bombers and destroying two.[50]

Even before the fighting was concluded in Málaga, the Nationalists had launched a new attack to the south of Madrid across the Río Jarama. This offensive, with the objective of flanking Republican defenses and cutting off the Valencia Road artery to the east, involved a force of five Nationalist brigades totaling thirty battalions, or somewhere between 18,000 and 25,000 troops, along with tank, artillery, and cavalry support. The Republicans had about fifty infantry battalions in the area, with an equal or perhaps larger total number of troops than those of the attackers.[51] Although the Nationalists lacked an advantage in numbers, they relied on surprise and superior skill and discipline, which had served them well in the early months of the war. In addition, since the bridges spanning the river served as bottlenecks, overall numbers became less important than the number of troops that could be concentrated in the areas around these crossings. The operation began on February 5, with the Nationalists driving to the banks of the Jarama. Their progress was steady, and they captured the Pedroque Bridge on February 11. Here they were met by the 11th Infantry Division of the Republicans, led by Colonel Enrique Líster (1907–94), a former quarryman and communist leader. Meanwhile, to the south the Nationalists had also crossed the San Martin de la Vega Bridge. The battle became one of attrition as the two forces ground together, each testing the other's endurance. Once again, the International Brigades were thrown into the breach, including the newly formed XV International Brigade, consisting of British, Franco-Belgian, and Balkan units, and later the American Lincoln Battalion. (The other American unit, the George Washington Battalion, would arrive in the summer.) The battle waged back-and-forth until February 27, when both forces withdrew to their respective lines. On this day, the Lincoln Battalion took part in the XV International Brigade's unsupported frontal assault, suffering 327 killed or wounded. The Nationalists had established a salient across the Jarama but achieved no breakthrough, at the cost of approximately 7,000 casualties. The defenders, meanwhile, had suffered 7,000 to 8,000 killed or wounded, and another 3,000 sick.[52]

Throughout the battle on the ground, another battle was taking place in the air. On February 12, five Heinkel He 51s fought seven I-16s, with the loss of two He 51s and one I-16. When the fighting resumed the next day, a Fiat squadron commander, Captain Luigi Lodi, was killed.[53] The Condor Legion conducted bombing operations throughout the battle, though it was becoming difficult to execute raids during the day. On one bombing run, forty Russian fighters attacked and scattered a Junker Ju 52 formation.[54] This necessitated a change in tactics. Thus, on February 15, the Ju 52s performed unescorted night bombing operations. A Spanish-piloted Junker group persisted in a daylight raid the next day, but the lead bomber and two He 51s went down in combat.[55] Rather than focusing solely on fielded forces in the short range, the bombing squadrons began to conduct interdiction missions, targeting the lines of communication between the battlefield and Madrid. On February 19, they raided a supply base at Albacete. They even attacked a chemical plant in distant Tarragona.[56]

Two famed air units met over the Jarama sector at this time. The Blue Patrol, consisting of Spanish Nationalist pilots flying Fiat CR.32s, had been formed the previous December in Córdoba under the leadership of García Morato.[57] They transferred to the Madrid sector on February 16. On the Republican side, Captain Andrés García LaCalle's squadron, consisting of Spanish and American pilots, had arrived in the area on February 11 and began operations from Azuqueca Airfield

(Campo X). On February 18, there was a large air battle consisting of the Italian Fiat group, the Blue Patrol, and a collection of Romeo Ro 37s and Junkers Ju 52s on the Nationalist side, against three fighter squadrons, including Captain LaCalle's, on the Republican side. It appears that the Republicans received the worst of the affair, losing eight fighters to the Nationalists' one. February 20 saw the last of the major air engagements, when 19 Fiats met 28 Republican fighters. In spite of the large numbers, apparently only one aircraft was shot down: one on the government's side.[58] Nevertheless, it appears that the presence of large numbers of Russian fighters in the area kept the Nationalists and their allies from conducting any significant missions to assist the ground forces in securing victory. The air superiority the Nationalists had enjoyed in Estremadura did not exist in the Madrid area.

DISPATCH FROM VALENCIA

By the end of February 1937, the war had been waged for seven months, and it was possible to begin considering what lessons could be learned thus far. At this time, Capt. Townsend Griffiss composed a lengthy and detailed analysis, entitled "Special Report on Spanish Government Air Force," which provided a wealth of information on airpower in the Spanish Civil War from an American perspective. Over the course of the winter, Griffiss had joined Fuqua in Valencia as full-time assistant military attaché to Spain. He set to work to study and understand all aspects of air operations during the war, utilizing as sources the Spanish Air Ministry and personal contacts.[59] His twenty-one page report covered an impressive variety of subjects from the history of airpower in Spain to the quality of aircraft, the quality of the pilots, tactics, the characteristics of the different nationalities, munitions, technology, and other miscellany.

The report began with background information on the operating environment of Spain that included a brief summary of the recent history of Spanish aviation: During the few years between the establishment of the Republic and the Civil War, there had been a push by administrators on both the left and the right to modernize Spanish airpower. The ultimate result of administrative reform, culminating in July

1935, had been a merging of the military, naval, and civil aeronautics divisions and the meteorological department under the name General Directorate of Aeronautics. By the start of the Civil War, Spanish aviation consisted of 500 aircraft and 5,450 personnel in the army, and 60 aircraft and 970 personnel in the navy. As discussed, Nieuport Ni-H 52s and Breguet XIXs were the key aircraft for the army, while Savoia-Marchetti SM.62s's, and Vickers Vildebeests were flown by the navy. Army aviation had been divided into three wings spread among twelve bases on the Peninsula, along with independent squadrons at six bases in Africa, while navy aviation was divided into independent squadrons at four bases. There were eleven civil air stations.[60]

To support the ambitious agenda of the reformers, there was a limited aircraft industry, which consisted of a handful of aircraft manufacturing plants and engine factories. Griffiss suggested that the lack of private-sector business weakened the industry's ability to quickly respond to high demand, writing, "Domestic manufacturing is dependent upon orders from the Government and these have been few and small." As for raw materials, limited gasoline production required importations or the use of inferior substitutes.[61] Griffiss concluded his introduction as follows:

> The above brief outline shows that the period April 1933 to July 1936 was for the Air Force one of reorganization and adjustment. The equipment in use was of obsolete types and the combat planes comparatively few in number. The Air Ministry had ordered airplanes from the United States and England, but this equipment was never delivered. It can be said that the efficiency and training of the personnel were far below the recognized standard. Aircraft manufacturing amounted to very little and the question of raw materials was serious.[62]

This was followed by a discussion of the current disposition of the Republican Air Force. In February 1937, Spanish military aviation, including French and Russian personnel and assets, were under the official control of the commander of Military Aviation, Lieutenant Colonel

Ignacio Hidalgo de Cisneros, based in Albacete. Although the air services had "general missions," including the prevention of Nationalist air supremacy and the interception of bombing raids, there was no clear doctrine of execution. Operations were defensive and reactionary, and assets were moved about as needed. Unit integrity had dissipated to the point that Griffiss referred to squadron status as "composite."[63]

There was then a status summary of Republican Spanish aviation personnel. Current numbers stood at a little over 10,000, with officers constituting about 12 percent of the total. There were 563 pilots. A third of these were enlisted men. The high proportion of enlisted pilots could be attributed to the fact that basic training schools were recruiting eighteen- to twenty-year-old men, giving them eighty hours of flight time, and appointing them as noncommissioned officer (NCO) pilots. The effectiveness of this system was questionable. As Griffiss observed, "A great deal of none too selective recruiting has been done with the result that the efficiency of the soldier personnel is extremely low." There were currently 500 student pilots in training: 100 in Spain, 200 in France, and 200 in Russia, though Griffiss's source had asked him to keep the Russian contribution a secret.[64] In spite of their efforts, the Republicans suffered grievously in the air fighting against the Nationalists. Spanish government aviation had almost ceased operations by the end of October 1936. With the defensive airpower on the verge of collapse, about 100 aircraft arrived from Russia, and the Soviets effectively, in Griffiss's words, "took command of the war in the air."[65]

The next several pages of the report were block-text encyclopedic-style assessments of the personnel and matériel of the foreign belligerents, starting with a discussion of the French. The French pilots were smart, experienced, and dedicated but lacked support from their own government. In order to uphold the façade of nonintervention, the French sent aircraft to Spain separately from their armaments, which often did not arrive. The planes were therefore equipped with old Spanish machine guns, placing them at a disadvantage when engaging the agile Italian Fiat CR.32s.[66] This contributed to the heavy attrition of French aviation: "It was not long before the French pilots had their backs to the wall. They suffered heavy combat losses, destruction of equipment from airdrome bombing raids as well as the loss of several planes by Spanish pilots who without authority took them for practice flights."[67]

The inventory of their most capable pursuit aircraft, the Dewoitine 371, had been lost completely. Similarly, the six Loire 46s were all gone. Of the original twenty, only four Potez 54 aircraft were combat-ready. The experimental Bloch MB.210 had crash-landed on the runway and was out of commission. A week before Griffiss wrote his report, a French-piloted Nieuport had crashed following a fly-over parade in Valencia. Of the forty-five French pilots who arrived since the beginning of the war, only seven remained.[68]

The French had originally assumed responsibility for the air defense of Madrid, but as casualties mounted and pilots and planes were not replaced, this role was taken over by the Russians. Griffiss was clearly most impressed by the Russian Air Force presence, intrigued all the more so by their "curtain of secrecy." According to an unofficial source, there were about 500 Russian pilots and mechanics (mostly pilots) in Spain. The typical Russian pilot was in his early twenties, apparently under strict orders not to wear a uniform, not to discuss air matters with foreigners (even allies), not to socialize with women, and not to allow foreigners to inspect his aircraft, let alone operate it. Only foreign pilots who had been trained at a flight school were allowed to fly Russian aircraft. In any event, Russian support was not provided freely. Soviet agents had gained considerable influence in the Spanish government and occupied several positions in the Air Ministry. "The Russians *are* the Air Force," Griffiss stated bluntly. The discipline of the Russians was remarkable. A rotation of pilots was kept in a state of readiness, sitting in the cockpits of their pursuit aircraft on the field, parachutes fastened, goggles on foreheads, poised to respond quickly to aerial attacks.[69]

There followed a discussion of aircraft and armaments, which has been and will be discussed elsewhere in this book. Griffiss then moved on to discuss other matters regarding air operations. He noted that neither radio nor photography had yet played a large role. Most aircraft, with the exception of larger platforms like the Potez 54s, were not equipped with radios. There were apparently too few aircraft available to dedicate to photographic collection missions. These two facts drastically reduced the effectiveness of reconnaissance missions, allowing neither direct communication with ground liaisons through radio nor visual support for planners through photography. Interestingly, Griffiss noted, almost in passing, that the Republicans were conducting experiments with a "heat ray" designed to halt aircraft engines in midair. These experiments were apparently being conducted at Albacete and Meneses Field near Valencia. He promised to follow up on these rumors when he had more information.[70]

Griffiss then turned to answering questions, apparently sent to him by the Military Intelligence Division. One question requested information on "attack" aircraft, to which he responded that the Russians were the only ones to have an aircraft designated to that mission, which he referred to as the "A-5" observation craft (almost certainly the R-5 Resantes). However, he noted that both pursuit aircraft and bombers were used in close air support, of which the Katiuskas appeared to be the most adept.[71] In response to a question about whether new tactics had been developed thus far in the war, the answer was a definitive negative. On the contrary, he stated: "It is reported by pilots who have had considerable experience in combat service in the Madrid area that no new method has been developed. In fact the reverse seems to be the case. The tactical teachings of several nations relative to the future war seem to have been completely shelved and the tactics in vogue are those of the period at the end of the World War."[72]

A question about close air support (or "ground attack," as it was called) drew an intriguing answer. The Nationalists had employed this tactic with great effectiveness near Madrid, particularly when field artillery failed to sufficiently weaken Republican lines. Attacks by German Junkers and pursuits at the same points succeeded to clear defenders from the line, and the Nationalist infantry was able to break through. An International Brigade soldier whom Griffiss interviewed confirmed that the impact of such attacks was more than merely physical, as "frequently their lines were [strafed] by enemy pursuit immediately prior to an infantry attack. This same man said that the morale effect was unbelievably severe and even though many casualties resulted the worst effect was the lowering of the will to resist." The only apparent antidote to this fear was the presence of friendly aircraft to provide cover.[73]

What was Griffiss's ultimate prognosis? It was grave for the Republic. Neither side had yet achieved air superiority, but the attrition of Republican Spanish, French, and Russian forces had favored the Nationalists. With the French divided over further support, the prospects seemed bleak for the government. Griffiss gravely observed, "Unless additional modern aircraft reaches the Air Force the Government's war in the air will come to a dismal close due only to the numerical strength of its enemy."[74] So much for Spanish fortunes. But what lessons could the United States derive from events in Spain? Griffiss provided points made to him in his conversations with air combat veterans: Bombers were not invincible and were particularly vulnerable to pursuit attack; and pursuits were superior to bombers at higher altitudes, thus precluding the practicality of high-altitude bombing. In a declaration that may have made the staff of the Chief of the Air Corps blanch, he stated, "The flying fortress died in Spain."[75]

What would be the consequences of these conclusions? If bombers were to conduct daylight missions, they must be faster and fly at lower altitudes; shielding must be strengthened, particularly to protect bomber pilots from attacks from the rear of the aircraft. There should be two types of pursuits: high speed monoplanes for bomber escorts, and rugged biplanes for defensive counterair ("alert"). Small-caliber, rapid-fire machine guns were more suited to aerial combat than high-caliber aerial cannons, for in the midst of battle, speed was more essential than power. Additional fields should be developed to compensate for the different radii of action of pursuit aircraft and bombers; and pursuits should escort bombers at a ratio of two-to-one.[76]

These were the initial observations by an American airman of Spanish Civil War air operations. How they would be modified or reinforced by events remained to be seen. Nevertheless, while Griffiss was drafting this report in Valencia, the Nationalists were planning one final push to encircle Madrid and cut the city off from the coast. Previous attempts had made progress but had failed to break through. If this next drive were successful, the end of the war with a Nationalist victory would finally be in sight.

GUADALAJARA

Following the victory at Málaga, the Corpo Truppe Volontarie started to assemble northeast of Madrid, near the town of Algora, by the Saragossa Road. The Italians were to lead this latest and likely final attempt to take Madrid through envelopment by advancing southwest to the city of Guadalajara, located on the Río Henares at the road junction linking Madrid to the east coast. For this purpose, General Roatta readied his three Fascist divisions: the 1st, Dio lo vuole (God wills it), commanded by General Silvio Rossi; the 2nd, Fiamme nere (Black Flames), under General Giovanni Coppi; and the 3rd, Penne nere (Black Feathers), under General Nuvolini. The officers of these divisions seemed more solidly grounded in Fascist ideology than sound military doctrine, but such was Italian confidence that their task was considered a simple one of marching to triumph. Their right flank would be shielded by the Nationalist Soría Division under Colonel José Moscardó, lately rescued from the siege of the Toledo Alcazár. The Italian regular army Littorio Division, commanded by the competent General Annibale Bergonzoli, was to be held in reserve. In support of the assault would be about 80 Ansaldo "tankettes," equipped with light machine guns, 200 mobile artillery pieces, 2,000 trucks, and a few armored cars and antiaircraft artillery pieces. About 60 aircraft were to provide close air support for the advancing columns. In all, about 50,000 men were organized on the front.[77]

In their path sat the 12th Republican Division under the command of Colonel Víctor LaCalle (not to be confused with Captain Andrés García LaCalle, who commanded the Spanish-American I-15 squadron). The Republicans were still recovering from the Jarama operation and were uncertain as to where the next hammer blow would fall. Thus, about 9,000 Republicans manned the front against a force more than five times their number. However, the defenders held two advantages that would become evident in the next few days: an incoming late-winter storm front and the Republican airfield at Alcalá de Henares. This airfield served as the headquarters of Colonel Yakov Smushkevich, a

Russian Air Force officer who operated in Spain under the curious nom de guerre of "General Douglas." Why he chose a British name rather than a Spanish one to allay suspicions of direct Russian involvement is yet another mystery of this strange war.[78]

On March 8, Coppi's Black Flames commenced their march southward toward Guadalajara. LaCalle's 12th Division was knocked back on its heels, unable to present an effective defense. The Italian infantry and vehicles were exhibiting a new type of warfare, *Guerra di rapido corso*, also known as blitzkrieg. However, blitzkrieg required rapid, maneuverable ground forces supported by air interdiction of enemy forces. As of the afternoon of the first day of the offensive, the Italians lost the key element of air support. Cold, stormy weather turned the hastily constructed airfields to mud and kept the Italian Fiats grounded.[79]

Nevertheless, the Italian Nationalist force gained ground on the second day of the offensive. Advancing on an eighteen-mile front, the Nationalists under Moscardó crossed the Henares River and seized Jadraque in the west while the Italians captured Brihuega in the east. This brought the Italians within twenty-one miles of Guadalajara. However, the cold rain continued to fall, making further advances difficult for the mechanized Fascist divisions. This delay gave the Republican government a chance to overcome its shock. General Miaja diverted troops to the area, where they began to concentrate around Torija and Trijueque, about seven miles southwest of the Italians.[80]

The Republicans formed the new IV Army Corps, commanded by Colonel Enrique Jurado. It consisted of the 11th Division under Líster, comprising the XI International Brigade, two Spanish Republican brigades, and a brigade led by Valentin González who was known as El Campesino ("The Peasant"); the 14th Division, commanded by the anarchist Cipriano Mera, together with the XII International Brigade and the 65th Republican Brigade; and LaCalle's 12th Division, with three Spanish Republican brigades. This brought Republican strength on the front to somewhere between 25,000 and 30,000.[81]

Colonel Jurado was corps commander, but any operational control he exercised was well-supervised and assisted by Soviet advisers. They positioned Líster's division on the main road connecting Madrid to Saragossa. Mera's division, positioned on Líster's right, occupied the road between Torija and Brihuega. LaCalle's division was to be held in reserve. LaCalle, claiming ill-health, was replaced by Nino Nanetti, an Italian communist. Dolores Ibárruri, the famed communist delegate known as "La Pasionaria," visited the troops at the front to fortify them with zeal for the cause of the workers. This force, thus organized and encouraged, awaited the arrival of the haughty Fascist columns.[82]

On March 10, Coppi's Black Flames moved at a snail's crawl from Brihuega, with a motorcycle patrol at point. This patrol made contact with a patrol from the Garibaldi Battalion, composed of leftist exiles from Mussolini's Italy. The Fascist patrol, however, was expecting to rendezvous with Nuvolini's division. Their confusion was due to the fact that the Italian command was unfamiliar with the lay of the land and was relying on 1:400,000 scale Michelin maps. So the Fascist patrol made friendly overtures to the Garibaldi advance party. They were met with hostile fire. When the Fascists discovered the true identity of their adversaries, they lost their nerve and surrendered. The rest of Coppi's division, alerted to the danger, engaged the Garibaldis in a firefight near the Ibarra Palace.[83]

The next day, Nuvolini's Division advanced southward down the Madrid–Saragossa Road. They captured Trijueque and came within fifteen miles of Guadalajara, until they were checked by the defenders.[84] The XI International Brigade, of which the Thaelmann Battalion was a part, had yet to recover from the fighting at Jarama and had been reinforced with Spanish rather than international replacements.[85] Regardless of their current composition, the Thaelmann troops held the Black Feathers at bay, supported by newly arrived Russian tanks. These were commanded by General Pavlov, who had assumed the name "General Pablo" (evidencing that he had a better grasp of Spanish naming conventions than did his air force counterpart, Smushkevich ["General Douglas"]). Pavlov's T-26 tanks with their 45-mm cannons were vastly superior in firepower and armor than the Italian Ansaldo tankettes with their machine guns.[86]

The Italian divisions soon realized they had more to worry about than the International Brigades and Russian tanks. Republican squadrons at airfields around Guadalajara had been thwarted the day before by inclement weather, but current conditions permitted them to operate over the battlefield without interference from enemy aircraft.[87] The defenseless Fascist forces could only take cover and hope that the poor weather would provide shelter for them, which it eventually did. The Italian leadership was still unchastened, but Republican airpower had made its presence felt. As Griffiss later wrote to the War Department, "The credit for the initial breaking of the Italian advance belongs to the Air Force."[88]

In the meantime, in spite of the forebodings across most of the front, the momentum of the Fascist attack had not yet completely expired. On the right flank of the Italians, the Nationalist Soría Division crossed to the right bank of the Henares River and captured Cogolludo.[89] At this crucial point in the battle, with two of his divisions engaged with the enemy, a third division turning the enemy's left flank, and two additional divisions in reserve, General Roatta made the seemingly inexplicable decision to call for an operational pause for the next day.[90]

However, events would not wait on Roatta's schedule. The Fiats of the Aviazione Legionaria were still grounded, but the Republican aircraft could fly. About thirty I-15s and I-16s attacked the Italian columns on multiple missions, dropping almost 500 bombs and expending 200,000 rounds of ammunition.[91] Líster's division, together with the XI International Brigade and El Campesino's brigade in the vanguard, launched a counterattack against Nuvolini's Black Feathers. The Italians were knocked backward, their 3-ton Ansaldo tanks being completely out-matched by the 20-ton Russian T-26s. By day's end, Trijueque was again in Republican hands. To the east, the Garibaldi Battalion forced back their Fascist co-nationals, and captured Ibarra Palace.[92] Only in the west, where there was minimal Republican presence, was Moscardó's Nationalist division able to make any progress. Moscardó's forces captured Espinosa de Henares, the location of an important railway junction. It seemed no one was willing or able to abide by General Roatta's instructions for an operational pause.[93]

On the following day, March 13, the tide turned decisively toward the Republicans. Líster's division continued to push the Italians back north, up the Saragossa Road, forcing General Roatta to throw in his reserve divisions, the Dio lo vuole Division and the Littorio Division, under Rossi and Bergonzoli, respectively.[94] Mera's 14th Division moved on Brihuega. Their advance was slowed by one of their own patrols, which prematurely blew up a bridge over the Río Tajuña.[95] Three German Junkers managed to enter the area but were soon chased off by Republican fighters. One of the Junkers, in retreat, managed to shoot down the plane of Antonio Blanche, who was leading one of the Republican patrols. Frank Tinker recalled watching in horror as Blanche's parachute did not open and he fell 6,500 feet to his death. The failure of the parachute was attributed to dampness, which resulted in a thorough check of all other parachutes in the squadron.[96]

The Republican counterattack recommenced on March 18, when Mera's division completed a pontoon bridge and crossed the Río Tajuña. On the main road, Pavlov's tanks led the advance of Líster's 11th Infantry Division. They met and drove back the Littorio Division. Líster then wheeled right, and he and Mera attempted a double envelopment of Brihuega. Coppi's 2nd Division (Black Flames), realizing its position had become untenable, fled the town before the trap was sprung.[97] General Roatta was in Salamanca at this time, imploring Franco to allow him to withdraw his forces from the front. Franco was reluctant to do so, but once news came of the attack on Brihuega, the order was given for a general withdrawal. The Italians retreated several miles before establishing some order in their lines. The battle was over.[98]

The Battle of Guadalajara—so-called, although it came no fewer than fifteen miles of the city—lasted eleven days and cost the Italians about 7,800 casualties (3,000 killed), while the Republicans suffered about 6,400 casualties (2,000 killed).[99] Hundreds of vehicles were lost by the Italians, and many of them were salvaged by the Republicans. Tinker noted that mechanics at Campo X kept a count of captured Italian trucks driving southward toward Guadalajara. Their tally amounted to more than eight hundred.[100] Spanish Nationalist losses were minimal. The Soría Division under Moscardó had acquitted itself well, withdrawing only after the rest of the offensive collapsed.[101]

Map 2. Nationalist-Republican Territory, March 1937

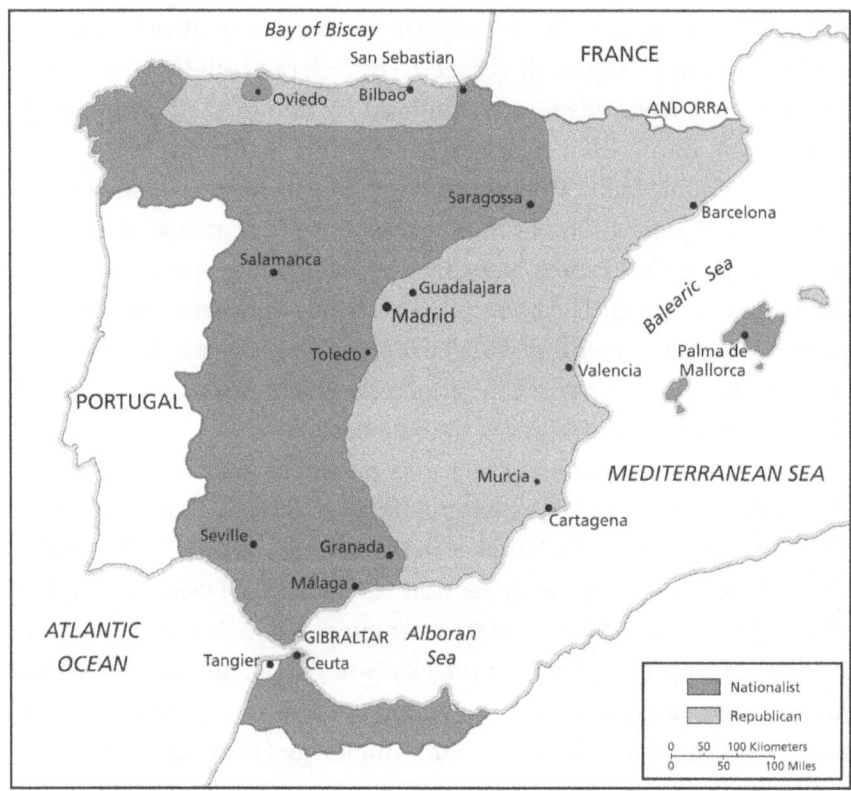

Thus concluded the final attempt of the Nationalists to capture Madrid in the spring of 1937. Although they had gained ground in each of the battles—the direct assault, Corunna Road, Jarama, and Guadalajara—they had failed to achieve their objectives. They achieved neither the occupation of Madrid nor its isolation. The critical role of airpower in this operation could not be denied, notably in the areas of counterair and close air support. Whether this operational victory would translate into a strategic advantage remained to be seen. Much of that depended on factors outside of the Republicans' control: the reaction of the Western democracies, the activities of their increasingly overbearing Russian benefactor, the subsequent actions of the Nationalists, and the continued support of Germany and Italy for Franco. But as the Nationalists turned their attention to the northern sector, it became clear to the Madrileños (with their absentee government in Valencia) and to the wider world that—against all expectations—Madrid was secure. The Madrileños had made good on La Pasionara's proclamation of "No pasarán!" (They shall not pass!).[102] Even more incredible was the rise of the unlikely hero of Madrid's stand: General José Miaja, the conservative career officer. According to an Easter-time *Newsweek* report, Miaja "gave his long-suffering followers a present more precious than eggs. He announced: 'Madrid is safe on all fronts.'"[103]

CHAPTER 5

INTERDICTION

> *Brutus : There is a tide in the affairs of men,*
> *Which, taken at the flood, leads on to fortune.*
> —SHAKESPEARE, *JULIUS CAESAR*

AMERICAN NEUTRALITY POLICY

We now pause from our historical narrative in order to focus on the exploits of American pilots who flew in the Spanish Civil War. Like their compatriots in the Lincoln and Washington Battalions of the International Brigades, these men came to Spain at considerable personal risk to serve—with one notable exception—the cause of the Republic. Yet compared to the legendary status of the International Brigades, these men were little known at the time and are now largely forgotten. Who were these men? What were their motivations? What contributions did they make? What lessons did they learn? We will examine these issues further in this chapter and shed some light on this interesting and somewhat mysterious collection of individuals.

First, we must consider the wider context of American foreign policy at this time, for that impacted the decisions made by these men on how they came to serve in Spain. American leaders were traditionally wary of both national and individual American involvement in foreign conflicts.

The original Neutrality Act dated back to the administration of George Washington, and the concept of nonintervention had since become a key, perhaps even a defining aspect of American foreign policy for most of the nation's history. As scholar George Finch explained nonintervention in a 1937 editorial for the *American Journal of International Law*, "The contribution of the United States to the development of this branch of international law is well known and generously acknowledged."[1]

Apart from the campaign against the Barbary Pirates in 1804–5, or the occasional naval mission during the War of Independence, the War of 1812, or the U.S. Civil War, or the early, abortive invasions of Canada, or the swift, successful invasion of Mexico, the United States had little occasion for fighting in foreign territory and thus little need for legislation regarding such operations. The outbreak of the Spanish-American War in 1898, with combat in the Caribbean and as far off as the Philippines, signaled the need for American leaders to consider the nation's standing with the rest of the world and to guard against involvement in distant foreign conflicts. Thus, legislative and executive actions were taken in the next several years to address this concern. On April 22, 1898, Congress passed a joint resolution authorizing the president to halt the exports of war material, specifically coal, from the nation's seaports; and on March 14, 1912, motivated by the chaotic situation in neighboring Mexico, Congress authorized the president to control the exportation of arms or munitions to nations in North and South America currently in the throes of civil disturbance.[2]

America's entry into the First World War was thus a departure from its long-held tradition of nonintervention. Though victorious in that conflict, the nation entered an interwar period of caution and restraint. Dismayed and disillusioned by their experience, the American people at large were determined to stay out of future foreign engagements, particularly those in Europe. By the 1930s, politicians were well-synchronized with this sentiment. It was the Great Depression, and Americans had problems of their own. A further series of legislative and executive action codified these sentiments. In 1932, President Herbert Hoover's secretary of state Henry Stimson halted arms shipments to Manchuria during the Japanese invasion of that territory, and he requested that Congress pass legislation authorizing the president to limit arms exports to any country, if deemed necessary—though Hoover's term ended before action could be taken. On May 28, 1934, Congress issued a joint resolution authorizing the president to embargo war material to Bolivia and Paraguay during those nations' Chaco War. And finally, in 1935, Congress passed a Neutrality Act in reaction to the international disturbances caused by the Italo-Ethiopian War; the act prohibited the shipment of arms to nations at war. It was under this authority that President Franklin Roosevelt embargoed war material to the belligerents, denying support to both attacker (Italy) and defender (Ethiopia) equally. Perhaps through oversight, the act failed to address the contingency of shipping such items to factions involved in a civil war.[3]

A few weeks after the outbreak of hostilities in Spain, Acting Secretary of State William Phillips acknowledged the civil war loophole of the Neutrality Act but expressed his expectation that Americans would keep to the spirit of the law:

> It is clear that our Neutrality Law with respect to embargo of arms, ammunition and implements of war has no application in the present situation, since that applies only in the event of war *between or among nations.* On the other hand, in conformity with its well-established policy of non-interference with internal affairs in other countries, either in time of peace or in the event of civil strife, this Government will, or course, scrupulously refrain from any interference whatsoever in the unfortunate Spanish situation. We believe that American citizens, both at home and abroad, are patriotically observing this well-recognized American policy.[4]

Phillips' faith in the patriotic cooperation of Americans was insufficient to stop businessman Robert Cuse from organizing the shipment of $2.8 million in aircraft and aircraft engines to the Basque port of Bilbao in December 1936. In statements released to the governments of Britain, France, the Soviet Union, Germany, Italy, and Republican Spain, the Department of State explained that it was legally unable to halt this shipment—and in fact was obliged to license it—but insisted it "sincerely regrets the unfortunate non-compliance by an American citizen with this Government's strict non-intervention policy."[5] As a consequence of this embarrassment, President Roosevelt mentioned the need to close this civil war loophole during his State of the Union address on January 6, 1937. Congress obliged the same day with a joint resolution specifically prohibiting arms shipments to the factions in Spain.[6] In May, the civil war loophole was definitively closed with the passage of the Neutrality Act of 1937.[7]

The above text describes restrictions on material support to belligerents, but American legislation also sought to curb personal service by individuals in foreign conflicts. The Citizenship Act of 1907 had forbidden Americans to take an oath to a foreign government under punishment of loss of citizenship. It was under this law that pilots serving in the Lafayette Escadrille during the First World War were charged, though their citizenship was restored in 1918, after the United States entered the war on the side of France and her allies. In 1934, several measures were established in Title 18 of the United States Code to deal with individual violations of the nonintervention policy. For instance, Americans who joined a foreign military risked a $1,000 fine and a prison term for up to three years; the fine could be up to $2,000, along with a possible three-year prison term if any American fought against a nation with whom the United States was not at war. There was also a ban against recruiting Americans for such warfare.[8]

According to official sources, twenty-nine American pilots served in Spain at some point during the civil war. Other sources suggest that it may have been as many as thirty-five.[9] It is unclear whether the American pilots who came to Spain in 1936 and 1937 were fully aware of the risks they were running by joining with a foreign air force. Due to the discrete methods many of them and their recruiters adopted to get them to Spain, it is clear they understood they were skirting American policy and law. Whether they thought they would be retroactively justified, like the flyers in the Lafayette Escadrille, is unclear. Yet, even had they been well-informed of the risks, the pilots who flew for Spain were not the sort to be swayed by such considerations. For the most part, these American flyers came to Spain with nothing to lose.

In September 1936, the first group of American pilots arrived in Spain to offer their services to the Republic. Their flying skills were found to be inadequate for combat, but they were kept on flying transports.[10] They were followed in November 1936 by a group of more skillful pilots, of whom Bertrand Acosta (1895–1954) might serve as representative. He was perhaps best known as a pilot for Commander Richard Byrd on his transatlantic flight in 1927. Up to the time of the Spanish Civil War, Acosta had an extraordinary career and was well-regarded by his fellow pilots. According to historian John Carver Edwards, "Over the course of his life, he had been a barnstormer, speed racer, test pilot aeronautical engineer, civilian flight instructor to Canadian flyboys during the First World War, failed entrepreneur, and always the aerial clown. Legend had it that Acosta once buzzed a huge clock on a New York City skyscraper when a passenger asked for the time."[11]

The experience of this wave of American pilots in Spain was inauspicious. According to one historian, "The Acosta Four were notorious in Spain for skills other than flying.... Drunken brawls, disputes with Spanish superiors, and an attempted desertion when pay was not forthcoming resulted in the first group leaving Spain by the end of 1936."[12] Frank Tinker, who arrived in Spain in January 1937, later learned of their exploits and expressed his disgust, going so far as to suggest they deserved to be executed.[13]

There are at least two sides to every story. Acosta and the others claimed that they arrived at the end of November 1936 in Basque Country, ready to fly; they were issued obsolete and unsafe aircraft, received no proper attire for flying, and were dispatched on dangerous and pointless missions. Under such conditions, the "Suicide Patrol" soon became disillusioned. Nevertheless, Acosta claimed to have downed an enemy aircraft by shooting the opposing pilot in the face when the latter, flying alongside Acosta's sluggish Breguet XIX to get a look at his prey, ventured within pistol range. On the same flight, Acosta's observer killed two other enemy pilots with his rifle. When they returned to their home field, they claimed three victories and the promised bonuses for each. The Spanish officials could not confirm the claims and refused to pay. Acosta and three other American pilots then attempted to leave; they were arrested for desertion and sent to Valencia for interrogation. The Republican government, in all probability loathe to imprison or execute Americans due to the likely international repercussions, instead deported them to France and considered the matter closed.[14]

On their way out of the theater, the mercenary pilots made some contact with Lt. Col. Sumner Waite, the assistant military attaché in Paris. In early January 1937, Waite spoke at some length with Frederick Ives Lord, a colleague of Acosta's. His story was consistent with that of Acosta's. Lord told Waite that the Republican Air Force was poorly equipped and even worse led. He mentioned that he and the other American flyers were assigned sport planes for combat and were obliged to drop bombs over the side of their craft, there being no other release mechanism. They claimed to have failed to receive the pay due to them and so had departed the war after only a few months. Lord made much of the growing Russian influence over air operations in Spain. Any payments that were made apparently had to be cleared through Russian authorities. The reasons for Lord remaining in France while Acosta and the other Americans returned to the United States were a mystery to Waite. He suspected that Lord, who had visited the Spanish embassy the night before, was attempting to get hired to ferry French bombers to the Republicans. Waite was not very impressed by the quality of Lord's character. "All of the above must be taken with several grains of salt," he concluded, regarding Lord's information. "It is believed that Lord is in the game for what he can get out of it."[15]

BAUMLER, TINKER, AND DAHL

While the previous, unsuccessful wave of American pilots was making its way out of the theater, a new wave was arriving. The motivations of each of the pilots differed, but on the whole, they were more willing to serve the cause of the Republic and more daring and adventurous in their attitudes toward flying. This may have been in part because they were generally less experienced than their predecessors, and thus less appreciative of the risks they were about to take. Or perhaps it was because they tended to be younger and thus had more energy to face those risks.

Characteristic of this adventurous spirit was Albert John "Ajax" Baumler (1914–73) of Bayonne, New Jersey. Twenty-two years old in December 1936, after four or five years with the New Jersey National Guard and Regular Army, he came to Spain with little more than his strong self-confidence and belief in his abilities.[16] Decades later, Gen. Earl E. Partridge, who would meet Baumler in October 1940, when Baumler worked as an instructor at Partridge's flying school at Barksdale Field, Louisiana, told interviewers a little bit about the character of this adventurer: "He was a very cocky fellow; he was very sure of himself, and his personal habits were such that he liked to drink and stay up late at night. He was so cocky that he got washed out just before graduation. I don't know the year, but I would guess it's about 1935. He went to Spain. He finagled his way over to Spain and he joined the Loyalists. He fought with them and did well; he was a *very* good pilot."[17]

Baumler volunteered for Spain and traveled across the Atlantic on the *Queen Mary* and through France accompanied by Augustin Sanz Sáinz, a former Spanish pilot and political refugee. He and another American, Charlie Koch, proved their abilities in test flights and were assigned to a Russian-led fighter squadron in Albacete.[18]

A short time after Baumler's arrival, Frank G. Tinker Jr. (1909–39), fated to become the best American pilot in Spain, arrived in the country. While Baumler could be considered strictly agnostic on the political matters of the conflict in which he was killing and risking death, Tinker shared some basic sympathies with the cause of his hosts. As he stated at the beginning of his memoir, *Some Still Live* (1938), he at first knew little about the cause of the war and had had no strong feelings toward or against either side. However, when Junkers were identified in the bombing of Madrid, Tinker assumed that Hitler was involved. The additional intervention of Mussolini and the Italian forces caused him to decide to throw in with the Republicans as a fighter pilot.[19] Tinker neglected to mention that, by the time war had erupted in Spain, his American military career had abruptly terminated due to some lapses in judgment.

Tinker was born in Louisiana in 1909 but spent his formative years in DeWitt, Arkansas, where his father, an engineer in the rice mill industry, brought the family in 1924. He attended the U.S. Naval Academy and graduated in 1933 with a Bachelor of Science; but he did not receive an active-duty commission right away due to austerity measures caused by the Great Depression. He thus started pilot training with the Army Air Corps but completed it with the Navy once his commission was finally approved. His career as a Navy pilot lasted less than a year, when he was compelled to resign his commission—or rather, had it terminated before he officially resigned—after a couple of serious infractions due to public drunkenness.[20]

When war broke out in Spain, Tinker took an interest in the conflict from afar. By late November 1936, he decided to become involved. He wrote to various Spanish officials in the United States and Mexico, and he eventually received an encouraging reply from the ambassador in Mexico City. On December 18, 1936, he arrived in the Mexican capital; the next day, he signed a contract that made him a second lieutenant, entitled to a salary of $1,500 per month, with a $1,000 bonus for every enemy aircraft he destroyed. If he did nothing but fly, he still would have made more money in three months than the average American household made in a year. Having secured this lucrative deal, he was sent back to the United States, and on Christmas Day he arrived at the Spanish general consul's office in New York City. There he received his Spanish passport and learned he was now "Francisco Gomez Trejo," an American of Spanish descent, coming to Spain to visit his grandparents. After leaving the consul's office, Tinker boarded the *Normandie*. The ship disembarked in Le Havre, France, and Tinker took a train to Paris, where he arrived on the evening of December 31.[21]

On New Year's Day, he traveled by train to the Spanish border. During the ride, he met and fraternized with a couple of Catalonian officials. This was fortuitous. At the border, when asked for his name, he gave it as "Francisco Trejo" (ignorant of the Spanish convention of using middle names as surnames). Tinker sensed that the guard was prepared to deny him entry, when one of his new Catalonian acquaintances vouched for him and gained his admittance.[22]

Of the other American pilots who reached Spain, perhaps the most notable was Harold "Whitey" Dahl (1909–56). By all accounts, Dahl was a roguish character, but like Baumler and Tinker, he could fly. He had been drummed out of the Army reserves for a civil court conviction the previous February. He had escaped further legal problems related to gambling by moving to Mexico and ferrying aircraft for shipment to Spain. From there, it was a simple act for him to talk his way into a contract with Spain to fly for them. It seemed to be the one thing he could do right, and he apparently needed steady employment to satisfy the spendthrift habits of Mrs. Dahl (Edith Rogers, neé Kaye), who lived in France while he fought across the Pyrenees. In December 1936, they had set sail with papers identifying themselves as Mr. and Mrs. Hernandez Diaz Evans. They arrived in France on the twenty-first of the month, and Whitey entered Spain five days later.[23]

There was also Ben Leider (1901–37) from New York, a short, stocky man in his mid-thirties who had been in Spain since September 1936. His family were Jewish refugees from a part of Russia that was to be ceded to Romania following the First World War. The Tsarist pogroms had caused them to flee Europe and come to America when Leider was a child. As he grew up, he developed an interest in flying, journalism, and politics. He worked as a reporter for the *New York Post*, became a member of the newspaper guild, and was instrumental in efforts to unionize other newspapers.[24] He also joined the American Communist Party. Perhaps more than any of the other American pilots, he was a true believer in the cause for which he fought. He volunteered for service in Spain for sergeant's pay rather than for mercenary pay. Originally assigned to transport aircraft, Leider persuaded Captain Andrés García LaCalle (1909–80) of the I-15 squadron to allow him a chance to fly in combat.[25]

Additionally, there was José Selles, who was not an American; but due to his fluent British-accented English, he was incorporated into the American Patrol. He was five-foot-four, of both Spanish and Japanese parentage, and raised in Japan—hence his nickname "Chang." He often served as an interpreter for the Americans, who were otherwise unable to understand the complicated rapid-fire Spanish orders they were given.[26]

Tinker and several of the Americans were now serving under twenty-seven-year-old LaCalle, flying I-15 Chatos, the Russian biplane pursuits.

The LaCalle Squadron began operations on the Jarama Front in February 1937. Their first several missions were against Nationalist ground targets.[27] Even such asymmetric actions carried risk for the flyers. On one of these missions, Tinker placed sixteen bullets into his own propeller before he realized his machine guns were unsynchronized.[28] Leider earned the first victory of the American Patrol when he was credited with the downing of an enemy fighter, a Heinkel He 51, which he pursued and fired upon until it crashed. As Tinker recorded, LaCalle was very proud of Leider's achievement, although Tinker suspected LaCalle may have wished that it had been he who had scored the first victory for the squadron. Tinker indicated that this was typical of LaCalle, who was always modest of his own achievements, despite already holding ace status.[29] There is an alternate version laid out by Richard K. Smith and R. Cargill Hall in their biography of Tinker, *Five Down, No Glory* (2011). According to Smith and Hall, Leider had broken formation to chase the Heinkel and was himself almost ambushed from the rear. LaCalle came to his rescue, chased off the pursuer, and then fired at the lead Heinkel until it lost control and crashed into the ground. In the meantime, Leider for some reason had failed to fire a shot. Back at the airfield, LaCalle upbraided Leider and threatened to have him transferred, until the latter expressed thorough contrition and LaCalle not only relented but gave credit of the victory to the American.[30]

Throughout the Jarama battle, the LaCalle Squadron undertook the interception of Junkers on their way to attack Republican positions. The German bombers were poorly equipped to defend themselves against direct attacks, and on February 16, LaCalle's squadron shot down two of them, sending the surviving ten back to Nationalist territory.[31] In the meantime, Baumler had been assigned to a Russian-led Chato squadron. This squadron, named Kosokov after its commander, shot down six Fiat CR.32s and four Junkers near Madrid on February 18.[32] However, that same day the American Patrol lost its first member to combat. Leider had been returning to base with LaCalle when the latter lost sight of him. Tinker claimed he saw Leider chasing an enemy fighter when he was ambushed by three others. Rather than bail out, he had attempted to land the aircraft but crashed into a hill. His death was confirmed the next day. Two other Americans, Whitey Dahl and Jim "Tex" Allison, were also shot down that same day, but both survived.[33] In the closing days of the battle, as the Nationalists were halted and slowly began to pull back, the LaCalle Squadron resumed attacks on enemy ground positions. On February 21, the squadron executed machine-gun strafing attacks on Nationalist infantry still on the eastern bank on the Jarama. This proved to be the final mission for the LaCalle Squadron at Jarama, as heavy rain kept the planes grounded thereafter.[34] The battle concluded six days later, with the Nationalists holding onto a bridgehead over the river but stopping far short of their objective on the Madrid-Valencia Road.

On February 25, 1937, Tinker, Dahl and Selles were granted a day's pass and set about visiting Madrid. On the way, they stopped at the infirmary at Alcalá de Henares to visit their friend Tex Allison, who was recovering from a leg wound. They then proceeded to the capital, where they checked into the Hotel Florida. By this time, they had acquired a number of champagne bottles, and while Tinker and Selles checked in, Dahl decided to head to the upper floors in the elevator. However, upon entering the conveyance, he realized that his hands were too full to press the buttons. At this time, another guest arrived and waited with increasing impatience to enter the elevator. He finally asked in Spanish why Dahl was not moving. Whitey snapped back in English that the guest should lend a hand instead of "standing there with his mouth full of teeth." The guest chastised him in fluent English, entered the elevator, and assisted a shocked Whitey in getting to his floor. He was none other than famed author Ernest Hemingway.[35] Hemingway was in Spain as a reporter for the North American Newspaper Alliance. When the pilots returned to Madrid a few days later, he hosted them at a soiree at which *New York Times* reporter Herbert Matthews and writer Martha Gellhorn were also present.[36] Apart from his novel *For Whom the Bell Tolls*, Hemingway would also write a number of short stories about the Spanish Civil War, one of which was "Night before Battle," which detailed an evening with American pilots. At one point, the narrator and his international brigadier friend meet a pilot named Baldy, who is attempting to operate an elevator while holding

INTERDICTION

six champagne bottles. When the narrator offers to assist him in his predicament, Baldy takes umbrage: "'I can fly anything,' said the woolly jacket man. 'And I can fly this old elevator. Want me to stunt it?'"[37] One of the themes of the story was the friction between the poorly paid, overworked International Brigade soldiers and the well-paid and somewhat frivolous mercenary pilots.

On March 10, LaCalle dispatched Dahl on a reconnaissance mission. The American spotted the Italian advance toward Guadalajara, but visibility was too poor for the rest of the squadron to follow up immediately on this information. The next day, in spite of continuing bad weather, the squadron took to the skies and strafed the Italian columns, crowded along the roads leading south.[38]

On March 12, Republican aircraft struck the wavering Italian Nationalist lines. I-15s and I-16s mercilessly hammered the enemy, who had limited defenses against the onslaught. The Republican troops recaptured Trijueque on the Saragossa-Madrid Road. Eventually, the Nationalist Air Force was able to take to the skies again to support the Italians' withdrawal. On March 14, Tinker got his first "kill" by shooting down a Fiat CR.32.[39] However, he then found himself separated from his squadron and hunted by five additional Fiats. He managed to maneuver away from the Italian fighters by diving and conducting a series of turns, corkscrew-fashion. The Fiats overshot his aircraft, and he escaped into the concealment of the clouds.[40]

On March 16, to the east of Trijueque, near Brihuega, there was a relatively large-scale aerial battle involving three Republican squadrons, including LaCalle's and Kosokov's. During this engagement, Baumler shot down a Fiat—though credit was shared with a Russian pilot.[41] Another American in the Kosokov Squadron, Charlie "Tiny" Koch, participated in several strafing runs, but by the end of the battle he was grounded with hemorrhaging due to stomach ulcers. He would later be discharged so that he could return to America for medical treatment.[42]

On March 17, General José Miaja, commander of the forces defending Madrid, paid a visit to the LaCalle Squadron. Tinker appreciated the unassuming and kind nature of the general, who commended the pilots in a short speech. When Dahl's patrol gave a display of readiness by manning their fighters and starting their engines within twenty seconds of an alarm sounding, Miaja made sure to congratulate each of the pilots personally. Tinker and his squadronmates were well-disposed toward the general after this visit.[43]

As discussed in the previous chapter, Guadalajara was considered a major victory for the Republican forces. Tinker capped this success on March 20 by shooting down a Fiat, his second aerial victory in Spain. The Fiat had been one of about twenty that were escorting three Junkers on a bombing mission. LaCalle's squadron checked their progress, causing the bombers to drop their payloads in their own territory and flee to safety.[44] Shortly after the battle, Dahl developed stomach problems and required hospitalization. In the meantime, Selles was summoned by the Russian squadron leader to Alcalá, under the pretense of performing translation work.[45] Tinker never saw him again.

APRIL DISPATCH

In Valencia the following month, Capt. Townsend Griffiss, the American assistant military attaché, crafted yet another lengthy, informative report on the situation in the air. It was primarily a summary of lessons learned up to that time. It seemed the Republican Air Force was having some difficulty in this regard. After nine months of war, the chief of Military Aviation, Colonel Ignacio Hidalgo de Cisneros, still had not completed a tactical doctrine for airpower, though he was apparently consolidating certain principles from experiences up to that date (April 25, 1937). Griffiss had consolidated his own principles after speaking with several pilots who had thorough combat experience in the theater. His findings can be summarized as follows:

1. Tactics are determined by equipment.
2. In peacetime, pilots need to be trained in basic aerial tactics.
3. In wartime, pilots need flexibility to adopt new tactics.
4. Training in aerial gunnery is of paramount importance.

For this last finding, Griffiss observed that most air forces neglected realistic training in aerial gunnery.[46]

The first principle, that equipment determined which tactics were used, had a major impact on Republican air operations early in the conflict. The variety of their aircraft at the outbreak of the war precluded the development of a uniform tactical doctrine. Further, their unfamiliarity with the Nationalist inventory of aircraft made it difficult to know what their enemies were capable of doing in the skies.[47] That problem had worked itself out with the arrival of the Great Powers and their air forces. The Republicans now relied almost exclusively on the Russian I-15 biplanes (Chatos) and I-16 monoplanes (Moscas) for their air defense. The biplanes, flying in V-formation, targeted the bombers while the monoplanes fended off the enemy's fighters. The I-15s attacked by flying directly at the lead bomber in a formation, machine gunning it before diving and turning almost 180 degrees back toward friendly territory. This was particularly effective because the gun turrets on the top and bottom of the fuselage of the Junkers Ju.52s were unable to defend against direct attacks from the front.[48]

Air missions were becoming large-scale events. During the Battle of Jarama, German bomber formations had grown, with one or two dozen Junkers flying in V or line formation, escorted by two to three times as many Heinkels flying in squadrons at different altitudes. This produced a fighting force of between 30 and 90 aircraft per air raid.[49] The Nationalists, or rather the Germans, developed a response to the tactics of the I-15s by luring them with a squadron of Heinkels flying below the bombers. When the Republican (or Russian) biplanes dove to engage the Heinkels, another squadron of Heinkels, flying above the bombers, would dive on the remaining biplanes that were still threatening the bombers. This tactic had only mixed results, since, according to Griffiss, "The Russian pilots never forget the mission of the moment."[50] The Russian I-16 monoplanes proved effective in targeting enemy pursuits, striking in two-plane teams with "scissor" attacks from both sides, utilizing tactics Griffiss described as "hit, run and cooperate."[51]

Griffiss discussed in detail the ground-attack functions of the Republican air forces. The pursuit pilots were proficient in both a "high attack" and a "low attack." In the high attack, the pursuits would dive from 14,000 feet to 4,500 feet—near the upper-limits of enemy anti-aircraft artillery range—dropping their 22-pound bombs and firing their machine guns at the enemy infantry. For the low attack, the pursuits would approach the target at 1,500 feet before diving to 100 feet and attacking the infantry with bombs and machine-gun rounds. A notable feature of the Russian I-15s created difficulties: the bomb release lever was located on the floor of the fuselage. This complicated matters, as pilots were required to reach down to trigger them, thus losing visibility.[52]

The Russians were the only belligerents with specific ground-attack aircraft. The latest version of the R-5 (or A-5 or 3-S) Resantes aircraft were equipped with formidable armaments, including four machine guns on their wings, a rear gun, twenty 22-pound bombs, and four 154-pound bombs. These aircraft would approach their targets in three-plane V-formations at 100 feet, climb to about 400 feet, and release their bombs. They would then dive and machine-gun the ground forces. A clever night tactic employed by the Russians was to fly a lone bomber ahead of the attack aircraft to draw the attention of searchlight crews. Once the searchlights were lit, the attack aircraft would strike and render the defenders blind. Additional Russian bombers would follow, now safely hidden from ground spotters.[53]

However, it seemed that for every tactic, a new countertactic was soon developed. For instance, the Russian scheme of baiting searchlights with a lone bomber before striking with attack aircraft led the Nationalists to place their searchlights on railcars and quickly maneuver them away from an attack.[54] New platforms were also beginning to make their appearance. Griffiss mentioned the arrival of the German Junker Ju 86 bomber. This aircraft would not boast of much success in the war, but it had one improvement over its predecessor—the presence of a front gun to counter head-on attacks. Republican pursuits were obliged to strike these new bombers from the rear.[55] Taking the above in consideration, Griffiss declared, "The most important development that has taken place in the government Air Force is the tactical coordination that now exists between the pursuit, bombardment, and ground-attack aviation. With internal understanding, it has been a great deal easier to build up coordination and cooperation between Air and Ground."[56]

Near the close of his report, Griffiss addressed some miscellany (summarized, not quoted, as follows):

1. Government aircraft were operating primarily out of temporary fields, with squadrons constantly shifting from one field to another.
2. The telephone high-rise building in Madrid, which had served as a point of reference and target for artillerymen in the Nationalist lines, housed the command post on its top floor.
3. Due to the general lack of communication equipment, the pilots communicated with each other and with the ground by signaling with their wings or waving their arms, keeping the methods as simple as possible.[57]
4. The Republicans (or more specifically, the Russians) had a firm grip on their pilots and made sure that they adhered to the demands of their duty. "Orders are also very clear that once an attack is launched it will be carried out no matter what develops," Griffiss noted, adding, "The punishment for the violation of these orders is extremely severe."[58]

Severe also was the combatants' growing hostility toward parachuting pilots. Both sides were now employing parachutes, hoping that a veteran pilot who lost an air duel would live to fly another day. However, their slow, defenseless descent made them tempting targets. How did pilots regard the legitimacy of striking a parachutist? There seemed to be a generational divergence of opinions on this matter. Younger pilots voiced little hesitation in categorizing parachutists as combatants and therefore as legitimate targets for hostile action. Veteran pilots saw this as dishonorable, declining to target a worthy adversary who, having already lost his aircraft, should not also lose his life in cold blood.[59] The opinions of the youths held the day, and parachutists were now considered fair game by both sides. Griffiss appeared to endorse this practice: "The aerial war of the future, as far as the combatants are concerned, will be void of all feeling and sentiment. Peace-time training should include every method for the destruction of the enemy and it is not going too far to recommend gunnery practice against dummies floating down in parachutes!—In Spain both Air Forces are shooting airmen dropping in parachutes."[60] He added that Russians seemed particularly adept at gunning parachutists in midair.[61]

On that coldly rational note, Griffiss concluded his nine-page report. It was clear that the trends in the air were toward uniformity in platforms, armaments, and tactics. With the commitment of Russian, German, and Italian airpower, a sense of order had arisen out of the original chaotic situation of the belligerent air forces from the previous July; and with this order, airpower could be more forcefully applied. This became evident one day after Griffiss's dispatch, when the Condor Legion bombed the Basque town of Guernica in what would become the most infamous event of the war. This will be discussed in the following chapter.

At the beginning of May 1937, the two leading American fighter pilots still in active service in Spain, Baumler and Tinker, were assigned together to a Russian-led squadron. There were some necessary adjustments to the new situation. Tinker's penchant for sarcasm almost caused serious trouble when he asked his Russian colleagues if Leon Trotsky was the leader of the Soviet Union. Nevertheless, their evident skill and the necessities of war overcame such conflicts, and the Americans were soon assigned to I-16 monoplanes, a considerable step-up from the I-15s.[62] Dahl, who had been out of country for an emergency appendectomy, returned in June 1937 and was assigned to an I-15 squadron.[63]

Shortly after joining the squadron, Tinker and Baumler were speaking to the commander, Kosokov, when the subject of spies arose. The Russian mentioned that one such spy had recently been discovered in LaCalle's squadron. Tinker soon realized he was talking about Chang Selles. In small consolation, Kosokov noted that Selles had not been spying for the Nationalists, but for the Japanese. Tinker was shocked and confused. As he recalled, "When we asked him what they had done with Chang, he pointed an imaginary pistol at his head and said, '*Fusilado*.'"[64] Nevertheless, Tinker considered the evidence and appeared to conclude it likely that Selles was a spy, for he was often writing letters, ostensibly to his sister in Japan. Also, he learned from Kosokov that

Selles could speak Russian, which was a surprise to Tinker and seemed to deepen the mystery around his former squadron-mate and friend.[65] Whether there were grounds for suspicion or whether this was merely wartime paranoia remains unclear. It is significant, though, that it was the Russians who were responsible for removing and punishing Selles, for it shows the extent to which the Russians were influencing Spanish Republican war policy with the sudden arrest and imprisonment of a Spanish pilot. (In a uniquely happy epilogue to this story, it appears that Selles, in fact, survived his captivity, having been released either shortly before or shortly after the end of the war. He was again arrested and interrogated by the Nationalist government, but once again managed to survive and was re-released circa 1944. He married and had children and lived in Valencia until his death in 1989. His minor claim to fame was that he apparently helped establish the first Judo club in that city.)[66]

RETURN TO AMERICA

For the remaining American fighter pilots who had arrived in the winter of 1936–37, the Battle of Brunete in July 1937 would prove to be their final mission in Spain. This Republican offensive was waged to the west of Madrid and was designed to divert the Nationalists from their activities in the north, where they had just captured the Basque capital of Bilbao. On the night of July 5, over 80,000 Republican troops struck at the left flank of the Nationalist salient. They attained surprise, and the defenders were hurled back, allowing the Republicans to capture Brunete, thirteen miles northwest of the capital.[67]

Early in the battle, the Americans were assigned to escort duty for the R-5 attack aircraft. However, over the course of the three weeks of battle, the skies became crowded and air-to-air encounters were numerous. On July 8, Baumler downed a Fiat. On two occasions, July 12 and July 17, Tinker shot down new Messerschmitt Bf 109Bs; he was the first American to do so, long before the U.S. Army Air Force pilots met the Messerschmitts in the European theater of the Second World War. However, on July 12, Dahl was shot down over enemy territory. His capture was later to become an international incident. Baumler was put out of commission due to an infected throat and had to be transferred to a hospital in Valencia. Tinker was now the lone active American fighter pilot left in Spain.[68]

By July 18, the Republican advance had been halted, and the Nationalist counteroffensive had commenced. Tinker flew three missions that day, totaling four hours, ten minutes of flight time. While escorting R-5s over Brunete, the squadron met with numerous aircraft. In one engagement, Tinker battled an experimental Heinkel He 112. This aircraft returned to its airfield and crashed on the runway. It was unclear to what extent Tinker deserves credit for this "kill." He did manage to shoot down another Fiat, his eighth and final victory in Spain. In this encounter, he dove on the Italian fighter at such a speed that he almost blacked out. By the end of the day, he collapsed onto his bed.[69]

By now, the Russian squadron commander had rotated out. Tinker assumed command of the fighters in the air, while a Russian officer commanded the squadron on the ground. According to Smith and Hall, Tinker's biographers, this was "probably the only occasion in the history of the Red Army Air Force when an American—and a graduate of the U.S. Naval Academy, at that—led one of its squadrons in combat."[70] Despite this distinction, Tinker had lost his passion for the war. His fellow Americans were gone, and none of the new Russian pilots could speak English or Spanish. On July 21, he issued his ten-day notice of termination of his contract. He had his last combat flight on July 28. On August 13, he crossed the border to France at Port Bou and never returned to Spain. He arrived in Paris on August 16 but soon discovered that Francisco Gomez's passport was not sufficient to get him back to America. Fortunately, he encountered Ernest Hemingway in Paris. The famous author vouched for Tinker to the American counselor and secured transportation for him aboard the *Champlain*, which left for the United States on August 26.[71]

Upon returning home, the American pilots, unemployed and under suspicion by their government, found themselves in desperate straits. Some attempted to regain the trust of the American government by providing information about their time in Spain. Of these, Baumler provided the most significant contributions. In the winter and spring of

1938, he corresponded with Maj. Edward Raley of the Intelligence Section, Information Division, of the Office of the Chief of the Air Corps. It appears Baumler had also provided a report to the Air Corps on March 11. On March 18, Raley contacted Baumler by mail, with a series of follow-up questions. On March 29, Baumler answered by mailing his hand-written responses back to Raley.[72]

Baumler provided a wealth of information, including details of the types of aircraft flown, the number of personnel from each nation, the estimated losses, the typical missions flown, and the flying formations of the squadrons.[73] Raley was also interested not just in Baumler's knowledge of facts but also in his opinion of aviation matters based on his experience. One such question asked what Baumler believed would be "the most desirable pursuit plane?"[74] Baumler replied that a lightweight, maneuverable monoplane with simple controls was the ideal pursuit aircraft. He suggested it include an air-cooled radial twin-row Hornet 1,500 hp engine. This engine would have made it twice as powerful as the I-16 Moscas he had flown in Spain, but otherwise his preferred design resembled that of the Russian monoplane. His suggestions included retractable landing gear, a radio receiver, flaps, and four guns: two .50-caliber machine guns on the fuselage and two .30-caliber machine guns on the wings, arranged to provide "intersecting lines of fire" creating a "cone of dispersion." He opposed the inclusion of bomb racks as too dangerous. He also suggested excluding most blind flight instruments and "excess" gasoline, noting "3 to 4 hours in pursuit is not necessary." For aircraft meant to serve at the front, it was best to sacrifice speed for maneuverability, but not more than 15–20 mph in the exchange.[75] He elaborated on ways to improve maneuverability by reducing weight: "Reduce structural strength to lower than the present factors of safety required by Air Corps specifications. A pilot, fighting for his life in the air is not interested in how many G's of dynamic loading his plane can stand. He wants performance and more performance."[76] He also recommended the use of synthetic woods in the fuselage and fabric-covered wings. As he admitted, "Such a plane would lack durability and length of life of metal, but would have *performance*."[77]

Raley made six copies of the transcript of Baumler's second statement. On April 6, he sent fives copies to his superior, suggesting one be circulated throughout the Office of the Chief of the Air Corps and the other copies forwarded to the General Headquarters Air Force, the Matériel Division, the Intelligence Directorate (G-2) of the Western European Section, and the Office of Naval Intelligence.[78] The same day, he sent a copy to Baumler, expressing his gratitude and telling him, "The stuff you sent was better than excellent and I can't thank you enough. You must have worn out a couple of pencils on that stuff, and believe me we are grateful for it."[79] Baumler, the pilot training washout and mercenary, was now in good standing with the U.S. Army Air Corps.

Tinker used his spare time, of which he now had plenty, to write a book about his experiences. *Some Still Live*, published in 1938 by Funk and Wagnall's, was a fairly honest and interesting account of an American's service in a strange land. His narrative has served as the model for subsequent writings on American pilots in the Spanish Civil War. At the time, it was serialized in the *Saturday Evening Post*, published in Britain by Lovat Dickinson, and translated into Swedish, although an effort to make a movie of it fell through.[80]

Tinker's writing caught the attention of Raley, who mentioned it to Baumler: "Last night read the first of the articles by F. G. Tinker Jr. in the *Saturday Evening Post*. Was about to suggest that you do something of the sort yourself, but it appears Mr. Tinker beat you to it. However, I believe there is still room for some articles of a little different sort—less along the line of personal experiences, and more of a discussion of the technique of the employment of aviation in war."[81] However, Baumler was not to imitate Tinker's literary success. He was a pilot, through and through, as subsequent events would reinforce.

Tinker, writing from his home in DeWitt, Arkansas, contacted the War Department in December 1938, sending a carbon copy to the State Department, and offering to serve as an American agent in Spain. Addressing his letter to the "Chief of Military Operations," he stated, "I know—and, in fact, personally trained—some of the Spaniards who are now running the Spanish Loyalist Air Force. In other words, if there is any information concerning Franco's planes to be gotten, I believe that

I can get it."[82] By what means he was to gather more information than the current military attachés in Spain and the rest of Europe had done thus far was unclear, particularly since the war was shifting irreversibly toward the Nationalist side and the Republican government was nearing collapse. He boasted of his knowledge of Castilian and the "least-known provincial dialects." In order to deflect suspicions, he recommended that his connections to the State Department remain "under cover." To further bolster his credentials, he noted that he had battled German Messerschmitts ("over-estimated") and added that he possessed several unfired rounds from a Heinkel machine gun, including a German tracer ("far superior" to the American variety).[83]

The letter was answered tersely by Col. E. R. W. McCabe, assistant chief of staff, G-2. He informed Tinker that the War Department could support only military attachés and civilian clerks on its payrolls. However, the G-2 office would be very interested in any information Tinker could provide from his time in Spain. This information would be kept "strictly confidential," but of course, only on a voluntary basis without any compensation. Also, the War Department would not be able to bring him to Washington for such a purpose. If Tinker responded to this letter, the present writer has not located such documentation. It is reasonable to suspect, however, that McCabe's answer was highly unsatisfactory and discouraging. One wonders if matters would have worked out differently had Major Raley been the one to respond to Tinker.[84]

Whitey Dahl was shot down during the Battle of Brunete on July 12, 1937. He landed in Nationalist territory and was taken prisoner. He regrettably failed to cover himself in glory during this time, apparently stating he was fighting only for money. He also purportedly implicated Griffiss, whom Dahl claimed intervened on his behalf with the Republican government regarding his pay. Dahl later retracted that statement, but in the interim, it created much trouble for the State Department, the War Department, and for Griffiss personally.[85] In an interview with George M. Graves, the American consul at Vigo, Dahl insisted that he was being "encouraged" to sign all sorts of statements implicating innocent persons of various controversial acts. A Nationalist judge told

Graves that he was waiting until the court-martial to make Dahl's signed statements public.[86] All this failed to endear Dahl to friend or foe, yet he always seemed to escape from the most perilous situations. He was sentenced to death on October 5, 1937, but the sentence was commuted by Franco to life imprisonment.[87]

The ultimate fates of Baumler, Tinker, and Dahl post-date the Spanish Civil War, and will be addressed later in this work. Instead, it is appropriate to conclude this chapter with a brief account of two other Americans who flew in Spain and whose stories are remarkable for reasons that will become clear. The first of these is Vincent Patriarca, the only American known to have flown for the Nationalists. The second is Derek "Dick" Dickinson, known for his alleged aerial duel with Mussolini's son, Bruno, in single air-to-air combat.

According to the Associated Press correspondent Edward Knoblaugh, Vincent Patriarca was an eighteen-year-old Italian American and son of a New York City barber. Patriarca lost his aircraft in combat and landed in Republican territory. He was seized by hostile civilians but, thanks to the intervention of Air Minister Indalecio Prieto, was handed over to Eric Wendelin, the American chargé d'affaires in Madrid. Patriarca remained at the embassy until transportation could be secured to take him to Valencia, and from there on a ship back to the United States.[88]

Patriarca was something of a spirited character, according to Knoblaugh: "He became one of the most animated of the embassy's guests. Having recovered something of his bravado, Patriarca would run out in the embassy gardens each time a 'dog-fight' was staged overhead and excitedly point out what he believed were faults in the manoeuvring [sic]. 'God, if I could only be up there, I'd show them,' he used to say, whereupon someone would promptly hush him up."[89] Nevertheless, the young man appears to have possessed some level of prowess in combat. According to Alfredo Logoluso, author of a history on Fiat CR.32s in Spain, on September 11, 1936, Patriarca shot down a Nieuport Ni-H 52 flown by British pilot Brian Griffin. He and another pilot were also credited with downing two more Nieuports on September 13. However, this appears to have been his undoing, as one of the lost Ni-H 52s crashed into Patriarca's Fiat, causing him to parachute into Republican territory.[90]

Finally, there is the intriguing case of Dick Dickinson, who upon returning to America from service in Spain published a report of his individual combat with none other than Bruno Mussolini, son of the Italian dictator. One version of his story, "As told to Edwin C. Parsons," appeared in *Reader's Digest* in its March 1939 edition. According to Dickinson, in August 1937, a challenge from Palma de Mallorca was broadcast over Nationalist radio that Mussolini would take on any five Republican pilots in aerial combat. Dickinson immediately took up the gauntlet, declining any assistance and instead demanding a one-on-one engagement. Mussolini responded favorably. On the appointed day, Dickinson took off with two accompanying aircraft to the rendezvous, flying a Mosca (I-16). Mussolini, flying a "Fiat Romeo monoplane with a 1300 h.p. Hispano-Suiza motor" was waiting for him with his entourage. The two engaged in aerial acrobatics that took their respective aircraft to their breaking points.[91] Dickinson, after sustaining a wound to his hand, and showered by bullets that crashed into his fighter, made one last attempt: "I pulled up as if starting a loop, then went into a hammerhead stall, half rolled, and came out on my back."[92] The maneuver was successful, and Dickinson was now behind Mussolini, ready to deliver the finishing blow. It was then that he saw a scarf and glove part from the enemy's craft, signaling surrender. The dictator's son dipped his plane's nose in salute, and both pilots flew off to their respective bases.[93] Historians have cast doubt on the veracity of this story. It will suffice to point out that there appears to be no independent verification of this incident apart from Dickinson's own recollections. It seems highly unlikely, but it doubtless thrilled American readers who wondered what firsthand aerial combat was like.

Much of this chapter covered events that occurred following the Battle of Guadalajara in March 1937. We will return to that occasion and resume the narrative of our history, in which Republican fortunes were at their high point; but their fortunes were soon to descend into irretrievable misfortune in the campaign for the Northern Sector.

CHAPTER 6

CLOSE AIR SUPPORT

It is of vital importance that the Air and Ground understand each other's problems, advantages, and limitations.

—TOWNSEND GRIFFISS

A PIVOT TO THE NORTH

The victory at Guadalajara ended the Nationalist offensive against Madrid in the winter of 1936–37. The Republic now had an opportunity to turn the tide and win the war, its best opportunity to do so since it thwarted the original coup attempt at the start of the war. However, as had been the case in July 1936, in March 1937 the leaders of the Spanish government were unable to exploit their advantages. In a visit to the front around Madrid, Col. Stephen O. Fuqua observed a general lack of offensive mentality among the Republican forces, in spite of the encouragement of their recent victories. As he wrote, "Unless the Militia are infused with the spirit of 'open warfare' and assume the offensive[,] their present trench psychology will in the end defeat them."[1] Consequently, the government's lack of initiative allowed the Nationalists to shift their focus from a target of strength to one of vulnerability:

the Northern Territory, comprising Basque Country, Cantabria, and Asturias. This pivot, and the Republican forces' relatively ineffective reaction, would set the stage for the Nationalists' ultimate victory in the war. It would also display both the terrible potential of aerial bombardment on undefended civilians and the benefit of its close coordination with ground forces, a function known as "close air support" in modern airpower literature.

On paper, it seemed like the Republicans held the numerical advantage even on the Northern Front. By March, the Nationalists had about 80,000 troops in the north, compared to 110,000 troops for the Republic. However, the Republicans figures may very well have been padded by local paymasters competing for resources from the central government.[2] Besides, the initial fighting in the eastern provinces of Basque Country were undertaken by about 39,500 on the Nationalist side against 37,000 Basques. The Nationalist force, named 1 Task Force and formed for this specific mission, consisted of Spanish and Italian troops, quickly merged after the Italian debacle at Guadalajara. They were led by Colonel José Solchaga (1881–1953), who himself answered to General Emilio Mola. In opposition, the Republican Northern Army was under the overall command of General Francisco Llano de la Encomienda (1879–1963), who had numerous resources on hand but lacked the foreknowledge of where the Nationalists would strike. He also lacked the confidence and support of Basque president José Antonio Aguirre, which disrupted the unity of command so badly needed at this time.[3]

Basque Country covered the three eastern provinces of the Northern Territory, with the city of Bilbao serving as its capital. Bilbao is located about six miles from the coast of the Bay of Biscay and bordered on the east by mountains. It was surrounded by a series of fortifications and trench works known as the Iron Ring, modeled after the Maginot Line currently under construction in France along its German border.[4] Historian E. R. Hooton describes the limitations of the Basque project: "Much of this effort, such as trench systems to cover the coastal road from Santander, was wasted while many pillboxes and bunkers were not camouflaged, either deliberately or through ignorance."[5] The setup of the fortifications were such that it was difficult to determine how a saboteur could have rendered them any less effectual. As Hooton continues: "Worse still, the designers placed the Main Line of Resistance (MLR) on forward instead of reverse slopes which exposed them to enemy fire. The need to hold a long perimeter meant that the system, at a kilometer deep, was eggshell thin and all of this was known to the Nationalists."[6]

The invasion of Basque Country commenced on March 31, 1937, in the southeast at Villareal, as Navarrese troops, supported by German bombers, pummeled the Basque lines and pushed ahead. However, resistance stiffened when they reached Mount Gorbea and the mountain passes of Barazar, Sumeltza, and Urquiola. These well-defended natural barriers, along with heavy rains, caused the Nationalist leadership to order an operational pause on April 5, after advancing nine miles from their starting positions. These lines would hold for two more weeks, and when the Nationalists recommenced their advance, it would be from the east, toward Elorrio.[7]

During the late afternoon of April 26 the aerial attack on Guernica, an ancient Basque village with a revered history, was initiated. Although the village had a population of about 7,000 residents, thousands of refugees from the front may have been present during the early evening when the attack began, thus increasing the confusion and subsequent carnage. The bomber force, including three squadrons of Junker Ju 52s, and additional Heinkel He 111s, employed at least thirty-four tons of incendiary bombs and high explosives. They were supported by strafing attacks from Messerschmitt Bf 109Bs and Heinkel He 51s, totaling forty-three aircraft from the Condor Legion. Italian Savoia-Marchetti SM.79 bombers and Fiat CR.32 fighters were also involved in the operation.[8] The attack killed three hundred people and destroyed about three-quarters of the buildings in the village.[9]

Many historians note that Guernica did serve a military purpose, as it was the location of a bridge used to supply forces in the area. In addition, Wolfram von Richthofen biographer James Corum notes that two Basque battalions were stationed at Guernica. As Corum states, "By all the rules of international warfare in 1937, Guernica was a legitimate target for aerial attack."[10] However, whatever military justification there may have been for the attack was overshadowed by the devastation wrought on the civilian population and their homes. Historian Xabier Irujo Ametzaga argues forcefully against the justification of the means employed. He charges that "crushing a town with three war hospitals and thousands of refugees, mostly civilians, for three hours in order to block troops from crossing a bridge is an atrocity."[11] It did not help the attackers' case that the bridge was left intact and undamaged.

The idea of a modern air force destroying a small, defenseless town shocked the Western world. Even those unfamiliar with any other aspect of the Spanish Civil War have heard of this event, because it was immortalized in Pablo Picasso's disturbing painting created later that year. As historian Michael Alpert states, to this day Guernica remains "the archetype of the destruction from the air of an undefended town for the purpose of terrifying its civilians."[12] Raymond Proctor succinctly summarizes the impact of the bombardment, "The Nationalists won territory, but the enemy had won the war of propaganda with Guernica."[13] Two lines of explanation and defense arose among the Spanish Nationalists: first, that it was the retreating defenders who had burned the town, not the attacking aircraft; second, that—even if it was German aircraft that had destroyed Guernica—the Franco regime did not know of or approve it. The first defense has been thoroughly discounted, most clearly by the Germans themselves, who wrote about the raid in their reports; it is recounted in Richthofen's diary as well. As for the second defense, Richthofen claimed to have conferred with Mola's chief of staff Colonel Vigón earlier on the day of the attack. How far up the chain this foreknowledge of the attack went is unknown, though Corum states that the Nationalist officials gave their "full approval."[14]

Despite the outrage it would cause, in the immediate aftermath, the Spanish government was unable to capitalize on the propaganda advantages surrounding the Guernica bombing because May 1937 would see the beginning of an internecine battle within the Republic that would plague it until the end of the war. The key political division was between those who believed the Communists held the key to victory through discipline and order and those (notably the Anarchists) who believed that advocacy for social and economic reform and the revolutionary fervor, which had motivated the initial resistance of the militias in July 1936, would see the Republic through to ultimate success. In the middle were those who trusted neither the Communists nor the Anarchists but who lacked the strength and credibility to keep the opposing forces from feuding. This middle category, which tended to be composed of leftist Republicans and Socialists, increasingly faded from influence in the conduct of the war.

The focal point for the political strife within Republican Spain was Barcelona. The city was home to a cross section of several political currents, notably of Anarchist, Communist, and Catalonian Nationalist factions. Heightened tensions seemed to suddenly snap on April 25, when prominent communist leader Roldán Cortada was murdered in the city. The murderers and their motives remain a mystery, but the assumption was that the Anarchists were responsible for the assassination.[15] Open fighting broke out on May 3, when the police attempted to seize the Telefonica building, controlled by the Anarchists, who resisted the authorities. Street battles and shootings between buildings continued until an uneasy truce was established on May 6, but the damage had been done.

Political unity within Spain, which would have been so vital at this critical time in the war, was shaken. The Partido Obrero de Unificación Marxista (POUM), a revolutionary organization of the far Left that stood apart from (and thus in opposition to) Stalinist influence, would be scapegoated for the fighting. Of more immediate relevance, Largo Caballero's administration lost its credibility, forcing his resignation on May 17. He was replaced by finance minister Juan Negrín (1892–1956), officially a Socialist, but one who was more amenable to Stalinist assistance and influence than Largo Caballero had been. It was Negrín, we may recall, who oversaw the transfer of the Spanish gold reserves to the Russian treasury for safekeeping during the war. He had been born into a wealthy family on the Canary Islands, received his higher education at German universities, and served as a professor of physiology at the University of Madrid until 1931, when he was first elected to the Cortes.[16] Negrín was the fifth prime minister of Spain since the uprising in July 1936, and he would remain in that position for the remainder of the war.

The circumstances he found himself in would have been difficult for any leader to overcome, but all the same he proved insufficient to the challenges before him and deserves his share of the blame for the ultimate failure of the Republican war effort.

While these political upheavals were happening in the Republican zone, the war continued to progress with some notable events. On April 29, the Nationalist battleship *España* sank in the Bay of Biscay. Initial reports claimed that Republican aircraft had bombed the ship and destroyed it, but subsequent reports determined that it was more likely the ship had struck a sea mine. This became a subject of some contention, with the Spanish government insisting that aircraft bombing had destroyed the ship, after all. A Spanish Navy official told Townsend Griffiss that the idea of a sea mine destroying the ship was nonsense, "For when a ship strikes a mine it goes down by the bow and not by the stern as the *España* did."[17] Yet both Griffiss in Valencia and Lt. Col. Horace Fuller in Paris received reports through British sources that the ship had indeed struck a mine, and the actual damage caused by the attacking bombers was indeterminate.[18]

On May 15, Valencia, the current seat of government, suffered an aerial bombardment for the first time in the war. Griffiss reported that six trimotor aircraft (likely Savoia-Marchetti SM.79s or SM.81s) had flown over the city at 7:50 p.m. and dropped twenty-two bombs of between 110 and 331 pounds each. On May 20, Griffiss and the French air attaché toured the area and found that additional bombs had fallen outside of the city in a path leading from the village of Saler on the coast. Their total tally was ninety bombs, mostly high-explosive types, but with eighteen incendiary bombs among them. The bombs caused about 250 casualties, though the government claimed less than half that number. For some reason, there was no antiaircraft fire, nor were any defensive counterair flights conducted.[19] The attack seemed to have come as a complete surprise to those tasked with defending the city. The east coast, previously a relatively tranquil part of Spain, now saw additional violence. Near the end of the month, Republican aircraft attacked the German patrol ship *Deutschland* in the Mediterranean. On May 30, Germany and Italy withdrew from the Non-Intervention Committee in protest of the attack.[20] The next day the Germans retaliated with a naval bombardment of Almeria.

In the meantime, in the Northern Territory, the Nationalists continued to close in on the Basque capital, Bilbao. On June 11, they resumed their offensive, breaking through the Iron Ring the following day. They accomplished this with the aid of the Nationalist bombers, which dropped 35–40 tons of bombs upon the defenders on June 11, and an incredible 100–110 tons on June 12.[21] This breach was detrimental to Basque morale. On June 14, Griffiss reported on a conversation he had with Captain Pearson, the British military attaché who had returned from a visit to Bilbao. It seemed that much of the effort to defend Basque Country was hindered by internal dissension, reinforcing the contemporary proverb, "Two Spaniards, one civil war." Largo Caballero, before his downfall, had dispatched an official to Bilbao to serve as minister of defense. The Basques, offended, had sent him back to Valencia. Air Minister Indalecio Prieto had attempted to reinforce the air forces in the north, but seventeen aircraft sent for that purpose were diverted into France by bad weather and the need to evade Nationalist patrols. There they were held and disarmed before being allowed to return to Spain. Griffiss concluded that the situation for the Basques looked grave if additional air support was not provided to them.[22] It proved so, and on June 19, the Nationalists marched into Bilbao. The city had been abandoned by its government and Republican forces and left to the civilians to face the Nationalists alone. In the retreat, Italian communist Nino Nanetti, a hero of Guadalajara, was killed in an air raid. He was one of the last of at least 30,000 casualties suffered by Republican forces in the invasion. The Nationalists, though victorious, suffered a comparable number of casualties.

General Emilio Mola would not see the Nationalists' day of victory. On June 3, the aircraft he was flying in crashed, killing him and all others on board. His sudden death was reminiscent to that of his former superior, General José Sanjurjo. Once again, airpower had brought about an unexpected turn of events in the narrative of the war. Franco appointed as Mola's successor General Fidel Dávila Arrondo (1878–1962), a sixty-eight-year-old staff officer who had come out of retirement to support

Photo 5. Generalissimo Francisco Franco attends the funeral of Emilio Mola, the second-most powerful general in Spain, killed in a plane crash during the Northern Campaign, June 3, 1937. *NARA*

the Nationalist coup in July 1936. He had never commanded troops in combat but had served as Franco's chief of staff and had his full confidence. Fuqua, learning of the appointment, noted, "He [Dávila] is said to be very intelligent, quite erudite, possessing wide culture and besides is classed as a hard worker."[23]

BRUNETE

By the end of June 1937, the balance of the struggle had tipped, once again, to the Nationalists. The loss of Bilbao, the first major city to switch hands since Málaga in February of that year, was a severe blow to Republican morale and unity. In addition, political changes within the Republic placed further stress on an already tense atmosphere. In mid-June, the government outlawed the POUM and began to arrest its leaders. This occurred while members of the POUM were fighting on the frontlines in the Battle of Huesca, which waged from June 12 through 19. One POUM member was George Orwell (1903–50), the famous British writer. He was struck through the neck by a sniper's bullet and was sent back to Barcelona to recover. Learning of the suppression of his militia, he narrowly avoided arrest and left Spain with his wife, events that he recorded in his memoir *Homage to Catalonia* (1938). The leader of the POUM, Andrés Nin, was not so fortunate and died in the custody of the NKVD, the Russian secret police. Communist propaganda claimed that Nin had escaped to Nationalist territory, thus explaining his disappearance. The NKVD even staged a "rescue" of Nin with German members of the International Brigades playacting as Nazis.[24] The Battle of Huesca itself turned out to be a fruitless waste. More than one thousand Republican troops were lost fighting for no gain. General Lukacs (real name Mata Zalka Kemeny of Hungary), an International Brigade commander, was killed when his vehicle was forced off the road by hostile fire. Antony Beevor reports it was due to artillery fire.[25] But Jesús Salas Larrazábal claimed that Captain Joaquín García Morato (the Nationalist pilot) had strafed a car similar to Lukacs's the same day.[26]

With the failures mounting and internal dissensions deepening, planners in the Republican military settled upon an offensive to break the Nationalist siege of Madrid and to relieve the defenders in the

Northern Territory by requiring the Nationalists to divert their forces to another front. The focus of this offensive would be the small town of Brunete, a municipality with little more than 1,500 people located fifteen miles to the west of Madrid. The Republican objectives were to seize this town and to use it as a springboard from which to break through the Nationalist defenses and encircle part of their army.[27] For this, the Republican forces, commanded by General José Miaja, had about 85,000 troops available, including 100 tanks and 133 aircraft. By contrast, the Nationalists, under Brigadier General Luis Valdés, had only 54,000 troops in the immediate region.[28] The fact that the government achieved a surprise was evidenced by the initial dominance enjoyed by their air force during the first couple of days of the offensive. As Jesús Salas Larrazábal noted of the defenders, "Troops fighting in the Las Rozas–Casa de Campo sector will never forget the large numbers of aircraft which passed over their heads to an unknown destination, presumably to attack their supply columns."[29] The Republican 11th Division, under Colonel Líster, led the assault, and captured Brunete on July 7. However, it was unclear whether his flanks were secure, and Líster paused for definite news. This decision proved fateful, as the initiative shifted away from the Republicans, not to return for the rest of the battle. Nationalist reinforcements arrived, and the Republicans could advance no further.[30]

Air operations during this time were significant and produced several notable events. American pilots Harold Dahl and Frank Tinker were both involved in the fighting: Dahl was shot down in his I-15 on July 12, while Tinker earned his final combat victory by shooting down a Fiat on July 18.[31] Russian Anatoly Serov and German Adolf Galland, who would each achieve fame flying for their respective nations, served in combat for the first time during the battle. Serov would fly offensive counterair missions in an I-15, while Galland would strafe flak guns in a Heinkel He-51. Both men would return from their respective missions with their crafts laden with bullet holes.[32] A Russian pilot by the name of Mikhail Yashukin would become the first to shoot down an enemy aircraft at night, when he downed a Junkers Ju 52 on the night of July 25–26.[33]

Messerschmitt Bf 109B fighters, bearing their *Zylinder Hut* (Top Hat) emblems on their fuselages, made their maiden combat appearances in Spain in the skies over Brunete.[34] Fuller, writing from Paris the following month, provided a report he received from an observer who was at the battle; it highlighted the difficulties Nationalist aircraft created for the Republican ground forces. The observer noted the consistent threat that the Nationalist aircraft posed to the Republican lines of communication. As he told Fuller, "It is significant that on July 10th one of our lorries, carrying the luggage of refugees, was crashed into between Madrid and Alcala by a Government munitions lorry which was being chased by Fiats. Unfortunately two persons in our lorry were killed in the crash."[35] Similar to Nanetti and (perhaps) Lukacs before him, Major George Nathan, chief of staff of the XV International Brigade, was killed in an air attack.[36]

As the power exerted by the Nationalist Air Force increased, the situation on the ground changed significantly. On July 12, Colonel Jurado, who had commanded the Republican forces at Guadalajara, was replaced as commander of the XVIII Corps by Colonel Segismundo Casado (1893–1968), a forty-four-year-old cavalryman who had served as a military staffer to President Manuel Azaña. He was consistently ill with ulcers, and thus not in the best condition to change the trajectory of the battle. Upon taking command, he soon realized the men were exhausted and demoralized, but he was nevertheless under orders to resume the offensive. By July 15, the Republicans had lost 11,100 men and the Nationalists had seized air superiority.[37] A counterattack commenced on July 18 in the sweltering heat. Temperatures were well over 100° F (37° C), and both sides suffered from dehydration. Líster's troops fought bravely to maintain the gains for which they had suffered so much, but they were gradually pushed back. On July 25, they were forced to abandon the Brunete cemetery, their last remaining possession in the town. The battle was over. For their efforts, the Republicans had gained about twenty square miles at the cost of between 17,000 and 25,000 casualties; the Nationalists suffered about 16,000 to 17,000 casualties. The Republicans lost around 50 aircraft compared to the Nationalists' 23 losses. It was therefore a largely wasteful effort that only partially achieved its objective of slowing the Nationalist drive in the north and that completely failed in breaking the Nationalist positions near Madrid.[38] Hooton considers this to have been "the decisive battle of the Civil War,"[39] perhaps because of the way the Republican wave crashed against the Nationalist wall with gross ineffectiveness, diminishing their ability to carry out major offensive operations thereafter. As Fuller reported in August, "There is no blinding the fact that the operations of 6–14 July constituted a noteworthy effort to pass from the defensive to the offensive and that at the first trial the Republican ground forces failed—and failed with heavy loss. Such a failure coming at such a time cannot augur well for the future."[40]

On Sunday, July 18, 1937, the *New York Times* marked the one-year anniversary of the start of the Spanish Civil War. A front-page Associated Press article provided the latest news from Spain, "600 Moors Slain in a Loyalist Trap." The headline came from a Spanish government report of a successful ambush of the Moroccan Regulares near Villafranca del Castillo. The article also passed on the general situation of the Battle of Brunete: the Republicans' attempt at encirclement; the heavy use of artillery and aircraft; the 15,000 to 25,000 Italian volunteers at Valladolid, and the war-weary American and Canadian volunteers who were ready for another charge into the breach. The article, continuing onto the second page, described the difficulties faced in supporting these large armies: "Supplies seep through at the risk of drivers' lives, since transport men must run a 100-yard gantlet of road exposed to Insurgent fire. They make it six times a day, although one truck already has been hit."[41]

Much of the second page was dedicated to the latest news on the Spanish Civil War. The key article, "Few Gains in Spain after Year of War," by Hanson Baldwin in Washington, D.C., assessed the "greatest conflict since the World War" during which "an estimated 50,000 on the fighting fronts, and other thousands of civilians behind the lines" had been killed.[42]

The article summarized the situation, with some editorializing and a few inaccuracies. Expert opinion placed the odds on a Nationalist ("Insurgent") victory "if foreign military aid to both sides is continued in the future at about the same scale as in the past."[43] Madrid itself had suffered greatly, with thousands of civilians killed or injured and 2,000 buildings demolished. The Republican forces had changed from a collection of "armed, but ill-equipped mobs" to a modern military, and both sides had received modern matériel from abroad. Franco had about 400,000 troops at his command, with tens of thousands of Italians and thousands of Germans in support, an unknown number of tanks, and about 400 aircraft. The Republicans boasted of 500,000 troops, but as many as a 100,000 of these were under autonomous Catalonian control and not necessarily coordinated with the Valencia government. As many as 40,000 troops were reportedly foreign volunteers in the International Brigades from over a dozen different nations (in fact, there were never more than half that number at any time during the war). Although the government proposed a goal of 1,000 aircraft for war, this number remained aspirational, and the inventory at the time was closer to 450. There seemed to be no financial strains on continued fighting, as the government controlled the gold reserves (Baldwin may have been unaware of the fact that these were now in Russian hands) while the Nationalists (or "Insurgents" as they were referred to throughout the article and newspaper) controlled many sources of raw materials. The current fighting in Brunete could be decisive for the entire war. The article concluded with three lessons from the fighting, paraphrased as follows:

1. Tanks and planes are both important to the war, but neither are decisive, and neither will by themselves shorten the war.
2. Swift deployment of troops is important, but mechanized infantry are vulnerable to airborne attacks.
3. Defensive tactics and technology hold a consistent advantage over the offensive.

We shall see to what extent these lessons are borne out by the circumstances of the war.[44]

AIR LESSONS FROM YEAR ONE

The *New York Times* had covered general lessons from the fighting in Spain, but to what extent were American sources deriving air lessons from Spain? It appeared that few were approaching the topic, making those who did all the more notable. In April 1937, an editorial appeared in *U.S. Air Services*, a publication dedicated to both civilian and military aircraft news. It was written in response to an editorial published in the January 1937 issue of *Literary Digest*. That piece, which appeared under the rather bold title, "Planes Debunked: As War Machines They Win in Theory but Fail in Practise," posited the thesis that the Spanish Civil War, coupled with the Italian-Ethiopian War, had proven the ineffectiveness of strategic bombing: "Actually, despite all the fanciful predictions that have been made, if the world's 38,150 military air-planes raided New York, each dropping the largest bomb it could carry, they could not wreak the havoc of the Yokohama earthquake of September 1, 1923, when 23,440 of a 620,306 population were killed."[45]

In reply to this, *U.S. Air Services* argued that strategic bombing, properly understood, was not used in the Spanish Civil War, nor could it be expected to be used. For one thing, Spain, like Ethiopia, lacked a modern industrial infrastructure and thus was not a proper setting for a test of strategic bombing. Further, as Spain was in a civil war, neither side would want to destroy property that they either owned or hoped soon to possess: "The civil war is between the HAVES and the HAVE-NOTS. We see here that the Fascists comprise or represent the owners of property in the cities." Also, since the war was "lacking in the chivalry heretofore expected," each side realized it was fighting for survival. This reduced the likelihood that bombing would result in a surrender, since a surrender might mean death. In short, strategic bombing could not be expected to be used in wars fought for total ends. Finally, Spain lacked the adequate munitions to carry off a proper strategic bombing operation. Taking all of this into consideration, the editorial summarized, it would be inappropriate to draw a general conclusion on the effectiveness of strategic bombing in the war.[46]

However, by late summer, the assistant military attaché for air in Spain, Captain Townsend Griffiss, was ready to draw some conclusions from the first year of air war in Spain. He produced and transmitted a ten-page, twenty-two section summary of air lessons, covering topics ranging from tactics and equipment to the future of air combat. As he noted in his introduction, "Many of the following points are elementary, but this very fact is impressive due to their past neglect and the importance of their development."[47] He commenced with a general view of air force composition, and noted that while tactics, training, and technology were all important in constituting an "Air Force of quality," numerical strength was the most essential element for achieving dominance in the air. In long wars, attrition was inevitable, and the quality of an air force could soon be negated by the numerical superiority of the opponent. Griffiss discussed at length the various types of aircraft and the function of each in the war. Low-wing monoplanes were becoming the prominent design among pursuits. (We will address technological advances in aircraft in greater detail in chapter 8.) The importance of the escort function of pursuits was evident, and a two-to-one ratio of pursuits to bombers now seemed to be standard.[48] Every bomber, no matter the design or skill of the pilot, had its blind spots. As Griffiss declared, "The peace time theory of the complete invulnerability of the modern type bombardment plane no longer holds." Griffiss summarized his view of aircraft design best suited for wartime conditions: "For all types of classes of aircraft the main points to stress are simplicity of design, easy field maintenance, sturdiness, serviceability and reliability. Simplicity of design should be made to cover the point of easy and rapid assembly."[49]

In his section on tactics, Griffiss noted—as he had in previous correspondence—that tactics often depended on the equipment used, adding that the equipment of the enemy was also a key factor. For bombing missions, the integrity of the formation was considered of utmost importance, and this was precisely what the attacking pursuit aircraft sought to disrupt. In turn, pursuit formations were also important in controlling the course of events and in most effectively driving home an attack. The Russians continued to use the standard three-plane V-formation for their aircraft, though the two-plane formation was becoming more and more commonplace on both sides. Whatever the advantage of different types of tactics, what was clearly most important was coordination of action. Griffiss wrote, "It is my opinion that the biggest and best lesson in tactics that can be learned from the Air War in Spain is the absolute necessity of unity of thought, effort and cooperation existing between the various components of an Air force."[50]

Griffiss then proceeded to a section he titled "Employment," in which he discussed the two key missions of the air forces in the war, which he named "Separate Striking Force" and "Ground Cooperation." This division mirrored the struggle going on in the U.S. military, with airpower advocates supporting an independently acting force and ground combat leaders supporting an air force focused on the support of ground forces. Griffiss's Separate Striking Force was not solely, or even primarily, dedicated to strategic bombing but rather to attacking and defending where necessary as events arose. By not tying the air force to any specific ground force, it would become a more flexible instrument, able to concentrate force where necessary. It was this strike force that would be responsible for attaining "Air Supremacy," which Griffiss observed would become both a more important but less attainable goal in the near future. As for ground support, Griffiss acknowledged that airpower contributed to the morale of both offensive and defensive troops when it was present overhead. However, airpower alone would not be able to change conditions on the ground unless the ground force itself showed initiative in seizing the advantages presented to it.[51]

There followed a lengthy discussion of bombardment. Griffiss listed common targets for bombing missions, including aircraft bases, ammunition dumps, bridges, railways, and city buildings. These targets differed in the level of protection they tended to receive and the precision needed to hit them. For instance, bridges and railways were high-value targets and were often not well-defended, but these were rarely prioritized (probably due to the precision needed to hit them.) Griffiss then considered the impact of striking battlefield targets, an approach that the Spanish government seemed to favor. This was actually more difficult than one would expect, for the Republicans' persistent attempts to dislodge entrenched troops west of Madrid had little success due to the precision needed to harm personnel within a trench. Griffiss acknowledged that the Nationalists had had success with bombing troops at Brunete, but this was due to the hasty and haphazard design of the Republican trenches there. Bombing missions against large targets behind the front lines—such as air bases, troop camps, and troop columns—seemed to yield more reliable results and thus were frequently conducted by both sides, but without the persistence needed to have their full potential impact. Targets within cities seemed to render the least payoff, as the targets were both well-defended and difficult to hit. Bombers seemed reluctant to expend their entire payload on such objects. As Griffiss observed, "The reason seems to be that the bombardment selected its targets against which but one or two bombs were dropped and unless a direct hit was made the results were slight."[52]

Several of the later sections of his report addressed a variety of topics in brief. Griffiss stressed the importance of practical training. Peacetime training needed to be conducted with the sense that wartime contingencies would require flexibility. Although a maneuver may work in practice, that did not mean it would work in war. Assumptions that new technology might have a certain effect in combat could build a "false sense of efficiency" and would not account for many of the stresses and environmental factors that also exist in real combat. Peacetime bases were insufficient in war and needed to be supplemented by temporary and emergency bases. Communication between these bases was essential in order to establish coordination in the use of airpower. Radio had not yet become a widely used technology in the air war, but Griffiss' contacts assured him that it was rapidly becoming highly advantageous. Field maintenance was important, too, since the demands of warfare did not always permit aircraft to be sent to factories for repair. As the capabilities of air forces were limited by weather, continuous and accurate meteorological information was of paramount importance. The Battle of Guadalajara, in which the Nationalist fighters were grounded while the government fighters could operate due to different air base conditions, was a key example of how weather could impact aviation in battle.[53]

Griffiss then detailed some of the limitations of airpower. One could not count on airpower shortening future wars. Rather, air forces must be capable of sustaining long wars and maintaining sufficient numbers of aircraft throughout the struggle without reliance on outside assistance. Antiaircraft weapons were becoming more of a factor in terms of accuracy and effectiveness. In order to best coordinate counterair defenses, a single authority over both antiaircraft and aircraft was necessary. Although there had been much news of air operations against sea targets, these had been exaggerated, and it was not yet evident that airpower could reliably dominate seapower. Griffiss used as examples the cases of the *España*, said to have been destroyed by aerial bombardment but likely sunk by sea mines, and the *Deutschland*, which was damaged by bombs but still operative. Whether future events would provide definitive evidence of airpower dominance was uncertain. Finally, the physical well-being of pilots was an important but easily overlooked factor in warfare. As Griffiss noted, "I have heard of many cases in which pilots have been at the front for months without a single day's rest. The effect on the squadron's efficiency is self evident." He recommended regular relaxation days for pilots, which would not only benefit them, but make them more effective in combat. He added, in anticipation of a possible objection, "Shortage of personnel is no argument."[54]

In conclusion, he repeated a contention he had made earlier in April:

> It is my opinion that in the future war the struggle in the Air will be shorn of all chivalrous acts. Many of the nicities of the Air War of 1914–1918 have already been thrown to the four winds in this struggle in Spain. One, for example, is the neutral zone of the parachute. In looking ahead to the vengeance with which the next Air War will be fought, it seems not only advisable but just to train our future pilots in the art of every anticipated form of combat.[55]

It was a bleak but sober conclusion by a veteran pilot who had witnessed the application of modern air forces in a large-scale, year-long struggle. The U.S. military had now been advised to prepare its pilots for the "vengeance" of the next war. It remained to be seen how much longer this struggle would continue and whether the lessons now identified would still be valid.

SANTANDER AND GIJÓN FALL

As Griffiss recorded these observations in his report, the Republican forces of the Northern Territory prepared themselves for the next strike from the encroaching Nationalist armies. General Mariano Gamir, who had replaced Llano de la Encomienda, commanded 80,000 men, though many of these were unarmed or otherwise unsuited for combat. There were also 260 artillery weapons, about 50 tanks or armored cars, and about 80 aircraft, though—like the men—not all of these assets were combat-capable. In opposition, General Dávila wielded a force of about 90,000 men, with 300 artillery pieces and 220 aircraft, including the planes of the Condor Legion and Aviazione Legionaria. Aside from raw numbers, the Nationalists also had advantages in discipline, high morale, initiative, and unity of effort.[56]

In July, the Battle of Brunete had managed to draw Nationalist troops from the north. However, the battle had ended within the month, and by mid-August, the Nationalists were ready to recommence their Northern Campaign. Beginning on August 14, they advanced on Santander. Their forces included highly motivated Navarrese and Italian troops, fresh off their successful capture of Bilbao. The defenders, by contrast, were demoralized and disorganized. On August 18, the Nationalists captured Escudo, forty miles south of Santander. On August 23, they cut off the road to Asturias in the west. Many of the Basques abandoned the defense and marched eastward to surrender on their home soil. With Santander surrounded and its fate sealed, the population panicked and the defense collapsed. The leadership abandoned the city, with General Gamir and Basque president Aguirre escaping by boat.[57] Hooton has called the taking of Santander, "the most spectacular success of the Civil War," for with the city the Nationalists took about 17,000 prisoners in addition to the tens of thousands of Basques who had already surrendered.[58] The defenders had squandered not only ground forces but airpower, for though they were outnumbered almost three-to-one in aircraft, they determined it appropriate to send their remaining fighter aircraft en masse against the Nationalists. The results were predictable, with the Nationalists claiming thirty aerial victories.[59] Gijón, about one-hundred miles west of Santander, stood alone as the last major Republican city in the north. Only a miracle could save it from a fate like Santander's and Bilbao's.

Nevertheless, the Republicans did their best to divert the Nationalists from Gijón by launching their own offensive against Saragossa. As with Brunete, the timing of the government's offensive was poor, uncoordinated with events in the north, and thus unable to effectively influence that front. At the time, it must have seemed like a worthwhile risk. The Republic was able to compile a force of 31 front-line brigades and 9 reserve brigades, consisting of 125,000 troops, along with over 100 each of artillery pieces and tanks. They also had about 200 aircraft, which was sufficient, at least initially, as the Nationalist Air Force was currently concentrated in the north. Against them was a Nationalist force of about half its size with minimal air support.[60] It appeared that the opportunity was strong for a quick, successful surprise attack.

With numerical advantages, local air superiority, and high hopes, the government launched its offensive on August 23, the same day the Republican leaders in Santander were abandoning the city. As with other such offenses launched by the government, there was steady progress in the first few days, followed by a loss of momentum in the face of stiffening resistance. On the left flank, the attackers crossed the Río Ebro south of Saragossa and captured Mediana. To the north they advanced about six or seven miles to Zuera but were halted there on August 27.[61] There was heavy fighting at Belchite, a town of about 3,800 people located twenty-five miles south-southeast of Saragossa. Here, the government forces found themselves faced with a small but fierce group of Carlists, conservative Catholics from Navarre who supported the institution of a rival monarchy to that of the Alfonsists. They had fought their own series of wars against the regime of Queen Isabella II during the nineteenth century, and their record of fighting for their beliefs against overwhelming odds had become a mark of regional pride. Here, they were standing in the midst of a massive government advance, attempting to hold ground until reinforcements could arrive. Franco had in fact diverted two divisions to Aragon from elsewhere on the Madrid front. He had also sent eighty aircraft to the aid of the defenders.[62] By August 30, a squadron of Junkers Ju 52s was operating against Republican forces besieging Belchite. According to Jesús Salas Larrazábal, "These operations were so effective that the attacking divisions complained bitterly of the lethal activities of the Nationalist Air Force."[63]

Such setbacks risked upending the entire campaign, yet the Republicans were able to regain their footing and heave forward, led by the 35th Division under the command of General Karol Swierczewski, the Polish officer known in Spain as "Walter." The attackers forced the surrender of the remaining defenders in Belchite.[64] However, that was the extent of the Republican gains. They were unable to pivot to the right and advance toward Saragossa. Nor were they able to divert significant enemy forces from the north, the key objective of the offensive. The battle ended in stalemate by September 28, with 15,000 Republican casualties compared to 7,500 Nationalists casualties. Two weeks later, there was an ill-advised charge by the International Tank Regiment at Fuentes de Ebro, which resulted in no gains and the loss of nineteen tanks. Líster called it "one of the stupidest operations of the entire war."[65] As with the battles of the Great War, at Belchite the attackers were worse off at the end than at the start, with only a few square miles to show for their sacrifices. Ultimately, they had failed to manufacture the miracle that could have saved Gijón, upon which the Nationalists were now approaching from multiple sides.

In Gijón, on August 29, President Belarmino Tomás (1887–1950) declared into existence the Asturian Republic. It was destined to survive less than two months, but it fought dearly for its life. Gamir had been replaced as commander of the Popular Army in the north by Colonel Adolfo Prada (1882/1883–1962), an officer of communist sympathies who had returned from retirement to active duty at the start of the war. He found swift promotion in service of the government.[66] His reward was a posting to a near-impossible situation with a degraded, demoralized force bracing itself for the coup de grace from the implacable enemy. The 80,000-man force the Republicans had possessed before the fall of Santander had, due to losses and defections, been reduced to fewer than 40,000. Their aircraft inventory had fallen from 80 to fewer than 20. With greater numbers, they had been unable to halt the Nationalists from achieving any of their objectives.[67] How could they possibly hope to stop them now?

Dávila gave them little time to contemplate their predicament. On September 1, the Nationalists commenced the final stage in what they could reasonably assume would be a swift victory with a two-pronged attack from the east and south. However, the defenders utilized the mountainous terrain and effective tactics that had successfully repelled the Moors twelve centuries prior, when the rest of Spain had been overrun. They also benefited from interior lines, and thus, as at Madrid, they were able to quickly deploy and reinforce faltering areas of the perimeter. There was greater unity of effort, for the defenders knew that there were no more cities to retreat to. By September 18, Colonel Solchaga, leading the Navarrese forces from the east, had advanced only seven-and-a-half miles along the coast. In the meantime, General Antonio Aranda's Castilian forces were stalled at Piedrafita, thirty-one miles south of Gijón.[68]

It was at this point that airpower started to clearly impact events on the ground. At Pico Gallo in the east, Nationalist aircraft kept up a steady harassment of Republican forces. This required them to fly at low altitudes, within range of ground fire. So impressive was their performance that they earned the praise of Navarrese brigade commander Colonel Muñoz Grandes, who declared, "During my long military career, I have seen many heroic acts achieved by our soldiers; but I have never seen courage to equal that shown by your pilots over the Espandes peaks."[69] In October, for their service at San Justo and Tarna to the south near the Río Nalón crossing, García Morato's Spanish-flown Fiat squadron earned praise from none other than the commander of the German Condor Legion, Major General Sperrle.[70] In the meantime, Condor Legion pilots, including young Adolf Galland, were experimenting with the concept of "carpet bombing." This involved indiscriminate bombing by aircraft flying at low altitude in close formation. The defenders could not resist the constant barrage from the skies and yielded ground. On October 15, Solchaga's and Aranda's forces met at Infiesto on the Río Piloña, nineteen miles southeast of Gijón.[71]

With the collapse of the defensive perimeter, all spirit of further resistance quickly vanished. On October 17, Tomás presided over the final meeting of the Council of Asturias and then fled by British ship.

Other leaders escaped by sea as well, including the commander of the defending forces, Colonel Prada.[72] He was fortunate to do so, for the Republican destroyer *Císcar* was sunk after an aerial attack by the Condor Legion on October 20.[73] Prieto had previously ordered this ship to depart, but Prada and his Soviet adviser Vladimir Goriev kept the ship in port.[74] Whether they believed the ship would be doomed on the open sea, or whether they had hoped to escape on it when necessary, is unclear. Ultimately, it proved to be another wasted resource, and perhaps the only solace was that it did not end up in Nationalist hands.

The Northern Campaign was a disaster for the Republicans that would ultimately prove fatal. Sources agree that almost a quarter of a million troops were lost: 33,000 dead, 100,000 wounded or missing, 100,000 taken prisoner. The Nationalists paid a high price, as well: 10,000 dead and another 90,000 to 100,000 wounded or missing. But for these losses they acquired the entire northern coast of Spain, along with its vast natural resources and industrial capabilities, which included most of the Spanish coal production and almost all of its steel.[75] Of the eighty aircraft in the Republicans' northern defense forces that August, only three managed to escape capture or destruction by flying to France. Another twenty-two fell into the hands of the Nationalists; the only consolation was that only eight of those twenty-two were modern Russian fighters, while the rest were legacy models or noncombat aircraft.[76]

Internationally, the situation was becoming bleaker for the Republic. On August 28, the Vatican had recognized Franco's regime as the legitimate government of Spain.[77] In France, Léon Blum's administration had fallen, replaced by that of Camille Chautemps, who had little sympathy for the Valencia government. The Soviet Union was going through dark changes of its own, creating more cracks in the broken reed upon which the Spanish Republic was leaning. In June, Stalin's purge reared its ugly head when Marshal Tukhachevsky, commander of the Red Army, was executed, along with other military leaders suspected of German sympathies. Soviet officials in Spain became suspect, too, perhaps due to their exposure to foreigners. Vladimir Antonov-Ovsëenko, consul-general in Barcelona; Jan Pavlovich Berzin, chief military adviser; and Arthur Stashevsky, economic councillor, were all recalled by Stalin and purged.

This was around the time the POUM was outlawed in Spain under the authority of the Soviet NKVD secret police.[78] How long would the Republican government yield to the influence of Stalinist paranoia?

Meanwhile, the Nationalists' allies were making some changes as well. Major General Sperrle was recalled to Germany, replaced by Lieutenant General Helmuth Volkmann. Born in Diedenhofen, Volkmann had served as a fighter pilot throughout the Great War. After the war, when Germany was forbidden from having an air force, he was assigned to positions in the infantry, artillery, and cavalry. At the time of his appointment to Spain, he was serving in the Luftwaffe Service Department. Volkmann was widely regarded as hard-working and honest. His lofty rank made a clear statement about Germany's continued commitment to supporting the Nationalists through airpower.[79] The Italians had also provided a flag officer to the effort. General Mario Bernasconi had arrived in May 1937 to command the Aviazione Legionaria and would remain in Spain until 1939.[80]

Franco, ever conscious of others encroaching on his territory, would continue to maintain a balance with his foreign benefactors, taking advantage of their assistance while ensuring that they did not interfere with his administration. Thus, the contrast between the two belligerents: the Republicans, divided among themselves and reliant on the overbearing and capricious influence of their ally, Soviet Russia; and the Nationalists, united and supported by allies who were limited in their influence in strategic decision-making.

Historian Hugh Thomas credited the victory in the north to the failure of cooperation within the Republican government rather than to any technological advantage the Nationalists may have possessed.[81] But could there be any doubt about the impact of airpower? With the bombing of Guernica, the reduction of the Iron Ring, the reverses at Brunete and Belchite, and the support airpower provided in the mountains near Gijón, the Nationalist air forces constituted a powerful force against the Republicans, who saw their fortunes fade as their own airpower weakened.

Yet, though the loss of the Northern Territory was critical, the Republican government still retained many resources in men and matériel, and the Soviets were still interested in opposing the spread of fascism to the Iberian Peninsula. The Republic thus could fight on for the time being, though the character of the war was shifting. As the Nationalist armies advanced, they did so with the increasing assurance that an air shield would cover their path to victory.

CHAPTER 7

AERIAL BOMBING

The completeness of the demolition and the general havoc caused by the projectiles in these raids, from all evidence obtainable, surpass anything that has occurred in this war.

—STEPHEN O. FUQUA

AFTERMATH OF THE NORTHERN CAMPAIGN

By the end of October 1937, the situation of Republican Spain looked bleak. During the Northern Campaign, it had failed to achieve any of its major objectives, even though Franco's forces were practically fighting a two-front war. All the Republican forces had managed to do was delay the consistent advances of the Nationalists in the north by making diversionary attacks in Aragón, capturing a few square miles of territory and militarily insignificant towns like Belchite. Otherwise, the Republican leaders had watched helplessly as Basque Country, Cantabria, and Asturias were, one-by-one, drawn into the Nationalist fold. Now, Franco could consolidate his forces and strike the Republic with the full weight of his resources. This included airpower, which was progressively seizing air superiority over much of the Peninsula.

Yet despite having every reason to despair, many on the Republican government's side, notably the foreign volunteers of the International Brigades, continued to believe in and champion its cause. This was evident in a report by Colonel Fuqua, issued after a visit to the XV International Brigade stationed at Quinto, a town twenty-seven miles southeast of Saragossa. His trip came at the invitation of Major Robert Merriman (1906–38), the chief of staff of the brigade and a fellow American. According to Fuqua, of the 2,000 American volunteers currently in Spain, approximately 900 were serving in a combat capacity. Of these combatants, about half were assigned to either the American-led Lincoln-Washington Battalion or the Canadian-led MacKenzie-Papinau Battalion of the XV International Brigade, while the other half were distributed among other combat branches.[1] Of the 1,100 American volunteers not active in combat units, 300 were in some type of convalescence, 300 were in training, and 500 were in noncombatant service such as the ambulance corps.[2]

Fuqua was able to meet a few interesting characters and see the quality of the men who were still fighting almost a year after the siege of Madrid. He was generally impressed, most notably by the character of his host. As he observed,

> Major Merriman is the backbone and moving spirit of the XV Brigade, he is addressed as "Camarada" by all except those near to him and to these he is known as "Bob." He is a fine manly type, over six feet in height, physically sound with the endurance of an ox, pleasing personality, filled with initiative, overflowing with energy, he moves about everywhere in the command honored and respected by all, he is unquestionably the [dominant] figure of the brigade, and the "Star" American in the "Volunteer" group.[3]

During his visit, Fuqua witnessed Merriman receive an award for valor earned in fighting at Quinto, Belchite, and Fuentes de Ebro.[4]

Regarding aviation, the troops Fuqua talked to downplayed its importance. He was informed that the International Brigade was repeatedly attacked during the Brunete battle by thirty aircraft that dropped an estimated total of 3,000 bombs, but these caused only a total of three casualties. Antiaircraft artillery had been used only a few times, but when it was, it appeared to be effective at deterring attacks. Fuqua recorded the general impression of the International Brigade troops, stating, "The plane is of little value in attacking trained ground troops deployed for the offensive or against defensive positions held by infantry." Interestingly, poisonous gas, whether delivered by aerial bombing or artillery shelling, was not a factor in the fighting, despite assumptions that it would play an important part in future industrial wars. Investigations of cases of asphyxiation in battle often revealed that this was caused by smoke and fumes from normal explosive projectiles and not from any deliberate poisonous substance.[5]

Back in Valencia, Townsend Griffiss was compiling a report on air activity from the previous month, which he issued on November 13. A brief review of the attacks and Griffiss's own summary made clear that the Nationalists and Republicans had a different set of priorities for their targeting. Attacks on foreign vessels traveling to and from the Republic were a particular focus for the Nationalists. On October 24, two planes struck and sunk the French merchant ship *Oued Mellah* along the Marseilles-Barcelona route. On October 30, the British merchant vessel *Jean Weems* was attacked in the same area. On November 4, another French ship, *La Corse*, was attacked near Mataró, though no harm came to it. While the Nationalists targeted the coast and nearby waters, the Republican Air Force conducted missions inland against troop concentrations and military installations. On October 15, while the battle in the Northern Territory was reaching its conclusion, 100 Republican aircraft raided the airdrome of Garrapinillos near Saragossa, for which they claimed the destruction of 30 Nationalist aircraft on the ground. On November 5, forty Republican aircraft bombed Saragossa. As Griffiss reported, "From all reports it is evident that many of the 'military objectives' were directly in the center of the city. Casualties are reported to have been severe and material damage heavy." Here Griffiss employed quotes around the words *military objectives*, implying some doubt as to the appropriateness of that classification. On November 11, ten Republican bombers struck Pamplona, about which Griffiss noted that Bilbao radio (now under Nationalist control) had reported that these aircraft approached from France. The next day, the Republican Air Force struck a convoy near Huesca and troop concentrations near Teruel and other nearby locations.[6]

After providing details of these attacks, Griffiss offered various observations. The first was his acknowledgment of the "unheralded work" of government reconnaissance to assist in the information gathering necessary for planning and preparing for the next stage in the war. He also noted with approval that the government was taking a more offensive approach to counterair, by striking enemy aircraft on the ground rather than waiting for an attack and utilizing pursuit and antiaircraft defenses. He hinted that Air Ministry communiqués, his primary formal source for information, had become less frequent and less reliable in reporting mission impacts, the implication being that government reports of enemy damage were to be taken with a grain of salt. This skepticism applied to both sides, as Nationalist radio transmissions (intercepted by Republican pilots) tended to claim their own downed aircraft as victories. On another topic, Griffiss hinted that Spain's reliance on Russian support was becoming increasingly tenuous, as the air force chief [probably Hidalgo de Cisneros] had told Griffiss that he had learned that matériel meant for Spain was instead being diverted to China to assist Russian forces in their fight with the Japanese. The Republic relied on continuous Russian shipments to replenish their inventory. Without this steady flow of support, the air force was vulnerable to a major Nationalist offensive.[7]

If Fuqua and Griffiss were wondering whether their reports were having any impact, they would have been interested to find that they were, in fact, the primary sources of a lengthy lecture held on December 1, 1937, at the Command and General Staff School in Fort Leavenworth, Kansas. While crediting the attachés for much of the information used, however, the lecturer was sure to point out that the opinions offered were his own.[8] Unfortunately, the identity of the lecturer eludes the author, and it may have been shielded out of respect for the academic tradition of nonattribution. Yet it is worth summarizing and quoting this work, since it was likely delivered to hundreds of mid-career Army officers, many of whom would likely command units or serve on headquarters staffs as lieutenant colonels, colonels, or perhaps even generals in the Second World War. The lecture covered all aspects of military operations, although the sections on air operations will be of most interest for the present purposes.

The lecture began with a summary of the start of the war and the intervention of Germany, Italy, Russia and France. This was followed by a discussion of Franco's relative success in uniting the Nationalists (here called "Insurgents") against the Republicans. Then there was an overview of the different ideological and regional loyalties of both sides. In particular, the stubborn independence of the Catalonians was illustrated by the remark, "In Spain they make the bitter joke that the only country to respect the non-intervention agreement is Catalonia." The lecturer then returned to the topic of foreign intervention, summarizing the contributions of the respective foreign benefactors.[9]

The lecturer then proceeded to summarize the early months of the war: the initial coup and Franco's crossing to the mainland; the advances of the Army of Africa and the relief of the Alcazar; and the early attempts to capture Madrid.[10] Notable attention was paid to air operations during these months. While discussing the Nationalists' assault on the capital, the lecturer made the following remarkable comment:

> In connection with the frontal attack, Franco tried, for the first time in history, the much discussed Douhet theory of massive bombing. During November, December and January, the Insurgent air force shuttled back and forth bombing Madrid. What was the result? Nothing. People shook futile fists at the murderers in the sky and muttered, "Swine." Madrid has now had a front line in it for over a year and during that year it has been bombed and shelled heavily. The results are 3,000 killed and 14,000 to 15,000 injured. A quarter of the city is in ruins.
>
> But streets are cleared, tramways and subways still run. In spite of broken windows, burning houses, gutted buildings and blocked streets, life in Madrid continues. 800,000 people live there now. Fires attract no spectators—they are quickly put out.[11]

Warming to his theme, he delivered what must have seemed to be a coup de grace to Douhetism:

> Bombing, far from softening the civil will, hardens it. Terrorism has finally been tried and found wanting. Murder of non-combatants increases resistance and lengthens war. Spain has given the world one great lesson—that the bombardment of so-called political objectives is futile; a waste of a powerful weapon. Mussolini has read the signs—he has announced to the world that Italy, the birthplace of Douhet, the prophet of aerial terrorism, will not wage war on the civil population.[12]

Having illustrated the futility of strategic bombardment, the lecturer continued with his narrative of the war, with which we are already familiar from previous chapters, in terms of the battles for Madrid and the attempted encirclement of the capital. In contrast to the futility of the Madrid bombing, he drew attention to the effectiveness of air operations against the Italian columns at Guadalajara, declaring, "It must be considered an air victory."[13]

From here, the lecturer proceeded to discuss the Northern Campaign. He acknowledged the wisdom of Franco's new strategy and condemned the failure of the defenders of Bilbao to properly prepare for the attack. The perimeter of the Iron Ring was so large, and the manpower available so limited, that there was no way to defend all parts of it effectively. The exploitation of these vulnerabilities was often left to Nationalist airpower, which bombed and softened defenses in preparation for the ground assault. This was possible due to the Nationalists' advantage in the air.[14] There followed a summary of the Battle of Brunete, the Republicans' initial gains with the support of aerial bombardment; the Nationalists' stiffening resistance, also supported by airpower; the huge air battle of July 21, featuring "three hundred and twenty planes"; the end of the battle with only slight Republican gains. The war narrative concluded there, without a discussion of Belchite, Santander, or Gijón. From here, the lecturer proceeded with what he considered to be the key aspects of the war.[15]

This led into a discussion of various air missions and their relative effectiveness. For instance, strikes against roads and rails had only temporary, limited impacts, as both tended to be swiftly repaired, and roads could still be used even when damaged. "Political bombardment," as earlier discussed, was ineffective and perhaps even counterproductive. As the lecturer warned, "The commander who orders the bombardment of the opposing capital is in reality issuing two orders: he orders his own capital to be bombed also." However, ground cooperation by airpower had proved to be extremely effective, due in part to its improvement of morale among the ground forces it supported. The bombardment of airdromes was impactful enough to cause squadrons near the front to move to new bases constantly and to adopt cover and camouflage measures. Bombers were repeatedly outclassed by pursuits in aerial combat, and even bomber crafts' traditional advantage of speed was being matched by newer pursuit models. Short-range missions thus required escorts, though bombers on longer-range missions could fly by themselves, due to the delay in employment of defensive counterair measures.[16] As for accuracy in bombing, the lecturer had some sobering news: "In the early phases of the war, Loyalist planes aiming at the Insurgents on the Spanish bank of the Bidassoa [boundary river) blew up a restaurant on the French bank in the village of Biratou. None of the bombs fell on the Spanish side. The joke at that time was that the Government could not even hit Spain with their bombs."[17] Nevertheless, airpower was important for any ground offensive; and in recognition of airpower's importance, the Nationalists had delayed their offensives in the Northern Campaign until the inclement weather had cleared sufficiently for aircraft to fly.[18]

In summary, the lecturer proclaimed the orthodox Army belief that airpower was properly used as a support to the main ground operations, while independent air missions were wasteful or even counterproductive. Granted, many of the events in the Spanish Civil War thus far supported that claim. Madrid had been bombed and had not surrendered; it had, instead, made the most determined stand yet seen in the fighting. Bombing accuracy was indeed still an ideal rather than an accomplished fact. Bombers were not invulnerable; they were instead plainly vulnerable to both airborne interception and antiaircraft weaponry. All this was true and had been made clear by the fighting. Yet, there were limits to the lecturer's insight. His discussion of Guernica (which he claimed was destroyed by Asturian arsonists) and the casualty estimate of Republican "assassinations" (300,000) were inaccurate and likely derived from sources other than Griffiss's and Fuqua's reports.[19] He only briefly discussed the airlift, perhaps the most important air mission of the war, and when he did, he underestimated the number of troops ferried across the straights by that method.[20] Overall, the lecture was an imperfect but generally fair assessment of the lessons learned of the first year of fighting; but the war was far from over. The composition of the war in the air was changing even as the lecturer was delivering his message, and these lessons would bear revisiting in the near future.

TERUEL AND THE ARAGÓN CAMPAIGN

Meanwhile, the Republican leaders, who had relocated to Barcelona in the fall of 1937, were preparing to put into motion their plan to break the Nationalist lines and turn the tide of the war. The focal point for the execution of this plan was the small town of Teruel, roughly ninety miles northwest of Valencia. Although it, by itself, was a militarily insignificant objective, it would allow for Republican troops from both the Central Zone and Catalonia to converge on a Nationalist salient. In spite of the failure of similar recent offensives, the planners must have expected the element of surprise combined with poor winter weather to give them a sufficient edge to catch the defenders off balance.

The commander of this operation was Brigadier General Juan Hernández Saravia (1880–1974), an artilleryman by training, who had long supported the Republican cause. At the outbreak of the war, he had been serving as Prime Minister Casares Quiroga's personal secretary, having returned from retirement when the Popular Front won the 1936 elections. His center-Left political connections made him one of the few high-ranking officers whom the Republican leaders could trust. He had held the rank of colonel until December 1937, when he was promoted to general specifically to take command of the Teruel offensive.[21] At his disposal was the Army of the Levant, 100,000 men strong, with

Map 3. Nationalist-Republican Territory, January 1938

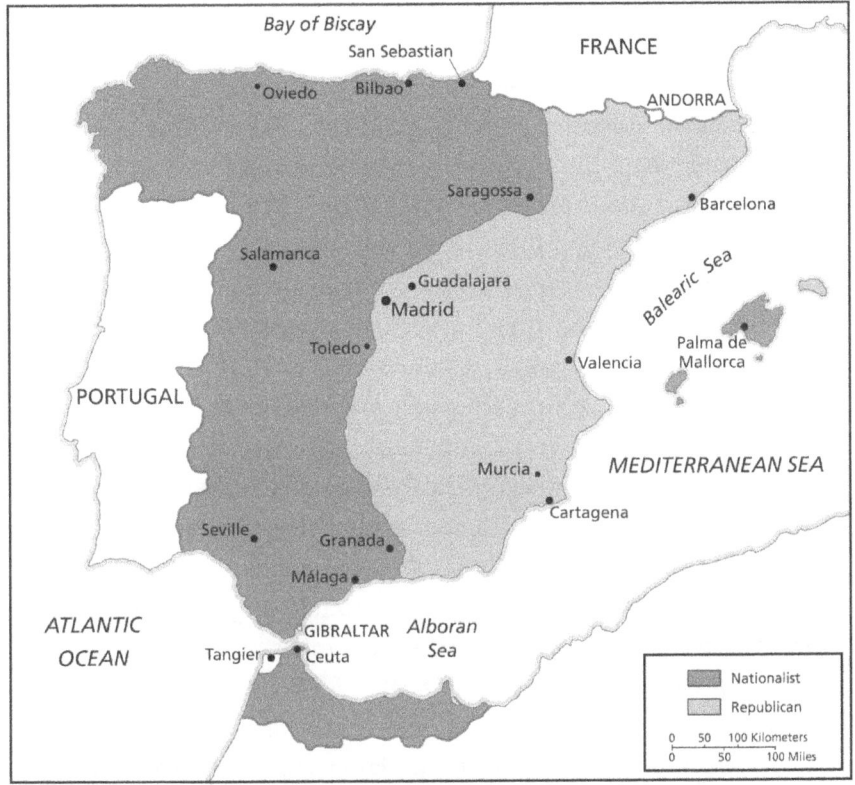

200 combat aircraft. By contrast, Teruel was garrisoned by fewer than 4,000 men. To capture it would seem to be a simple thing, and from there, one victory could lead to more, and perhaps reverse the momentum of the war.

The offensive commenced on December 14.[22] By all indications, the surprise worked. It took the Nationalists two weeks to deploy two corps to the area to check the Republican advance. The weather conditions were harsh, in the exact opposite way as those at Brunete from five months prior. Whereas men at Brunete were dropping from dehydration and heat exhaustion, at Teruel they were succumbing to the harsh cold. Temperatures fell to −0.4 °F (−18 °C) and snow piled up to men's knees. Yet the Republicans pushed their way ahead through force of will and weight of numbers. They eventually overwhelmed the stalwart defenders of Teruel on January 8, 1938; but as with other such endeavors, their advance then stalled. What should have been the mere first phase of a thrust into Nationalist territory turned into the high-water mark of the campaign. The fighting settled into a stalemate. A month later, the Nationalists forces, now with sufficient reinforcements to match the exhausted Republican troops, counterattacked at several points along the front, both north and south of Teruel. The Republicans were driven back, abandoning the town by the end of the battle on February 22. Casualty estimates vary, but it was clearly one of the bloodiest battles of the war thus far, with about 98,000 casualties: 54,000 attributed to the Republicans and 44,000 to the Nationalists. While it is difficult to visualize the loss of so many men, one may more readily comprehend the shifts of the lines on a map of Spain, and these were significantly in the Nationalists' favor. The Republicans had been pushed back across the Río Alfambra, with the hard-charging Nationalist cavalry under General José Monasterio playing a prominent role in the action. According to Hugh Thomas, in two days of fighting, February 7 and 8, 1938, the Nationalists captured 500 square miles of territory.[23]

The Republicans had timed their battle for bad weather to give them cover from Nationalist air attacks, and for the first several days conditions were too poor for significant aerial missions to take place. Once the weather improved, however, large formations were again able to take to the skies. According to Griffiss, now writing from Barcelona, "On the 30th it is reported that the Nationalists had in the air at one time 150 pursuits protecting 40 bombers"[24] However, the government antiaircraft assets may have saved the day for the Republicans and kept a withdrawal from becoming a rout. The costs wrought by these weapons were consistent and widespread enough to make them a factor for which attacking aircraft had to account. Griffiss detailed Republican claims of aircraft destroyed by antiaircraft artillery, which amounted to seven aircraft in the two-week period between December 19, 1937, and January 1, 1938, with another bomber destroyed near Rubiales on January 11.[25] Poor visibility made friendly and enemy identification difficult. Commander Ibarra, a Fiat squadron leader, had his craft shot down near Teruel by friendly fire from antiaircraft artillery, though he parachuted to safety.[26] The threat of fratricide went from air-to-ground as well as from ground-to-air. For instance, in early February 1938, Condor Legion aircraft mistakenly attacked a Nationalist division, killing or wounding four hundred.[27]

Finally, the Battle of Teruel is notable for the introduction of the Junkers Ju 87 *Sturzkampfflugzeug* (Stuka) dive-bombers. The compact (45 ft. 3.5 in. [width] × 35 ft. 5 in. [length] × 12 ft. 9.5 in. [height]) inverted wing, two-man, all-metal bombers, each equipped with a 7.9-mm MG 17 forward machine gun and a MG 15 machine gun for the observer, were infamous for the loud shrieking sound they made while diving. Three of them had been shipped to the Condor Legion for experimentation, and their first combat appearance was on February 17, 1938.[28] Apart from the fact that they were used at Teruel, little else is known of their performance in the battle.

The Nationalists now launched a counteroffensive with a forcefulness that threatened to collapse all cohesive resistance and end the war. General Dávila was invested with the responsibility of the offensive and

Photo 6. The infamous Junkers Ju 87 "Stuka" dive-bombers made their first combat appearance in Spain in early 1938. *Hoffman Prints, NARA*

had about 160,000 troops at his command. About 70,000 Republican troops stood in their way.[29] Many of these men were battle-fatigued, ill-prepared for a sudden assault coming so quickly on the heels of the previous battle, and without sufficient equipment to resist even a much smaller force.[30] They now faced the brunt of their enemies' power. The Nationalists launched the offensive on March 9 and a day later captured Belchite, which had been in Republican hands since the previous summer. By March 12, the left flank of the three-pronged attack, Yagüe's Moroccan Corps, reached Escatrón on the Río Ebro, twenty-four miles east of Belchite.[31] On the right flank, Aranda's Galician Corps captured Montalbán on March 13, about ten miles east of the Nationalists' starting point.[32]

On March 16, a brave defense was put up by the XV International Brigade at Caspe, southeast of Escatrón on the Ebro River. However, a single brigade was insufficient to sustain a shattered front, and the troops were soon overwhelmed. By March 22, the Nationalists corps were advancing on an eighty-mile front, cutting a large swath through Republican territory. During the night of March 30 alone, the Navarrese Division advanced twelve miles.[33] On April 3, the XV International Brigade—which had regrouped at Gandesa—was routed, with the survivors narrowly escaping capture by swimming across the Ebro River.[34] That same day, the Nationalists captured the provincial capital of Lérida.[35] Finally, on April 15, Good Friday, Spanish Nationalists reached Vinaròs on the Mediterranean coast. Republican territory had been split in two, with Catalonia and its capital of Barcelona in the north, and the Central Territory, with Madrid and Valencia, in the south. The campaign cost the Nationalists 21,000 killed and wounded. In turn, the Republicans had 34,400 killed and wounded, and another 53,900 captured.[36] The Republican government's defeat seemed absolute.

The impact of airpower was clear. On March 9, the first day of the operation, Nationalist aircraft mercilessly bombed Republican positions at Huerva and Herrera and continued to bomb the defenders as they withdrew.[37] Over the course of the next several days, the two sides fought fiercely for air dominance. On March 12, thirty-eight biplane fighters (eighteen Fiats and twenty I-15s) engaged in battle above Híjar, with the Republicans losing five aircraft. On March 14, ninety aircraft were involved in air combat, with seven losses for the Republicans and four for the Nationalists. On March 24, fifty-nine fighters fought, with five Republican aircraft shot down and another two colliding with each other. From that point on, the Republicans were less likely to engage in the skies and relied more on antiaircraft fire, while the Nationalists began to focus on ground targets. This likely explains the losses the Nationalist Air Force suffered in the following days; they lost two Savoia-Marchetti SM.81s and one Romeo Ro 37 on March 28, a Breda Ba 65 on March 30, a Heinkel He 111 and Messerschmitt Bf 109B on April 1, and a Fiat piloted by Italian group commander Aiello that same day. The Republicans made a last-ditch effort to halt the Nationalists on April 14 over Tortosa, when fifteen I-16s engaged seventeen Fiats, with the loss of three Moscas.[38] The next day, the Nationalists reached the sea.

On April 9, Fuqua visited the front in the Falset–Mora la Nueva sector, where the XV International Brigade was located. (He had apparently obtained a *salvoconducto*, which gave him carte blanche authorization to visit all fronts—an impressive concession by the Spanish government to a foreign military officer.) He spoke with the International Brigade commander Lieutenant Colonel Vladmir Copic and was informed that Merriman had been missing since the rout at Gandesa. During the fighting, the International Brigade had lost 700 men in all, including 200 Americans and 300 British volunteers, though many of the latter were assumed to have been taken prisoner. In meeting with the remaining volunteers, Fuqua found them badly shaken and weary but still willing to fight. He compared them to a badly beaten boxer, who nonetheless had at least one good punch left in him. In traveling around the sector, escorted by British volunteer Captain Hugh Slater, Fuqua found the highways populated by refugees.[39]

The shifting character of the air war in Spain was made clear in an incident Fuqua experienced while on the highway: "While nearing the front line, escorted by Capt. Slater, eight planes were noted approaching overhead, concerning which the Captain remarked 'I suppose they are ours as we have not opened fire upon them' to which I merely replied

'I hope so.' When the planes flying in two groups of five and three were at our zenith, a terrific firing from the anti-aircraft guns opened upon them. Later the Captain remarked 'Do you hear the bees[?].'"[40] As the antiaircraft fire intensified, shell fragments fell about their vehicle. Fuqua, upon inquiring whether there were any safety measures to be taken on such occasions, and finding there were none, took charge and led Slater away from the highway and to a nearby wall, against which they secured themselves until the shooting was over:[41] "It might be well, for the 'safety' regulation writers of the future in covering the means to employ against artillery shells and airbombs to include this item of protection against the 'bees.' Would suggest if such writer ever reads these notes, he emphasize the fact that safety is best secured against the 'bees' by seeking vertical protection trees, slopes or buildings standing upright on the side of the 'cover' away from the direction of the flight of the planes."[42]

Fuqua later met with the antiaircraft artillery commander and was informed that he had originally assumed the aircraft were friendly and had therefore held his fire. Once he had discovered his error, he made up for it by firing on the enemy with a high intensity of fire with his six guns. It was this firing, rather than projectiles from the enemy aircraft, which so harried Fuqua and his driver.[43]

In the meantime, events on the European stage were shifting further to the disadvantage of the Spanish Republic. British Foreign Minister Anthony Eden, who had become increasingly sympathetic to the Republican cause and increasingly upset over the reluctance of His Majesty's government to directly address the blatant violations of the Non-Intervention Agreement, resigned on February 20, two days before the end of the Battle of Teruel. His departure hardly seemed to phase the Tory administration, as his successor, Edward Frederick Lindley Wood, Lord Halifax (1881–1959), proceeded to finalize the Anglo-Italian Treaty on April 16, a day after the Nationalists reached the Mediterranean Sea at Vinaròs. One of the conditions of the treaty was the allowance for the Italians to maintain their troops in Spain until the end of the conflict.[44] But the most significant event on the European scene was Nazi Germany's Anschluss of neighboring Austria on March 12. The absorption of one sovereign nation by another in the center of the continent was accomplished without any serious opposition or objection. If the Western Democracies were so little concerned with the fate of Austria, how much less so would they be with the fate of Republican Spain, on the verge of complete destruction at the hands of the Nationalists and their German and Italian allies? The one bright spot for the Republic came from neighboring France, where Léon Blum again became prime minister on March 10 and opened the border soon after.[45]

Meanwhile, some of the air powers with forces in Spain were undergoing some notable personnel changes. In January 1938, Colonel Richthofen returned to Germany, replaced as chief of staff of the Condor Legion by Major Hermann Plocher, who had helped organize the units sent to Spain at the start of the war.[46] In April, seemingly less significant at the time but ultimately of greater consequence, Lieutenant Werner Mölders arrived to join the Condor Legion. He would replace Adolf Galland as squadron commander the following month.[47] The leading pilots of the Nationalists received some much-deserved recognition at this time. On March 18, at Castejón, Kindelán presented Captain Joaquín García Morato with the Laureate Cross of San Fernando. On April 11, Ángel Salas Larrazábal was promoted to the rank of major in the presence of his entire group.[48] Meanwhile, on the Republican side, Prieto, his nerves broken by the failure and reverse of the Teruel operation, resigned as Minister of Defense. He joined the chorus of voices within the Republic declaring the war to be lost and advocating the need to broker an immediate peace.[49] Little encouragement was coming from the Soviet Union, which was still churning under the military purge. In December 1937, around the time of the start of the Teruel offensive, General Yakov Alksnis, commander of the Red Army Air Forces, had been arrested by the Stalin regime.[50]

BOMBING ASSESSMENTS

While the Nationalists were conducting their legendary March to the Sea, a remarkable event occurred in the aerial warfare waged in Spain. From March 16 to March 18, Barcelona was subject to repeated bombardments by Savoia-Marchetti SM.81s from the Aviazione Legionaria.

Fuqua, who had been transferred to Barcelona together with the Republican government, described the onslaught in a dispatch dated March 25, 1938. As he stated, "These bombardments in intensity, number of casualties and material damages have surpassed all previous attacks of this character since the beginning of the war." Over the course of the three days, 276 high explosive bombs, varying in size between 110 and 220 pounds, were dropped by aircraft operating out of Mallorca. Officials from the Defensa Especial Contra Aeronaves (DECA) reported that 875 people were killed (including 118 children), another 1,600 were wounded, 48 buildings were destroyed and another 71 damaged. Fuqua had a close call on the afternoon of March 17, when two bombs landed about 250 yards from his office. He had been standing by the window and was thrown back by the force of the explosions. Fortunately, apart from a bruised shoulder, he escaped unharmed.[51]

Nevertheless, Fuqua was clearly affected by the experience and what he witnessed in the aftermath of the attacks: "From the point of casualties, property damages and morale destruction of a people stand as the most severe, probably, in the all time recorded history of airplane bombing. . . . The true story of the effect upon the people, their life and morale, requires for portrayal the pen of a newspaper genius as well as the brush of a master artist."[52]

The physical damage was evident, but what about the psychological impact? Was it the case—as had been insisted upon by the lecturer at Fort Leavenworth—that the people's resolve was reinforced by the bombing? Did they shake their clenched fists in the air and declare renewed vigor for their cause? Fuqua suggested otherwise: "It might be recorded here that for several days following the raids the city was in a state of panic, thousands left their business and homes for subway safety or [for] the protection offered by the near-by hills and country. The economic and industrial life of the city were completely paralyzed and the masses of the people thoroughly demoralized."[53]

Here was a firsthand account of the results of the continuous bombing of a vulnerable city. It suggested a dramatic change in the character of aerial warfare in Spain and gave reason to reconsider whether Douhet's theory of strategic bombing should be dismissed, after all.

By coincidence, in the same month, the *Saturday Evening Post* published an article that all but insisted that, indeed, Douhetism could be dismissed. The article was titled "Preview of Armageddon" and was written by Maj. Thomas R. Phillips, from the faculty of the Command and General Staff School. An editorial note at the beginning was sure to clarify that Phillips's opinions were his own and not those of the War Department. Yet, his points so closely resembled those of the lecturer from December 1937 as to suggest he was either the selfsame lecturer or had been highly influenced by him. Phillips opened with a description of Douhet and his theory and his appeal to airpower advocates. He pointed out that the bombing of Madrid in the winter of 1936–37 was a testing of that very theory, and that the results were a solid refutation of it, for "bombing, far from softening the civil will, hardens it."[54]

Instead, Phillips advocated for increased investment in American ground-based defense, arguing that this would allow aircraft to focus on other missions. As he suggested, "With the homeland well defended by antiplane gunners, the air force is freed to fly out after the enemy."[55] In the meantime, the proper role for aircraft would be not to bomb cities or lines of communication but to support ground troops directly. As he stated, "Although attacks on scattered troops often do not do a large amount of damage, the moral effect is overwhelming."[56] The air force, therefore, was best used as a supplement to artillery. Phillips advocated for the production of "attack" aircraft built specifically for close air support.[57]

Such opinions were no longer confined to the halls of professional military education institutes. They were now open for the public and political leaders to consider. Thus, they required a public response. An editorial in *U.S. Air Services* provided such a response in its April 1938 issue. The author (probably the editor, Earl Findley) first pointed out that Phillips's background was in the Coast Artillery Corps, implying that his opinions of airpower could hardly be disinterested. He then threw down the gauntlet, declaring that Phillips's "barrage of words against Air Force accomplishments in Spain, Ethiopia and China stimulates this reprisal of editorial bombs aimed at the major's gun emplacements."[58]

Douhet, the editorial reminded its readers, when developing his theory, used as his model the nations of central Europe in the 1920s. He was envisioning a war between developed, democratic nations, not a civil war. By contrast, the war in Spain was a civil war between two totalitarian forces. Hence, although the will of the population may be wrecked by bombing, the respective leaders would be better insulated from any political consequences. When responding to critics who cited Madrid as an example of a population being fortified rather than broken by aerial bombing, he reminded the readers that Madrid had also been subjected to artillery bombardment. One could just as easily argue that this was evidence of the ineffectiveness of artillery. He concluded his discussion of Spain, before moving on to discuss the Sino-Japanese war, by stating the situation in Spain, "does not furnish a reliable basis for learning what may be expected when modern 'western' nations resort to war."[59]

The following month, the editor of *U.S. Air Services* received some lofty support, this time from the assistant chief of the Air Corps, Brig. Gen. Henry "Hap" Arnold (1886–1950). The article was a transcript of his address to the Bond Club in Philadelphia, where he was preparing to oversee Air Corps maneuvers in the northeastern United States that same month. After his opening remarks, in which he lauded the performance of aircraft in Spain, he came to the heart of the matter, noting that observers in military circles had pointed to the failure of aircraft for not delivering on the loftier promises of airpower advocates.[60]

Having acknowledged the existence of such critics, Arnold proceeded to explain how airpower advocates distinguished different types of air operations. According to him, there were two categories: the first being the support of the ground forces, the second being "Air Force Operations," consisting of strikes deep within enemy territory designed to disrupt and demoralize the adversary, making it impossible to carry on the war. Arnold declared, "The truth of the matter is that in Spain practically all air operations have been of the former character and category."[61]

Hence, strategic bombing, or Douhetism, had not failed in Spain, but rather had not been truly attempted. Neither side wished to unleash the full capability of airpower upon the other side because they had sympathizers within enemy territory, and because they one day hoped to take possession of the structures within enemy territory.[62] Not only did the belligerents decline to utilize strategic bombing, they were unable to do so even if they tried, because they lacked sufficient resources to carry out such a mission. Thus, regarding actual air force operations, Arnold announced, "our primary lesson from the Spanish conflict is to draw no lesson on the power and limitations of Air Forces from that conflict."[63] It is significant that Arnold equated the term "Air Force" with a force capable of strategic bombing. The lack of such a force in Spain thus rendered the question of air force lessons moot.

Even so, Arnold did not neglect to mention perhaps the most significant air operation of the war: the airlift. As evidenced by the Command and General Staff School's lecture and Arnold's speech, American military leaders were aware of Operation Magic Fire, though the extent of their knowledge was unclear. Arnold mentioned that the first aircraft used for transport were German airliners, but he did not mention that the additional aircraft were supplied by the German military. He mentioned only that these additional aircraft were originally used as bombers and were better suited for the mission than the converted civilian models. The implied lesson from this was that aircraft built specifically for the military are much more useful in war than civil aircraft converted to military use in contingencies.[64]

He followed this with a discussion of the Sino-Japanese war and an observation that in light of the recent wars, developed nations throughout the world had attempted to build sizable combat aircraft inventories. How could this be, if modern wars had disproved the effectiveness of air forces? In light of this new arms race, Arnold proceeded to describe the three ways in which air force power was measured: first, by number of aircraft suitable for combat; second, by number of personnel, not just pilots and crew but also mechanics and other supporting members; and third, by the number of high-capacity air bases. By these metrics, the United States ranked no better than fourth, behind Great Britain, Italy, and Russia. Germany may even have surpassed the United States by this point.[65] However, the War Department hoped to rectify this situation by building an air inventory of 2,320 aircraft by June 30, 1940.[66] (There were 1,719 serviceable aircraft in 1938.)[67] On a positive note, while the number of aircraft in the United States currently lagged behind that of other powers, American technology and the quality of its personnel were the match of those of any other nation. However, if it was to sustain itself in a long war—and protect its citizens and industry from aerial attacks—more would need to be invested into it to develop a sufficient inventory and infrastructure.[68]

Whether subsequent events in Spain would reinforce or reject the various opinions outlined in this section remained to be seen. Although Republican Spain appeared to be on the brink of destruction, final victory for the Nationalists was still elusive, and much fighting lay in the future.

THE LEVANT

In April 1938, Franco and the Nationalists found themselves in a similar position to where they had been in November 1936, on the verge of winning the war. With the Republic split in two and its armies badly beaten and demoralized, the Nationalists could put their full weight against either the Northern or Central Zone and crush it before forces within the other zone could launch an effective offensive to the rear. Barcelona, the current seat of the Republican government, would appear to be the logical objective. Yet rather than pivoting north into Catalonia, Franco ordered his forces south along the Mediterranean coast, toward Valencia.

Charles Esdaile suggests this may have been due to concerns over French intervention, or due to the need to allow Varela and his Castilian Corps an opportunity to achieve further glory, or due to the belief that capturing Valencia would sufficiently shut off supplies so that the Central Zone would soon fall completely.[69] The first of these reasons seems preeminent, as Léon Blum was still in office in France and had opened the border with Spain. Germany's Anschluss of Austria had occurred the previous month, and the risk for another European-wide war must have seemed palpable. This reticence, then, to provoke the French would be in keeping with Franco's tendency to avoid making enemies unnecessarily. In any event, Barcelona, still recovering from the Italian bombing operation from the month before, and the Negrín government, still clinging to a hope for victory through endurance, were spared a direct assault in the spring of 1938. Instead, Valencia was to become the objective of a new campaign known as the Levant Offensive.

For this operation, Franco assigned two Spanish Corps, the Castilian (under General José Varela) and the Galician (under General Antonio Aranda), along with a "Liaison Task Force" under Colonel Rafael Garcia-Valiño and a cavalry brigade, for a total of about 81,000 men. On the Republican side were two corps of the Army of the Levant under Hernández Saravia, the recent commander of the Teruel offensive, and two corps of the Reserve Army under Colonel Leopoldo Menéndez, for a total of about 96,000 troops.[70] The defenders had the burden of guarding a 126-mile-long front; but still, it was remarkable that Franco assigned a relatively small force to this operation that, if successful, could have ended the war. The Nationalists may have been relying on the evidently superior morale of their troops, following up on a very successful campaign; but the Republicans were more familiar with the terrain and possessed the desperation of knowing that they were now fighting for survival.

The offensive commenced when Varela's Castilian Corps, the westernmost of the Nationalist forces, advanced southeast from Montalbán, capturing Aliaga on the Río Guadalupe on April 24. Jorcas, between the Río Guadalupe and Río Alfambra, fell three days later. Heavy storms slowed Varela's advance in early May, but Garcia-Valiño's Liaison Task Force, between Varela and Aranda's corps, advanced twelve miles to Canta Vieja by May 17. In the east, Aranda's Galician Corps pushed the defenders down the coast, with the Liaison Task Force supporting its right flank. On June 8, the Liaison Task Force took Adzaneta, twenty-seven miles from their starting position.[71] Castellón, the provincial capital, fell to Aranda's troops on June 14. But soon after this, the lines stabilized, and for the next month no significant developments arose along the front.[72]

The Republicans did not squander this opportunity. While Franco's troops consolidated their gains and prepared to lunge forward once again toward Valencia, the Republicans deployed reinforcements into the sector. By July, ten extra divisions had been added to the original defensive force.[73] In addition, far behind the front lines, the Republicans were building a line of trenchworks and fortifications as a literal last-ditch effort to halt the imminent Nationalist assault. Work on this project had commenced on May 8, after the first phase of the Nationalist offensive had slowed. Between 14,000 and 20,000 workers were assigned to the construction effort, a combination of military and civilian professionals, volunteers, and prisoners. By mid-July, a winding path stretched from the Río Turia Valley south of Teruel to the coast south of Nules, about eighty-four miles of trench lines, with pillboxes, artillery placements, and other structures. It became known as the XYZ Line, an impressive example of what determined defenders can do when faced with the threat of annihilation.[74]

By this time, the Nationalist ranks had swelled with the addition of the newly formed Turia Corps under Colonel José Solchaga, along with an additional division added to Garcia-Valiño's force and Italian troops from the Corpo Truppe Volontarie. The Nationalist total now numbered 150,000 troops, nearly double the size of the original force. The defenders numbered 120,000.[75] The offensive recommenced on July 5 with the Nationalist left flank continuing to push down the coast. Eight days later, the right flank advanced southeastward from Teruel.[76] There was some initial success, with the fall of Sarrión on July 14, but then further progress ground to a halt. The Republicans had now occupied the XYZ Line, and the Nationalist frontal assaults were repulsed with heavy casualties. On July 25, news came of a sudden Republican incursion in the north across the Río Ebro, and the Levant campaign ended in stalemate.[77] Valencia had been saved. Nationalist losses from April to July ranged between 15,000 to 20,000, compared to 5,000 losses for the Republican defenders.[78] It was as if the clock had been turned back twenty years, to a battle from the Great War, where attackers suffered heavy losses in vain attempts to break through fortified defenses. The contrast between the success of the XYZ Line and the failure of the Iron Ring was stark and likely confused observers as to the extent that tactics had progressed since Verdun.

Where was the Nationalist airpower that had breached the perimeter defenses around Bilbao? A review of air operations from April through July 1938 makes it evident that the Nationalists had not yet achieved a sufficient level of air dominance to focus on close air support for their ground forces. Inclement weather made flying perilous and kept the respective air forces grounded during key periods of the battle.[79] The Condor Legion found itself short of supplies, while the Republicans were equipped with new Super Moscas (I-16 Type 10s) from Russia.[80] Ground fire over the battlespace appeared to be very effective. A Heinkel He 45 reconnaissance biplane was destroyed by such means on April 29. On May 14, another He 45 was lost, along with two Heinkel He 51s. Airborne defenses were effective, as well. There was a great deal of air-to-air combat on May 23, with the Republicans claiming victory over seventeen Fiat CR.32s, two Savoia-Marchetti SM.79s, and three other aircraft. The results seemed too good to be believed, which they may have been. Jesús Salas Larrazábal wrote of a Republican government official, who happened to be the father of a fighter pilot, excitedly visiting an aerodrome near the fighting, hoping to see the wreckages of the seventeen Fiats. He was disappointed by the lack of evidence of such a resounding victory, and Salas Larrazábal remarked that only three Fiats had actually been lost. The Nationalists claimed that five I-16s and six I-15s were destroyed, though a Republican pilot remarked that the losses amounted to one Katiuska and three I-16s (Moscas).[81]

One may have noticed, throughout the history as recorded in this book, the stark contrast between Republican and Nationalist claims. To the point, on July 18, 1938, Fuqua issued a report entitled "Claims of Contending Parties Concerning Airplanes Brought Down during June, 1938." In it, he reported that the Nationalists claimed the destruction of 51 Republican aircraft and acknowledged 5 losses in aerial combat. Meanwhile, the Republican government claimed the destruction of 42 Nationalist aircraft and acknowledged the loss of 18 aircraft of its own. Fuqua made note on the disparity of claims, which tended to place the best light on whoever was estimating victories and losses.[82] It is reasonable to conclude that these reports were optimistic for each reporting side and served a propaganda purpose. However, inaccurate estimates may not have been solely propaganda, but the result of limited information on the enemy's condition. As Jesús Salas Larrazábal explained, "In attempting to make sense of these claims and counterclaims, it should be remembered that during the Spanish War any aircraft which was forced to land outside its own airfield was classified as being shot down. Conversely, the loss of an aircraft was only admitted if it had been destroyed."[83]

Nevertheless, the fighting was fierce and both sides continued to struggle for advantage in the air. On June 14, Nationalist bombers were attacked by over forty fighters, with Messerschmitt Bf 109s coming to the aid of the bombers. In spite of the crowded airspace, Proctor reported only one aircraft from each side being brought down in the subsequent fighting.[84] There was an air battle over the Valencian area on June 18 between ten Fiats and twenty-seven Republican fighters, in which six of the Republican aircraft were destroyed. Major Salas Larrazábal had led the Fiats but was rendered defenseless when his guns malfunctioned. His aircraft was hit five times in the fighting, but he was fortunate to make it through the battle.[85] Near the end of the campaign, on July 15, Lieutenant Mölders led his squadron of Bf 109s into a battle against twenty-five I-15s. It was in this engagement that he earned his first victory by sneaking up behind an I-15 and firing continuously as it plummeted to earth.[86] There was a large air battle above Segorbe on July 18, with the Nationalists claiming ten victories and three losses, and Republican veteran Francisco Tarazona claiming ten victories for his side. On July 21–22, four Fiats were lost by the Nationalists, leading up to the ultimate air battle on July 23, when three Bf 109B squadrons engaged about forty Republican fighters, with the Germans claiming six victories.[87] Nevertheless, the Republican Air Force, at great cost, had done its job, and kept the Nationalists from concentrating on striking the fielded forces along the XYZ Line.

However, Republican pursuits could not be everywhere. As the Levant campaign drew to a close, Fuqua sent a report on the results of the bombing of the CAMPSA factory in Barcelona on the night of June 7–8. He explained that the information obtained for this dispatch came to him through unofficial channels. The attack was executed by four trimotor bombers, probably Savoia-Marchetti SM.81s, which had three engines and were often used by the Italians for night missions. Forty bombs in all were dropped, with one causing a conflagration upon striking a gasoline tank. About 41,000 to 45,200 tons of gasoline and other types of oil were destroyed in the inferno, more than three-fifths of the total inventory. Of the storage capacity, more than four-fifths was completely or partially destroyed. Overall, it was a spectacular payoff from a single bombing mission, one that would certainly have far-reaching effects on the ability of Catalonia to defend itself or even continue to operate at normal efficiency. It is no wonder Fuqua had to rely on unofficial sources for this report, for an official acknowledgment would have been too demoralizing.[88]

But was this an aberration? Soon after, the Americans came into possession of a translation of a report issued by the Spanish Republican government's Chief of the Information Service of the Anti-Aircraft Defense. It contained accounts of aerial bombings by the Nationalists and the response by the Republican antiaircraft batteries, covering the period of July 27 to August 2. The report gives one an idea of the accuracy and effectiveness of the typical bombing mission as well as of the effectiveness of antiaircraft defense. In short, bombing runs often seemed to involve great effort, risk, and cost for little payoff. For instance, on July 28, five Junkers dropped 70 bombs of 221 pounds each in Tarragona, resulting in a total of two casualties. Later that day, in Estremadura, five bombers with four pursuits dropped 100 bombs on Cabeza del Buey, wounding one person.[89] And so on. The author of these reports made sure credit was given where it was due, writing, "The action of our aad [anti-aircraft defense] batteries was brilliant. On most occasions they frustrated the designs of rebel aviation and it may be said that the latter did not attain any of its objectives."[90] But this was not the case on every occasion. On July 28, the port of Valencia was bombed by six aircraft, killing five and wounding twenty-five others. Among those killed was K. A. Moyell, a member of the Non-Intervention Committee.[91] The next day, ten Junkers bombed Falset, killing thirty-five, wounding ninety, and damaging thirty buildings. That was just one of more than thirty recorded attacks on that day, executed with varying degrees of

Map 4. Nationalist-Republican Territory, July 1938

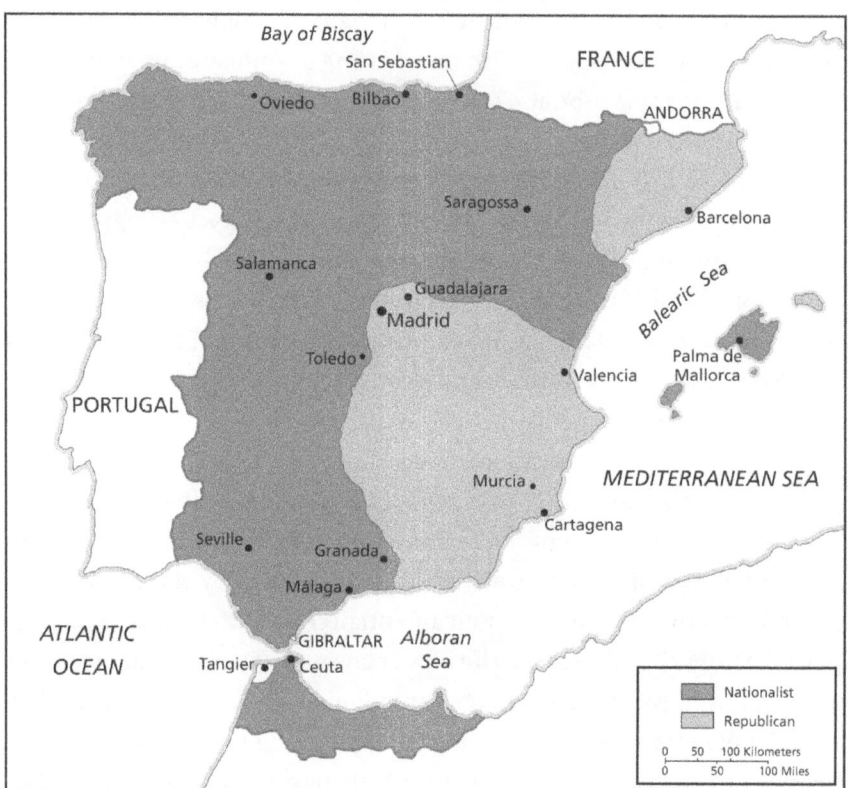

effectiveness.⁹² What the Nationalist bomber force was lacking in performance, it was making up for in frequency, increasing its odds of occasionally striking a vulnerable target.

Although the Republic had escaped total collapse with its stand at the XYZ Line, the overall outlook for the Republican government was grim in the mid-summer of 1938. Edouard Daladier had assumed the prime ministership in France and had closed the border once again in June.⁹³ On July 5, the Non-Intervention Committee, in typical half-measured fashion, called for the partial withdrawal of foreign troops from Spain.⁹⁴ Could one expect Italy and Germany, now so close to seeing their beneficiary triumph, to yield to such an appeal? In Russia, General Vseyelod Lopatin (also known as "General Montenegro"), who had commanded the Soviet air contingent in Spain, was executed.⁹⁵ It was as if association with Spain were enough to raise the suspicions of Stalin and his inquisitors. Still, Juan Negrín believed that victory was attainable: If the increasingly shaky peace among the Great Powers of Europe suddenly broke out into general war, the Spanish Peninsula would become an essential front. We have the benefit of hindsight to see that this idea was not so far-fetched; but when one's contingency plan relies upon the outbreak of a world war, one is in dire straits, indeed.

CHAPTER 8

AIRCRAFT TECHNOLOGY

"Science," the king cried presently, "is the new king of the world."
—H. G. WELLS, *THE WORLD SET FREE*

THEORIES OF THE HISTORY OF TECHNOLOGY

We once again pause from the narrative of our history, this time to discuss the role of technology. The Spanish Civil War developed the reputation as the test arena for European military technology, for good reason. There was no shortage of innovations that each side hoped would shift the course of the war in its favor. New technologies had to be matched, or bested, and tactics had to be altered to compensate for those innovations. Thus, the dogfighting fabric-covered biplanes with small-caliber, rapid-firing machine guns began to give way to dueling metal-plated monoplanes with larger-caliber cannons. Incendiary bombs became a commonly used munition in bombing raids, causing not only destruction but terror beyond the immediate, targeted location. Antiaircraft artillery became more accurate and lethal, firing shells at ever higher altitudes and shaking bomber pilots out of their assumed security. From the cauldron of war sprung forth a great variety of aircraft and armaments. How could one determine which provided the best solution? What constituted the best solution? Was the best solution the same for all involved? As a field, the history of technology offers a couple of approaches to this question.

The first of the schools of thought is known as *technological determinism*, which historian Merritt Roe Smith of the Massachusetts Institute of Technology defined as, "The belief in technology as a key governing force in society."[1] Famed American economist Thorstein Veblen (1857–1929) obliquely referred to the way technology drove societal change in his book *The Theory of the Leisure Class* (1899). In his introduction, Veblen discussed how societies at various stages of economic development distinguish between the upper "exploit" classes and the lower "drudgery" classes, and how this delineation proliferates as the society advanced from savagery to barbarism to modernity.[2] The culmination of Veblen's views on technology came with his book *Engineers and the Price System* (1921), in which he called for a "Soviet of technicians" to guide a ruling cohort of "production engineers."[3] His colleague at the New School for Social Research, Charles Beard (1874–1948), further developed this concept, framing technology as a positive good with a specific path of progress.[4]

Veblen and Beard have long since departed, and one would be hard-pressed to find a self-declared hard-line technological determinist today. Yet, arguably, determinism is the default position of many Americans, not just among those of a leftist bent (like Veblen and Beard) but also among free-market entrepreneurs, military professionals, or anyone who equates technological development with progress. In the introduction to the Westvaco Corporation's anthology on American invention, *Innovation and Achievement* (1987), John C. Callihan wrote: "Innovation and achievement, together, are America's powerful engine of progress which helps create our quality of life. They give us the economic advantages which we enjoy. They are the reasons that our progress and results are almost unrivaled by the other societies of the world."[5]

American and British airpower historians have also contributed to this implicit determinism, as can be witnessed by the use of the words "obsolete" or "obsolescence" when describing legacy aircraft.

For example, from a contribution to Bernard Nalty's edited history of the U.S. Air Force, *Winged Shield, Winged Sword* (1997), we learn that the Air Corps' failure to acquire more aircraft in the late 1920s was a blessing in disguise: "The Air Corps was not saddled with too many aircraft that would soon be obsolete. Just beyond the horizon lay all-metal, multiengine bombers and monoplane fighters, aircraft whose performance would far surpass the performance of the lumbering bombers and biplane pursuits of the late 1920s."[6]

Of course, an idea as expansive as determinism is certain to call forth a rival theory. Thus, an alternative to technological determinism has arisen in the form of *social constructionism*. The theory is a postmodern one, introduced in the past half-century and enjoying significant prominence in academic circles. The characteristics of this vantage point were described by the editors of a collection of academic essays, entitled *The Social Construction of Technological Systems* (1987), as follows:

> Key concepts within this approach [the sociology of scientific knowledge] are "interpretative flexibility," "closure," and "relevant social groups." One of the central tenets of this approach is the claim that technological artifacts are open to sociological analysis, not just in their usage but especially with respect to their design and technical "content."[7]

In short, the social context in which technological development takes place is of the highest importance, and certain organizations or institutions within that social context have overwhelming influence as to which type of technology is adopted. By implication, in a different context, a different technological path could have been undertaken. Social constructivism runs counter to the technological deterministic theory in that it does not recognize a single, best technological path.

One finds something to value and something to criticize with both approaches. In the context of aerial technology during the Spanish Civil War, the determinist view would hold that technology would develop in such a way that would enable one side or the other to gain aerial dominance and destructive firepower to bring about a Douhet-type victory.

Thus, those technologies that made aircraft more capable of surviving and triumphing in combat, and that made their payloads more lethal and expansive, would become the desired and dominant technologies. Seen in this light, the streamlining of aircraft through retractable landing gear, the increased survivability provided by metal armoring, and the expansive and enduring destructiveness of incendiary bombs would support the determinist view that technology was advancing confidently toward an as-yet unseen but nonetheless certain end.

The social constructionist viewpoint would appear to explain why different nations adopted different technologies during this period. For instance, during this period the French went through several changes in their conception of what constituted "successful aerial characteristics." In part, this was because—unlike Germany, Italy, and the Soviet Union—France was a republic subject to routine political changes. The French Air Force was established as an independent organization in 1933 and was heavily influenced by the ideas of the Italian Giulio Douhet. However, by 1936, aerial assets were placed under the tactical control of ground commanders. The new minister of air, Pierre Cot, reversed this course, grouping bombers and fighters under different commands. This decision was reversed once again in 1938, when Cot left office, and aircraft were once again assigned to ground commanders.[8] This dissonance of purpose, combined with the financial constraints of a depression-burdened economy, resulted in a heterogeneous mix of airframes and limited quantities of each.[9] Meanwhile, the Italians were committed to speed as part of a nationalistic ideology called *Futurismo* that, according to historian Michael Alpert, "admired speed, technology, violence and the new machine of speed, the aeroplane."[10] The Italians were also driven by financial considerations, and thus in spite of the appeal of developing strategic bombers and fast pursuits, they often selected instead a cost-effective solution, measuring success by how much use they could get out of their existing platforms. Granted, this second motivation would appear to point more to an economic motivation rather than social one.[11]

Perhaps the greatest shortcoming of both technological determinism and social constructivism is both theories' diminishment of the individual. Yet we see, time and again, where an individual is of consequence, sometimes in defiance of the time and place in which the person lived. Many had tried, but it was the Wright brothers who had solved the riddle of flight. And it was the tenacity of the Wrights, not the obstinacy of the U.S. Army bureaucracy, that eventually led to the military's adoption of the aircraft. Aircraft designers such as Andrei Tupolev, Nikolai Polikarpov, and Hugo Junkers left their marks and, in part, their identities upon the history of aviation. To fail to acknowledge this would be akin to dismissing the importance of Francisco Franco, Juan Negrín, Benito Mussolini, León Blum, or Josef Stalin in the history of the Spanish Civil War generally. Individuals were responsible for this technology, and they may have been influenced by the values of relevant social actors, or they may have been driven by an abstract idea of progress, but they ultimately used their unique skills and talents, not to mention their hard work, to develop a technology that would impact the course of aviation and military history.

Ultimately, military technology is meant to win the current war first and to set the combatant up for victory in the next. How did the aerial technology used in the Spanish Civil War measure against these standards? While there were discernible trends in aviation technology, it was unclear to what extent any of these trends could guarantee victory in the war to come. Each nation had its own criteria for the successful use of aviation. This complicated the direction of the aerial arms race between the Great Powers of Europe and America in the interwar period.[12] Airpower was still a relatively new asset, and the way that it fit into Industrial Age warfare was not yet established.[13] We will examine each nation's approach, its contributions, and its relative success in the next two sections of this chapter, before concluding with a review of the armaments utilized by the belligerents.

GERMAN AND ITALIAN AIRCRAFT

After the First World War, Article 198 of the Versailles Treaty prohibited Germany from having an air force.[14] Subsequent mandates imposed strict limitations on civilian aviation. It was not until 1926, when the Locarno Treaties admitted Germany into the League of Nations, that the Germans were allowed to construct commercial aircraft without restrictions.[15] However, the Germans had not sat idly by, waiting for the victors of the last war to be willing to offer concessions. They had already engaged in some of their own crafty diplomacy with another pariah state. In 1922, Germany recognized the Soviet Union, and German officers began to coordinate with the Russians in the development of aviation out of the sight of the Allied observers.[16] In 1927, the Germans inaugurated a "training and experimental flying centre" at Lipetsk, in southern Russia.[17] The rise of Adolf Hitler and his Nazi regime signaled the end of international oversight of German rearmament. In 1935, Hitler reinstated the German Air Force, the Luftwaffe. In 1936, the mighty dirigible *Hindenburg* appeared in the German skies. That March, the Germans remilitarized the Rhineland. In August, Berlin hosted the Olympic games, with military aircraft performing aerobatics for the assembled multitudes. By then, German bombers and fighters were intervening directly in the tumult in Spain.[18]

Previous chapters have discussed the use of the Junkers Ju 52 (introduced in 1930) and Heinkel He 51 (introduced in 1933) in the early stages of the war, precluding the need to do so here in detail. It will suffice to acknowledge that each air platform had its shortcomings, which soon became evident when confronted with serious opposition in the form of the Russian I-15 (Chato) and I-16 (Mosca) pursuits. The Germans responded to their earlier experiences with the introduction of new assets, including the Junkers Ju 86 bomber, the Heinkel He 111 bomber and the Messerschmitt Bf 109 fighter. Their incorporation into the conflict revealed that the Germans were seeking to test their capabilities in actual combat.

The Junkers Ju 86D-1s were, like the Heinkel He 51s, designed to circumvent Versailles Treaty restrictions by assuming the pretense of civilian-use aircraft.[19] They were powered by two 592 hp diesel Junkers Jumo engines that enabled them to reach maximum speeds of 202 mph, rise to a ceiling of 19,357 feet, and carry 1,764 pounds of bombs. They had a range of 709 miles. They were smaller in size and capacity than the Ju 52s, but they were faster and more durable. In April 1937, Townsend Griffiss reported on the arrival of the Ju 86s in theater. They had three machine guns, with one placed in a front turret, allowing them to counter head-on attacks and thus rectifying one of the vulnerabilities of the Ju 52s. Unfortunately, a blind-spot remained in the direct rear of the aircraft, and Griffiss remarked in April 1937 that he was aware of reports that "four or five of this type of Junker have already been shot down."[20]

The Heinkel He 111s arrived in Spain in February 1937, along with the Ju 86s and Dornier Do 17s, as part of the Experimental Bomber Squadron. Their design preceded the start of the war, but the models used in Spain (which included the He 111B-2s) were developed after the fighting was underway. The He 111B-2s were powered by two 950 hp Daimler-Benz DB 600 CG engines, which gave them a maximum speed of 230 mph, a ceiling of 22,967 feet, and a range of 566 miles with an impressive bombload of 3,308 pounds. They were far superior to the other German bombers, and too fast for most enemy pursuits to intercept. They took part in the fire-bombing attack on Guernica in April 1937, and their distinctive ("fishlike silhouette") appearance made them infamous. As historian Gerald Howson observed, "These sleek but sinister-looking bombers came to be popularly identified as symbols of Nazi aggression, and of the fearsome innovation of concentrated terror-bombing of defenceless civilians."[21]

A replacement fighter for the Heinkel He 51 came in the form of the Messerschmitt Bf 109. Originally designed in 1935, it was a low-wing, all-metal monoplane (although the earliest versions included wooden propellers), with a retractable undercarriage. As with the Heinkel He 111, the models used by the Condor Legion were introduced after the start of the war. The first such model to see action in Spain was the Bf 109B, equipped with a Junkers Jumo 210D liquid-cooled engine (720 hp) that could reach speeds of 289 mph and had a range of 429 miles and a ceiling of 26,904 feet. These were significant improvements over the He 51's capabilities, and enemy pilots were obliged to change their tactics.[22] However, German engineers continued to improve on the design, though they traded some range for speed. The E model, introduced in late 1938, included a Daimler-Benz DB 601A liquid-cooled inverted V-12 engine (1,175 hp), and it could reach maximum speeds of

347 mph, with a ceiling of 34,400 feet and a range of 410 miles. According to Howson, "The Messerschmitt Bf 109 is generally regarded as one of the two greatest fighter aircraft ever built, the other claimant being its classical opponent in the Second World War, the Supermarine Spitfire."[23] Although the Heinkel He 51 had a lower wing loading compared to the Messerschmitt Bf 109B (14.3 lb./sq. ft. to 27.2 lb./sq. ft.)—one of the characteristic advantages of a biplane over a monoplane due to its association with maneuverability—the Bf 109B far exceeded the He 51 in maximum speed and range.[24] The Germans had found the fighter they wanted.

Due to the character of the Spanish Civil War, developments in transport, reconnaissance, and naval aircraft were more limited. There was one notable exception. Late 1938 saw the arrival of four small, fabric-covered staff transport aircraft. They were lightweight, only 2,910 pounds fully loaded; lightly armed, with a single 7.2-mm MG 15 machine gun and a 330-pound bombload; and slow, with a maximum speed of 109 mph. Yet, according to the editor of a recent compendium of military aircraft, this model was "so perfect at what it did that even if it was designed today, 60 years after its first flight, it could not be improved."[25] This was the Fieseler Fi 156 Storch. It was well-named and flew like a stork, for it had a 165-foot takeoff distance and a 50-foot landing distance in an 8 mph headwind—at higher headwinds it could make a virtually vertical landing. It was arguably the first short takeoff/landing (STOL) aircraft to be used in war. Over 2,500 would be produced, and it would become the ideal craft for special operations.[26]

The use of photography in aerial reconnaissance became a significant factor in the Spanish Civil War as well. The ability of the Nationalists to collect, compile, organize and analyze data from such reconnaissance gave them valuable information about Republican troop movements.[27] Spanish scholars Diego Navarro Bonilla and Guillermo Vicente Cano summarize the impact of aerial photography as follows: "The superior photographic information at the operational and tactical levels, centralized in the Generalissimo's headquarters in Burgos, allowed the Nationalists to have a better knowledge of the terrain and enemy forces. The air superiority acquired by Nationalists in early 1937 was parallel with the information superiority enjoyed by Franco's army."[28]

Two of the more notable aerial reconnaissance aircraft were the Heinkel He 45 and He 70. The He 45, called the "Pavo" (Turkey) in Spain, had been introduced in 1932. It was a biplane with wooden wings, a steel tube fuselage, and fabric covering. Its 750 hp BMW VI-12 cylinder V-type engine could reach a maximum speed of 180 mph. Its range was 746 miles, making it suitable for long-range missions. It provided material support for the Nationalist march to the sea in 1938. As with most reconnaissance aircraft, its design allowed for the installation of a camera in lieu of a bombload.[29] The Heinkel He 70 Rayo (Lightning) also appeared in 1932, but it was a very different aircraft. It was designed in response to a Luft Hansa solicitation for an aircraft comparable to the Lockheed Orion. The result was a monoplane with an all-metal fuselage and wooden wings. It had retractable landing gear and a 750 hp BMW VI 7.3 Z engine. It could reach a maximum speed of 221 mph and had a ceiling of 19,686 feet; its range of 497 miles made it appropriate for short-range reconnaissance. As many as thirty-one He 70s were sent to Spain, where they were used in the Northern Campaign against the Basque Country and Asturias and in the battles of Teruel and the Ebro.[30]

Since Germany had prioritized building the Wehrmacht and Luftwaffe rather than the Kriegsmarine (Navy) during the interwar period, it did not focus heavily on the development of naval aircraft.[31] Yet, it did have some assets to contribute to the Spanish Civil War. The Arado Ar 95s served a minor role operating out of Majorca. These were metal-framed, mostly metal-covered biplane torpedo-bombers that could operate with either floats or wheels for landing. Their 845 hp BMW 132Dc radial engine allowed for a maximum speed of 171 mph (standard for seaplanes during the war), but it had an impressive 23,951-foot ceiling and a range of 1,094 miles. Only the Italian Cant Z 506B Airone could boast better statistics. Not many were built, perhaps eleven in all, but they paved the way for the Arado Ar 196 (introduced in 1939), which did not appear in Spain, but would serve aboard German capital ships in the Second World War.[32]

Table 3. Naval aircraft employed in Spain during the civil war

Designation	Name	Year introduced	Nation	Horsepower (total)	Max speed (mph)	Ceiling (ft)	Range (miles)
Dornier DoJ	Wal (Whale)	1922	Italy/Germany	1200	112	16,405	622
CASA-Vickers	Vildebeest	1929	Britain (Spain)	600	137	14,272	746
Savoia-Marchetti SM.62		1929	Italy (Spain)	600	137	14,765	746
Heinkel He 59B		1932	Germany	1320	111	11,484	1,088
Cant Z 501	Gabbiano (Seagull)	1934	Italy	900	171	22,965	1,000
Arado Ar 95A		1937	Germany	845	171	23,951	1,094
Cant Z 506B	Airone (Heron)	1937	Italy	2250	280	24,600	1,370

Italy, unlike Germany, had been on the winning side of the Great War. Yet, just as the punishment meted out by the Allies to Germany was much harsher than that nation expected, the spoils granted to Italy were meager compared to what that nation desired. Thus, under dictator Benito Mussolini, the Italian Air Force, the Regia Aeronautica, became a tool to assist in the development of a new Fascist Empire. Italo Balbo, who served as Mussolini's minister of air and later as air marshal, was restrained by budgetary concerns from developing a force that could implement General Giulio Douhet's vision of victory through strategic bombing. Instead, the Regia Aeronautica, though an independent armed force, was built with an inventory suitable to make it a supporting arm of the army and navy.[33]

In previous chapters, we were introduced to the Fiat CR.32s and the Savoia-Marchetti SM.81s. The Fiats made a strong impression on friend and foe alike, but the strain of a contested air environment convinced the Italians that the SM.81 was not the ideal bomber for modern warfare. Fortunately, Savoia-Marchetti had developed another bomber concurrently with the SM.81, the SM.79. Equipped with three Alfa Romeo 126 R.C.34 radial piston engines producing a total of 2,340 hp, it could reach speeds of 267 mph and had a ceiling of 21,327 feet and a range of 1,181 miles. It had a bombload of 2,756 pounds and was armed with one 12.7-mm machine gun each in the cabin and in the dorsal and ventral turrets. The first SM.79s assigned to Spain arrived at Majorca in February 1937.[34] Rather than replacing the SM.81, the SM.79 shared the burdens of service with its predecessor throughout the rest of the war. According to Lt. Col. Henry B. Cheadle, Fuqua's successor as military attaché in Spain, the Italian bombers based in Majorca divided their tasks into day bombing (the SM.79s, named Sparvieros, or "Sparrowhawks") and night-bombing (SM.81s, appropriately named Pipistrellos, or "Bats."). This division of labor was probably due not to any specific feature that made the SM.81s superior at night but rather to their comparatively slow speed (211 mph vs. 267 mph for the SM.79s) which made them more vulnerable during the day to fighter interception.[35]

Italian operations in the Mediterranean provided cause for the use of sea-based planes. Two notable Italian naval aircraft were by the Cantière Riuntini dell'Adriatico (United Adriatic Shipyard), or Cant, for short. These were the Z.501 Gabbiano (Seagull) flying boat and Z.506B Airone (Heron) float plane.[36] Both were of mostly wooden construction, the Gabbiano had plywood covering on the fuselage and fabric covering on the wings; the Airone had fabric covering all over. The Gabbiano was powered by a 900 hp Isotta-Franchini Asso XI R2C-15 liquid-cooled V-engine positioned on the parasol wing centered above the fuselage. The low-wing monoplane Z.506B Airone was its intended replacement. The Airone's three Alfa Romeo 126 R.C.34 radial engines produced 2,250 hp, which gave it a maximum speed of 280 mph, a ceiling of 24,600 feet, and a range of 1,370 miles. Its wings spanned 86 feet, 11 inches, a good 13 feet longer than those of the Cant Z.501, and its length of 63 feet, 1.5 inches exceeded the Gabbiano by 16 feet. The Nationalists acquired four of the Airones in June 1938 and used them primarily in reconnaissance and search-and-rescue missions. It was in one of the Airones, on October 28, 1938, in which the hero of the *Plus Ultra* flight, Ramón Franco, and his crew crashed into the sea and were killed.[37]

If the Germans were an example of earnestness and ambition in regard to aerial technological development, the Italians were a model of contentment, keeping to their more modest advances. Historian Brian R. Sullivan assigns two key reasons for this. First, Italy was under severe economic constraints. The Regia Aeronautica alone had spent 650 million lira in its first year of engagement in Spain (estimated at $3,208 million in 2025 U.S. dollars). This was the equivalent of its entire 1939 aircraft procurement budget. Second, General Giuseppe Valle, the chief of staff for Air, did not want to commit to a strategic bombing force (as advocated by Douhet) or to a force designed to work in close support of the army and navy (as advocated by Brigadier General Amedeo Mecozzi, Douhet's contemporary and "theoretical adversary"). General Valle was inclined to favor Mecozzi, but this would have upset Mussolini, an admirer of the late Douhet; so no strategic path was adopted.[38]

The Italians made some innovations in the bomber category, though these were employed on a limited basis in Spain. The Fiat Br 20 Cignona (Stork), a medium bomber, was introduced in 1936. It had retractable landing gear, a metal frame, duralumin skin, and a fabric-covered aft and controls. It was powered by two Fiat A.80 R.C. 41 radial engines for 2,060 hp, capable of reaching 267 mph (the same as the SM.79), with a ceiling of 23,623 feet and a range of 1,865 miles (superior to the SM.79 and the SM.81). It could carry over 3,500 pounds of bombs, making it the bomber with the heaviest payload. Only about thirteen or fourteen were sent to Spain, where they contributed to the fighting from Belchite to Catalonia.[39] Their performance appeared to be satisfactory, but only about 600 were ever produced, compared to the more than 1,300 SM.79s made during the same period. A light bomber, the Caproni Ca 310 Libeccio (South-West Wind), introduced in 1938, made an appearance in Spain in small numbers near the end of the war.[40] Although the Ca 310s were far inferior to the SM.79s in speed (232 mph versus 267 mph) and range (637 miles versus 1,181 miles) and carried a fraction of the bombload (706 pounds versus 2,756 pounds), Italy would ultimately produce 2,400 of them. This is probably because their wood, metal, and fabric construction was more affordable than the steel and duralumin-built SM.79s.

As for fighter aircraft, the strong performance of the Fiat CR.32s convinced the Italians that biplanes with mixed-material construction (metal frames with fabric covering) were still practical assets in a modern air force. Hence Italy's reliance on the Fiat CR.42 Falco (1939) in the aftermath of the civil war for fighter operations. The Italian tendency

Table 4. Bomber aircraft employed in Spain, 1937–39

Designation	Name	Year introduced	Nation	Mission	Horsepower (total)	Max speed (mph)	Ceiling (ft)	Range (miles)	Bomb load (lbs)
Savoia-Marchetti SM.79	Sparviero (Sparrow)	1934	Italy	Bomber, medium	2,340	267	21,327	1,181	2,756
Heinkel He 111B-2	Pedro	1936	Germany	Bomber, medium	1,900	230	22,967	566	3,308
Fiat Br 20	Cignona (Stork)	1936	Italy	Bomber, medium	2,060	267	23,623	1,865	3,528
Junkers Ju 87B	Stuka	1937	Germany	Bomber, dive	1,200	236	26,576	497	1,103
Junkers Ju 86D-1	Jumo	1937	Germany	Bomber, medium	1,184	202	19,357	709	1,764
Caproni Ca 310	Capronchino; Libeccio (South-West Wind)	1938	Italy	Bomber, light	940	232	22,956	637	706

was apparently to avoid any development, particularly if it meant an increase in cost, until it proved itself to be clearly superior to the status quo. As the Italians proved with the Macchi MC 202 Folgore (1939)—which was not used in Spain—their engineers were certainly capable of producing a high-quality metal monoplane fighter; but success in the civil war and budgetary constraints limited the urgency in focusing on such advancements.

RUSSIAN AND FRENCH AIRCRAFT AND SPANISH PRODUCTION

Josef Stalin's mercurial relationship with his aeronautical experts, both civilian and military, had a serious impact on the course of Soviet aviation before the Second World War. Although there was never a safe time for a prominent Russian to come to Stalin's attention, the periods of 1928–32 and 1937–41 were particularly perilous. In the earlier of these two periods, the suspicions of the OGPU—a predecessor to the NKVD—first fell on engineers. In April 1928, Peter Palchinsky (1875–1929), the supposed leader of the insurgent Industrial Party, was arrested at his home and had his papers seized. His wife heard no more of him until, thirteen months later, she read about his execution by firing squad for treason. In November 1930, a group of engineers, accused of belonging to the Industrial Party, was put on trial, with Palchinsky tried posthumously as the conspiracy's leader.[41] That same year, the OGPU had commenced Operation Vesna (Springtime) targeting military specialists suspected of being counterrevolutionaries or even monarchists. These specialists received the blame for the failure of the Soviet economy to meet its promised level of prosperity. The fact that many acknowledged their complicity in anti-Soviet plots gave credence to the OGPU's accusations and reinforced Stalin's fears.[42]

Aircraft designers were swept up in this terror, including Nikolai Polikarpov (1892–1944), who was imprisoned in the early 1930s. Of course, incarceration was no excuse to postpone important work. Good aeronautical engineers were hard to find. Polikarpov and others were therefore taken to a special prison, TsKB-29, to develop new aircraft.[43] Successful projects helped many of them recover the good graces of the secretary general. One of Polikarpov's fellow inmates, Aleksandr Vasil'yevich Nadashkevich, recalled a briefing they delivered to Stalin personally. "When we had finished—and we were standing off by ourselves then—Stalin asked, 'They don't make it oppressive for you here, do they?' For ten years this phrase hasn't given me any peace. Was he being a hypocrite or an actor?"[44]

The Great Terror, or Purge, which started in 1937, was much more comprehensive in scope and severe in magnitude. Once again, aircraft designers fell subject to Stalin's wrath. Andrei Tupolev's days as a free man were numbered when, in August 1937, a modified Tupolev TB-3 aircraft disappeared shortly after crossing the North Pole. Tupolev had nothing to do with the modifications or the experimental flight, but he was nonetheless arrested two months later. His colleague and later biographer, L. L. Kerber, was to have been the radio operator on the fateful flight, but he had been replaced the night before. His good fortune only went so far, and he was arrested the following April.[45]

Once again, an aircraft design department was established for the imprisoned engineers, this time at the Central Aero-Hydrodynamics Institute (TsAGI) in Moscow.[46] Kerber recalled his arrival there:

[The guard] led us to the dining area. As the door opened, about a hundred men sitting at tables covered with snow-white tablecloths turned their heads at the same time. Someone yelled, someone else ran toward us. There were many well-known, friendly faces, and friendly hands reached out to us. It is difficult to describe this meeting or the emotion it generated in us all. . . . At various tables we saw Andrei Nikolayevich Tupolev, Vladimir Mikhaylovich Petlyakov, Vladimir Mikhaylovich Myasishchev, Josef Grigor-yevich Neman, Sergei Pavlovich Korolyov, Aleksandr Ivanovich Putilov, Vladimir Antonovich Chizhevskiy, Aleksei Mikhaylovich Putilov, Dmitriy Sergeyevich Markov, and Nikolai Il'ich Bazenkov—in short, the cream of the Russian aeronautical world.[47]

In how many nations could the prison population be the prime recruiting ground for aircraft designers? The Soviets had (perhaps inadvertently) developed an unnerving but effective system to prevent the outflow of skilled engineers.

The introductions of the impressive I-15 Chato, I-16 Mosca, R-5 Resantes, and SB-2 Katiuska have been recorded in previous chapters. The technological innovation of the Russians slowed after this first wave, doubtless due to the impact of Stalin's purge of engineers. New versions of the I-15 and I-16 were introduced, but the only completely original aircraft to appear in Spain was the R-Z Natacha. The R-Zs were first developed in 1935 by Dmitry S. Markov (later imprisoned) and A. A. Skarbov; they were biplanes of a similar design to the R-5 Resantes. They included a liquid-cooled Mikulin M-34RN engine that produced 750 hp and could reach speeds of 180 mph. This was still slow, but markedly faster than the R-5s. Similar to the original R-5s, the R-Zs were armed with a forward-facing machine gun and an observer's machine gun. The R-Zs also carried up to 882 pounds of bombs. They first arrived in Spain in January 1937, but did not see action until March.[48]

The I-15s (Chatos), for all their impressive performance in combat, received criticism from pilots for their difficulty in landing. This was attributed in part to their upper wings, each of which curved upward from the fuselage, giving it a birdlike, or "gulled," shape, which hindered

Table 5. Pursuit and attack aircraft employed in Spain, 1937–39

Designation	Name	Year introduced	Nation	Mission	Horsepower (total)	Max speed (mph)	Ceiling (ft)	Range (miles)
Polikarpov R-5	Resante (Skimming)	1928	Russia	Attack	680	158	21,327	684
Polikarpov R-Z	Natacha	1935	Russia	Attack	750	180	26,248	622
Polikarpov I-152 (bis)	Super Chato	1937	Russia	Fighter	775	226	31,170	280
Messerschmitt Bf 109B		1937	Germany	Fighter	720	289	26,904	429
Messerschmitt Bf 109E-1	Emils	1938	Germany	Fighter	1,175	347	34,400	410
Polikarpov I-16 Type 10	Super Mosca	1938	Russia	Fighter	750	276	27,134	497

the pilot's visibility when descending or landing. A new model, the I-152 (Super Chato) was thus designed with a straight upper wing; its production began in 1937, but the model was not sent to Spain until November 1938, when the situation was becoming increasingly hopeless for the Republic.[49] The I-152 had an upgraded engine, a 775 hp M-25 Wright Cyclone, which increased its maximum speed by 10 mph (to 226 mph). Its ceiling increased by about 1,000 feet (to 31,170 feet). However, the new Super Chatos were apparently more difficult to handle and were not popular with Spanish pilots, apart from their speed and the well-made clock installed on the instrument panel of each plane. At the end of the war, when Spanish Republican pilots flew their aircraft to France for refuge, many removed the clocks to keep as souvenirs, but their commander, Captain Emilio Galera Macías, confiscated them on behalf of the (then exiled) Spanish Republican government.[50]

The I-16 Type 10 Super Mosca made its appearance in Spain in March 1938. Its key advancements over previous versions were the inclusion of the 750 hp Shvetsov M-25 V radial engine, which allowed for a maximum speed of 276 mph and a ceiling of 27,134 feet. These statistics were actually *lower* than those of the Type 5 model (a regular Mosca) (282 mph, 30,448 feet, respectively), probably due to the addition of two more machine guns to the front fuselage, which increased its total loaded weight to 3,782 pounds, up from 3,219 pounds. The Super Moscas were featured prominently in the Battle of the Ebro in the summer and autumn of 1938, when more than 200 aircraft were involved in each of several engagements. The magnitude of these air battles, according to Howson, was "a scene not equaled again until the Battle of Britain."[51]

The purging of the Soviet military and engineering field certainly seems to have wiped out any possible lessons learned from the Spanish Civil War. It was certainly a major reason why the Russians were not able to match the innovations introduced by the Germans throughout the conflict. However, the significant introduction of new designs in the years preceding the German invasion of the Soviet Union (1939–41) are impressive and suggest that the Russians appreciated the need to continuously adapt. Aircraft developed during this period included the Petlyakov Pe.2 dive bomber (introduced 1940; 11,425 produced), the Ilyushin Il-4 medium bomber (1940; 5,256 produced), the Yakovlev Yak-7 fighter (1941; 5,000 produced), the Mikoyan-Gurevich MiG-3 fighter (1941; 3,120 produced), the Lavochkin LaGG-3 fighter (1941; 6,258 produced), the Tupolev ANT-58 heavy bomber (1941; 2,527 produced), and the Ilyushin Il-2 attack aircraft (1941; 36,163 produced). All these planes had retractable landing gear. Most of them had mixed-material designs, likely due to cost restrictions. Their powerplants varied from 1,240 hp (the LaGG-3) to 3,700 hp (ANT-58), a significant advance compared to the aircraft used in the Spanish Civil War, which varied from 680 hp (R-5 Resantes) to 1,660hp (SB-2 Katiuska). They increased in speed as well, with the Yak-7 reaching 400 mph, compared to the fastest Russian aircraft in the civil war, the I-16 Mosca Type 5, which could reach 282 mph. This impressive output redounds to the credit of the Russian engineers working under difficult and perilous conditions.

The problems facing French engineers were equally consequential, though unlike their Russian counterparts, they were spared the threatening menace of tyrannical scrutiny. Even in the late 1920s, when the Germans were still restricted to civilian flying, many in France became concerned with the ease with which German civilian aircraft could be transitioned into bombers (as would eventually happen with such aircraft as the Junkers Ju 52). In 1932, a French translation of Douhet's *Command of the Air* became available. In the book, the Italian general presented a hypothetical scenario in which a French-Belgian alliance was quickly subdued by German air superiority and strategic bombing. This scenario was the source of a great deal of anxiety among military and political leaders. At this point, a young, talented and ambitious man, Pierre Cot, became air minister. While the army remained committed to a defensive ground strategy vis-à-vis Germany, Cot advocated for an offensive air strategy, with aircraft ready to enter enemy air space and bomb key targets.[52] Organizational reform assisted in the manifestation of this policy. The French Air Force, the Armeé de l'Aire, achieved independence in 1933. In 1936, Cot took further steps to centralize the operational control of air assets by establishing two Air Corps: one for most of the bombers, and one for most of the fighters.[53] The advantages and disadvantages of such an approach are evident: each type of aircraft would be able to focus on its core mission, but when cooperation between fighter and bomber was needed, bureaucratic barriers would have to be overcome.

Earlier chapters have examined France's uneven support for Spain during the civil war. This lack of a consistent policy resulted in France sending to Spain a mixture of aircraft, both old and new, high quality and low quality. The Potez 54 was discussed in chapter 3, but not the Potez 25, which also had a role—or perhaps only a cameo—in the Spanish Civil War. These were single-engine biplane bombers with wooden frames and fabric covering, powered by 500 hp Farman 12We water-cooled engines. Introduced in 1925, they could reach maximum speeds of only 143 mph with a ceiling of 24,279 feet and a range of 373 miles. Griffiss noted that the Potez 25s sent to Spain "never appeared on the Madrid front," and believed they were sent only as a cover for the delivery of more recently developed, higher quality aircraft like the Potez 54s.[54]

In February 1937, when Griffiss was listing fighters in terms of quality, he placed the Loire 46 above the Heinkel He 51. The Loire 46 C1, a gull-winged monoplane fighter, had been introduced in 1934. It had a 930 hp Gnome-Rhône 14Kfs 14-cylinder air-cooled engine, and could reach speeds of 255 mph, with a ceiling of 34,450 feet and a range of 466 miles. It was intended to have four wing-mounted MAC 34 7.7-mm machine guns; but as with the other French aircraft, these were not included in shipments, and Vickers guns had to be installed instead. According to Howson, all five of the Loire 46 C1s sent to Spain in September 1936 were destroyed by the end of October, so it seems odd that Griffiss would mention them at all. Howson suggested that there may have been a sixth one, or that the fifth one was erroneously listed as destroyed, since apparently a Loire 46 C1 was at Manises Airfield near Valencia as late as December 1936. In spite of their brief appearance, a Loire 46 C1 has the distinction of being the first to shoot down a Junkers Ju 52 in the war.[55]

Although there were no Spanish-designed aircraft in the war, there were several Spanish-*produced* aircraft. Most of these aircraft were of French-design, such as the Breguet XIX bombers built at the Construcciones Aeronáutica S.A. (CASA) factory in Madrid, and the Nieuport-Delage Ni-H 52 fighters constructed at the Hispano-Suiza Sección de Aviación factory in Guadalajara.[56] Aircraft from these plants constituted the largest portion of the Spanish military aviation inventory at the start of the war. These two types of aircraft have been examined in previous chapters; they were found to be insufficient for their missions and unpopular with their crews.

As the war progressed and the Nationalists captured more territory, the Republican government moved aircraft production to the eastern coast. Several factories were constructed by the German engineer Antonius Raab, at least until September 1937, when he was arrested by the Soviet NKVD (secret police) for employing anarchists and anti-Stalinists—a typical self-defeating measure that the Republican government was obliged to condone.[57] In addition to Breguets XIX and Nieuport Ni-H 52s, the Spanish also began to manufacture the I-15 Chatos. Russian colonel Yakov Smushkievich, who became the de facto commander of Republican air operations, established the program in February 1937. Over the next two years, until the factories were captured by the Nationalists, they produced 237 Chatos for use by the Spanish.[58] These undoubtedly helped keep the Republicans competitive in the air, especially as the number of aircraft imported from the Soviet Union began to decrease.

Spanish factories were capable of producing naval aircraft, too, as was the case with the British-designed CASA-Vickers Vildebeest, which has been discussed previously. The original production license was granted in 1929, and aircraft construction took place in Getafe, near Madrid. However, only two dozen or so had been produced by the start of the civil war. Whatever strong qualities they may have possessed, by 1936, these were largely irrelevant. As Howson remarked, "It was the misfortune of the Vildebeest that, in the two theatres of war in which it saw action, in Spain in 1936 and in Malaya in 1942 [by the British against Japanese forces], it was obsolete and completely outclassed and outnumbered by the enemy it had to face." But the Republicans put some to good use, both over sea and land. Vildebeests were involved in the Republican victory at Guadalajara. By April 1938, only six remained operational.[59]

In contrast, the Nationalists did not have any factories for the production of their own aircraft. The Hispano-Suiza and CASA factories in Seville and Cádiz, respectively, repaired or upgraded existing aircraft but did not manufacture any new ones. A CASA factory near Seville made preparations to produce Heinkel He 111 bombers, but the war ended before it could commence operations.[60]

ARMAMENTS

For almost the entirety of the war, smaller-caliber machine guns (those firing rounds less than 20 mm in diameter) were preferred over cannons as aerial armaments. This had been the preference in the Great War, as well, and in spite of some efforts to incorporate the larger-caliber weapons into aircraft, by the mid-1930s their use was still limited.[61] The British perhaps typified the opinion of most air powers, as historian Harry Woodman notes: "The belief held [by government officials] in Whitehall was that a single-seat fighter was too light to accommodate cannon, a view that was radically revised in 1938."[62] There were, of course, exceptions, but lack of real-world demonstrations placed their utility in question. The French Dewoitine 500 series of aircraft were built to employ "motor cannons," which fit into the valley of a V-shaped in-line engine and fired through a hole at the center of the propeller. However, the Dewoitine D.510s sent to Spain, like other French aircraft, lacked these armaments.[63]

For the most part, the pilots and crews of the belligerent air forces were accustomed to the rifle-caliber machine guns and developed their tactics accordingly. As Griffiss observed in a March 13, 1937, dispatch, "From what I have heard of the Russians of their tactics and combat spirit I am convinced that the slow firing rate of the larger calibers would never blend with their temperament."[64] In Paris, Lt. Col. Horace Fuller gathered information from a "reliable British source," about the ongoing developments in air operations. According to this source, while the Russian aircraft were lauded for their superior speed, the pilots themselves credited their rapid-firing armaments for their effectiveness in thwarting Nationalist attempts at attaining air superiority.[65]

The two featured Russian pursuits, the I-15 and I-16, were indeed impressive in their rate and volume of fire. The I-15 had four PV-1 machine guns ringed around the front fuselage. Each of these could fire 780 rounds per minute (rpm), for a total of over 3,120 rpm. However, the aircraft carried a maximum of 4,000 rounds, so after a little more than one minute of firing, the guns would be empty. This required the pilots to fire for only a few seconds at a time and to use only two of the guns until they were assured of hitting the target.[66] Even more remarkable was the I-16's rate of fire. Its two wing-mounted 7.62-mm ShKAS machine guns fired up to 1,800 rpm apiece, for a total rate of fire of 3,600 rpm. However, this rate of fire was merely theoretical, since the I-16 was loaded with only 900 rounds per gun. Thus, after half a minute of firing, a pilot might find himself unarmed. In addition, gun barrels were ill-designed for such a rapid-firing mechanism, the heat of which caused warping that limited the lifespan of these weapons. However, bursts of a few seconds were all that was necessary or even possible, since combat in the I-16s, with a maximum speed of over 270 mph, gave the pilots little time for aiming and shooting.[67]

There was a steep learning curve in the use of such weapons. Frank Tinker, who had the distinction of being one of two Americans (Albert

Baumler was the other) to fly an I-16 noted the difficulty of controlling the powerful mechanism in a dogfight against a Fiat CR.32. After shooting an enemy's motor, he had intended to cease firing but was unable to stop until after he had struck the pilot. He regretted the incident but admitted, "There was nothing to do about it but hope that it might have been one of Mussolini's relatives."[68] Word of these impressive weapons spread beyond the battlefield. Griffiss referred to a "Special" Russian machine gun that could fire 1,800 rounds per minute.[69] Fuller's source informed him about the discretion exercised by the Russians, who were clearly jealous of their technological edge in this aspect of aviation. Even the pilots were not allowed near the weapons between flights.[70]

Most of the machine guns fired rounds ranging in caliber from 7.62 mm (0.3 in.) to 12.7 mm (0.5 in.) Griffiss noted that the "outstanding machine gun" among the Nationalists (up to March 1937) was the Italian Breda. He may have been referring to the armaments of the Fiat CR.32 Chirris, certain series of which were equipped with two 12.7-mm Breda machine guns. Griffiss included in his March 13, 1937, report a mentioning that none of the pilots he interviewed had fired a "large caliber machine gun." These pilots were not averse to such a weapon, so long as it was included with "two or more rapid firing small caliber machine guns."[71]

In November 1937, Griffiss reported that "the only motor-cannon-guns known to be in Spain are the ones mounted on the German Messerschmitt pursuit and the French guns now being tested by the Government Air Force."[72] Whether any of the Messerschmitt Bf 109B series aircraft sent to Spain came equipped with a cannon is unknown, but unlikely. Howson made no mention of cannons on the Messerschmitt Bf 109Bs. Griffiss may actually have meant the Heinkel He 112, an experimental aircraft that arrived the previous December with a 20-mm cannon mounted on its engine.[73]

Although the Messerschmitt Bf 109Bs in Spain were not armed with cannons, later series of the Bf 109 probably were. Raymond Proctor, the author of *Hitler's Luftwaffe and the Spanish Civil War* (1983), wrote of the D series, "The first models had three machine guns synchronized through the propeller. As time went on, additional machine guns were installed in the wings, and eventually two 20 mm cannons."[74] In June 1937, a squadron of Heinkel He 59 seaplanes were armed with 20-mm cannons on their noses. Howson noted that these weapons "proved extremely useful against small ships and railway locomotives."[75]

As the caliber of rounds increased, so too did the weight and destructiveness of bombs. According to Griffiss, during the Madrid campaign of the winter of 1936–37, the Nationalists had employed bombs mostly weighing between 110 and 441 pounds (50 to 200 kilograms), while the Republicans countered with bombs varying in size between 22 and 220 pounds (10 to 100 kilograms).[76] The limited capacity of the bombers influenced what types of bombs were used and how they were used. The Katiuska, the standard bomber for the Republican side, was a light bomber, but even the heavier bombers of the Spanish Civil War had bombloads that would place them in the medium-bomber rather than the heavy-bomber category. The German Junkers Ju 52 could carry a metric ton of bombs (1,000 kg, or 2,205 lb.), as could the French Potez 54 class and the Italian Savoia-Marchetti SM.81. As the war progressed, bombers were introduced that were capable of holding greater bombloads. Nevertheless, the heaviest of the bombers, the Italian Fiat Br 20 (with a bombload of 3,528 pounds), the German Heinkel He 111B-2 (with a bombload of 3,308 pounds), and the Italian Savoia-Marchetti SM.79 (with a bombload of 2,756 pounds), were all still within the range of what would later be deemed the medium-bomber class, from 1,650 to 5,999 pounds.[77]

The increased use of incendiary bombs is one of the more significant features of the Spanish Civil War. Their initial deployments against airdromes and cities were not impressive. According to a dispatch from Fuller in March 1937, a British source reported that many of the incendiaries failed to ignite. Whatever fires they started were easy to contain and extinguish, so long as authorities used sand, not water, to smother the flames.[78] Guernica was the setting of the first effective use of incendiary bombs in Spain. In spite of the moral outrage it incurred, it convinced air forces throughout the world that incendiaries were practical weapons of warfare. From Berlin, American military attaché Maj. Truman Smith forwarded a translation of an article written by a

Colonel Rudolf Xylinder of the Kriegsakademie, published in the *Militär Wochenblatt*. Xylinder noted how "Thermite bombs, developing a heat of 3000° were successfully employed by the nationals [Nationalist forces] in the Basque province for the purpose of setting fire to the forests in the enemy terrain." Xylinder used this example to advocate for wider area, less-discriminate bombing tactics.[79]

Perhaps the most remarkable advancement in weaponry came in the field of antiaircraft artillery. Douhet had been skeptical of the effectiveness of any type of asset designed specifically for air defense. The inaccuracy of antiaircraft weaponry during the Great War made such weapons particularly objectionable (to him).[80] However, in the eighteen intervening years, the technology seemed to have matured, at least on the Nationalist side. Of the 385 land-based antiaircraft artillery used by the Nationalists during the war, the most common were the 20-mm FLAK30 (116 guns). However, it was the German-built 88-mm FLAK18 (79 guns) that were the prize of the ground-based air defense units. The first four of these arrived in late 1936, and were manned by Spanish crews.[81] More artillery and personnel to man them arrived, and with the formation of the Condor Legion, a Flak Group (F/88) was formed with 88-mm, 37-mm, and 20-mm guns.[82] In January 1937, Lt. Col. Raymond Lee, the U.S. military attaché in Great Britain, passed on information from "an unbiased source in London enjoying unusual facilities for obtaining reliable information." According to this source, the four guns of each battery manned by Germans were arranged in a square formation, each side 250 yards long, firing streams of shells into the air. These guns could be used reliably against targets flying at 12,000 feet, though it was possible to strike objects at an even higher altitude.[83]

The deficiency of the Spanish Republican government's antiaircraft weaponry, particularly early in the war, was remarkable. Of the 351 antiaircraft guns possessed by the Republicans, almost two-thirds of these (around 210) were 20-mm Oerlikon.[84] According to Col. F. H. Lincoln, the U.S. Army assistant chief of staff, G-2, the twenty-one daylight raids on Madrid between November 1 and December 22, 1936, were an indication that the antiaircraft defense of the city failed to deter Nationalist aggression.[85] From Paris, Fuller noted that according to his

British source, ground-based aerial defenses consisted of "several quick firing pom-poms [evidently so called because of their sound] in Valencia which one can hear firing when there is a raid either by sea or by air," but these were considered insufficient.[86] When discussing the air raid on Valencia on May 15, 1937, Griffiss observed that the antiaircraft batteries were unable to commence firing before the attack was over.[87] A total of sixty-four 76-mm Soviet M1931 guns were provided to the Republican government, but half of these did not arrive until the French reopened the border with Spain in March 1938, when the situation was becoming desperate, if not hopeless, for the Republicans.[88] Nevertheless, as we saw in the previous chapter, Republican antiaircraft fire was effective in the battles of Teruel and the Levant and helped stave off total dominance of the air by the Nationalists into the last year of the war.

The desire for a technological edge is perhaps best captured by the remarkable case of the heat ray. In his February 21, 1937, dispatch, Griffiss made a striking claim in which he stated, "Six weeks ago I was told that one of the reasons for the great secrecy that surrounded air activities in the vicinity of Albacete was on account of experiments being made with a certain type of heat ray to stop aircraft engines in flight." He noted that such research was being conducted at Manises Field near Valencia. He promised to provide more details when he had them.[89] As it turned out, these additional details were provided by Fuller's British source, whose report Fuller forwarded in April 1937:

> An Englishman who came here [to Spain] under the name of Mr. Charles Way, arrived in January claiming that he had an electrical apparatus to bring down aircraft. He took great trouble to tell everybody that it was a closely guarded secret of the British Government. The authorities were deceived into erecting a tower for his apparatus at Manises onto which he fitted a searchlight made by FIAT, Italy, and dated 1913. He then left the country on the pretext of fetching more equipment and shortly afterwards English papers published accounts of very similar activities by an Englishman in Paris. I never met Mr. Way but know many people who did, and he appears to be rather an adventurous rogue.[90]

AIRCRAFT TECHNOLOGY

It is not stated how much the authorities paid for Mr. Way's services, nor is it clear how he convinced the authorities that he knew what he was talking about. Nor is the ultimate fate of Mr. Way at all indicated. The case remains shrouded in mystery. If true—and it certainly seems to be the type of scheme that arises during wartime when state dollars are flowing freely toward defense projects—it stands as a testament to the desire for a new technology to bring down attacking aircraft. One wonders how familiar Mr. Way was with the advances being made in both Britain and Germany toward the development of radar, which, while not bringing down aircraft directly, would make it easier for friendly aircraft to locate and attack enemy aircraft.[91] But the use of radar would have to wait for the next war.

CHAPTER 9

AIR SUPERIORITY

Neither armies nor navies can exist unless the air is controlled over them.

—WILLIAM MITCHELL, *WINGED DEFENSE*

THE EBRO OFFENSIVE

Lost causes are romantic; losing causes are not. As evidence of this, coverage of the second anniversary of the Spanish Civil War was limited to the eighth column of the front page of the *New York Times*, and it spilled onto page 8. "Rebels Smash On as Spain Observes War Anniversary" was the headline for William P. Carney's article, written the day before in Burgos. Carney told of the capture of the Mora de Rubielos salient, forcing back the reinforcements of Líster and El Campesino. As a consequence, "The Nationalists' drive now may roll downhill all the way to Valencia before it can be checked."[1] Herbert Matthews from Valencia gave the other side of the story, based on editorials from Republican newspapers commemorating the anniversary of the start of the war. Matthews noted, "The keynotes of all editorials are pride and determination. The Loyalists are proud of the fact that without a professional army and with relatively little outside help they have stood off virtually all of Spain's professional military forces, enormously strengthened by aid from Italy and Germany."[2]

The "pride and determination" masked an increasingly desperate situation for the Republic. Nevertheless, the war was not yet lost, and a good deal of fighting spirit remained in Republican Spain. In fact, plans were being put into motion to halt the Nationalist threat to Valencia, to drive a salient into a vulnerable part of their lines, to unite Catalonia with the Central Zone, and perhaps at long last turn the tide of the war. The Battle of the Ebro was about to commence.

While to the south the Nationalists were grinding away at Republican defenses on the XYZ Line, the newly formed Army of the Ebro began to assemble on the east bank of that river. It consisted of the V Army Corps (under Líster), the XV Army Corps (under Manuel Tagüeña) and the XII Army Corps (under Etelvino Vega), with the XVIII Army Corps (under José del Barrio) in reserve, a total of 80,000 troops in all. There were also about 150 artillery pieces, including antiaircraft artillery, 60 tanks, and 110 aircraft, including the most recent models of the I-15s and I-16s, the Super Chatos and Super Moscas, respectively.[3] It was impressive that so late in the war and after so many disastrous turns, the Republicans were able to muster such a formidable force, giving them at least temporary superiority over their opponents. For on the Nationalist side sat three divisions of Yagüe's Moroccan Corps, with 40,000 men.[4]

The initial crossing by boat occurred on the night of July 24–25. The night operation caught the Nationalists by surprise, and Republican advances were swift and effective. Further successful crossings followed, with pontoon bridges laid for vehicles. By early August, the Republicans had advanced to the outskirts of Gandesa, twelve miles from their starting point. The territory captured during this time consisted of two salients west of the Ebro River: a northern one from Mequinenza, stretching to west of the Mount Auts and curving back to the Ebro north of Fayón, covering forty-five square miles; and a larger southern one, stretching from the convergence of the Río Matarrana with the Ebro, southward to the east of Villalba de los Arcos and Gandesa, and along the Río Canaletas to where that river converged with the Ebro, about

166 square miles. However, that is where the offensive ground to a halt; the Army of the Ebro would never advance another foot. Franco had enough time to send in his reinforcements, including the other divisions of the Moroccan Army Corps along with the Maestrazgo Corps under García Valiño. These troops, along with the Nationalist Air Force, were sufficient to halt the momentum of the attack. The fighting in the rocky terrain in the summer heat was brutal. Within the first two weeks, both sides had suffered thousands of casualties. A Nationalist counterattack began on August 6 and would soon recapture the northern pocket of the Ebro salient. Throughout September and October, the Nationalists made halting progress in retaking the lost territory in the southern salient. The Republicans would fight for every inch, assisted by inclement weather, the potent but unreliable ally of defenders throughout history. In early September, the Nationalists had pushed back the lines about three miles, recapturing Corbera in the center of the front. By the end of October, the Nationalists were closing in on Pinell in the south and threatening to envelope the remaining Republican forces west of the Ebro.[5]

The Ebro Offensive seemed about as well planned as the Republicans could have hoped for in terms of their operational objectives. Whether their forces would have been better off on a strategic defense with bite and hold tactics along the front in both zones, keeping the Nationalists too busy to focus on a new major offensive and thus prolonging the war in the hope of eventual relief through an international crisis (i.e., a continental or world war), is interesting to ponder; but conditions were such that the odds were against the Republicans whatever they did. A major reason was the decisive shift in the air in favor of the Nationalists. Raymond Proctor estimates that the Nationalist forces had 434 aircraft on hand: 70 for the Condor Legion, 170 for the Nationalist Spanish pilots, and 194 for the Italians.[6] Republican air assets, though reinforced, amounted to only 200 aircraft by early August, giving the Nationalists more than a two-to-one advantage.[7]

The crowded battlespace presented threats to the pilots from both the air and the ground. During one of the early engagements, Fiat squadron commander Captain Gautier was killed by ground fire. However, on August 1, a Fiat group and squadron managed to destroy seven of twelve I-15s in the air, with now-Major Joaquín García Morato and Captain Julio Salvador each gaining one victory. A Heinkel He 51 was destroyed the same day, and a Dornier Do 17 was shot down on August 5, while the Republicans lost an I-16 and a Katiuska.[8] Then the Messerschmitt Bf 109s arrived on August 12 and destroyed seven I-16s and three Katiuskas in their first engagement. A day later, the latest model of the I-15s, the Super Chatos, joined battle. There was a large air battle of about 100 aircraft on August 14, in which the Republicans claimed to have destroyed three Fiats and one He 111. There were four battles on August 23, in which one Fiat was destroyed, but the Nationalists claimed to have downed eleven I-16s and two Katiuskas. On August 24, there was a tradeoff of one I-15 and one I-16 for two Fiats.[9] Apparently, the Junkers Ju 87 Stuka dive-bombers made an appearance at this time, and though they were used sparingly, they had considerable success in striking the bridges over the Ebro.[10]

Col. Stephen Fuqua visited the front in early September and found the troops of the XV Corps demoralized by the all-too-familiar experience of a stalled offensive. He breakfasted with corps commander Lieutenant Colonel Tagüeña, a twenty-five-year-old former schoolteacher. Tagüeña expressed displeasure with the orders to retreat and was highly critical of the high command for its failure to ensure steady supplies to the front lines. During their conversation, Fuqua mentioned that the cloudy weather might reduce the likelihood of enemy air attacks, to which Tagüeña replied bluntly, "They come in all kinds of weather, even if it snows." Conversely, the commander had no faith in the Republican Air Force and, according to Fuqua, believed that their action reports were "greatly exaggerated." Fuqua proceeded to the 3rd Division headquarters west of Faterella, positioned nonchalantly on a hill, with a single antiaircraft gun positioned next to the commander's quarters. Members of the staff lounged around the grounds, showing little situational awareness of the proximity to the front, a mere kilometer away. While Fuqua was there, news came of the fall of Corbera. He visited the headquarters of the XV International Brigade, but learned the Lincoln Battalion had been sent to the front line before his arrival. On his return trip on September 8 at 1:45 p.m., he crossed the Ebro via the 360-foot-long trestle bridge at Mora la Nova, the main connection over the river. The bridge guard assured Fuqua that it was safe to cross as the Nationalists did not conduct bombing missions during lunch.[11] Once over, Fuqua paused to examine the arrival of a convoy of troops being brought to the front:

> Evidently, they had not had the guard's "assurances as to the fascists' consideration for the lunch hour," or disbelieved him, as these soldiers detrucked on the left bank of the river, ran furiously and disorderly across the bridge and later, when the empty trucks crossed, entrucked and went on their way. We were told this was to avoid the probability of being hit with a bomb, but as a safety measure the procedure seemed a farce, as it was noted that all of the men grouped on the right bank of the river awaiting the trucks and thus made a most vulnerable target. Fortunately, the guard's analysis of the situation was correct for this occasion.[12]

Fuqua observed that the Nationalist aircraft dominated the skies, forcing supply trucks to travel by night: "The bombers, pursuit and reconnaissance planes were hovering overhead practically the whole time after 8:00 a.m. and would have been out before except that the earlier part of the day was quite windy with threatening weather."[13]

During Fuqua's last night in the sector, at Villanueva y Geltrú, an enemy aircraft dropped five bombs near his quarters, damaging a railroad building. The red tracers of the antiaircraft Maxim gun provided spectators with an impressive display. "Thus closed what might be called from a standpoint of 'action' a 'perfect day' at the front," Fuqua concluded.[14]

Despite the criticism of the Republican Air Force, it continued to operate in the increasingly perilous skies. About once a week, the Republicans were able to collect enough pilots and aircraft to challenge Nationalist air superiority. On September 5, there was an air battle involving over fifty fighters, Messerschmitt Bf 109s from the Condor Legion against I-15s and I-16s. On September 13, Lieutenant Mölders' squadron, escorting a squadron of bombers, was attacked by twenty-five Republican I-16s; four of the Moscas were destroyed that day. A week later, about thirty aircraft were engaged in fighting with the loss of an I-15. On October 4, a Republican bombing raid at La Cenia Airfield damaged four aircraft and destroyed a Bf 109.[15] In none of these encounters were the Republicans successful enough to shift the balance of power in the air. But by engaging the enemy in the skies, they were at least providing some respite to the troops on the ground. Their efforts and sacrifices often went unheralded, and to those like Tagueña, they were hardly worthy of acknowledgment.

Before we close this part, with the Army of the Ebro demoralized but still resisting Nationalist attempts to seize what the Republicans had so dearly and so recently paid for, the international context should be acknowledged. While visiting the front, Fuqua spoke to several officers about the international situation, noting, "It is believed that many of them, although perhaps not wishing a European clash of arms, hoped that in some way the Czechoslovakia imbroglio would afford a 'way out' for Spain. Answers to such questions as 'Why are the "democracies" so interested in Czechoslovakia and not in Spain?' were not attempted."[16]

The extent of the democracies' interest in Czechoslovakia was made explicit by the end of the month with the Munich Agreement, in which the crisis over the heavily German-populated Czech territory of the Sudetenland was decided by the leaders of Britain, France, Germany, and Italy, with the Czech government a passive observer. The Sudetenland would soon join Hitler's Reich and the chances of an outbreak of general war seemed averted, at least for the time being. Much of Europe and the rest of the world breathed a sigh of relief, but it knocked the wind out of the Spanish Republican hopes for outside intervention and salvation.

CATASTROPHES, REAL AND IMAGINED

By the time of Fuqua's visit to the Ebro front, his assistant military attaché Townsend Griffiss had left Spain. He returned to the United States for his next assignment as a student at the Air Corps Tactical School (ACTS). But before he left, Griffiss completed a report entitled,

"The Air Warfare in Spain and Its Effect upon the Air Rearmament of France." The report encapsulated Griffiss's views on aerial warfare during his time in Spain, and he drew some conclusions that may have been surprising to those at the Military Intelligence Division who received it. Regardless, it was a timely analysis by a subject matter expert, a fighter pilot with direct experience with the conflict in Spain.

Griffiss acknowledged early in the report that air operations had failed to achieve the promises of Douhet in swiftly ending the war. However, Griffiss emphasized the importance of context. "Jumping at conclusions in the use of aircraft in this war and applying them without careful study to a rearmament program might be disastrous," he noted.[17] He agreed with the opinion of French General Armangaud, formerly of the Armée de l'Aire, that the composition of air forces in Spain was not suited for a true test of aerial principles, notably strategic bombing. As Griffiss added, "[The Air Forces in Spain] have been criti[ci]zed and placed in the same category as one field gun that fails to accomplish a mission requiring a whole regiment."[18]

He followed this up with a general recounting of the war up to that point, stressing the importance of coordination between land and air forces in all aspects of the fighting. As he summarized, "Any story of the Spanish War, no matter how much in detail or how general in scope, shows the absolute dependency of Ground Forces upon Air Action and also that Air Operations in order to be successful on the field of battle must have ground support."[19] He repeated his earlier belief that the Republican air assets were far outnumbered by Nationalist air assets, and that this difference in quantity, rather than a difference in quality, accounted for the steady Nationalist gains in air dominance. This air dominance, in turn, was key to continued success on the ground. Wrote Griffiss, "Above all[,] the activities in Spain have shown that even though an Air Force alone will not win a campaign, the side whose Air Force is licked will certainly lose."[20]

He then proceeded to discuss the different missions conducted by the air forces. He noted that bombardment on the battlefield, while lacking "precision and accuracy" had a great impact on morale, perhaps a greater impact than that of artillery due to its ability to reach greater distances and to be followed with strafing attacks on enemy positions. The Germans, in particular, had worked to perfect the coordination between air and ground elements. As Griffiss observed, "Today it seems that the Germans are studying the possibility of giving an overwhelming superiority to attack over defense by using at the same time artillery, tanks and airplanes."[21] As for pursuit, he noted, "Since Guadalajara no battle has been launched without pursuit being called to cover it by the establishment of a net of patrols protecting attacking troops." He placed emphasis on the importance of a sizable pursuit inventory, due to their relative simplicity and affordability as compared to bombers. They were also important for establishing air superiority, which was necessary for conducting offensive operations, but which came at a high cost in aerial combat.[22]

His discussion of strategic bombing was the most interesting. In short, while it was true that strategic bombing had failed to win the war, it was also true that strategic bombing had not really been attempted. According to Griffiss, "The terrific power of bombardment striking forces has never been unleashed on rear area objectives." There had been operations deep within enemy territory, but they were not sufficient in scope and magnitude to bring about the needed results.[23] In discussing the raids on Republican ports in the fall of 1937, he stated, "These raids were cautious, extremely limited and very poorly psychologically spaced." Nevertheless, they discouraged shipping activity for a while, until the long intervals between bombings allowed dockworkers and shippers to regain their nerve and continue to operate at full capacity. Overall, he insisted, "Bombardments of port sections and coastal cities have not been failures when the limited means employed and purposes are taken into consideration."[24] While not pushing the Douhetian idea that the people would demand peace as soon as bombing commenced, he also discounted the idea that bombing produced the opposite effect of hardening the will of the people over the long term: "It is true that the initial bombardments of the cities proper have angered the people and in many instances have aroused an otherwise dormant will to resist. But in the few cases when the raids have been prolonged that first prompted 'will to resist' has been turned to 'terror' and then to 'panic.'"[25] He cited the raid on Valencia in May 1937 and the attacks on Barcelona in March 1938 as evidence of how a populace, particularly if it is relatively secure from other types of attacks, could descend into panic if it is struck from the air.[26]

Griffiss dedicated the rest of the report to how the governments of France and Belgium were reacting to news from the war. Having served as assistant military attaché to both nations, he had convinced his official contacts to provide information on the progress of their military readiness. Both nations had developed a passive defense infrastructure, but the appearance of high explosives in the Spanish war suggested that these defenses were now outdated. The Belgian government was restrained in further development of either defensive or offensive counterair assets due to its limited finances. France was hindered by its frequent changes in government, which resulted in a lack of consistency in policy. The French had commenced the construction of a "large retaliatory bombardment force," in 1933, and by 1936 had accumulated an impressive inventory. However, political shifts and the nationalization of the aircraft industry derailed this effort. The recent rise of Édouard Daladier to the premiership had restored somewhat the drive to develop the French Air Force, which had set a goal of producing 1,750 additional aircraft by April 1939, many of which were to be pursuit aircraft.[27]

These nations, and Britain as well, had concluded that the best method for destroying enemy bombardment was "by attacking the enemy aircraft in the air by one's own Air Force." This was a departure from the Douhetian idea of destroying the enemy air force on the ground at its bases. Instead, as Griffiss noted, "Dispersion of equipment, numerous landing fields and rapidity of movement have made this maneuver [destruction of enemy air forces on the ground] impossible upon which to depend." Pursuits, supported by antiaircraft artillery, proved to be a formidable instrument of air defense. Consequently, according to Griffiss, "Both France and England have launched tremendous pursuit programs supported by anti-aircraft defenses." Belgium was also considering such a strategy.[28]

With this summary of his wartime observations, Griffiss concluded his mission in Europe. His message was that the character of warfare had changed, that a strong aviation arm was essential to success on the ground, that a bomber striking force could bring about terror in targeted cities, and that a sizable pursuit force could seize control of the air and make other missions possible. He returned to America as his nation's foremost authority on air operations during the Spanish Civil War. His career had been one distinguished success after another. Where would his bright prospects take him next?

In September, tragic news came when Maj. Gen. Oscar "Tubby" Westover (1883–1938), chief of the Air Corps, was killed in a plane crash while visiting a Boeing plant in California. During his tenure as leader of the air branch, he had favored working within the system to develop airpower and to cooperate with the other branches rather than agitating for independence, as Brig. Gen. Billy Mitchell had done in his speech and writing. One U.S. Air Force historian, in a summary echoed by other reports, discussed Westover's temperamental conservatism: "A rather humorless, austere person, Westover believed in complete loyalty to superior authority, whether to the Chief of the Air Corps or to the General Staff; to denounce Army policy, as Mitchell had done, was unthinkable."[29] He was succeeded by Maj. Gen. Henry "Hap" Arnold (1886–1950), a very different type of officer.

Arnold had earned his wings in 1911, while stationed with the Signal Corps at Governor's Island. By 1917, he had his first command position in charge of the 7th Aero Squadron in the Canal Zone. His first base command came in 1929 at Fairfield Air Depot, and he was in command of the 1st Wing at March Field, California, by the time of his appointment as assistant chief of staff of the Air Corps.[30] His impressive climb up the military ladder belied a rocky and controversial career, for he was decidedly (and publicly) in the Mitchell school of airpower preeminence, much to the chagrin of his early commanders. A review of Arnold's fitness reports by his superiors could provide a sufficient synopsis of his career and his character:

> 1916: "Never seemed loyal and willing to cooperate. He is not suited for an independent command. . . . An able young officer of good habits but a trouble maker."[31]

1918: "Inferior in judgement and common sense. . . . Inclined to be disloyal to his superiors and prone to intrigue for his own advantage."[32]

1926: "In my opinion, during the period covered by this report, in judgment and common sense he fell below average. . . . My confidence in him was greatly shaken. I should now hesitate to entrust to him any important mission."[33]

Any of the above would be sufficient to detonate the career of a twenty-first century military officer, but Arnold would ultimately earn his "Hap" call sign, as happenstance mixed with determination led to a series of successful assignments and supportive superiors:

1927: "An exceptionally able air officer. He has an excellent observation squadron, and it is in excellent state of preparedness for any duty."[34]

1928: "An exceptionally high-grade officer. . . . Possesses lots of good hard common sense. . . . General officer, Air Corps, in peace or war."[35]

1931: "Superior officer. Qualified for any duty in the Air Corps."[36]

As for his opinion of himself at this time: "I assure you that I am not modest when it comes to getting things for myself. . . . I have a background . . . that few Air Corps officers have. I also believe that I am well qualified to be a Brigadier General."[37] By late 1935, when he was nominated as Westover's assistant chief of staff, he had attained that promotion.[38]

As assistant chief of staff, he had to deal with the limited resources available for military investment during the Great Depression and with the balancing act of shared authority between the Air Corps and the General Headquarters Air Force (GHQAF). He accumulated adversaries within the airpower community due to his lukewarm commitment

Photo 7. After a turbulent first half of his career, Henry "Hap" Arnold rose to the level of Chief of Staff of the Air Corps. Here he is in 1932, during the upward trajectory of his fortunes, hosting actress Bebe Daniels at Long Beach, California. *U.S. Air Force*

to the B-17 (he was concerned about investing so heavily in a single platform). In fact, so fierce was the antagonism toward Arnold that rumors were spread of him being a drunkard when his nomination to chief of staff appeared imminent. Nevertheless, he attained his new rank and position.[39] It was a time of great anxiety and shifting priorities for the U.S. government, for that very week the Munich Agreement was announced. It was this diplomatic coup by the Nazis that convinced President Franklin Roosevelt of the need to strengthen the airpower of the United States after witnessing the way Hitler had leveraged the looming threat of the Luftwaffe to gain his objectives. For Arnold, as one historian noted, "Problems changed overnight from a lack of money to a lack of time."[40]

The stress of the international arena and the threat of danger from above, as witnessed in the Spanish Civil War, seemed to have an unsettling impact on the American psyche. This may explain the reaction to a very unusual CBS radio broadcast on the evening of October 30, 1938, which purported to document a Martian attack on New Jersey. It was in fact a dramatization based on novelist H. G. Wells' *War of the Worlds* put on by the Mercury Theatre and starring actor Orson Welles. Welles' delivery must have been convincing; the program caused an outbreak of hysteria that seems hard to explain when removed from the wider context. The police switchboards in Manhattan, Queens, the Bronx, Brooklyn, Mount Vernon, Newark, East Orange, and Maplewood were flooded with calls either requesting information or passing on "news" of the attacks. The *New York Times* itself received 875 calls of this nature. In an encouraging testament to the American spirit, hundreds of doctors and nurses came forward to volunteer to assist in the treatment of casualties.[41]

The anonymous reporter for the *New York Times* may have had his finger on the pulse of those made fearful by the program, writing: "Despite the fantastic nature of the reported 'occurrences,' the program, coming after the recent war scare in Europe and a period in which the radio frequently had interrupted regularly scheduled programs to report developments in the Czechoslovak situation, caused fright and panic throughout the area of the broadcast."[42]

It is interesting that, three days earlier, CBS radio had broadcast another dramatization that caused little or no disturbance yet had featured a much more believable scenario. Archibald MacLeish's *Air Raid* was about an attack on a fictional southeastern European village. MacLeish had been influenced to write the script by Picasso's *Guernica* painting. Unlike *War of the Worlds*, MacLeish's *Air Raid* seemed to result in no controversy and, in fact, garnered a great deal of critical praise from such outlets as the *New York Times* and *Time* magazine.[43] This may have been because the fictionalized danger was far away and thus more abstract to its listeners. Still, it was emblematic of the tense atmosphere and widespread anticipation of a serious international crisis. Historian Lisa Jackson-Schebetta, writing of the broadcast, notes the influence of the changing character of war and communication on audiences throughout the developed world: "During the Spanish Civil War, two technologies combined to affect how the public imagined warfare and themselves in relation to it: radio and the airplane. . . . The interplay of the two technologies reached a synergistic culmination during the Spanish Civil War."[44]

On October 30, 1938, the same day as the *War of the Worlds* broadcast, a true catastrophe befell the Spanish Republic: the Nationalists resumed their counteroffensive. Their advance was steady, and they captured town after town, reducing the bridgehead the Republicans had captured and held desperately since July. The defenders could no longer rely on the shock troops of the International Brigades because the Republican government—in a show of faith with nonintervention efforts (and for propaganda purposes)—had dismissed them from further service. Similarly, the Italians had withdrawn 10,000 troops from the war. The final air battle of the Ebro occurred on November 12, when twenty-four Fiats, escorting a bombing force, engaged about six I-16s, escorting their own bombing force; the Republicans lost an I-16 and Katiuska in the struggle.[45] On November 16, the last Republican unit withdrew over the Ebro, back into Republican territory. The lines of July had been reestablished, and the Battle of the Ebro was over. The Republicans suffered 70,000 casualties, with 15,000 killed and 20,000 taken prisoner. The Nationalists were similarly hard-pressed, with 60,000 casualties and 6,000 killed. The Republicans had also lost 100 aircraft—compared to 40 aircraft lost by the Nationalists—at a time when Nationalist air superiority was becoming an assumed condition of battle.[46]

There followed a month and a half of relative calm, as the government in Barcelona considered its predicament and wondered where the Nationalist counterstrike would ultimately fall. By the end of the year, they realized that their seat of government was once again imperiled as Nationalist troops crossed the Ebro.

THE FALL OF BARCELONA

Modern airpower doctrine defines *air superiority* as the "degree of control of the air by one force that permits the conduct of its operations at a given time and place without prohibitive interference from air and missile threats."[47] By contrast, *air supremacy* is now defined as a more absolute version of air superiority in which "the opposing force is incapable of effective interference within the operational area using air and missile threats."[48] This is a much narrower definition of air supremacy than that employed before the Second World War as a synonym for *air dominance*. Presumably, the use of the term *supremacy* has fallen out of favor as too conclusive a statement in the uncertainty of war.[49]

As the situation stood in Spain in late 1938, the Nationalists certainly had achieved what would now be defined as air superiority, and they were trending toward air supremacy. After the Battle of the Ebro, the Nationalists had on hand 500 aircraft, mostly fighters and bombers, to bring to bear on Catalonia, while the defenders could barely scrape together 100 to 125 aircraft.[50] An example of the air superiority of the Nationalists was their ability to bomb Republican territory with increasing frequency with fewer and fewer losses of their own. The military attaché in Barcelona provided the Military Intelligence Division a summary of such bombardments against Catalonia from July to October 1938: There had been 627 aerial bombardments during this period, with 16,138 bombs dropped from the air. When coupled with the eighteen sea bombardments conducted during the same period, the result was 4,018 killed, 6,174 wounded, and 5,936 buildings either totally or partially destroyed. Barcelona alone had been subjected to 160 aerial attacks, resulting in 2,500 dead and 3,200 wounded, along with 1,200 buildings destroyed.[51]

This report was not submitted by Col. Stephen Fuqua, who had been obliged to retire at long last from the U.S. Army, but rather by his successor in the position of military attaché, Lt. Col. Henry B. Cheadle (1891–1959). Born in Cannon Falls, Minnesota, Cheadle was a career infantry officer, a West Point graduate, and a veteran of both the Mexican campaign and the Great War. Prior to his transfer to Barcelona, he had served as assistant military attaché in Budapest, Hungary. The arrival of Cheadle did not conclude Fuqua's involvement in Spain. The now retired colonel remained on staff in a civilian capacity, committed to standing his post to the bitter end.[52]

The bitter end appeared to be approaching quickly. The Republic had been in similar positions before, both in the fall of 1936, when the Nationalists were at the gates of Madrid, and in the spring of 1938, when the Nationalists were storming down the Mediterranean coast toward Valencia. In both cases, Republican resourcefulness and tenacity had saved the day. But now both resources and morale were in short supply in Catalonia. There were over a million refugees in Barcelona, displaced farmers and villagers from the areas recently captured by the Nationalists or those fleeing from the imminent advance of the enemy.[53] The loss of farmland, along with the increasingly obstructionist blockade, resulted in food shortages and high inflation. As for matériel, Hidalgo de Cisneros was obliged to travel to Moscow to make a personal appeal to Stalin for renewed support. He received a promise of 250 aircraft, 250 tanks, 650 artillery pieces, and 4,000 machine guns, though how they would arrive in time to make any difference was left undetermined.[54]

In the meantime, the Nationalists prepared for their Catalonian offensive under the overall command of General Dávila. A total of 340,000 troops were made available for the operation, led by the Moroccan Corps and the Corpo Truppe Volontarie. These were accompanied by 135 tanks and 1,400 artillery pieces. In defense, Hernández-Saravia had on hand 220,000 troops, still recovering from the reverses at Ebro, along with about 40 tanks and 173 artillery pieces, many of which were dilapidated.[55] The attack commenced on December 23, when the Nationalists crossed the Río Segre, north of the Ebro.[56] For the first week of the fighting, the Republicans managed to hold their own. However, in the skies above the battlefields, the Nationalist dominance became manifest. At the beginning of December, Wolfram von Richthofen had returned to Spain to assume command of the Condor Legion. He now launched an aggressive campaign to clear the skies of Republican aircraft. In three days of fighting, December 28–31, the German pilots destroyed twelve Republican aircraft in the air with the loss of one Messerschmitt.[57] The Germans employed a variety of platforms in their operations. Cheadle passed on this summary, either in his own words or those of his Spanish source: "It may be seen that there exists an extraordinary number of models which no doubt adversely affects the tactical employment of aviation, however, it is felt that by testing such a variety of models, Germany is deriving profitable experiences from this war."[58]

During this time, the Italian As de Bastos group claimed fourteen victories, all I-15s, while the La Cucaracha group claimed ten. In each encounter, the Nationalist losses were one Fiat each. On the Republican side, García LaCalle, now the commander of the Republican fighter units, realized his remaining veteran pilots were rendered as helpless by exhaustion as much as by enemy bullets. He ordered that they take a rest while the newly trained pilots took their places.[59] Was he trying to improve morale and allow his veterans to recover, or did he realize that all was lost, and was he trying to spare those pilots who had served the Republic for so long while sacrificing the green pilots to almost certain annihilation? The dire situation left him bereft of easy decisions.

On January 3, 1939, the front broke. The losses for the Republic at this time were critical. Líster, who had been in charge of holding the line, later estimated that about 70,000 Republican casualties were suffered during the first twenty days of the campaign.[60] Borjas Blancas fell within days. On January 12, the Nationalists captured Montblanc; Tarragona and Valls were taken later that week. On January 25, the Nationalists commenced crossing the Río Llobregat, bordering Barcelona on the west.[61] The morale among the defenders could be summarized by the experience of Tomás Roig Llop, a conservative Catalan, whose plight was documented by Charles Esdaile in his *Spanish Civil War*: Llop had been called up in the conscription to join in the defense of the city. When he arrived at the barracks, he saw that the situation was one of total chaos. A man who promised freedom and safety took command and marched the men (Llop included) out of the barracks. Once the column had turned a corner, out of sight of the guards, it dissolved, and the conscripts fled in all directions.[62] The internecine fighting from a year earlier had taken its toll. As E. R. Hooton observes in *Spain in Arms*, "Any hopes of emulating the defense of Madrid by mobilizing the population collapsed under the burden of falling morale following the undermining of Catalan nationalism and Communist machinations against the Trotskyists and Anarchists."[63]

On January 26, the Nationalists entered Barcelona. There was no effective resistance and, in fact, crowds gathered to welcome the conquerors and cheer them on to victory. The day before, Cheadle, along with the staff of the U.S. embassy (presumably including Fuqua) embarked upon the American cruiser *Omaha*, which had conveyed them safely to Marseilles. There was some risk involved in this action. While the ship itself was not directly attacked, bombs fell near the whaleboat that had carried passengers from the Spanish shore to the ship.[64] The Republican government had fled north to Figueras. There the Cortes held its final meeting on February 1, 1939, and Negrín vowed to continue the fight from the Central Zone. Cheadle, writing as "M.A. Perpignan," observed the likelihood of success in Negrín's plan: "Furthermore, it is not certain that representatives of this [Catalonian] Government would be welcomed by authorities in power in southern Spain. For these reasons it appears very doubtful if the present Government can survive the loss of Catalonia."[65]

By now, there was no cohesive defense in Catalonia. Figures vary, but it is estimated hundreds of thousands of civilians and troops, perhaps as many as 500,000 or more, crossed the border into France during this period. On February 5, they were joined by Negrín, Azaña, Martínez Barrio, Giral, and other members of the disintegrating government.[66]

Air operations during this time displayed the extent of the dominance the Nationalists had achieved. The Condor Legion harassed the Republican forces retreating northward.[67] They were now piloting their latest Messerschmitt model, the Bf 109E. Like previous models, these were low-wing metal monoplanes with retractable landing gear. However, the E models were equipped with 1,175 hp Daimler-Benz DB 601A liquid-cooled V-12 engines. These could reach speeds of 347 mph (a 58 mph increase over the B models, which had been the first to appear in Spain) and a ceiling of 34,400 feet (an increase of 7,800 feet). They were armed with four machine guns that fired 7.9-mm bullets. By the time of their arrival, air superiority had been secured. In spite of Franco's apparent protests, the Condor Legion pilots displayed no hesitation in attacking the refugees who remained in the province. Relations between Richthofen and the Nationalist command had been strained throughout much of the campaign, with Richthofen at one point threatening to halt operations.[68] This quarreling provided the Republicans no relief. On February 3, those Republican aircraft that could fly were ordered to France. Those that could not were to be destroyed.⁶⁹ Those that tarried, regretted it. On February 5, Republican pilot Francisco Tarazona landed at the airfield near Figueras, finding it in a state of chaos. Soon after his arrival, Fiats and Messerschmitts attacked, destroying much of the aerodrome. A day later, thirty-five fighters and two bombers were destroyed on the ground at Vilajuiga. Only five fighters managed to take off.⁷⁰ Incredibly, the Republicans scored perhaps their final air victory of the war when an I-15 flown by José Falco shot down a Bf 109E, whose pilot was killed by German bombs before he could escape the crash.⁷¹ That same day, February 6, the Condor Legion struck the town of Figueras in its final raid of the war.⁷²

On February 9, the Nationalists reached the French border. Catalonia was conquered, and the battle was over.

THE FALL OF MADRID

In February 1939, there were four armies and 500,000 troops in the Central Zone of what remained of Republican Spain. There were also about 27 attack aircraft (Natachas), 18 bombers (Katiuskas), and 30 fighters (I-15s and I-16s), along with several miscellaneous combat aircraft and another 100 fighters nearing completion at the Alicante factory.⁷³ Could the Republicans have fought on with such a force for another three months? Six months? More? On paper, the answer would be yes. They could have employed tactics similar to those that had saved them in the winter of 1936–37, when the Nationalists had threatened Madrid, or similar to those employed in the spring of 1938, when the Nationalists had advanced toward Valencia. The defenders could have used interior lines to reinforce weak points in the salient; used urban environments to lure the enemy into door-to-door fighting; and exploited their knowledge of the local topography to defend in depth and force a war of attrition. The attackers would have had to fight for every inch of territory. The Republican antiaircraft artillery could have provided significant coverage against enemy bombers, and even the diminished air force could have achieved some check on Nationalist air dominance, if used wisely. The Republicans might have even executed diversionary attacks, as they did during the Northern Campaign, to at least delay a final assault.

Something similar, in fact, had been attempted in the winter of 1938–39, when General Vincente Rojo finally was able to launch his Estremaduran-Andalusian offensive, variously referred to as Pozoblanco, or Peñaroya. The campaign met with some initial success, and it took a few weeks for the Nationalists to attain local air superiority. At the beginning of the battle, there was only a single mixed group of aircraft and one Fiat squadron in the sector. On January 23, the Republicans shot down an aircraft and found in the uniform of the dead pilot a cigarette case with García Morato's initials engraved upon them. They thus assumed they had killed the greatest of Nationalist aces. The pilot was in fact Captain Mánuel Vázquez Sagastizábal, himself an ace to whom García Morato had given his cigarette case as a gift. The Republicans had killed Patroclus but not Achilles. Eventually, Nationalist reinforcements arrived in the air and ground, and the Republicans were driven back to the original starting lines by February 4, taking some 40,000 casualties.[74]

Could further, less costly offensives have been conducted to keep the Nationalists off balance and oblige them to reinforce areas of the front threatened by sudden Republican advances? Again, theoretically, this would have been possible. In reality, apart from Negrín and those in his immediate sphere, few in Republican Spain had the spirit to continue the war. At the time of the conquest of Catalonia, in early February 1939, the garrison of Minorca rebelled and surrendered to the first Nationalist officer they could find. The spirit of defeat seemed to have infected the highest ranks of the military, leaving few who supported any continued resistance. This became clear on February 16, when Prime Minister Negrín met with his commanders at Albacete. With the remarkable exception of Miaja (now Generalissimo of Republican forces), the commanders favored an immediate call for peace.[75] These appeals fell on deaf ears. Negrín rejected their advice and encouraged his commanders to continue to hold out. He established his new capital at Elda, near the coast. There may have been legitimate reasons for selecting such a location, but it was far from the front and, once again, suggested that the Republican leadership had one foot out of Spain while encouraging the people and troops to endure.

Consequently, Negrín's arguments held no sway with most of the officers, who considered the war lost and calls for further resistance delusional. Foremost among these was Colonel Segismundo Casado, the commander of the Army of the Center, headquartered in Madrid. He had served with the Republicans throughout the war and was known for his hard work and efficiency. He did not trust Negrín or the communists, whom Casado assumed controlled him, and he came to see continued resistance as cruel and hypocritical.[76] After the fall of Barcelona, Casado's primary efforts were to broker a peace with the Nationalists. He initiated contact, and on February 20 met directly with Franco's agents. His plan was simple: seize control of the government, subdue the communists, and call for an immediate cease fire and negotiations for peace. He was not subtle in his machinations. He attempted to bring Hidalgo de Cisneros into the conspiracy, but Hidalgo instead informed Negrín, who took no action.[77] It is unclear whether Negrín was biding his time until he could more confidently crush Casado, whether he thought he could win Casado back into the fold, or whether he realized there was nothing he could do. Regardless, time was running out on the Negrín administration. On February 27, 1939, France and Great Britain recognized the Franco regime.

March 5 was the fateful day. Casado and a socialist politician named Julián Besteiro announced the illegitimacy of Negrín's authority and established the National Council of Defense in Madrid. Insurgents rose up and seized control of key locations in Cartagena. The Republican fleet sailed to Bizerta in French-controlled Tunisia. Also that day, a Bf 109B flown by a German officer named Von Bonin shot down an I-15 over Alicante, the final aerial victory of the war.[78] In spite of all the misfortune for Negrín's government, there were still loyal units, particularly among the communist forces. The new insurgents (or Casadists) had to fight to establish their hold on power. The prime minister, for his part, was not present to encourage his champions in their struggle. On March 6, he held a meeting with other leaders, including La Pasionaria, to consider their options. They apparently decided that all they could do within Spain had been done, and that prudence dictated an immediate egress. They then promptly departed the country by aircraft—aviation

Map 5. Nationalist-Republican Territory, March 1939

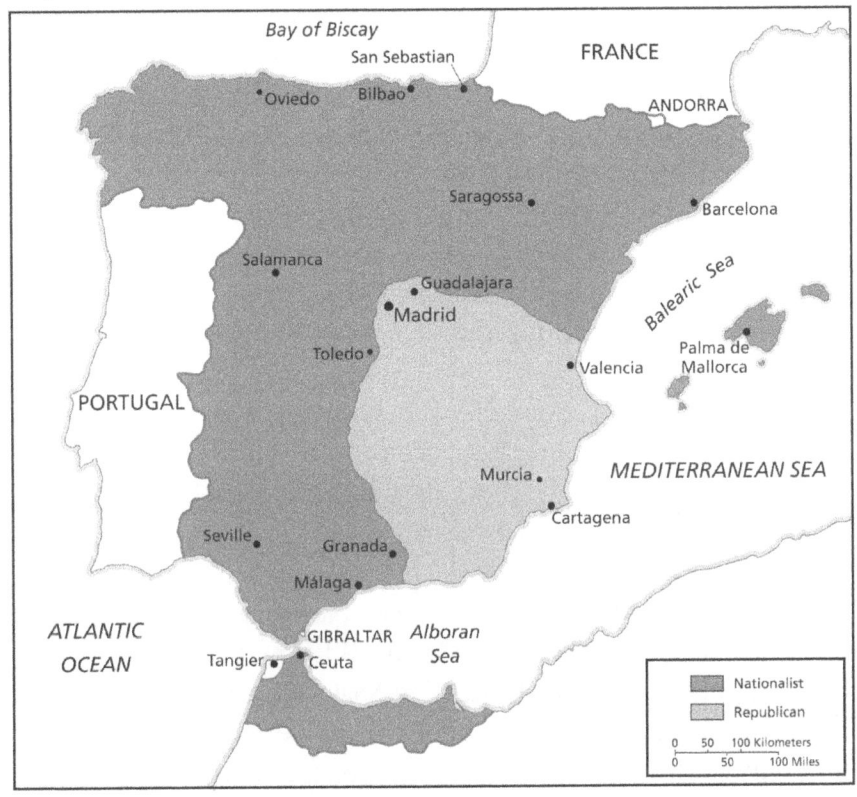

once again having a clear impact on the course of events in this war. Miaja yielded to the necessity of the moment, remained behind, traveled to Madrid, and assumed a leading position in the National Council.[79] With the situation in Spain in hand, the Germans were on the move elsewhere. On March 15, Nazi troops marched into Prague, absorbing the remainder of Czechoslovakia and making a mockery of the much-heralded Munich agreement. Great Britain and France were humiliated and angered. The much-anticipated continental war seemed imminent, but it would not come soon enough for Republican Spain.

The internecine fighting in the Central Zone could be interpreted as a replay of the fighting in Barcelona in May 1937: The Casadists were largely anarchists and their opponents were largely communists. This time, however, the results were reversed, and the communists were defeated. Communication with the Nationalists resumed and negotiations commenced in Burgos. If Casado thought that his accommodationist approach would win any concessions from Franco, he was soon disillusioned. On March 25, the Nationalists called off negotiations. The next day, their armies advanced on all fronts. Under such circumstances, how could any Republican officer rouse his men to hold off the relentless foe? Doubtless some tried, and many brave men followed, and many were wounded or killed; but their efforts and sacrifices were subsumed in the flood of defeatism and surrender. The Republican Army quickly dissolved. The next day, Casado, finding his schemes gone awry, fled to Valencia.[80] Then, on March 28, the Nationalists marched into Madrid, a city that had resisted assault and siege for two-and-a-half years. Miaja, the master survivalist, managed to escape by plane to Oran, while Casado exited Spain on the British vessel HMS *Galatea*. On March 30, Valencia, which had stood strong and defiant behind the XYZ Line in the spring of 1938, yielded to the triumphant Nationalists, who took an estimated 35,000 prisoners.[81] Cartagena, the last key city in Spain, was secured the next day.[82] On April 1, after thirty-three months of fighting, Franco declared that all of Spain was under the control of his forces. Cheadle, in his dispatch sent two days later, summarized the conflict when he wrote, "This war, which lasted for 989 days, has been one of the longest, bloodiest, costliest and most brutal internecine struggles of modern history."[83] As the Nationalists themselves declared in a communiqué, "The red army having been captured and disarmed and the last military objectives attained, THE WAR IS OVER."[84]

CHAPTER 10

AFTER-ACTION REPORT

'Tis sunset of life gives me mystical lore,
And coming events cast their shadow before.

—THOMAS CAMPBELL, "LOCHIEL'S WARNING"

U.S. AIRPOWER, APRIL 1939–DECEMBER 1941

A Francoist peace had come to Spain, but peace in Europe was tentative and fleeting. Germany's seizure of the remnant of Czechoslovakia, followed soon after by Italy's occupation of Albania, put Britain and France on notice that the Axis powers were emboldened and expansive, and that further appeasement, like that offered at Munich, would offer only temporary respite from further aggression. On September 1, 1939, German troops invaded Poland, and Britain and France declared war. (The Soviet Union also invaded Poland, and later Finland, but these aggressions went unchallenged by the Allies.) Events followed in rapid succession until Germany and its ally Italy were in control of much of Europe, including a defeated France. The cause of the Allies was saved in the summer of 1940 with the British victory in the Battle of Britain, an exclusively aerial conflict between the RAF and the Luftwaffe. The Axis invasion of the Soviet Union on June 22, 1941, seems to have been the height of insanity or hubris, but it initially succeeded in conquering large swaths of territory and destroying much of the Red Army. Meanwhile, in the Pacific, Germany's fellow Axis member Japan continued its conquest of mainland China. Thus, an ultimate Axis victory on all fronts seemed a likely outcome. It was at this point that eyes turned toward the one world power that had thus far maintained its neutrality: the United States.

The leaders of America had not remained idle during the course of these world-shaking events. Particularly, the need for a strong Air Force had been made clear by the wide-ranging global crisis. As early as January 1939, President Roosevelt announced his determination to increase the size of the U.S. aircraft inventory. He set a goal of 6,000 aircraft, and an obliging Congress appropriated $300 million to the Air Corps ($6,723 million in 2025 dollars). The United States had much ground to make up compared to other leading powers. In September 1939, there were only 800 modern combat aircraft in the American inventory; Britain had 2,000; France, 1,700; and Germany, 3,600.[1] In May 1940,

Photo 8. On May 5, 1939, waves of aircraft flew over Madrid, not in aggression, but in celebration of the Nationalist Victory. *Hoffman Prints, NARA*

Roosevelt increased the objective to 11,000 total aircraft, with 50,000 as a stretch goal upon the full mobilization of the domestic aircraft industry. Aircraft production expanded by a great degree during this period. In November 1940, American factories were turning out 50 military aircraft per week, a rate that would produce 2,600 aircraft per year. In 1941, this rose to an average of 365 aircraft per week, for a total of 19,000 for the entire year, more than a sevenfold increase.[2]

Being a constitutional republic that honored property rights and free enterprise, the American government could not merely will these aircraft into existence; instead, it had to work closely with industry to make Roosevelt's goal a reality. As such, at the end of July 1940, General H. H. Arnold met with the presidents of Douglas, Curtiss, Consolidated Aircraft, North American Aviation, Martin, and Lockheed and the vice president of Boeing to discuss their plans for facility expansion to meet the government demand. Arnold explained to the industry heads that the Army required 6,882 aircraft by April 1, 1941, and another 6,002 within the following twelve months. The businessmen unanimously replied to the Air Corps chief that they would require cost plus fixed fee (CPFF) contracts to mitigate the risks of undertaking such orders.[3]

With CPFF contracts, the contractors would be reimbursed for their expenses (up to a not-to-exceed amount, and with certain conditions as to which type of expenses were allowable) and also receive a set dollar amount as a fee for profit over and above their expenses. Such contracts remain highly appealing to industry as they help share the risk between buyer and seller, particularly when the ultimate cost of a project is unknown at time of contract award. And they are attractive contracts, especially in contrast to firm fixed price (FFP) contracts, in which the final price (including both cost and profit) is established up front, regardless of contractor expenses. At the National Defense Council meeting on July 2–3, 1940, the War Department had expressed its opposition to CPFF contracts for acquisitions other than construction contracts.[4] However, Arnold now urged the secretary to reverse that policy, an action indicative of the urgency of the situation.[5]

Fortunately for Arnold, he benefited from his close working relationship with Army chief of staff General George Marshall. Their informal agreement was that aviation strength and philosophy, including support for strategic bombing, would become military priorities, while the push for Air Corps independence would be postponed. Both Marshall and Arnold held to this arrangement, and American aviation received a priority, if not a preeminence, in American strategic alignment. In June 1941, the U.S. Army Air Forces (USAAF) was formed, absorbing the General Headquarters Air Force (GHQAF; rechristened "Combat Command") and the Air Corps. Arnold retained his Air Corps command while also assuming the position of chief in the USAAF. Thereafter, he would be included in Combined Chiefs of Staff meetings, taking a seat alongside the chiefs of the Army and Navy in their meetings with their British counterparts.[6]

Thus supported in its priorities and administrative integrity, the Air Corps/USAAF grew at a startling rate in both manpower and matériel. Total personnel increased from 26,000 in September 1939 to 300,000 in December 1941.[7] As for combat ready aircraft, a report from Arnold's office sent to Assistant Secretary of War Robert Lovett indicated that, as of January 31, 1941, the GHQAF could field two groups of heavy or medium bombers (B-17s and B-23s), two groups of pursuits (P-40s and P-39s), and a squadron of A-20A light bombers, constituting 279 aircraft in all.[8] A month later, this number had grown to 348 aircraft.[9] By April 1942, the USAAF possessed a total of 14,397 aircraft (up from 1,709 in July 1939), of which 4,310 were combat capable (only 1,239 had previously been combat capable), along with 22,057 flight school graduates (2,457 previously), 99 flight schools (11 previously), and 217 bases (69 previously).[10]

If the USAAF inventory was not growing at an even faster pace, it was due to the United States' support of Britain in its war against Germany. Since the beginning of the war, the United States had moved from a position of committed neutrality to a condition of virtual alliance with Britain and near belligerency toward the Axis powers. It had started cautiously by selling aircraft to Britain and requiring the British representatives to retrieve the deliverables at the factories themselves.[11] In the summer of 1940, during the Battle of Britain, representatives from the U.S. Army (including Arnold) and Navy met with representatives from Britain to discuss quantities to be purchased and possible standardization in design to meet British specifications.[12] As a result of these discussions, a tentative agreement was reached in which 14,375 aircraft would be delivered to the British by April 1, 1942, while 12,884 were to be supplied to the U.S. Army and 6,208 to the Navy. Such figures caused much concern in American military circles, as the number to be supplied to the Army was "the minimum required for the augmentation of tactical squadrons essential to the National Defense," according to Assistant Secretary of War Robert Patterson.[13] Nevertheless, this policy set the stage for more overt support. In March 1941, the U.S. government enacted the Lend Lease Act, which allowed it to "lend" rather than sell matériel to Britain for the duration of the war. Starting in May 1941, U.S. Air Corps pilots began to fly aircraft from the factory to the hand-off point.[14] The U.S. support to Britain was so extensive that Arnold attempted to raise alarm with his superiors as to the risks incurred to American military readiness. As he wrote to Stimson on October 16, 1941,

> These efforts in the diversion of aircraft from the Army Air Forces is having a disastrous effect on the organization of an effective United States Army Air Force. The lack of airplanes in our tactical units is highly destructive to the morale of our flying personnel.
>
> The state of mind of the American public also is to be considered in this situation. They are expending billions of dollars anticipating the organization of an efficient Army Air Force and unless the United States Army Air Forces are furnished with the proper equipment, this public will be confronted with a net result of having a lot of trained pilots with very poor morale, trained only on primary and advanced training planes.[15]

These concerns would soon be overcome by events. Within six weeks of Arnold's warning, the Japanese would attack the American fleet at Pearl Harbor, and the United States would be plunged into the war as a full-fledged belligerent.

CHAPTER 10

CONCLUSIONS

With this history having reached America's entry into the Second World War, it is now appropriate to take a final look at the air operations of the Spanish Civil War and to consider what relevance that conflict held for American airpower then, and now.

Airpower played a critical role in the Spanish Nationalists' victory. This is not to claim that it was the decisive factor, for that would be the comparative *unity of effort* achieved by the Nationalists, centered around the person of General Francisco Franco. However, airpower was a key *contributor* to the decisive factor, as it enabled Franco's rise to paramountcy in the Nationalist cause. His flight upon the Dragon Rapide brought him from isolation on the Canary Islands to Morocco, to take control of the army there. The airlift brought that army to the mainland and changed the balance of forces on the Peninsula. When Franco's troops swept through Andalusia and Estremadura on the way to Madrid, they were supported by air cover. The aircraft that provided airlift and air cover were provided mostly by Germany and Italy, whose governments pledged their support to Franco personally, not to the Nationalist cause generally. Further support was thus contingent on his leadership in Spain.

Aircraft also contributed indirectly to clearing the field of potential rivals to Franco's preeminence: Sanjurjo, the would-be leader of the coup, was killed when his aircraft crashed while attempting to take off from a runway near Lisbon, Portugal; Mola, Sanjurjo's right-hand man and Franco's leading competitor, was killed in the summer of 1937 when his aircraft crashed during the Northern Campaign; Goded's flight from the Balearics (where he had successfully taken over Mallorca) to Barcelona resulted in his arrest and later execution. These key flights and airpower in general thus enabled Franco to become the unrivaled generalissimo of the military and caudillo of the government early in the war. Together, these events brought cohesion to the disparate elements of the Nationalist cause and united their resources for the common objective of victory. By contrast, the Republicans underwent five changes in government within the first year of the war and were unable to achieve a long-term unity that was necessary to defeat the Nationalists.

AFTER-ACTION REPORT

As for airpower functions and their relative impact: the airlift conducted August through October 1936 was the most consequential air mission of the entire war. The transport of 13,000 troops from Africa to the Peninsula shifted the balance of forces on the mainland and allowed Franco to seize the initiative, capture much of Estremadura, and threaten Madrid. A sea convoy did carry about 3,000 troops across the Straits of Gibraltar in early August, but this was not repeated due to the risk presented by the Republican-dominated navy. By transporting a major portion of the Army of Africa across the straits in two months, the airlift provided critical support to the Nationalists at their most vulnerable time early in the war.

Although some air operations in the Spanish Civil War resembled those of the First World War or other earlier conflicts, they were distinguishable from those conflicts in the following ways:

1. The strategic impact of the airlift;
2. The consistently successful use of both airborne and ground-based counterair measures against bombers;
3. The prominent use of large-caliber aircraft cannons and incendiary bombs;
4. The extensive use of aerial photography; and
5. The increased acceptance of the machine-gunning of pilots parachuting from their damaged aircraft.

This work has focused on American observations of the conflict. Thus, the opinions of Capt. Townsend Griffiss, as assistant military attaché for air for Spain, are of particular interest. Several of the direct lessons from the use of airpower in Spain came from his dispatches. These lessons included the following:

1. Air superiority was key to victory on the ground;
2. Bombers, being vulnerable to interception, required their own pursuit escorts;
3. Speed was more important than firepower in aerial combat;

4. Tactical coordination between the different air functions of pursuit, bombing, and attack was highly effective; and
5. Training must resemble combat as closely as possible.

Aside from military attachés' observations, American pilots who flew in Spain obviously came away with their own unique perspectives. Albert "Ajax" Baumler was one of the top two American fighter pilots to fly in Spain, the other being Frank Tinker. Unlike Tinker, who decided to write an adventurous memoir of his time there, Baumler agreed to divulge his knowledge in his lengthy correspondence with intel officer Maj. Edward Raley. His answers to Raley's inquiries can thus be considered representative of the American airmen's experience in Spain. His responses were generally more tactical in nature but had some operational or strategic implications.

Baumler favored specialization in aircraft, with high-speed monoplanes providing counterair defenses and maneuverable biplanes providing offensive counterair and close air support.[16] When asked to describe his ideal pursuit aircraft, should only one type be possible, his description closely resembled the I-16 Mosca: a monoplane with four machine guns, a radio receiver, and retractable landing gear. However, he desired a high-powered machine of 1,500 hp, which neither the I-16 nor contemporary American pursuits could match.[17] The North American P-51 Mustang (introduced in 1940) seems to have most closely resembled Baumler's ideal.

Baumler further indicated that bombings of runways tended to have more definitive impacts than attacks on roadways. When asked by Raley to elaborate, he stated that although vehicles on roads can drive around bomb craters, such detours are not possible for aircraft taking off or landing on runways.[18] He also refuted the notion that bombers were invulnerable to interception. As for defensive counterair, he noted, "Bombers, caught by pursuit, and having no pursuit escort will invariably try to escape. I have never heard of a bombing squadron completing a mission when pursuit was present, at their altitude and location."[19]

The issue of what airpower lessons American military leaders may have learned from the war is the key and most difficult question. For one must consider both what American officers said and what they did. General Arnold, in his speech to the Bond Club in Philadelphia in May 1938, minimized any lessons that could be learned from the Spanish Civil War, because aircraft there were used for general support operations rather than as independent striking forces.

Similarly, Maj. George Kenney, who would become a general and Air Force commander in the Pacific during the Second World War, minimized the impact of air operations in an article for *U.S. Air Services* in July 1938. For him, the lessons from the war were limited due to the small size of the forces involved (numbering at most 1,000 at any one time). There was some evidence of improvement in the effectiveness of antiaircraft weaponry, but this could be matched and overcome by increases in bomber speed. Kenney acknowledged the importance of the airlift, yet he also qualified it as hardly unique, considering that airlift missions had been previously executed by the British in the Middle East, the Italians in Ethiopia, and the Japanese in Manchuria. He did stress that the Spanish Civil War had shown, to his satisfaction, that a nation cannot rely on the conversion of commercial aircraft to military use in wartime. Yet, his ultimate assessment was a common one in the U.S. Air Corps, "Air Power has not been tested in Spain to date."[20]

Yet, if the leadership of U.S. Air Corps, and later the U.S. Army Air Force, were outwardly dismissive of the significance of the Spanish Civil War, they seemed to have somehow internalized some of its lessons. For instance, they recognized that aircraft other than medium and heavy bombers were important. Several pursuit models were introduced in the United States during the period from 1936 to 1941. These included the Curtiss P-36 (introduced 1937), Seversky P-35 (1937), Lockheed P-38 (1938), Bell P-39 (1939), Curtiss P-40 (1939), North American P-51 (1940), and Republic P-47B (1941). In 1940, although the Air Corps plans included a quintupling of the number of heavy bombers from 38 to 178, and more than a doubling the number of medium bombers, from 225 to 562, they also included a near tripling in the number of pursuit aircraft, from 393 to 1,094.[21] As late as February 1941, the first line combat strength of the USAAF included 208 pursuits and 101 heavy and medium bombers, approximately a two-to-one ratio.[22]

This was the ratio recommended by Griffiss in his "Special Report" of February 1937.²³

Moreover, the importance of transport aircraft was recognized by Arnold, and during his tenure the purchase of aircraft dedicated to that purpose increased significantly. At the end of 1939, there were only 78 such aircraft in the regular Air Corps inventory, with only 5 more planned for 1941.²⁴ However, between September 1940 and September 1941, the Air Corps/USAAF ordered 1,282 transport aircraft, including C-46s, C-47s, C-53s, and C-54s. Several of these models were originally intended for civilian use but were subsequently diverted to military purposes during production.²⁵

A major consideration was the extent to which the effectiveness of strategic bombing was proven or disproven by the war. Douhet's theory, strictly interpreted, was not sustainable following the Spanish Civil War. He had anticipated that the civilian populations and political classes of both sides would clamor for peace upon the first bombing of their cities. This did not happen. He argued that defensive counterair was wasteful, based on his assumptions that attacking bombers could not be consistently intercepted or shot down by antiaircraft weaponry. Yet in Spain, pursuits were often able to intercept bombers and antiaircraft artillery struck a number of targets with increasing accuracy and range. Thus the short, decisive air war described by Douhet did not come to pass, and bombers did not have free rein over the skies.

However, was the opposite true? The lecturer at the Command and General Staff School at Fort Leavenworth insisted in December 1937 that bombing only strengthened the resolve of the targeted populations and prolonged the war. This, too, was not supported by evidence. One must consider the results reported by Stephen Fuqua of the bombing of Barcelona in the spring of 1938, where Italian raids caused widespread panic and resulted in the shut-down of many of the city's operations for several days.

Nor should the qualifying circumstances mentioned by other airpower advocates, like Arnold, Kenney, and the editors of *U.S. Air Services*, be dismissed. A civil war is different from a foreign war. If one is attempting to unite a country and possess its property at the end of the war, it is reasonable that one would be reluctant to fully unleash the destructive power of aerial bombardment. At the siege of Madrid, Franco had restricted bombing by declaring a safe zone within the city. As the American journalist Edward Knoblaugh pointed out, the defenders were more than satisfied to take full military advantage of this guarantee. Further, it is a legitimate qualification that each side in the war lacked a large-scale striking force capable of sustaining a bombing operation. American airpower leaders were not strict adherents to Douhetism—many may not have read him before the appearance of the 1942 English translation of his *Command of the Air*. They adopted instead a more nuanced approach that saw airpower being used as an instrument of indirect warfare, causing critical damage to industry and infrastructure and thus making sustained warfare impossible for the defender. Of course, this required a certain level of precision, which Griffiss indicated was not readily apparent in bombing operations during the Spanish Civil War. The case of Guernica, where the village was destroyed but the targeted bridge left intact, pressed home this point. In summary, the Spanish Civil War did not give a decisive answer to the full capabilities of strategic bombing. That would have to await the next war.

As for the development of aerial technology: It was a very important factor in the war. The aircraft that were flown in Spain represented the latest advances in the field of aeronautical engineering. The trends from wood to metal, biplane to monoplane, fixed landing gear to retractable landing gear, and even from machine gun to cannon were evident over the course of the three years of fighting. These changes in design drove changes in tactics that, in turn, exposed new vulnerabilities that would need to be compensated for. For instance, the original German bombers in Spain, the Junkers Ju 52, were vulnerable to attacks from the front due to their relative slowness and lack of a forward-facing turret. These aircraft were therefore replaced by the Junkers Ju 86, which was faster than the Ju 52 and had a forward-facing turret. And these were then replaced by the Heinkel He 111, which was faster still than the Ju 86 and could fly at a higher ceiling. A similar improvement in capabilities marked the replacement of the Heinkel He 51 fighter with the Messerschmitt Bf 109. The timely arrival of the Russian I-15 Chato biplanes and I-16 Mosca monoplanes helped save Madrid from occupation in the fall of 1936 and represented the advantages of simple-construction, single-purpose platforms. It was a similar case with the R-5 Resantes and R-Z Natachas, which were the only dedicated ground-attack aircraft to appear in Spain in significant numbers. However, the Russian inability to innovate as quickly as the Germans, due in part to Stalin's purge of engineers, eventually tipped the scales in aerial technology in the Germans' favor. The gradual air superiority verging on air supremacy achieved by the Nationalist air forces owes much to this growing disparity in technologies.

Not only were changes in aerial platforms significant, but changes to munitions and air defense were significant as well. The trend toward incendiary bombs as opposed to high-explosive bombs indicates that aerial bombing could have effects on targets long after the bombings took place. It was insufficient to merely escape the initial impact and blast; those on the ground now had to deal with quickly spreading fires that could cost more lives and severely damage infrastructure. Guernica was perhaps the starkest example of the potency of aerial bombardment with incendiaries. Just as impactful to air operations were the improvements to the accuracy and range of antiaircraft artillery. These provided a new factor for attacking aircraft to consider. Early in the war, ground fire could reach up to 4,500 feet. By 1939, German 88-mm FLAK artillery possessed an effective range of 12,000 feet. A city defended by sufficient antiaircraft artillery could thus pose a threat to low-flying daylight bombers. This again drove a change in tactics to night bombing or high-altitude bombing and negated Douhet's assumption that such defenses were unreliable.

In several ways, the airpower experiences of the Spanish Civil War were applicable to the Second World War. These included the following: the effectiveness of antiaircraft defense; the need for pursuit escorts; the importance of airlift and transport aircraft; the effectiveness of single-role aircraft; the advantages of streamlined pursuits; the importance in redundancy in airfields and lines of communication; and the lack of precision in combat bombing. However, we see among American military leaders that these lessons were unacknowledged, if not outright disregarded. In part, this was because there were a mere five months between the end of the war in Spain and the beginning of the Second World War. It was from this larger conflict among the major powers that American observers were more likely to draw lessons, particularly in regard to the role that aircraft played in the blitzkrieg and the Battle of Britain. The fact that many of these lessons were similar to the ones on display in Spain suggests that lessons of the earlier conflict should have been more greatly appreciated.

However, it is a legitimate argument that strategic bombing as envisioned by airpower advocates was not truly tested in the Spanish Civil War and would have to await a conflict of a much larger scale. For instance, the May 1937 bombing of Valencia was conducted by six medium bombers dropping 90 bombs, totaling about 15 tons. Outside Bilbao at the Iron Ring on June 12, 1937, a total of 100–110 tons of bombs were dropped on multiple defensive positions along the front. By contrast, during the "Big Week," of February 19–26, 1944, Allied bombers would unleash 19,000 tons of bombs on 20 industrial targets in Germany, averaging 118–35 tons per target per day.[26]

Finally, the airpower lessons of the Spanish Civil War are still applicable today. We saw repeatedly how air superiority proved decisive in several battles, including at Teruel and in the Aragon Campaign, until it eventually became impossible for an army to take the field against an enemy with air superiority. Apart from the obvious benefits of close air support, aircraft proved that they could operate in ways unique to the air domain to bring about operational and even strategic-level effects through the functions of airlift and reconnaissance. Even strategic bombing, though not of the magnitude envisioned by airpower advocates, proved to have an outsized effect on its targets. Tactically, Werner Mölders's "finger four" pattern, in which two pairs of aircraft, each consisting of a lead and a wingman, operated in coordination, replaced the traditional three-plane V-formation. It would be adopted by the British RAF during the Second World War and then passed onto their American allies. U.S. fighter pilots would continue to use this tactic throughout the Cold War.[27]

Ultimately, the Spanish Civil War proved that airpower could execute a spectrum of different, unique capabilities in warfare. It could (on the two extremes) provide direct support to ground forces or perform long-distance bombing missions; but it could also conduct offensive and defensive counterair operations, the interdiction of reinforcements, aerial reconnaissance of enemy territory, and the airlifting of friendly troops. And these functions consistently contributed to the success of the entire force. Thus, the theories of Mecozzi, Slessor, and Chennault were vindicated by the events of 1936–39 in Spain.

FATES, UP TO DECEMBER 1941

The participants and observers of the Spanish Civil War did not have long to contemplate their lot. Several of them would be swept into the global crisis of the Second World War. Many would lose their lives. The frequency of noncombat deaths among the pilots is striking and indicative of the inherent risk involved in flight—a fact evident since the death of Lieutenant Selfridge back in 1908, when Orville Wright's Flyer crashed to the ground. What follows is a short summary of the fates of several individuals who appeared in the above narrative, in rough chronological order of events.

Joaquín García Morato: On April 4, 1939, a mere three days after the end of the Spanish Civil War, Nationalist Spain's greatest ace pilot participated in flying stunts for the filming of a movie about the Condor Legion. During a climb, his Fiat stalled and fell to the earth. It shattered on impact and García Morato was killed instantly.[28]

Anatoly Serov: On May 11, 1939, General Anatoly Serov was killed in a test crash along with famed aviatrix Polina Osipenko. In spite of his wartime heroics and high rank, it was Serov's copilot whose death garnered greater attention from the Soviet authorities. Stalin even served as a pallbearer at Osipenko's funeral.[29]

Frank Tinker: During the afternoon of June 13, 1939, a bellhop of the McGehee Hotel in Little Rock, Arkansas, was dispatched to check on a guest in Room 1013. That morning, the hotel's switchboard had gone out. When it had come back on, it was seen that the phone in this guest's room was off the hook. The bellhop arrived at the door and knocked repeatedly. Upon receiving no answer, he entered and found Tinker lying unconscious on his bed. Blood was on the sheets and a

.22 caliber pistol was on a chair near the bed. Medical assistance was summoned, but the patient died before appropriate treatment could be rendered. A gunshot wound was located below his heart. His death was ruled a suicide. He was buried in DeWitt Cemetery under a stone with the phrase "¿Quién Sabe?" ("Who Knows?").[30]

Stephen Fuqua: Having retired from active service and completed his civilian role in Spain, Fuqua returned to the United States with his wife and daughter. He would put his vast experience and knowledge to use writing a military column for *Newsweek*, analyzing the progress of the Second World War.[31]

Indalecio Prieto: Bereft of a country, Spanish Republican officials in France loaded many of their valuables onto the ship *Vita*, which proceeded across the Atlantic Ocean to Mexico. Prieto, former minister of Maritime and Air, was waiting for the ship to arrive and took possession of it, controversially establishing his influence over the Republican government-in-exile there.[32]

Alfredo Kindelán: The chief of the Nationalist Air Force, having seen the success of his side and of his champion, Francisco Franco, expected an immediate restoration of the monarchy. When this did not happen, Kindelán began to lobby more insistently, but unsuccessfully. Nonetheless, he still, for the time, retained the good graces of his caudillo and was promoted to lieutenant general in 1940.[33]

Ernest Hemingway: In 1940, Hemingway published the Spanish Civil War novel *For Whom the Bell Tolls*. The hero of the story, Robert Jordan, is an American volunteer and explosives expert sent to blow up a bridge behind enemy lines with the assistance of a guerrilla unit. The moral of the story is the importance of duty and selflessness in the face of increasingly hopeless odds. Hemingway's characters are vivid, particularly the shady guerrilla leader Pablo and his spirited *mujer* Pilar. The book features some of the most riveting scenes in American literature, such as the murder of the "fascists" in Pilar's home village and the mental breakdown of Pilar's ex-lover, a *matador de toros*.

Harold "Whitey" Dahl: The true-life story of Whitey Dahl would match any fiction Hemingway could have devised for him. Dahl had survived gambling debts, military discharge, a shoot-down, an escape back to friendly territory, the Hotel Florida's elevator, a debilitating stomach ailment, and another shoot-down, this time resulting in his capture. He was convicted of rebellion by a Nationalist court-martial and sentenced to death; but that sentence was commuted in apparent response to the appeals of his wife, the actress Edith Dahl neé Rogers, and his mother—though some behind-the-scenes cajoling by the State Department certainly played a role. His life spared, no one seemed eager to secure his release. He instead sat out the rest of the war in captivity, but also in relative comfort. It was not until February 21, 1940, that he was released. He disembarked in New York City on March 18. As he waited for Edith to arrive, Dahl regaled reporters with stories of his six aerial victories, though the actual figure may have been between two or four. When his wife finally arrived, she stayed only briefly for a photo opportunity before departing. They both later claimed their marriage had never been legitimate. Two days later, he was arrested for writing bad checks on his old debts; but he was released due to the excessive costs of extraditing him to California to stand trial. A less spirited man would have counted himself fortunate and resigned himself to a quiet, humble life of freedom. But Dahl was an adventurer, and for all his faults, he could fly. He moved to Canada, found love, married, and joined the Royal Canadian Air Force as a flight instructor. He would later become a squadron leader of an air transport unit. His adventures did not end there, but one must consult other histories for them.[34]

Werner Mölders: Like García Morato, Mölders was the leading ace among his nation's pilots during the Spanish Civil War, having won fourteen victories. Like Serov, he had attained the rank of general following his service in the war, as commander of Luftwaffe fighters. And like both of them, he died in a noncombat accident, crashing in Czechoslovakia in 1941, on his way to attend the funeral of General Ernst Udet.[35]

Wolfram von Richthofen: The former commander of the Condor Legion found further opportunities, advancements, and (initially) success with the Luftwaffe throughout the Second World War. In September 1939, he commanded an air division in the invasion of Poland; in May 1940, he commanded VII Air Corps, providing air support for the blitzkrieg through the Ardennes, outflanking the French Army; and starting in the summer of 1941, he served first as an air corps commander and then as an air fleet commander against the Soviet Union. The forces under von Richthofen's command crippled and almost destroyed the Soviet Air Force, the VVS, in the early stages of the invasion.[36]

Bruno Mussolini: On August 7, 1941, twenty-three-year-old Bruno Mussolini was test-piloting a heavy bomber in Pisa. He lost control and the aircraft crashed, injuring five and killing three, himself included. Il Duce, as soon as he was notified of his son's death, traveled to Pisa with his family to view the corpse in the hospital and to preside over the funeral the next day. The coffin was buried at Predappio, Romagna, the traditional home of the Mussolini clan.[37]

Yakov Smushkevich: Stalin's purges had taken a toll on the readiness of the Soviet Air Force, the VVS. By June 22, 1941, 43 percent of the officers of the VVS had less than six months experience. Its aircraft inventory was quickly becoming obsolete. Twenty-five percent of its fighter aircraft were biplanes. The monoplane I-16 Moscas, so impressive in the Spanish Civil War, were the most numerous fighters in the VVS, but the development of their capabilities had not kept pace with the latest in aviation technology. Consequently, on the first day of the Nazi invasion, 336 aircraft were destroyed in the air and another 800 were destroyed on the ground.[38] The blame for this catastrophe obviously could not be placed on Stalin, so another sacrifice was required. The burden fell on Smushkevich. Unlike other high-ranking military officers, he had prospered after his service in the Spanish Civil War. Upon returning to Russia in 1937, he was hailed as a Hero of the Soviet Union and was appointed to the position of deputy chief of the VVS. In 1940, he had been promoted to inspector general. Ultimately, this only set him up to be held accountable for the subsequent disaster, and he was shot on Stalin's order on October 28, 1941.[39]

Francisco Franco: Nationalist Spain became a fascist dictatorship in all but name under Franco's rule. On August 8, 1939, the "law of head of state" gave him sole power to institute laws. A council of ministers was available in an administrative capacity, but this could be dispensed with at Franco's prerogative. There was little doubt as to where true power resided. The government assumed direct control over much of the economy, particularly in terms of the raw material markets and manufacturing. However, the economy was not socialistic; private property was preserved, and the wealthy and well-connected were privileged. Five large banks were granted a virtual oligopoly over the national finances. Private contractors were awarded state contracts for which they could utilize prisoners-of-war—of which there were some 500,000 by the end of the war.[40] Yet, Franco exercised a shrewdness that likely would save his regime and spare his nation from the horrors of the Second World War. He allowed volunteers to serve in the Blue Division during the invasion of the Soviet Union, in apparent revenge for the Russian intervention in the Spanish Civil War. However, he held back from a formal declaration of war against the Soviet Union, let alone against the Western Allies. He thus avoided the opprobrium in the West that met Mussolini when he cast his and Italy's lot with that of Hitler and Nazi Germany.[41]

Albert "Ajax" Baumler: Of all the American flyers who served in the Spanish Civil War, Baumler had undoubtedly the most successful post–civil war career. His correspondence with Maj. Edward Raley of the Intelligence sector must have assisted in his repatriation. He was welcomed back into the U.S. Army and earned promotion to first lieutenant. In October 1941, he was accepted into Maj. Claire Chennault's American Volunteer Group (AVG) in China. In December 1941, he crossed the Pacific on way to this new assignment, stopping at Wake Island before continuing. Subsequent developments would interrupt his plans.[42]

Edward Raley: In 1941, then-Lt. Col. Edward Raley was assigned to G-2 of the Hawaiian Air Force. In that capacity, he made contact with Lt. Cdr. Edwin Layton, an intelligence officer with the U.S. Pacific Fleet. According to Layton, he and Raley (whom he mistakenly called "Edwin") were in constant communication in late November 1941 regarding Japanese activity.[43] Due to bureaucratic complexities, the amount of information they could exchange was limited. However, some of the information, such as suspicions of a Japanese plan to provoke an incident with the British in Malaya in December 1941, would later become a topic of interest to the Congressional Pearl Harbor Board.[44]

Photo 9. Unlike his fellow American mercenaries, Albert Baumler had a successful return to American service as a pilot. Here, Lieutenant Colonel Baumler *(front-left)* with fellow officers in China, 1943. *U.S. Air Force*

TOWNSEND GRIFFISS' FINAL FLIGHT

On May 12, 1939, Captain Townsend Griffiss graduated from the Air Corps Tactical School (ACTS) along with seventy-five fellow officers. Maj. Gen. Henry "Hap" Arnold delivered the baccalaureate address, having personally flown his Douglas B-18 to Maxwell Field the day before.⁴⁵ He offered congratulations to the graduates, and dedicated much of his speech to describing the plans for Air Corps development in the near future. These included an aircraft inventory growth from 2,300 to 5,500 and an enlisted personnel increase by 25,000 men in two years, along with a 90 percent increase in the officer corps over the course of ten years. As he explained, these decisions were not made in a vacuum but in response to the changing nature of global politics and national security concerns. Arnold noted, "Even the casual student of world affairs must be cognizant of the tremendous change which air armaments have brought to bear on national policy, international negotiations and current diplomacy."⁴⁶

However, since airpower had reached a new level of prominence in military circles, there was now increased pressure to perform up to expectations. He added, "Now that we have sold a new idea in warfare, we must make doubly sure that it is not unsold by the poor performance of our air units."⁴⁷

As he drew to a close, he provided a hopeful vision of the near future: "Undoubtedly we shall be called upon for great effort during the next two years, but the result will justify your effort. The President's Air Program will be accomplished and we shall have covered the first mile in providing this nation with an adequate Air Defense."⁴⁸

With that, the graduates of ACTS were sent forth to enter the next stage of their careers as squadron and group commanders or as staff officers, forming the backbone of the military's most innovative branch. These men were in a unique situation, for theirs was the final class before the outbreak of general war in Europe. A year later, as practical training began to take precedence over education, ACTS itself would close.⁴⁹

Following his graduation, Griffiss continued to find himself billeted to plum assignments with high visibility and lucrative opportunities for advancement. He traveled to the nation's capital and served as air aide first to the Secretary of War and then to General Jacob Devers, who had been tasked with establishing bases on islands offered by the British for American use.⁵⁰ In May 1941, Griffiss, now a major, received orders to report to Maj. Gen. James Chaney in London, England, as a special Army observer.⁵¹ It was in this capacity that, on October 30, 1941, Griffiss was officially notified by the Office of the Adjutant General that he was to travel to Kuibyshev in the Soviet Union to "carry out the instructions of the Deputy Chief of Staff of the Army." He was to depart London on November 3—a mere four days hence—and was authorized to travel by any means, military or civilian, that would get him to his destination.[52]

A cablegram from Arnold to Brig. Gen. Joseph McNarney in London from October 28 clarified Griffiss's mission. He would be sent to receive from the Russians information on potential air routes for the transfer of aircraft and other supplies from the United States to the Soviet Union. Three routes were identified, all with ultimate destinations in Kuibyshev: two from Nome, Alaska, traveling westward across the Pacific and the expanse of Asian Russia; and one from Basra, Iraq, northeast to Askhabad on the Soviet side of its border with Iran, and then north to the final destination. The "courier" (i.e., Griffiss) was authorized to notify the Russian officials that the expeditious delivery of aircraft depended on such information. He was encouraged to stress the importance of the Siberian routes.[53]

Griffiss promptly set about executing his orders. He departed London on November 3, landing at Fownes, Ireland, later that day; the next morning, he flew to Lisbon. From there, he proceeded to Gibraltar, then Malta, and then to Cairo, arriving in the early morning of November 9. The next day, November 10, he flew to Habbiyina, Iraq. On November 12, he arrived in Tehran, Iran.[54] There he received a message from Chaney instructing him to "not quit the vicinity of Tehran" until notified to proceed into Russia.[55]

On November 21, a cable from the adjutant general informed Griffiss that he had been promoted to the temporary rank of lieutenant colonel.[56] It had taken him nineteen years as a commissioned officer to reach this level. Though the promotion was a temporary one, it would in all likelihood have been just the first step on a continuous, swift ascendency into the upper ranks of the American military, similar to what would also happen to other officers during the Second World War. Had it not been for the notoriously glacial pace of interwar promotions, Griffiss would probably already have been a permanent lieutenant colonel or even a full colonel.

Finally, on November 24, Griffiss received permission to enter the USSR, and had only to await Soviet-provided transportation.[57] On November 28, he departed Tehran, arriving first at Baku and then Astrakand, and finally at his long-awaited destination, Kuibyshev, on November 30. Upon arriving and speaking with officials at the American embassy, Griffiss learned that the Soviets had already received inquiries on air routes from three other sources: the American ambassador, the military attaché, and Col. Philip Faymonville of a Special Mission group. By the time Griffiss arrived, the Soviets had declined to provide any such information to the ambassador and had not responded to the request of the military attaché. They told Faymonville that they would be willing to accept aircraft at their borders, or to send pilots to retrieve the aircraft at the Persian Gulf. The implication to Faymonville was that the Soviets did not want foreigners flying aircraft into Russia.[58]

Griffiss was thus at a disadvantage by the time he arrived, hoping to attain information that had three times before been refused or ignored. Nevertheless, he pressed on with his mission. On December 2, he, Faymonville, and Lt. Col. Joseph Michela, the military attaché, visited the Soviet Liaison Office, where Griffiss presented his requests. He had no greater success than the other Americans. The Soviets accepted his papers but provided no response until December 26, when they declined to provide any such information to Griffiss. At the end of the year, Griffiss received orders from Maj. Gen. J. E. Chaney in London to terminate his mission and return to England.[59] By this time, the United States was at war with the Axis powers.

An unsigned report found in Griffiss's papers and dated January 3, 1942, likely an unsent memorandum, provides an analysis of why the Russians declined to assist him. He believed that the Soviets were well-aware not only of the importance they played in the overall war effort against Nazi Germany but also that the Western Powers regarded them as wartime allies but peacetime adversaries. Thus, the Russians welcomed aid for the sake of national survival but were reluctant to fully trust Britain or the United States. This innate suspicion was not alleviated by some of the initial shipments of P-40s from England to Archangel. These aircraft had lacked a modification for the generator that the

British had installed on their own aircraft. Even after these parts had been shipped to Russia, several aircraft still did not work in the freezing Russian climate. To make matters worse, the P-40s lacked spare parts along with operation and maintenance information.[60]

As a solution, Griffiss suggested that the needed material be shipped as expeditiously as possible, and that American aircraft be provided with American personnel.[61] What did he believe the result of this to be? Griffiss wrote: "It is felt that this gesture would have immediate results in correcting any doubt in the Soviet mind as to our sincerity which would have a most beneficial influence on Soviet-U.S. relations. In addition, vigorous and rapid action on our part at this time could well smooth over any misunderstanding which might arise from possible future curtailment of equipment."[62]

His assessment revealed a keen appreciation for the strategic situation. Yet his own transportation out of Russia was long in coming. In the meantime, Griffiss appeared to chafe under the perceived failure of his mission and his impatience to get back to his home assignment in England. An incident with Faymonville appears to have upset him to an uncharacteristically high degree. In a telegram to Chaney on January 12, 1942, Griffiss stated that he had become aware that Faymonville had contacted Chaney directly to request that he (Griffiss) join him in Moscow. Griffiss insisted to Chaney that he was unaware of such a request and was very much opposed to it. "I urgently desire to return to my post and I have already wasted six weeks in Russia. The situation today for a change in Soviet policy is less favorable than ever before." He went so far as to state, "I am mighty —— AT__AT** Faymonville reported action and I sincerely hope that you will not be influenced by it." What Griffiss meant by "—— AT_AT**" is unclear (a typist's note stated that this part of the message could not be deciphered) but Griffiss' annoyance is evident.[63] In any event, Chaney appeared to have taken prompt action. In Griffiss's personnel file, there is a handwritten note dated January 15, 1942, stating, "MA [Military attaché] received cable from Gen. C [Chaney] to advise F [Faymonville] he had no authority to change my orders. —Another to advise me no change and that F had been notified."[64]

During further delays, Griffiss typed out additional notes in a heavily edited draft, summarizing much of what he had written on January 3, but elaborating somewhat, again revealing his frustration with his situation. While granting that Soviet dissatisfactions with aircraft shipments were justified, he seemed generally less charitable toward the gamesmanship of his hosts: "Soviet[-]American relations in Russia at low ebb and show down will come in very near future. United States should deal firmly with Soviets and if sincere in aid effort state forc[i]bly reasons for non[-]delivery and show what can be done in present emergency. (We must avoid any indication of weakness and must transact business in Soviet style)."[65] He concluded with further complaints about the lack of transportation, writing, "Last plane left here for Tehran December twenty-ninth and have high hopes for another January twenty-seventh. Bad weather exceptionally low temperatures and lack [of] Soviet cooperation causes for maddening delay."[66]

Griffiss's high hopes were insufficient to get him on a plane on January 27. However, according to his handwritten notes, he finally departed Kuibyshev for Astrakand on January 29. The next day, he flew to Baku and then Tehran. On February 4, he departed Tehran for first Habbaniya, then Leida, and finally Cairo.[67] He seemed to have developed a bad cold during his travels and was obliged to spend a couple of days in bed. On February 8, 1942, he wrote, "Sunday. Up at 1100 AM, drove to Pyramids, [Lambert] and Norman—Lunch Shepheard's—Norman and Col Kemp?"[68] This was the last entry in his handwritten notes. A week later, he would depart on a long flight out of Cairo.

On February 17, a cable from Cairo was received at the Adjutant General's Office at the War Department in Washington: "FOR ARNOLD FROM ADLER RAF REPORT COLONEL TOWNSEND L GRIFFISS UNITED STATES ARMY AIR CORPS MISSING ON FLIGHT CAIRO TO ENGLAND PERIOD FURTHER INFORMATION LATER UPON CONFIRMATION PERIOD [.]"[69]

The same day, Chaney cabled the Adjutant General's Office that Griffiss had been a passenger on a British aircraft that had been missing since February 15.[70] Two days later, Chaney reported to the Adjutant General's Office that the aircraft, a B-24 Liberator, had been reported to have crashed off the southeast coast of England on February 15.[71] On February 23, a radiogram from Cairo to the Intelligence Division (G-2) of the War Department, passed on a message from the Middle East RAF, noting that the Liberator had reportedly been shot down.[72] On March 9, Chaney cabled the adjutant general that he was awaiting the completion of the British official report of the crash, but confirmed that the plane wreckage and Griffiss's briefcase had been recovered. He was presumed dead, though the body had not been found.[73]

A Court of Enquiry was convened and found that Liberator AM918 had been shot down on the morning of February 15 by two Polish pilots in the service of the RAF.[74] The court identified the pilots as Flight Sergeant Brzeski and Sergeant Malinowski of the 317th Squadron out of Exeter. According to the court, weather and visibility at that time would have allowed for correct friend-or-foe identification. Therefore, the pilots' failure to properly identify the Liberator was the primary cause of the incident. However, the court also placed responsibility on the ground organization for the "lack of exercise of effective control" over the situation. It was found that the Group Operational Staff had not forwarded information regarding the Liberator to the Fighter Sector. The receiver-transmitter (R/T) and controller's logs were not well-kept. There was a "Noticeable lack of R/T discipline, both in the air and on the ground." Also, the forward Relay Station had not been utilized. All of these were contributing factors to the fratricide. The court recommended greater attention to identification of civil aircraft and that "Scale models as well as Silhouettes and photographs should be provided in the case of both military and civil aircraft."[75] These were sensible recommendations, but obviously too late for Griffiss and the other passengers and crew of Liberator AM918. Chaney recommended in his dispatch to Arnold that "no publicity be given to findings court of enquiry."[76] Thus the terrible accident would be subsumed in the larger carnage and tragedy of the Second World War.

Griffiss died a single man, so his next of kin was his mother, Mrs. Katherine H. W. Griffiss, who lived in a house on Delaware Avenue in Buffalo, New York.[77] After the war, she would receive Griffiss's last will and testament, along with the condolences of the adjutant general.[78]

CHAPTER 10

In July 1942, Lt. Gen. Henry "Hap" Arnold, commanding general, U.S. Army Air Forces, was requested to provide input to support the posthumous award of the Distinguished Service Medal for Griffiss.[79] He replied the next month. In recounting the deceased's career, Arnold made note of his contributions as a military attaché during the Spanish Civil War:

> From 1935–1938 Lt. Col. Griffiss served as Air Attache to France, and for a large part of this period observed and analyzed the lessons of the Spanish War. His analyses and reports were of considerable use to the War Department and the Army Air Forces on the subjects of the coordination between ground and air arms, the armament of pursuit aircraft, and the development of aerial tactics.[80]

It was now left to the living to put those lessons to "considerable use." For Griffiss, his life of dedicated service to his country was at an end.

Hail and farewell, Lieutenant Colonel Griffiss.

NOTES

CHAPTER 1. AIRPOWER

Epigraph: "We Make Progress Unhindered by Custom," in Finney, *History of the Air Corps Tactical School*, v.

1. Kinney, *Airplanes*, 8–9.
2. McCullough, *The Wright Brothers*, 93, 96–100.
3. Kelly, *The Wright Brothers*, 38–39.
4. Fritzsche, *A Nation of Fliers*, 7; Kelly, *Wright Brothers*, 45.
5. Lilienthal, "Practical Experiments," 154.
6. W. Wright, "Some Aeronautical Experiments," 28.
7. W. Wright, "Some Aeronautical Experiments," 28.
8. Kelly, *Wright Brothers*, 49–51.
9. McCullough, *Wright Brothers*, 69–70.
10. Kelly, *Wright Brothers*, 80–83.
11. McCullough, *Wright Brothers*, 86–87; Kelly, *Wright Brothers*, 85–86.
12. Kelly, *Wright Brothers*, 86–90. Regarding the chain and sprocket, see National Air and Space Museum, "1903 Wright Flyer," accessed March 16, 2024, https://airandspace.si.edu/collection-objects/1903-wright-flyer/nasm_A19610048000.
13. Kelly, *Wright Brothers*, 86, 90, 96–100; McCullough, *Wright Brothers*, 105. Regarding the wood and fabric design, see National Air and Space Museum, "1903 Wright Flyer."
14. O. Wright and W. Wright, "The Early History of the Airplane," 12–13.
15. Kelly, *Wright Brothers*, 101–2; McCullough, *Wright Brothers*, 105–6.
16. Kelly, *Wright Brothers*, 148–50; 154–55; 161–65; 207; 208–12.
17. "Wright Aeroplane Flies at Capital," *New York Times*, September 4, 1908. For a description of the launching mechanism, see McCullough, *Wright Brothers*, 115–16.
18. "Wright Aeroplane Flies at Capital."
19. "Wright Flies Over an Hour," *New York Times*, September 10, 1908.
20. "Fatal Fall of Wright Airship," *New York Times*, September 18, 1908; "Fatal Tumble out of Sky," *Evening Star* (Washington, D.C.), September 18, 1908, https://chroniclingamerica.loc.gov/lccn/sn83045462/1908-09-18/ed-1/seq-1/.
21. Ennels, Kane, and Wueschner, *Cradle of Airpower*, 2.
22. Hurley and Heimdahl, "Roots of U.S. Military Aviation," 18–20.
23. Kinney, *Airplanes*, 33.

24. Mets, "Army Roots," 11.
25. Kinney, *Airplanes*: Crissy, 33; Hurley and Heimdahl, "Roots of U.S. Military Aviation," 27 (Gavotti).
26. Boyne, *Influence of Air Power*, 57–58 (Marne); 76–77 (Fokker); 109–11 (Gothas).
27. For biographical information on Foulois, see U.S. Air Force, "Major General Benjamin Delahauf Foulois," accessed November 15, 2020, https://www.af.mil/About-Us/Biographies/Display/Article/107091/major-general-benjamin-delahauf-foulois/.
28. Mets, "Army Roots," 12.
29. Hurley and Heimdahl, "Roots of U.S. Military Aviation," 30–33.
30. Mortensen, "Air Service in the Great War," 52–53.
31. Mortensen, "Air Service in the Great War," 44–49.
32. Mets, "Army Roots," 14; Mortensen, "Air Service in the Great War," 49.
33. Mortensen, "Air Service in the Great War," 65; Boyne, *Influence of Air Power*, 79, 97.
34. Mortensen, "Air Service in the Great War," 69.
35. Courtwright, *Sky as Frontier*, 70–77; for the elder Lindbergh's political views, see Berg, *Lindbergh*, 34–36.
36. Edwin L. James, "Crowd Roars Thunderous Welcome," *New York Times*, May 22, 1927; and Carlyle MacDonald, "Could Have Gone 500 Miles Farther," *New York Times*, May 22, 1927.
37. "Lindbergh Triumph Thrills Coolidge," *New York Times*, May 22, 1927.
38. Meilinger, "Trenchard and 'Morale Bombing,'" 247–48.
39. Meilinger, "Trenchard and 'Morale Bombing,'" 248–50.
40. Meilinger, "Trenchard and 'Morale Bombing,'" 251–52.
41. Meilinger, "Trenchard and 'Morale Bombing,'" 250, 253–59.
42. Meilinger, "Trenchard and 'Morale Bombing,'" 268–69.
43. Boyne, *Influence of Air Power*, 136–38.
44. Douhet, *Command of the Air*, 181.
45. Douhet, *Command of the Air*, 184, 189–91.
46. Douhet, *Command of the Air*, 49–54.
47. Douhet, *Command of the Air*, 95.
48. Douhet, *Command of the Air*, 128–29.
49. Douhet, *Command of the Air*, 20.
50. Douhet, *Command of the Air*, 58.
51. Boyne, *Influence of Air Power*, 142. "Gen. Mitchell Dies; Air Leader in War," *New York Times*, February 20, 1936.
52. Mortensen, "Air Service in the Great War," 43–44.
53. Mortensen, "Air Service in the Great War," 60.
54. Mortensen, "Air Service in the Great War," 65–68.
55. Boyne, *Influence of Air Power*, 144–47.
56. Mitchell, *Winged Defense*, xiii–xv.

57. Mitchell, *Winged Defense*, 120–21.
58. Mitchell, *Winged Defense*, 199, 213.
59. Mitchell, *Winged Defense*, 215.
60. Boyne, *Influence of Air Power*, 143.
61. Mitchell, *Winged Defense*, 126–27.
62. Slessor, *Air Power and Armies*, 214. Regarding his relationship to Trenchard, see Phillip S. Meilinger's foreword in Slessor, *Air Power*; see also Boyne, *Influence of Air Power*, 119.
63. Slessor, *Air Power and Armies*, 8–9.
64. Slessor, *Air Power and Armies*, 4.
65. Slessor, *Air Power and Armies*, 10.
66. See Slessor's conclusions in *Air Power and Armies*, 202–14.
67. Slessor, *Air Power and Armies*, 65–66.
68. Sganga, Tripodi, and Johnson, "Douhet's Antagonist," 6.
69. Sganga, Tripodi, and Johnson, "Douhet's Antagonist," 8–11.
70. Kelley, *Claire Lee Chennault*, 4–5; and Benton, *They Served Here*, 21.
71. Chennault, *Role of Defensive Pursuit*, 3.
72. Chennault, *Role of Defensive Pursuit*, 7.
73. Chennault, *Role of Defensive Pursuit*, 12–13, 18.
74. Chennault, *Role of Defensive Pursuit*, 24–25, 31–32.
75. Chennault, *Role of Defensive Pursuit*, 39.
76. Chennault, *Role of Defensive Pursuit*, 22–23.
77. Kelley, *Claire Lee Chennault*, 5–6.
78. Boyne, *Influence of Air Power*, 148; Shiner, "Heyday of the GHQ Air Force," 102–4.
79. Maurer, *Aviation in the U.S. Army*, 475–76.
80. U.S. Air Force, *Statistical Digest, Fiscal Year 2008*.
81. Moy, "Transforming Technology," 306–7.
82. Morris, *Origins of American Strategic Bombing Theory*, 163–69.
83. Morris, *Origins of American Strategic Bombing Theory*, 172.
84. Moy, "Transforming Technology," 309.
85. Maurer, *Aviation in the U.S. Army*, 388.
86. Moy, "Transforming Technology," 326–27
87. Shiner, "Heyday of the GHQ Air Force," 140–44.
88. Berg, *Lindbergh*, 291–92.
89. Berg, *Lindbergh*, 293.
90. Shiner, "Heyday of the GHQ Air Force," 124–25; Mets, "Army Roots," 24.
91. Berg, *Lindbergh*, 292–96.
92. "Action on Air Mail Unfair, Lindbergh Tells President," *New York Times*, February 12, 1934.
93. Berg, *Lindbergh*, 296.
94. Shiner, "Heyday of the GHQ Air Force," 125–29.

95. "Chief of the Air Corps Declares GHQ Air Force a Forward Step," *Air Corps Newsletter* 18, no. 2 (February 1, 1935), 31.
96. Shiner, "Heyday of the GHQ Air Force," 127–28.
97. "Gen. Mitchell Dies; Air Leader in War," *New York Times*, February 20, 1936.

CHAPTER 2. SORTIES

1. "Telephone Service with Spain Shut Off; Gibraltar Hears of Revolt in Cartagena," *New York Times*, July 18, 1936, Late City Edition.
2. Cortada, *Modern Warfare in Spain*, xxiii.
3. "Army and Navy: General Managers," *Time*, April 8, 1929, http://content.time.com/time/magazine/article/0,9171,732215,00.html.
4. "Major Gen. Fuqua Is Dead Here at 68," *New York Times*, May 13, 1943; Cortada, *Modern Warfare in Spain*, xxiii.
5. "Stephen Ogden Fuqua," Hall of Valor, Military Times, accessed March 19, 2017, https://valor.militarytimes.com/recipient/recipient-17560/.
6. "Army Men Criticize Fuqua Promotion," *New York Times*, April 2, 1929.
7. "Fuqua Is Confirmed as Major General," *New York Times*, May 5, 1929.
8. Cortada, *Modern Warfare in Spain*, xxiii.
9. U.S. War Department, Adjutant General's Office, *Army List and Directory*, 59.
10. Juntunen, "U.S. Army Attachés," 7, 10–11.
11. Bowers, *My Mission to Spain*, 123.
12. U.S. War Department, Adjutant General's Office, *Army List and Directory*, 58–59.
13. *Princeton Union* (Princeton, Minn.), 30 July 1896; Licata, "Cicero J. Hamlin's Descendants."
14. Mulvey, "Townsend Griffiss."
15. U.S. War Department, Adjutant General's Office, *Army List and Directory*, 58–59.
16. Griffiss, *When You Go to Hawaii*, 180.
17. Oscar Westover to Townsend Griffiss, "Commendation," November 4, 1936.
18. For a history of Spain during these years, see Carr, *Spain*, chaps. 9–14.
19. For a history of Spain during the Second Republic, see Beevor, *Battle for Spain*, chaps. 3–5; or Hugh Thomas, *Spanish Civil War*, chaps. 3–12.
20. Thomas, *Spanish Civil War*, 98–100.
21. Thomas, *Spanish Civil War*, 131–32, 135–36.
22. Thomas, *Spanish Civil War*, 138, 142–45.
23. Beevor, *Battle for Spain*, 34–38.
24. Thomas, *Spanish Civil War*, 168.
25. Stephen O. Fuqua to Military Intelligence Division, "Trial of Officers Charged with Undue Acts of Repression during the October Revolt," received April 2, 1936, RG 165 M-1445, Roll #7, NARA.
26. Preston, *Franco*, 90–91.
27. Thomas, *Spanish Civil War*, 173–74.

28. Thomas, *Spanish Civil War*, 206–8. Some biographical information on Calvo Sotelo is available on pages 7–8.
29. Stephen O. Fuqua to Military Intelligence Division, M.A. Madrid Report No. 6379, "Assassination of Señor Calvo Sotelo," July 14, 1936, RG 165 M-1445, Roll #7, NARA.
30. Stephen O. Fuqua to Military Intelligence Division, M.A. Madrid Report No. 6387, "Military Uprising against the Government," August 10, 1936, p. 1, RG 165 M-1445, Roll #7, NARA.
31. Thomas, *Spanish Civil War*, 210–11.
32. Thomas, *Spanish Civil War*, 215.
33. Thomas, *Spanish Civil War*, 215–19.
34. See Thomas, *Spanish Civil War*, chaps. 14–16; and Beevor, *Battle for Spain*, chaps. 6–7.
35. "Phone Calls Censored," *New York Times*, July 18, 1936.
36. William P. Carney, "Spain Checks Army Rising as Morocco Forces Rebel, 2 Cities in Africa Bombed," *New York Times*, July 19, 1936. The Government also denied that Franco had joined the rebellion, "Phone Calls Censored," *New York Times*, July 18, 1936.
37. Beevor, *Battle for Spain*, 61–63.
38. These numbers are a composite developed from the following sources: "The Spanish Situation—August 6, 1936," RG 165 M-1445, Roll #7, NARA; Beevor, *Battle for Spain*, 79; Proctor, *Hitler's Luftwaffe*, 12–13; Quesada, *Spanish Civil War 1936–1939 (1): Nationalist Forces*, 8–9; Quesada, *Spanish Civil War 1936–1939 (2): Republican Forces*, 11; and Thomas, *Spanish Civil War*, 328–29. By these figures, there is a difference of about 10,000 soldiers unaccounted for between those on duty, those on leave, and those who joined one side or the other in July 1936. This may be attributable to the general confusion of the time and thus lack of accountability, the uncertainty of the loyalties of troops in contested areas, desertion, or some other explanation that the author has been unable to identify.
39. Quesada, *Nationalist Forces*, 14.
40. Thomas, *Spanish Civil War*, 163n2.
41. Esdaile, *Spanish Civil War*, 45.
42. Thomas, *Spanish Civil War*, 315–16.
43. Fuqua to Military Intelligence Division, M.A. Madrid Report No. 6387, "Military Uprising," 5.
44. Thomas, Spanish Civil War, 204.
45. Beevor, *Battle for Spain*, 72.
46. The details on the division of the Navy are a composite from the following sources: Esdaile, *Spanish Civil War*, 332–34; Salas Larrazábal, *Air War over Spain*, 48; Quesada, *Spanish Civil War 1936–1939 (1): Nationalist Forces*, 34–35; Quesada, *Spanish Civil War 1936–1939 (2): Republican Forces*, 24, 33; and Thomas, *Spanish Civil War*, 328–29, 331–32.

47. Stephen O. Fuqua to Military Intelligence Division, M.A. Madrid Report No. 6382, "Spanish Situation—Military," July 23, 1936, RG 165 M-1445, Roll #7, NARA; regarding lack of officers, see Thomas, *Spanish Civil War*, 332.
48. The details on the division of the Air Force is a composite from three sources: Howson, *Aircraft of the Spanish Civil War*, 20, 301–5; Salas Larrazábal, *Air War over Spain*, 44–46, 48–49; and Thomas, *Spanish Civil War*, 330–31.
49. Beevor, *Battle for Spain*, 68–69.
50. The *New York Times* printed an Associated Press report that the plane exploded twenty feet over Cascares Bay. "Noted Spaniard Killed," *New York Times*, July 21, 1936. On the Puss Moth, see Howson, *Aircraft of the Spanish Civil War*, 97–98.
51. Bowers, *Mission to Spain*, 245.
52. Macklin, "Major Hugh Pollard," 277–78.
53. Macklin, "Major Hugh Pollard," 277.
54. Macklin, "Major Hugh Pollard," 279.
55. Howson, *Aircraft of the Spanish Civil War*, 104.
56. Howson, *Aircraft of the Spanish Civil War*, 104–8.
57. Alpert, *Franco and the Condor Legion*, 4.
58. Proctor, *Hitler's Luftwaffe*, 4–6.
59. Proctor, *Hitler's Luftwaffe*, 6.
60. Beevor, *Battle for Spain*, 49.
61. Preston, *Franco*, 1–10.
62. Preston, *Franco*, 18.
63. Thomas, *Spanish Civil War*, 141.
64. Preston, *Franco*, 27.
65. Preston, *Franco*, 42–48.
66. Preston, *Franco*, 90, 103–5.
67. Preston, *Franco*, 120 (appointed to Canary Islands).
68. Preston, *Franco*, 136–37.
69. Preston, *Franco*, 140.
70. Thomas, *Spanish Civil War*, 217, 231.
71. "Rebels in Morocco Reported at Helm," *New York Times*, July 19, 1936, Late City Edition.
72. Macklin, "Major Hugh Pollard," 278.
73. Bowers, *Mission to Spain*, 241–43, 249.
74. Townsend Griffiss to G-2, M.A. Paris and Madrid Report No. 22,693-W, "Account of the Situation on the North Coast of Spain and Its Relation to the Safety of the American Ambassador to Spain," August 3, 1936, p. 1, RG 165 M-1445, Roll #7, NARA.
75. Griffiss to G-2, M.A. Paris and Madrid Report No. 22,693-W, "Account of the Situation," 2–3.
76. Bowers, *Mission to Spain*, 249–51.
77. Bowers, *Mission to Spain*, 246.

78. Griffiss to G-2, M.A. Paris and Madrid Report No. 22,693-W, "Account of the Situation," 3–4.
79. ⁹ Bowers, *Mission to Spain*, 253. Griffiss had a somewhat different account. Griffiss to G-2, M.A. Paris and Madrid Report No. 22,693-W, "Account of the Situation," 4–5.
80. As quoted in Bowers, *Mission to Spain*, 254.
81. Bowers, *Mission to Spain*, 254.
82. Quesada, *Nationalist Forces*, 4.
83. Kelly, *The Wright Brothers*, 252.
84. Salas Larrazábal, *Air War over Spain*, 14.
85. Salas Larrazábal, *Air War over Spain*, 14–16.
86. Alpert, *Franco and the Condor Legion*, 8; Howson, *Aircraft of the Spanish Civil War*, 115.
87. Salas Larrazábal, *Air War over Spain*, 20. Preston, in *Franco*, called the family "lower middle class gentility" (3).
88. Thomas, *Spanish Civil War*, 514n2.
89. Griffiss to Military Intelligence Division, M.A. Valencia Report No. 6471, "Special Report," 1–2.
90. Howson, *Aircraft of the Spanish Civil War*, 10–11.
91. Griffiss to Military Intelligence Division, M.A. Valencia Report No. 6471, "Special Report," 4.
92. Beevor, *Battle for Spain*, 66.
93. Salas Larrazábal, *Air War over Spain*, 44–49; Howson, *Aircraft of the Spanish Civil War*, 301–4.
94. Howson, *Aircraft of the Spanish Civil War*, 8–9 (CASA-Breguet, Hispano-Nieuport); 81 (CASA-Vildebeests).
95. Howson, *Aircraft of the Spanish Civil War*, 115–16.
96. Aircraft specifications for here and throughout the book are drawn from eight key secondary sources: Angelucci, *Rand McNally Encyclopedia of Military Aircraft: 1914–1980*; Angelucci, *Rand McNally Encyclopedia of Military Aircraft: 1914 to the Present*; Howson, *Aircraft of the Spanish Civil War*; Jarrett, *Biplane to Monoplane*; Murphy and McNiece, *Military Aircraft, 1919–1945*; Nalty, *Winged Shield*; Winchester, *Classic Military Aircraft*; and Winchester, *Military Aircraft Visual Encyclopedia*.
97. Howson, *Aircraft of the Spanish Civil War*, 190.
98. Tinker, *Some Still Live*, 29–30.
99. Howson, *Aircraft of the Spanish Civil War*, 81.
100. Howson, *Aircraft of the Spanish Civil War*, 115–17. For "flying boat," see Barfield, "The Age of the Flying Boat," 89–106, 89.
101. Salas Larrazábal, *Air War over Spain*, 57. Salas Larrazábal noted he was unable to independently confirm this claim.
102. Salas Larrazábal, *Air War over Spain*, 38–43.

103. Salas Larrazábal, *Air War over Spain*, 54–55.
104. Howson, *Aircraft of the Spanish Civil War*, 12.
105. Howson, *Aircraft of the Spanish Civil War*, 116 (Dornier); 120 (Douglas); 143 (Fokker).
106. Thomas, *Spanish Civil War*, 341–42.

CHAPTER 3. AIRLIFT

1. Townsend Griffiss to G-2, M.A. Paris Report No. 22,693-W, "Account of the Situation on the North Coast of Spain and Its Relation to the Safety of the American Ambassador to Spain," August 3, 1936, p. 8, RG 165 M-1445, Roll #7, NARA.
2. Griffiss to G-2, M.A. Paris Report No. 22,693-W, "Account of the Situation," 9.
3. Griffiss to G-2, M.A. Paris Report No. 22,693-W, "Account of the Situation," 9.
4. Stephen O. Fuqua to E. T. Conley, Telegraph No. 98, August 13, 1936, RG 165 M-1445, Roll #7, NARA.
5. Alpert, "Clash of Spanish Armies," 333; "Aerial Warfare in Spain," 185.
6. Howson, *Arms for Spain*, 21–25, 38–39; Alpert, *Franco and the Condor Legion*, 67–69.
7. Townsend Griffiss to Military Intelligence Division, M.A. Valencia Report No. 6471, "Special Report on Spanish Government Air Force," February 21, 1937, p. 10, IRISREF A2873, Frames 2264–287, AFHRA.
8. Salas Larrazábal, *Air War over Spain*, 65–66.
9. Howson, *Aircraft of the Spanish Civil War*, 251–52.
10. Howson, *Aircraft of the Spanish Civil War*, 110–12.
11. Griffiss to Military Intelligence Division, M.A. Valencia Report No. 6471, "Special Report," 13–15.
12. Thomas, *Spanish Civil War*, 341.
13. Thomas, *Spanish Civil War*, 353.
14. Howson, *Aircraft of the Spanish Civil War*, 274.
15. Howson, *Aircraft of the Spanish Civil War*, 276.
16. Logoluso, *Fiat CR.32 Aces*, 9–11.
17. Salas Larrazábal, *Air War over Spain*, 79. Jesús Salas Larrazábal's eldest brother, Ángel, was an ace Fiat pilot for the Nationalists (9).
18. Salas Larrazábal, *Air War over Spain*, 75.
19. Norman E. Fiske to Military Intelligence Division, M.A. Rome Report No. 15,646, "Military Operations—General; Military, Naval and Air Operations, Spanish Civil War," November 27, 1936, p. 3, RG 165 M-1445, Roll #7, NARA.
20. Howson, *Aircraft of the Spanish Civil War*, 206–7.
21. Proctor, *Hitler's Luftwaffe*, 18–19.
22. Thomas, *Spanish Civil War*, 357–58; Jaeneke, "Part Played by the Condor Legion," 52. The particular version consulted was a draft of the work: History of the Air War Study Group, 1957, IRISREF K1026T, AFHRA.
23. Proctor, *Hitler's Luftwaffe*, P.20.

24. Howson, *Aircraft of the Spanish Civil War*, 207; Proctor, *Hitler's Luftwaffe*, 22. Proctor notes that the aircraft may have taken off from Friedrichshafen instead.
25. Jaeneke, "Part Played by the Condor Legion," 52; Howson, *Aircraft of the Spanish Civil War*, 207; Proctor, *Hitler's Luftwaffe*, 21.
26. Jaeneke, "Part Played by the Condor Legion," 52–52a; Howson, *Aircraft of the Spanish Civil War*, 207–8.
27. Howson, *Aircraft of the Spanish Civil War*, 207.
28. Howson, *Aircraft of the Spanish Civil War*, 116–17, 146.
29. Proctor, *Hitler's Luftwaffe*, 22.
30. Alpert, *Franco and the Condor Legion*, 53–55.
31. Munson, "Biplane's Fall from Favour," 15–16.
32. Howson, *Aircraft of the Spanish Civil War*, 206.
33. Townsend Griffiss to Military Intelligence Division, M.A. Valencia Report No. 6530, "Organizational Training, Tactics Employed," April 25, 1937, p. 2, Call #248.282–23, IRISREF A2817, Frames 1425–1433, AFHRA.
34. Proctor, *Hitler's Luftwaffe*, 22.
35. Howson, *Aircraft of the Spanish Civil War*, 172.
36. Figures from the airlift come from Proctor, *Hitler's Luftwaffe*, 22–31.
37. Proctor, *Hitler's Luftwaffe*, 36.
38. Thomas, *Spanish Civil War*, 391.
39. Proctor, *Hitler's Luftwaffe*, 30–31.
40. Handwritten memo by Edward Raley, citing M.A. Paris, Report No. 23,475-W, June 8, 1937, IRISREF A1398, Call # 145.91–135O, Frame 1016, AFHRA.
41. Howson, *Aircraft of the Spanish Civil War*, 274.
42. E. O. Sawyer to E. W. Raley, Letter regarding Spanish Airlift, October 25, 1937, IRISREF A1398, Call # 145.91–135O, Frame 1017, AFHRA.
43. Sawyer to Raley, Letter regarding Spanish Airlift, October 25, 1937.
44. Thomas, *Spanish Civil War*, 373–78.
45. Stephen O. Fuqua to Military Intelligence Division, "The American Embassy as an Information Center," August 15, 1936, RG 165, Box 1544, NARA.
46. Fuqua to Military Intelligence Division, "American Embassy as an Information Center."
47. O.N.I. Report No. 57, August 31, 1936, "Miscellaneous Documents concerning Spanish Civil War—Plans Division," p. 1, Call #145.91–135MM, IRISREF A1399, Frames 685–86, AFHRA.
48. O.N.I. Report No. 57, August 31, 1936, "Miscellaneous Documents," 2.
49. O.N.I. Report No. 57, August 31, 1936, "Miscellaneous Documents," 1–2. See also Howson, *Aircraft of the Spanish Civil War*, 301–6.
50. Salas Larrazábal, *Air War over Spain*, 72–73.
51. Salas Larrazábal, *Air War over Spain*, 55.
52. Salas Larrazábal, *Air War over Spain*, 67–68.
53. Salas Larrazábal, *Air War over Spain*, 75.

54. Proctor, *Hitler's Luftwaffe*, 29.
55. Thomas, *Spanish Civil War*, 386.
56. Salas Larrazábal, *Air War over Spain*, 87.
57. Thomas, *Spanish Civil War*, 194.
58. Salas Larrazábal, *Air War over Spain*, 78.
59. Thomas, *Spanish Civil War*, 411.
60. Salas Larrazábal, *Air War over Spain*, 82.
61. Preston, *Franco*, 172.
62. The principles of war are listed in Joint Publication 1, *Doctrine of the Armed Forces of the United States*, figures I-1, I-3.
63. Salas Larrazábal, *Air War over Spain*, 81.
64. Salas Larrazábal, *Air War over Spain*, 81-82.
65. Salas Larrazábal, *Air War over Spain*, 72.
66. Salas Larrazábal, *Air War over Spain*, 82–83.
67. Salas Larrazábal, *Air War over Spain*, 89.
68. Thomas, *Spanish Civil War*, 436.
69. Salas Larrazábal, *Air War over Spain*, 92.
70. Thomas, *Spanish Civil War*, 430–31.
71. Hooton, *Spain in Arms*, 81.
72. Hooton, *Spain in Arms*, 42.
73. Salas Larrazábal, *Air War over Spain*, 85–86.
74. Thomas, *Spanish Civil War*, 436–37.
75. Howson, *Arms for Spain*, app. III (derived from the Russian State Military Archives), 278–79.
76. Salas Larrazábal, *Air War over Spain*, 90.
77. Howson, *Arms for Spain*, 129.
78. Lannon, *Spanish Civil War*, 46–47.
79. Proctor, *Hitler's Luftwaffe*, 55.
80. Thomas, *Spanish Civil War*, 338–40.
81. Beevor, *Battle for Spain*, 157.
82. Thomas, *Spanish Civil War*, 392–93.
83. Howson, *Arms for Spain*, 125–26. The full Russian name for GRU is *Glavnoye Razvedyvatelnoye Upravlenie*, Main Intelligence Directorate.
84. These numbers are calculated from Thomas, *Spanish Civil War*, 448–49n1. Of the 2.367 billion Spanish pesetas (which Thomas equates to $788 million [at a 3 peseta/$ exchange rate]), 257 million were kept in French banks from before the war, and another 470 million were sent to France after the outbreak of hostilities, leaving 1.64 billion in Spain.
85. These figures are calculated from Salas Larrazábal's estimate of 1,500 kilograms (3,308 pounds) shipped July 30, 1936, and 7,000 kilograms (15,435 pounds) shipped in August; 8.5 metric tons are approximately 9.5 tons in the English (American) system. Salas Larrazábal, *Air War over Spain*, 65.

86. Beevor, *Battle for Spain*, 153–54, 467–68n13.
87. Howson, *Arms for Spain*, 121.
88. Howson, *Arms for Spain*, 128–29.
89. Beevor, *Battle for Spain*, 154.
90. Knoblaugh, *Correspondent in Spain*, 43.
91. I use the term "broken reed" in the biblical sense, from 2 Kings 18:21. It is a reference to Egypt, which Judah was hoping would support it against the Assyrians. The term means an unreliable ally.
92. Salas Larrazábal, *Air War over Spain*, 95–96.
93. Howson, *Aircraft of the Spanish Civil War*, 193, 198, 277; Salas Larrazábal, *Air War over Spain*, 95.
94. Griffiss to Military Intelligence Division, M.A. Valencia Report No. 6471, "Special Report," 9.
95. Howson, *Aircraft of the Spanish Civil War*, 192–93.
96. Tinker, *Some Still Live*, 31.
97. Howson, *Aircraft of the Spanish Civil War*, 194.
98. Howson, *Aircraft of the Spanish Civil War*, 197–98.
99. Townsend Griffiss to Military Intelligence Division, M.A. Valencia Report No. 6491, "Armaments and Equipment, Russian Pursuit," March 14, 1937, p. 2, RG 165 M-1445, Roll #7, NARA.
100. Griffiss to Military Intelligence Division, M.A. Valencia Report No. 6491, "Armaments and Equipment," 2.
101. Albert Baumler to Edward Raley, March 29, 1938, "Albert J. Baumler," p. 1 (Frame 880), IRISREF A1399, Frames 834–94, AFHRA.

CHAPTER 4. COUNTERAIR

Epigraph: Townsend Griffiss, M.A. Valencia, Report No. 6471, "Special Report on Spanish Government Air Force," February 21, 1937, p. 21, Call #248.501–79, IRISREF A2873, Frames 2264–287, AFHRA.

1. Knoblaugh, *Correspondent in Spain*, 58.
2. Knoblaugh, *Correspondent in Spain*, 58.
3. Bolloten, *Spanish Civil War*, 284–85.
4. Bolloten, *Spanish Civil War*, 285, 291–95.
5. F. H. Lincoln, Assistant Chief of Staff, G-2, to Chief of Staff, G-2, "American Embassy, Madrid," November 24, 1936, NARA, RG 165, Box 1544, 2610-S-50-015.
6. Claude Bowers to Secretary of State, Correspondence, October 12, 1936.
7. F. H. Lincoln to Chief of Staff, "Request of Military Attache, Spain, to be Detailed as Military Observer in Spanish Civil War upon Departure of American Embassy," October 14, 1936, NARA, RG 165, Box 1544, 2610-S-50-010.
8. John Morgan to Claude Bowers, telegram, October 15, 1936.
9. Knoblaugh, *Correspondent in Spain*, 232.

10. Knoblaugh, *Correspondent in Spain*, 232.
11. Beevor, *Battle for Spain*, 176–77.
12. Thomas, *Spanish Civil War*, 480–83, 487.
13. Beevor, *Battle for Spain*, xiii, 180.
14. Thomas, *Spanish Civil War*, 485–87.
15. Alpert, *Franco and the Condor Legion*, 91.
16. Salas Larrazábal, *Air War over Spain*, 99–101.
17. Salas Larrazábal, *Air War over Spain*, 101; Proctor, *Hitler's Luftwaffe*, 64–65.
18. Proctor, *Hitler's Luftwaffe*, 64–65.
19. Salas Larrazábal, *Air War over Spain*, 104–5.
20. Proctor, *Hitler's Luftwaffe*, 66.
21. Beevor, *Battle for Spain*, 182.
22. Knoblaugh, *Correspondent in Spain*, 100–1.
23. O. S. Wood to M.A. London, "Military Information on Civil War."
24. Wood to M.A. London, "Military Information on Civil War."
25. Beevor, *Battle for Spain*, 199.
26. Logoluso, *Fiat CR.32 Aces*, 32–33.
27. Sullivan, "Fascist Italy's Military Involvement ," 719.
28. Corum, *Wolfram von Richthofen*, 119.
29. Corum, *Wolfram von Richthofen*, 1–7.
30. Corum, *Wolfram von Richthofen*, 11–12.
31. Hooton, *Spain in Arms*, 6–9.
32. Howson, *Aircraft of the Spanish Civil War*, 263–64.
33. Salas Larrazábal, *Air War over Spain*, 107.
34. Howson, *Aircraft of the Spanish Civil War*, 264.
35. Hooton, *Spain in Arms*, 8–12.
36. As quoted in Thomas, *Spanish Civil War*, 494.
37. Beevor, *Battle for Spain*, 192.
38. Hooton, *Spain in Arms*, 12–14.
39. Hooton, *Spain in Arms*, 14.
40. Stephen O. Fuqua to Assistant Chief of Staff, G-2, M.A. Valencia Report No. 6453, "Madrid Map Showing Air Raids from November 1st to December 22d, 1936 and Madrid City Map," January 8, 1937, RG 165 M-1445, Roll #7, NARA.
41. Sumner Waite to Military Intelligence Division, M.A. Paris Report No. 23,106-W, "Revolutionary Movements; Spain," January 18, 1937, p. 4, RG 165 M-1445, Roll #7, NARA.
42. Waite to Military Intelligence Division, M.A. Paris Report No. 23,106-W, "Revolutionary Movements," 6.
43. H. H. Fuller to Military Intelligence Division, M.A. Paris Report No. 23,126-W, "Major Operations, Operations in Spain," January 26, 1937, RG 165 M-1445, Roll #7, NARA.

44. Raymond E. Lee to Military Intelligence Division, M.A. London Report No. 38512, "Employment of Troops in Domestic Disturbances," January 25, 1937, p. 1, RG 165 M-1445, Roll #7, NARA.
45. Lee to Military Intelligence Division, M.A. London Report No. 38512, "Employment of Troops," 2.
46. Thomas, *Spanish Civil War*, 573.
47. Beevor, *Battle for Spain*, 200.
48. Thomas, *Spanish Civil War*, 582–86.
49. Proctor, *Hitler's Luftwaffe*, 101–2.
50. Salas Larrazábal, *Air War over Spain*, 117.
51. Hooton, *Spain in Arms*, 15; Johnston, "Jarama, Battle of," 276; and Beevor, *Battle for Spain*, 209.
52. For details of the battle, see the following histories: Hooton, *Spain in Arms*, 17–23; Thomas, *Spanish Civil War*, 588–96; Beevor, *Battle for Spain*, 209–14; Johnston, "Jarama, Battle of," 276–77; and Bradley, *International Brigades in Spain*, 21–24. For the George Washington Battalion, see Esdaile, *Spanish Civil War*, 356.
53. Salas Larrazábal, *Air War over Spain*, 120.
54. Proctor, *Hitler's Luftwaffe*, 104–5.
55. Salas Larrazábal, *Air War over Spain*, 120–21.
56. Proctor, *Hitler's Luftwaffe*, 107.
57. Salas Larrazábal, *Air War over Spain*, 108.
58. Salas Larrazábal, *Air War over Spain*, 118–22.
59. Townsend Griffiss, M.A. Valencia. Report No. 6471, "Special Report on Spanish Government Air Force," February 21, 1937, p. 21, Call #248.501–79, IRISREF A2873, Frames 2264–287, AFHRA.
60. Griffiss, M.A. Valencia. Report No. 6471, "Special Report," 1–3.
61. Griffiss, M.A. Valencia. Report No. 6471, "Special Report," 4.
62. Griffiss, M.A. Valencia. Report No. 6471, "Special Report," 4.
63. Griffiss, M.A. Valencia. Report No. 6471, "Special Report," 6.
64. Griffiss, M.A. Valencia. Report No. 6471, "Special Report," 7–8.
65. Griffiss, M.A. Valencia. Report No. 6471, "Special Report," 9–10.
66. Griffiss, M.A. Valencia. Report No. 6471, "Special Report," 10.
67. Griffiss, M.A. Valencia. Report No. 6471, "Special Report," 10.
68. Griffiss, M.A. Valencia. Report No. 6471, "Special Report," 10–11. Griffiss stated the aircraft was a Nieuport 62, but Howson does not list any Nieuport 62s or French Nieuport-Delage NiD 52s as being deployed to Spain during the civil war.
69. Griffiss, M.A. Valencia. Report No. 6471, "Special Report," 11–12.
70. Griffiss, M.A. Valencia. Report No. 6471, "Special Report," 16.
71. Griffiss, M.A. Valencia. Report No. 6471, "Special Report," 18.
72. Griffiss, M.A. Valencia. Report No. 6471, "Special Report," 18.
73. Griffiss, M.A. Valencia. Report No. 6471, "Special Report," 20.
74. Griffiss, M.A. Valencia. Report No. 6471, "Special Report," 20.

75. Griffiss, M.A. Valencia. Report No. 6471, "Special Report," 21.
76. Griffiss, M.A. Valencia. Report No. 6471, "Special Report," 21.
77. Thomas, *Spanish Civil War*, 596–97.
78. Thomas, *Spanish Civil War*, 597–99 The typical Republican infantry division comprised three mixed brigades, each with four battalions of 650 men apiece, or 7,800 men at full strength; Quesada, *The Spanish Civil War 1936–1939 (2)*, 14–17. The author estimates that support personnel may have raised this total to 9,000.
79. Thomas, *Spanish Civil War*, 597–98; Sullivan, "Fascist Italy's Military Involvement," 706.
80. Stephen O. Fuqua to Military Intelligence Division, M.A. Valencia Report No. 6505, "The Guadalajara Drive—Italian Participation Therein," April 2, 1937, p. 1, RG 165 M-1445, Roll #7, NARA. Hooton has Brihuega falling on the morning of March 10. See Hooton, *Spain in Arms*, 28.
81. Bradley, *International Brigades*, 24.
82. Beevor, *Battle for Spain*, 217.
83. Thomas, *Spanish Civil War*, 599–603; Bradley, *International Brigades*, 8.
84. Thomas, *Spanish Civil War*, 600.
85. Bradley, *International Brigades*, 24.
86. Quesada, *Republican Forces*, 18.
87. Edwards, *Airmen without Portfolio*, 62–63.
88. Townsend Griffiss to Military Intelligence Division, M.A. Valencia Report No. 6514, "Air Combat Operations," April 7, 1937, p. 1, RG 165 M-1445, Roll #7, NARA, 1.
89. Fuqua to Military Intelligence Division, M.A. Valencia Report No. 6505, "Guadalajara Drive," 1.
90. Thomas, *Spanish Civil War*, 600.
91. Griffiss to Military Intelligence Division, M.A. Valencia Report No. 6514, "Air Combat Operations," 2.
92. Thomas, *Spanish Civil War*, 601.
93. Fuqua to Military Intelligence Division, M.A. Valencia Report No. 6505, "Guadalajara Drive," 1.
94. Thomas, *Spanish Civil War*, 601.
95. Beevor, *Battle for Spain*, 219–20.
96. Tinker, *Some Still Live*, 134–35.
97. Beevor, *Battle for Spain*, 220.
98. Thomas, *Spanish Civil War*, 602.
99. Thomas, *Spanish Civil War*, 602.
100. Tinker, *Some Still Live*, 149–50.
101. Thomas, *Spanish Civil War*, 602.
102. "They shall not pass!" Delores Ibarurri, "La Pasionaria," made this statement during a radio address during the coup attempt in Madrid the previous July.

It was an unattributed Spanish translation of General Henri Philippe Pétain's declaration at Verdun in 1916, "Il ne passeront pas." Bartlett, *Bartlett's Familiar Quotations*, 570, 692.
103. *Newsweek*, April 3, 1937, 15.

CHAPTER 5. INTERDICTION

Note: Much of this chapter is taken from a paper submitted for a Master's level history class: Christopher G. Marquis, "'¿Quién Sabe?' U.S. Airmen in the Spanish Civil War," paper submitted for Master's-level course, Auburn University, 2018.

1. Finch, "United States and the Spanish Civil War," 75.
2. Finch, "United States and the Spanish Civil War," 79.
3. Finch, "United States and the Spanish Civil War," 74–77, and 77n5.
4. William Phillips to All Consulates in Spain, Department of State Circular Telegram 852.00/2510a, August 7, 1936, https://history.state.gov/historicaldocuments/frus1936v02/d389.
5. Department of State Press Release, December 30, 1936, quoted in Finch, "United States and the Spanish Civil War," 74–75.
6. Finch, "United States and the Spanish Civil War," 80.
7. W. M. Smith, "Mercenary Eagles," 53.
8. W. M. Smith, "Mercenary Eagles," 24–28.
9. W. M. Smith, "Mercenary Eagles," 84n92.
10. Edwards, *Airmen without Portfolio*, 24–25.
11. Edwards, *Airmen without Portfolio*, 28–29.
12. W. M. Smith, "Mercenary Eagles," 60.
13. Tinker, *Some Still Live*, 33–34.
14. Edwards, *Airmen without Portfolio*, 29–31.
15. Sumner Waite to Military Intelligence Division, M.A. Paris Report No. 23,066-W, "Air Combat Operations; Aviation in Spain," January 7, 1937, RG 165 M-1445, Roll #7, NARA.
16. "Albert John Baumler," Hall of Valor, *Military Times*, https://valor.militarytimes.com/recipient/recipient-29666/.
17. Earle E. Partridge, interview by Tom Sturm and Hugh N. Ahmann, April 23–25, 1974, Colorado Springs, CO, US Air Force Oral History Program, K239.0512-729, AFHRA, 224–25. Underlined wording is from the original text.
18. Smith and Hall, *Five Down, No Glory*, 132–33; Tinker, *Some Still Live*, 19.
19. Tinker, *Some Still Live*, 1.
20. This biological information is found in Smith and Hall, *Five Down, No Glory*, chaps. 2 and 3. Much of their information is gathered from Tinker family papers and letters, see 344n1. Specific references are as follows: early life, 17–19; Naval Academy, 33–35; commissioning, 42–43; assignment, 46–47; end of career in Navy, 50–54.

21. Smith and Hall, *Five Down, No Glory*, 74–76; According to Internal Revenue Service records, the average net income in 1936 was $3,554. See U.S. Treasury Department, Bureau of Internal Revenue, *Statistics of Income for 1936, Part I*, 83.
22. Tinker, *Some Still Live*, 6–7.
23. Edwards, *Airmen without Portfolio*, 4–5.
24. Edwards, *Airmen without Portfolio*, 25–27.
25. Smith and Hall, *Five Down, No Glory*, 94–95.
26. Tinker, *Some Still Live*, 38, 56–57.
27. Edwards, *Airmen without Portfolio*, 42.
28. Tinker, *Some Still Live*, 70.
29. Tinker, *Some Still Live*, 72. Tinker consistently misspelled his name as "Lieder," perhaps not realizing that the Germanic long-*i* sound is made with the "ei" spelling, while "ie" makes the long-*e* sound. Interestingly, *leider* is German for "unfortunately" while *Lieder* means "song."
30. Smith and Hall, *Five Down, No Glory*, 111–12.
31. Smith and Hall, *Five Down, No Glory*, 115.
32. Smith and Hall, *Five Down, No Glory*, 115; Edwards, *Airmen without Portfolio*, 41
33. Tinker, *Some Still Live*, 84–85, 91.
34. Edwards, *Airmen without Portfolio*, 57.
35. Tinker, *Some Still Live*, 110–11.
36. Smith and Hall, *Five Down, No Glory*, 130.
37. Hemingway, "Night before Battle," in *The Complete Short Stories of Ernest Hemingway*, 437–59, 452.
38. Tinker, *Some Still Live*, 123–25.
39. Edwards, *Airmen without Portfolio*, 63–66.
40. Tinker, *Some Still Live*, 138–39.
41. Smith and Hall, *Five Down, No Glory*, 156–57.
42. Edwards, *Airmen without Portfolio*, 68.
43. Tinker, *Some Still Live*, 147–48.
44. Tinker, *Some Still Live*, 154–55.
45. Smith and Hall, *Five Down, No Glory*, 164.
46. Townsend Griffiss to Military Intelligence Division, M.A. Valencia Report No. 6530, "Organizational Training, Tactics Employed," April 25, 1937, p. 1, Call #248.282-23, IRISREF A2817, Frames 1425–33, AFHRA.
47. Griffiss to Military Intelligence Division, M.A. Valencia Report No. 6530, "Organizational Training," 1.
48. Griffiss to Military Intelligence Division, M.A. Valencia Report No. 6530, "Organizational Training," 2–3.
49. Griffiss to Military Intelligence Division, M.A. Valencia Report No. 6530, "Organizational Training," 2.
50. Griffiss to Military Intelligence Division, M.A. Valencia Report No. 6530, "Organizational Training," 3.

51. Griffiss to Military Intelligence Division, M.A. Valencia Report No. 6530, "Organizational Training," 5.
52. Griffiss to Military Intelligence Division, M.A. Valencia Report No. 6530, "Organizational Training," 5–6.
53. Griffiss to Military Intelligence Division, M.A. Valencia Report No. 6530, "Organizational Training," 6–7.
54. Griffiss to Military Intelligence Division, M.A. Valencia Report No. 6530, "Organizational Training," 7.
55. Griffiss to Military Intelligence Division, M.A. Valencia Report No. 6530, "Organizational Training," 8.
56. Griffiss to Military Intelligence Division, M.A. Valencia Report No. 6530, "Organizational Training," 8.
57. Griffiss to Military Intelligence Division, M.A. Valencia Report No. 6530, "Organizational Training," 8–9. Regarding the Telefónica building serving as a target, see Beevor, *Battle for Spain*, 176.
58. Griffiss to Military Intelligence Division, M.A. Valencia Report No. 6530, "Organizational Training," 9.
59. Griffiss to Military Intelligence Division, M.A. Valencia Report No. 6530, "Organizational Training," 9.
60. Griffiss to Military Intelligence Division, M.A. Valencia Report No. 6530, "Organizational Training," 9.
61. Griffiss to Military Intelligence Division, M.A. Valencia Report No. 6530, "Organizational Training," 9.
62. Edwards, *Airmen without Portfolio*, 83–86.
63. Smith and Hall, *Five Down, No Glory*, 246.
64. Tinker, *Some Still Live*, 227.
65. Tinker, *Some Still Live*, 227–28.
66. Corral, "A Ukulele, a Torture Box and a Judo Black Belt."
67. Edwards, *Airmen without Portfolio*, 91.
68. Edwards, *Airmen without Portfolio*, 92–95.
69. Smith and Hall, *Five Down, No Glory*, 265–67.
70. Smith and Hall, *Five Down, No Glory*, 270.
71. Smith and Hall, *Five Down, No Glory*, 270–83.
72. Albert J. Baumler and E. W. Raley, Correspondence, 1938, IRISREF A1399, AFHRA, Frames 835–38.
73. Baumler to Raley, Correspondence, 1938, Frames 850–60.
74. Baumler to Raley, Correspondence, 1938, Frame 868.
75. Baumler to Raley, Correspondence, 1938, Frames 868–69.
76. Baumler to Raley, Correspondence, March 29, 1938, Frame 870. For a comparison to the I-16, see Howson, *Aircraft of the Spanish Civil War*, 197–201.
77. Baumler to Raley, Correspondence, March 29, 1938, Frame 885.
78. Raley cover letter, Correspondence, April 6, 1938, Frame 838.

79. Raley to Baumler, Correspondence, April 6, 1938, Frame 839.
80. Smith and Hall, *Five Down, No Glory*, 287.
81. Raley to Baumler, Correspondence, April 6, 1938, Frame 839.
82. F. G. Tinker Jr. to Chief of Military Operations, United States War Department, "Letter Offering of Services to War Department and State Department," December 9, 1938, RG 165 M-1445, Roll #8, NARA.
83. Tinker to Chief of Military Operations, "Letter Offering of Services," December 9, 1938.
84. E. R. W. McCabe, Assistant Chief of Staff, G-2, to F. G. Tinker Jr., December 20, 1938, RG 165 M-1445, Roll #8, NARA.
85. W. M. Smith, *Mercenary Eagles*, 92–95; see also Smith and Hall, *Five Down, No Glory*, 285.
86. Graves, "Consul at Vigo to the Secretary of State," Telegram, July 27, 1937, 530–31.
87. W. M. Smith, *Mercenary Eagles*, 98.
88. Knoblaugh, *Correspondent in Spain* , 114–15.
89. Knoblaugh, *Correspondent in Spain*, 114.
90. Logoluso, *Fiat CR.32 Aces*, 16.
91. Dickinson and Parsons, "My Air Duel with Bruno Mussolini," 34–37, 34–35.
92. Dickinson and Parsons, "My Air Duel with Bruno Mussolini," 36.
93. Dickinson and Parsons, "My Air Duel with Bruno Mussolini," 37.

CHAPTER 6. CLOSE AIR SUPPORT

Epigraph: Townsend Griffiss to Military Intelligence Division, M.A. Valencia Report No. 6514, "Air Combat Operations," April 7, 1937, p. 10, RG 165 M-1445, Roll #7, NARA.

1. Stephen O. Fuqua to Military Intelligence Division, M.A. Valencia Report No. 6506, "The Military Situation," April 4, 1937, pp. 3–4, RG 165 M-1445, Roll #7, NARA.
2. Thomas, *Spanish Civil War*, 542, 612, and 612n2.
3. Hooton, *Spain in Arms*, 81, 84–86.
4. Hooton, *Spain in Arms*, 86.
5. Hooton, *Spain in Arms*, 87.
6. Hooton, *Spain in Arms*, 87.
7. Hooton, *Spain in Arms*, 87–88.
8. These details are found in Thomas, *Spanish Civil War*, 624; Alpert, *Franco and the Condor Legion*, 125–27; and Irujo Ametzaga, "Special Feature."
9. The 300-person death toll appears to be the agreed-to number among recent historians, despite early reports of more than 1,000 dead. See, for instance, Beevor, *Battle for Spain*, 232; or Hooton, *Spain in Arms*, 94. However, Irujo Ametzaga ("Special Feature") believes many of these statistics, including people killed, buildings destroyed, and aircraft used, to be underestimates.

10. Corum, *Wolfram von Richthofen*, 134.
11. Irujo Ametzaga, "Special Feature."
12. Alpert, *Franco and the Condor Legion*, 125.
13. Proctor, *Hitler's Luftwaffe*, 131.
14. Corum, *Wolfram von Richthofen*, 134 and n.53.
15. Beevor, *Battle for Spain*, 263.
16. Bolloten and Esenwein, "Negrín, Juan," 360–62.
17. Townsend Griffiss to Military Intelligence Division, M.A. Valencia Report No. 6546, "Air Combat Operations," May 6, 1937, p. 6, RG 165 M-1445, Roll #7, NARA.
18. Townsend Griffiss to Military Intelligence Division, M.A. Valencia Report No. 6554, "Air Operations, Official Report on España," May 26, 1937, p. 4, RG 165 M-1445, Roll #7, NARA; H. H. Fuller to Military Intelligence Division, M.A. Paris Report No. 23,508-W, "Major Operations, Notes on Basque Front," June 22, 1937, p. 2, RG 165 M-1445, Roll #7, NARA, 2.
19. Townsend Griffiss to Military Intelligence Division, M.A. Valencia Report No. 6552, "Air Operations, Valencia Bombardment," May 17, 1937, RG 165 M-1445, Roll #7, NARA.
20. Beevor, *Battle for Spain*, 288–89.
21. Salas Larrazábal, *Air War over Spain*, 165–66.
22. Townsend Griffiss to Military Intelligence Division, M.A. Valencia Report No. 6569, "Distribution of Troops, Air Situation at Bilbao," June 14, 1937, RG 165 M-1445, Roll #7, NARA.
23. Stephen O. Fuqua to Military Intelligence Division, M.A. Valencia Report No. 6571, "General Davila Replaces General Mola Killed in Air Accident," June 16, 1937, RG 165 M-1445, Roll #7, NARA.
24. Thomas, *Spanish Civil War*, 705–6; Beevor, *Battle for Spain*, 273. The Russian name for NKVD is *Narodnyy Komissariat Vnutrennikh Del*, People's Commissariat for Internal Affairs.
25. Beevor, *Battle for Spain*, 277.
26. Salas Larrazábal, *Air War over Spain*, 162.
27. Thomas, *Spanish Civil War*, 710.
28. Hooton, *Spain in Arms*, 119–24.
29. Salas Larrazábal, *Air War over Spain*, 174.
30. Beevor, *Battle for Spain*, 279.
31. Salas Larrazábal, *Air War over Spain*, 174–76.
32. Alpert, *Franco and the Condor Legion*, 150–51; Proctor, *Hitler's Luftwaffe*, 149.
33. Alpert, *Franco and the Condor Legion*, 151.
34. Howson, *Aircraft*, 232–33.
35. H. H. Fuller to Military Intelligence Division, M.A., Letter, 23,694-W, August 28, 1937, p. 3, RG 165 M-1445, Roll #7, NARA.
36. Esdaile, *Spanish Civil War*, 259; Proctor, *Hitler's Luftwaffe*, 150–51.

37. Hooton, *Spain in Arms*, 135–37.
38. Information for this battle is taken primarily from Hooton, *Spain in Arms* (chap. 4); Thomas, *Spanish Civil War* (chap. 40); and Beevor, *Battle for Spain* (chap. 24).
39. Hooton, *Spain in Arms*, 143.
40. H. H. Fuller to Military Intelligence Division, M.A., Letter, 23,694-W, p. 8.
41. Associated Press, "600 Moors Slain in a Loyalist Trap," *New York Times*, July 18, 1937, Late City Edition, 1.
42. Hanson W. Baldwin, "Few Gains in Spain after Year of War," *New York Times*, July 18, 1937, Late City Edition.
43. Baldwin, "Few Gains in Spain."
44. Baldwin, "Few Gains in Spain."
45. "Planes Debunked: As War Machines They Win in Theory but Fail in Practise," *Literary Digest* 123, no. 4 (January 23, 1937): 13–15, 13.
46. "Air Warfare in Ethiopia and Spain, and Other Editorials," *U.S. Air Services* 22, no. 4 (April 1937): 9.
47. Townsend Griffiss to Military Intelligence Division, M.A. Valencia Report No. 6648, "Air Lessons of War, First Year," August 17, 1937, p. 1, RG 165 M-1445, Roll #7, NARA.
48. Griffiss to Military Intelligence Division, M.A. Valencia Report No. 6648, "Air Lessons," 2.
49. Griffiss to Military Intelligence Division, M.A. Valencia Report No. 6648, "Air Lessons," 3.
50. Griffiss to Military Intelligence Division, M.A. Valencia Report No. 6648, "Air Lessons," 4–5.
51. Griffiss to Military Intelligence Division, M.A. Valencia Report No. 6648, "Air Lessons," 5.
52. Griffiss to Military Intelligence Division, M.A. Valencia Report No. 6648, "Air Lessons," 6–7.
53. Griffiss to Military Intelligence Division, M.A. Valencia Report No. 6648, "Air Lessons," 8–9.
54. Griffiss to Military Intelligence Division, M.A. Valencia Report No. 6648, "Air Lessons," 9–10.
55. Griffiss to Military Intelligence Division, M.A. Valencia Report No. 6648, "Air Lessons," 10. [Misspelling left as is.]
56. Force estimates are compiled from the following sources: Beevor, *Battle for Spain*, 237; Hooton, *Spain in Arms*, 102–3; Salas Larrazábal, *Air War over Spain*, 177–79; and Thomas, *Spanish Civil War*, 717–18.
57. Thomas, *Spanish Civil War*, 718–20.
58. Hooton, *Spain in Arms*, 107.
59. Salas Larrazábal, *Air War over Spain*, 180–81.
60. There seems to be a wide range in force estimates for the Republicans. Hooton's estimates in *Spain in Arms* (144–45) are the most recent and are therefore

primarily relied upon in this section. Other references were incorporated, including Salas Larrazábal, *Air War over Spain*, 186, Beevor, *Battle for Spain*, 297, and Thomas, *Spanish Civil War*, 725.
61. Thomas, *Spanish Civil War*, 725 (Mediana); Salas Larrazábal, *Air War over Spain*, 186 (Zuera).
62. Thomas, *Spanish Civil War*, 726.
63. Salas Larrazábal, *Air War over Spain*, 186.
64. Bradley, *International Brigades in Spain*, 48.
65. Hooton, *Spain in Arms*, 147–48; 148 (quote from Enrique Lister, *Nuestra Guerra*).
66. Hooton, *Spain in Arms*, 110.
67. The following sources are used for these figures: Salas Larrazábal, *Air War over Spain*, 187–88; Hooton, *Spain in Arms*, 111; Beevor, *Battle for Spain*, 301.
68. Salas Larrazábal, *Air War over Spain*, 188; Hooton, *Spain in Arms*, 108, map 8.
69. As quoted in Salas Larrazábal, *Air War over Spain*, 188.
70. As quoted in Salas Larrazábal, *Air War over Spain*, 189.
71. Thomas, *Spanish Civil War*, 730.
72. Hooton, *Spain in Arms*, 113; Thomas, *Spanish Civil War*, 731.
73. Salas Larrazábal, *Air War over Spain*, 193.
74. Thomas, *Spanish Civil War*, 731.
75. Thomas, *Spanish Civil War*, 733.
76. Salas Larrazábal, *Air War over Spain*, 195. The mention of three surviving aircraft is from an excerpt of Francisco Tarazona's book, *Sangre en el Cielo* that is reprinted in Salas Larrazábal's *Air War over Spain*.
77. Thomas, *Spanish Civil War*, 697.
78. Thomas, *Spanish Civil War*, 702–5.
79. Proctor, *Hitler's Luftwaffe*, 171–72.
80. Hooton, *Spain in Arms*, 65.
81. Thomas, *Spanish Civil War*, 733.

CHAPTER 7. AERIAL BOMBING

Epigraph: Stephen O. Fuqua to MID, M.A. Barcelona Report No. 6803, "Air Operations, Barcelona Bombardment," March 25, 1938, p. 3, RG 165 M-1445, Roll #7, NARA.
1. Stephen O. Fuqua to Military Intelligence Division, M.A. Valencia Report No. 6711, "Three Day Visit to the Eastern Front," November 1, 1937, RG 165 M-1445, Roll #7, NARA. There had once been separate Lincoln and Washington Battalions, but they had been so badly attrited during the Battle of Brunete that the two were combined in July 1937.
2. Fuqua to Military Intelligence Division, M.A. Valencia Report No. 6711, "Three Day Visit to the Eastern Front."
3. Fuqua to Military Intelligence Division, M.A. Valencia Report No. 6711, "Three Day Visit to the Eastern Front," 2. Brackets to indicate spelling correction.

4. Fuqua to Military Intelligence Division, M.A. Valencia Report No. 6711, "Three Day Visit to the Eastern Front," 2.
5. Fuqua to Military Intelligence Division, M.A. Valencia Report No. 6711, "Three Day Visit to the Eastern Front," 11–14.
6. Townsend Griffiss to Military Intelligence Division, M.A. Valencia Report No. 6721, "Air Combat Operations, October 12th–November 12th," November 13, 1937, pp. 2–3, RG 165 M-1445, Roll #7, NARA.
7. Griffiss to Military Intelligence Division, M.A. Valencia Report No. 6721, "Air Combat Operations. October 12th–November 12th," 3–5.
8. Lecture, "Lessons from the Spanish Civil War," Command and General Staff School, December 1, 1937, p. 16, RG 165 M-1445, Roll #7, NARA.
9. Lecture, "Lessons from the Spanish Civil War," 1–2.
10. Lecture, "Lessons from the Spanish Civil War," 3.
11. Lecture, "Lessons from the Spanish Civil War," 3.
12. Lecture, "Lessons from the Spanish Civil War," 3–4.
13. Lecture, "Lessons from the Spanish Civil War," 4–6.
14. Lecture, "Lessons from the Spanish Civil War," 6–8.
15. Lecture, "Lessons from the Spanish Civil War," 9–10.
16. Lecture, "Lessons from the Spanish Civil War," 11–12
17. Lecture, "Lessons from the Spanish Civil War," 12.
18. Lecture, "Lessons from the Spanish Civil War," 12.
19. Lecture, "Lessons from the Spanish Civil War," 15.
20. Lecture, "Lessons from the Spanish Civil War," 2.
21. Boyd, "Hernández Saravia, Juan," 256–57.
22. Information about the Battle of Teruel is taken from the following sources: Beevor, *Battle for Spain*, 313–22; Esdaile, *Spanish Civil War*, 251–58; Hooton, *Spain in Arms*, 157–74; Salas Larrazábal, *Air War over Spain*, 207–17; Thomas, *Spanish Civil War*, 788–94.
23. Thomas, *Spanish Civil War*, 793.
24. Townsend Griffiss to Military Intelligence Division, M.A. Barcelona, Report No. 6756, "Air Combat Operations, Teruel Offensive," January 12, 1938, p. 1, RG 165 M-1445, Roll #7, NARA.
25. Griffiss to Military Intelligence Division, M.A. Barcelona, Report No. 6756, "Air Combat Operations, Teruel Offensive," 2–3.
26. Salas Larrazábal, *Air War over Spain*, 213.
27. Proctor, *Hitler's Luftwaffe*, 180–81.
28. Salas Larrazábal, *Air War over Spain*, 216.
29. Hooton, *Spain in Arms*, 174–75.
30. Thomas, *Spanish Civil War*, 798.
31. Salas Larrazábal, *Air War over Spain*, 224.
32. Thomas, *Spanish Civil War*, 799.
33. Salas Larrazábal, *Air War over Spain*, 226.

34. Bradley, *International Brigades in Spain*, 46; Esdaile, *Spanish Civil War*, 269–70.
35. Thomas, *Spanish Civil War*, 802.
36. Hooton, *Spain in Arms*, 181, 187.
37. Proctor gives the total of bombs dropped by the Condor Legion as 160 tons (*Hitler's Luftwaffe*, 191–93); Salas Larrazábal puts the total for all Nationalists at 210 tons (*Air War over Spain*, 227).
38. These events are recorded in Salas Larrazábal, *Air War over Spain*, 227–32.
39. Stephen O. Fuqua to Military Intelligence Division, M.A. Barcelona Report No. 6813, "Visit to the Ebro Sector—Eastern Front," April 12, 1938, RG 165 M-1445, Roll #7, NARA.
40. Fuqua to Military Intelligence Division, M.A. Barcelona Report No. 6813, "Visit to the Ebro Sector," 2. Bracketed punctuation added by present author.
41. Fuqua to Military Intelligence Division, M.A. Barcelona Report No. 6813, "Visit to the Ebro Sector," 3.
42. Fuqua to Military Intelligence Division, M.A. Barcelona Report No. 6813, "Visit to the Ebro Sector," 3.
43. Fuqua to Military Intelligence Division, M.A. Barcelona Report No. 6813, "Visit to the Ebro Sector," 3.
44. Beevor, *Battle for Spain*, 337–38.
45. Hooton, *Spain in Arms*, 188.
46. Proctor, *Hitler's Luftwaffe*, 177–78.
47. Alpert, *Franco and the Condor Legion*, 183.
48. Salas Larrazábal, *Air War over Spain*, 229–31; Salas Larrazábal, or his translator, referred to the rank as commander, but this is almost certainly meant to be *comandante*, the Spanish equivalent of major.
49. Beevor, *Battle for Spain*, 335–36.
50. Boyne, *Influence of Air Power*, 164.
51. Stephen O. Fuqua to Military Intelligence Division, M.A. Barcelona Report No. 6803, "Air Operations, Barcelona Bombardment," March 25, 1938, RG 165 M-1445, Roll #7, NARA.
52. Fuqua to Military Intelligence Division, M.A. Barcelona Report No. 6803, "Air Operations, Barcelona Bombardment," 2.
53. Fuqua to Military Intelligence Division, M.A. Barcelona Report No. 6803, "Air Operations, Barcelona Bombardment," 4.
54. Phillips, "Preview of Armageddon," 12.
55. Phillips, "Preview of Armageddon," 96.
56. Phillips, "Preview of Armageddon," 97.
57. Phillips, "Preview of Armageddon," 97–98.
58. "What Lessons from Air Warfare?," *U.S. Air Services* 23, no. 4 (April 1938): 7–8; 7.
59. "What Lessons from Air Warfare?," 7–8.
60. Arnold, "Air Lessons from Current Wars," 17.
61. Arnold, "Air Lessons from Current Wars," 17.

62. Arnold, "Air Lessons from Current Wars," 17.
63. Arnold, "Air Lessons from Current Wars," 17.
64. Arnold, "Air Lessons from Current Wars," 17–18.
65. Arnold, "Air Lessons from Current Wars," 18.
66. Arnold, "Air Lessons from Current Wars," 18.
67. Maurer, *Aviation in the U.S. Army*, 352.
68. Arnold, "Air Lessons from Current Wars," 32.
69. Esdaile, *Spanish Civil War*, 271.
70. These figures come from Salas Larrazábal, *Air War over Spain*, 237, and Hooton, *Spain in Arms*, 190, 194. It is estimated that the Nationalists had ten divisions, each with about 7,900 troops, along with a 2,600-troop cavalry brigade. Hooton, *Spain in Arms*, 198; Quesada, *The Spanish Civil War 1936–1939 (1)*, 11.
71. Hooton, *Spain in Arms*, 190, 194–96.
72. Thomas, *Spanish Civil War*, 830.
73. Hooton, *Spain in Arms*. 192.
74. Hooton, *Spain in Arms*, 190, 196–99; Esdaile, *Spanish Civil War*, 273.
75. Hooton, *Spain in Arms*, 197–98.
76. Thomas, *Spanish Civil War*, 832.
77. Hooton, *Spain in Arms*, 198–99.
78. Casualty totals from Beevor, *Battle for Spain*, 347; and Hooton, *Spain in Arms*, 199.
79. Proctor, *Hitler's Luftwaffe*, 207–9.
80. Thomas, *Spanish Civil War*, 830.
81. Salas Larrazábal, *Air War over Spain*, 238–40.
82. Stephen Fuqua to Military Intelligence Division, M.A. Barcelona Report No. 6853, "Claims of Contending Parties Concerning Airplanes Brought Down during June, 1938," July 18, 1938, RG 165 M-1445, Roll #8, NARA.
83. Salas Larrazábal, *Air War over Spain*, 240.
84. Proctor, *Hitler's Luftwaffe*, 211.
85. Salas Larrazábal, *Air War over Spain*, 243–44.
86. Proctor, *Hitler's Luftwaffe*, 214–15.
87. Salas Larrazábal, *Air War over Spain*, 248–50.
88. Stephen Fuqua to Military Intelligence Division, M.A. Barcelona Report No. 6855, "Results of the Destruction by Rebel Aviation Bombing of the CAMPSA Storage Plant in Barcelona Harbor," July 20, 1938, RG 165 M-1445, Roll #8, NARA.
89. Office of the Chief of the Information Section of Anti-Aircraft Defense, "Extract from the Record of Enemy Aerial Activity Summarized in the Bulletin of Anti-Aircraft Defense," July 27, 1938, pp. 2–4, RG 165 M-1445, Roll #8, NARA.
90. Office of the Chief of the Information Section of Anti-Aircraft Defense, "Extract from the . . . Bulletin of Anti-Aircraft Defense," 11.
91. Office of the Chief of the Information Section of Anti-Aircraft Defense, "Extract from the . . . Bulletin of Anti-Aircraft Defense," 4.

92. Office of the Chief of the Information Section of Anti-Aircraft Defense, "Extract from the ... Bulletin of Anti-Aircraft Defense," 4–7.
93. Thomas, *Spanish Civil War*, 825.
94. Beevor, *Battle for Spain*, 363.
95. Alpert, *Franco and the Condor Legion*, 190.

CHAPTER 8. AIRCRAFT TECHNOLOGY

Note: Much of this chapter is taken from the author's master's thesis: Christopher G. Marquis, "American Aerial Perspectives: Observations on the Technological Development of Military Aviation during the Spanish Civil War, 1936–1939," MA thesis, Auburn University, 2020.

1. Merritt Roe Smith, "Technological Determinism in American Culture" in M. R. Smith and Marx, *Does Technology Drive History?*, 2.
2. Veblen, *Theory of the Leisure Class*, 1–8.
3. See Schatzberg, "Technik Comes to America," 505–6.
4. Schatzberg, "Technik Comes to America," 508–10.
5. Callihan, foreword to *Innovation and Achievement*, 13.
6. Shiner, "Coming of the GHQ Air Force," 108.
7. Bijker, Hughes, and Pinch, *Social Construction of Technological Systems*, xlii.
8. Corum, "Spanish Civil War," 322–24; Baughen, *Rise and Fall of the French Air Force*, 69–70.
9. Murphy and McNiece, *Military Aircraft*, 91, 136–38.
10. Alpert, *Franco and the Condor Legion*, 48.
11. Sullivan, "Fascist Italy's Military Involvement," 723–25.
12. For a discussion of the concept of an arms race in the Industrial Age, see McNeill, "Industrialization of War."
13. For a description of what is meant by "Industrial Age," see "Industrial Age" in Hines, *Webster's New Reference Library*, 918–20.
14. Statistics on the aircraft in the following sections are compiled from these sources: Howson, *Aircraft of the Spanish Civil War*; Jarrett, *Biplane to Monoplane*; Murphy and McNiece, *Military Aircraft*; Nalty, *Winged Shield, Winged Sword*; Angelucci, *Rand McNally Encyclopedia of Military Aircraft: 1914–1980*; Angelucci, *Rand McNally Encyclopedia of Military Aircraft: 1914 to the Present*; Townsend Griffiss to Military Intelligence Division, M.A. Valencia Report No. 6471, "Special Report on Spanish Government Air Force," February 21, 1937, IRISREF A2873, Frames 2264–87, AFHRA; and Winchester, *Classic Military Aircraft*. On the Treaty of Peace with Germany (Treaty of Versailles), June 28, 1919, see Bevans, *Treaties and Other International Agreements*, 2:129.
15. Murphy and McNiece, *Military Aircraft*, 94; Fritzsche, *Nation of Fliers*, 106–7.
16. Murphy and McNiece, *Military Aircraft*, 24–25.
17. Alpert, *Franco and the Condor Legion*, 30.
18. Fritzsche, *Nation of Fliers*, 187–90.

19. Murphy and McNiece, *Military Aircraft*, 138
20. Townsend Griffiss to Military Intelligence Division, M.A. Valencia Report No. 6530, "Organizational Training, Tactics Deployed," April 25, 1937, p. 8, IRISREF A2817, Call # 248.282–23, Frames 1425–33, AFHRA.
21. Howson, *Aircraft of the Spanish Civil War*, 181–82.
22. Howson, *Aircraft of the Spanish Civil War*, 232.
23. Howson, *Aircraft of the Spanish Civil War*, 231, 235
24. Wing loading is calculated by dividing gross weight by wing area. See Kenneth Munson, "The Biplane's Fall from Favour," in Jarrett, *Biplane to Monoplane*, 11; and Cavagnaro, "Performance."
25. Winchester, *Classic Military Aircraft*, 164.
26. Howson, *Aircraft of the Spanish Civil War*, 139.
27. Navarro Bonilla and Cano, "Photographic Air Reconnaissance," 379.
28. Navarro Bonilla and Cano, "Photographic Air Reconnaissance," 379.
29. Howson, *Aircraft of the Spanish Civil War*, 169–70.
30. Howson, *Aircraft of the Spanish Civil War*, 179–80.
31. Murphy and McNiece, *Military Aircraft*, 216.
32. Winchester, *Classic Military Aircraft*, 26–27.
33. Murphy and McNiece, *Military Aircraft*, 21.
34. Howson, *Aircraft of the Spanish Civil War*, 272.
35. H. B. Cheadle to Military Intelligence Division, M.A. Barcelona Report No. 6972, "Foreign Nationalist Aviation," December 31, 1938, RG 165 M-1445, Roll #8, NARA; and Howson, *Aircraft of the Spanish Civil War*, 274–75.
36. A *flying boat* has been defined as an "aircraft in which the fuselage formed the hull for landing and taking-off from water," while a *floatplane* has been defined as an aircraft "with a separate pontoon-type alighting structure." Aircraft that incorporate one of these characteristics, along with a retractable landing gear, are called *amphibians*. See Barfield, "Age of the Flying Boat," 89.
37. Howson, *Aircraft of the Spanish Civil War*, 72–73.
38. Sullivan, "Fascist Italy's Military Involvement," 723–25. This amount was calculated by first converting 650 million 1937 Italian lira to 30,910,025 gold grams, utilizing Rodney Edvinsson's "Historical Currency Converter (Test Version 1.0)," Historicalstatistics.org, January 10, 2016; then by multiplying the grams by the current U.S. dollar price of gold, which was $103.793 per gram on April 11, 2025, according to Chards, https://www.chards.co.uk/gold-price/daily-gold-price-per-gram-us-dollars.
39. Howson, *Aircraft of the Spanish Civil War*, 131–32.
40. Howson, *Aircraft of the Spanish Civil War*, 75.
41. L. R. Graham, *Ghost of the Executed Engineer*, 1, 45. The full Russian name of the OGPU is the *Obyedinyonnoye gosudarstvennoye politicheskoye upravleniye* (United State Political Directorate).
42. Whitewood, *Red Army and the Great Terror*, 128–30.

43. Kerber, *Stalin's Aviation Gulag*, 155. The full Russian name of the TsKB is the *Tsentralnoye konstruktorskoye byuro* (Central Design Bureau).
44. Kerber, *Stalin's Aviation Gulag*, 170.
45. Kerber, *Stalin's Aviation Gulag*, 143–47.
46. Kerber, *Stalin's Aviation Gulag*, 149–50. The full Russian name of the TsAGI is the *Tsentral'nyy Aerogidrodinamicheskiy Institut*.
47. Kerber, *Stalin's Aviation Gulag*, 151.
48. Howson, *Aircraft of the Spanish Civil War*, 265.
49. Howson, *Aircraft of the Spanish Civil War*, 193, 196.
50. Howson, *Aircraft of the Spanish Civil War*, 196–97.
51. Howson, *Aircraft of the Spanish Civil War*, 200.
52. Baughen, *Rise and Fall of the French Air Force*, 63, 69–73.
53. Corum, "Spanish Civil War," 322–23.
54. Griffiss to Military Intelligence Division, M.A. Valencia Report No. 6471, "Special Report," Frames 2274–75, 9–10.
55. Howson, *Aircraft of the Spanish Civil War*, 224–27.
56. Howson, *Aircraft of the Spanish Civil War*, 8–9.
57. Howson, *Aircraft of the Spanish Civil War*, 25.
58. Howson, *Aircraft of the Spanish Civil War*, 195.
59. Howson, *Aircraft of the Spanish Civil War*, 81–82.
60. Howson, *Aircraft of the Spanish Civil War*, 28.
61. Woodman, "Armaments Development," 189.
62. Woodman, "Armaments Development," 190.
63. Howson, *Aircraft of the Spanish Civil War*, 114–15. See also Townsend Griffiss to Military Intelligence Division, M.A. Valencia Report No. 6717, "Armament and Equipment, Moto-Cannon," November 9, 1937, RG 165 M-1445, Roll #7, NARA.
64. Townsend Griffiss to Military Intelligence Division, M.A. Valencia, Report No. 6490, "Machine Guns and Ammunition," March 13, 1937, RG 165 M-1445, Roll #7, NARA.
65. Horace H. Fuller to Military Intelligence Division, M.A. Paris Report No. 23,345-W, "Air Combat Operations, Operations in Spain," April 10, 1937, pp. 1–2, RG 165 M-1445, Roll #7, NARA.
66. Smith and Hall, *Five Down, No Glory*, 92.
67. Smith and Hall, *Five Down, No Glory*, 218.
68. Tinker, *Some Still Live*, 236.
69. Griffiss to Military Intelligence Division, M.A. Valencia, Report No. 6490, "Machine Guns and Ammunition."
70. Fuller to Military Intelligence Division, M.A. Paris Report No. 23,345-W, "Air Combat Operations," 2.
71. Griffiss to Military Intelligence Division, M.A. Valencia, Report No. 6490, "Machine Guns and Ammunition."

72. Townsend Griffiss to Military Intelligence Division, M.A. Valencia Report No. 6717, "Armament and Equipment, Motor-Cannon," November 9, 1937, RG 165 M-1445, Roll #7, NARA.
73. Howson, *Aircraft of the Spanish Civil War*, 184, 231–33.
74. Proctor, *Hitler's Luftwaffe*, 90–91.
75. Howson, *Aircraft of the Spanish Civil War*, 177.
76. Griffiss to Military Intelligence Division, M.A. Valencia Report No. 6471, "Special Report," Frame 2285, 20.
77. For a classification of bomber payloads, see T. Hooton, "Military Aviation—the Slow Developer," 66 fn.
78. Horace H. Fuller to Military Intelligence Division, M.A. Paris Report No. 23,265-W, "Major Military Operations, Air Combat Operations—Air Equipment and Tactics," March 10, 1937, pp. 1–3, RG 165 M-1445, Roll #7, NARA.
79. Truman Smith to Military Intelligence Division, M.A. Berlin Report No. 15,397, "Experiences with Modern Weapons," July 16, 1937, pp. 1–2, RG 165 M-1445, Roll #7, NARA.
80. Douhet, *Command of the Air*, 37.
81. Esdaile, *Spanish Civil War*, 340; 141 (arrival of first 88-mm FLAK18s).
82. Proctor, *Hitler's Luftwaffe*, 60.
83. Raymond E. Lee to Military Intelligence Division, M.A. London Report No. 38512, "Employment of Troops in Domestic Disturbances," January 25, 1937, p. 1, RG 165 M-1445, Roll #7, NARA.
84. Esdaile, *Spanish Civil War*, 345.
85. F. H. Lincoln to Assistant Chief of Staff, WFD, "Antiaircraft Artillery in Spain," March 12[?], 1937, p. 4, RG 165 M-1445, Roll #7, NARA.
86. Fuller to Military Intelligence Division, M.A. Paris Report No. 23,345-W, "Air Combat Operations," 2.
87. Griffiss to Military Intelligence Division, M.A. Valencia Report No. 6552, "Air Operations, Valencia Bombardment," May 17, 1937, p. 4, RG 165 M-1445, Roll #7, NARA.
88. Esdaile, *Spanish Civil War*, 282, 345.
89. Griffiss to Military Intelligence Division, M.A. Valencia Report No. 6471, "Special Report," Frame 2281, 16.
90. Fuller to Military Intelligence Division, M.A. Paris Report No. 23,345-W, "Air Combat Operations," 3.
91. Way may have been influenced by Nicola Tesla's theoretical "death ray," or the heat rays used by the Martian tripods in H. G. Wells's *The War of the Worlds* (1898).

CHAPTER 9. AIR SUPERIORITY

1. William P. Carney, "Rebels Smash On as Spain Observes War Anniversary," *New York Times*, July 18, 1938, Late City Edition, 1.

2. Herbert L. Matthews, "Loyalists Remain Determined," *New York Times*, July 18, 1938, Late City Edition, 1, 8.
3. Force estimates are gathered from the following sources: H. Thomas, *Spanish Civil War*, 835; Esdaile, *Spanish Civil War*, 283–84; Beevor, *Battle for Spain*, 350; Hooton, *Spain in Arms*, 206 (tables 6.1 and 6.2), 209–10; and Proctor, *Hitler's Luftwaffe*, 221–23.
4. Beevor, *Battle for Spain*, 350; Hooton, *Spain in Arms*, 206 (table 6.2).
5. Information of the Battle of the Ebro is found in the following sources: Thomas, *Spanish Civil War*, 835–57; Esdaile, *Spanish Civil War*, 281–94; Beevor, *Battle for Spain*, 349–58; Hooton, *Spain in Arms*, 205–27; Proctor, *Hitler's Luftwaffe*, 218–36; and Salas Larrazábal, *Air War over Spain*, 254–83.
6. Proctor, *Hitler's Luftwaffe*, 223.
7. Hooton, *Spain in Arms*, 224–25.
8. Salas Larrazábal, *Air War over Spain*, 258.
9. Salas Larrazábal, *Air War over Spain*, 258–62.
10. Beevor, *Battle for Spain*, 352–53.
11. Stephen O. Fuqua to Military Intelligence Division, M.A. Barcelona, Report No. 6895, "Visit to the Ebro Front," September 13, 1938, pp. 1–3, 6, RG 165 M-1445, Roll #8, NARA.
12. Fuqua to Military Intelligence Division, M.A. Barcelona, Report No. 6895, "Visit to the Ebro Front," 5.
13. Fuqua to Military Intelligence Division, M.A. Barcelona, Report No. 6895, "Visit to the Ebro Front," 5.
14. Fuqua to, Military Intelligence Division, M.A. Barcelona, Report No. 6895, "Visit to the Ebro Front," 8.
15. Proctor, *Hitler's Luftwaffe*, 231–33; Salas Larrazábal, *Air War over Spain*, 264.
16. Fuqua to Military Intelligence Division, M.A. Barcelona, Report No. 6895, "Visit to the Ebro Front," 7.
17. Townsend Griffiss, "The Air Warfare in Spain and Its Effect Upon the Air Rearmament of France," August 11, 1938, p. 1, RG 165 M-1445, Roll #8, NARA.
18. Griffiss, "Air Warfare," 2–3.
19. Griffiss, "Air Warfare," 4–5.
20. Griffiss, "Air Warfare," 7–8.
21. Griffiss, "Air Warfare," 11–12.
22. Griffiss, "Air Warfare," 14–15.
23. Griffiss, "Air Warfare," 17.
24. Griffiss, "Air Warfare," 19.
25. Griffiss, "Air Warfare," 19.
26. Griffiss, "Air Warfare," 24.
27. Griffiss, "Air Warfare," 20–25.
28. Griffiss, "Air Warfare," 21–23.
29. Shiner, "Coming of the GHQ Air Force," 131.

30. Arnold, *American Airpower Comes of Age*; the first part of this series, likely written by editor John W. Huston, gives Arnold's biographical information. The information here is taken from pages 4–39, specifically pages 4, 8, 25, and 37.
31. As quoted in Arnold, *American Airpower Comes of Age*, 9.
32. George O. Squier, *Efficiency Report*, 1919, as quoted in Arnold, *American Airpower Comes of Age*, 10.
33. Mason M. Patrick, *Efficiency Report*, 1926, as quoted in Arnold, *American Airpower Comes of Age*, 20.
34. E. E. Booth, *Efficiency Report*, 1927, as quoted in Arnold, *American Airpower Comes of Age*, 23.
35. Charles J. Symmonds, *Efficiency Report*, 1928, as quoted in Arnold, *American Airpower Comes of Age*, 23.
36. H. C. Pratt, *Efficiency Report*, 1931, as quoted in Arnold, *American Airpower Comes of Age*, 26.
37. Henry H. Arnold to E. E. Adler, April 28, 1932, as quoted in Arnold, *American Airpower Comes of Age*, 26.
38. Arnold, *American Airpower Comes of Age*, 37–39.
39. Arnold, *American Airpower Comes of Age*, 42–52.
40. Mets, "Army Roots," 26–27.
41. "Radio Listeners in Panic, Taking War Drama as Fact," *New York Times*, October 31, 1938, 1; and "Geologists at Princeton Hunt 'Meteor' in Vain," *New York Times*, October 31, 1938, 1, 4.
42. "Radio Listeners in Panic," 4.
43. Jackson-Schebetta, "Companies to Keep," 39–43.
44. Jackson-Schebetta, "Companies to Keep," 34.
45. Salas Larrazábal, *Air War over Spain*, 282.
46. Casualties from Ebro come from the following sources: Thomas, *Spanish Civil War*, 855; Beevor, *Battle for Spain*, 358; Esdaile, *Spanish Civil War*, 291; Hooton, *Spain in Arms*, 227–29; and Proctor, *Hitler's Luftwaffe*, 235–36.
47. Joint Publication 3-01, *Countering Air and Missile Threats*, GL-8.
48. Joint Publication 3-01, *Countering Air and Missile Threats*, GL-8.
49. An example of the use of "air supremacy" in its earlier sense—i.e., as a synonym for air dominance—is found in Griffiss's declaration in April 1937 that "the Government has gained Air Supremacy," following the Battle of Guadalajara. Townsend Griffiss to Military Intelligence Division, M.A. Valencia Report No. 6514, "Air Combat Operations," April 7, 1937, RG 165 M-1445, Roll #7, NARA, 10.
50. See Beevor, *Battle for Spain*, 372; Proctor, *Hitler's Luftwaffe*, 240; and Salas Larrazábal, *Air War over Spain*, 285.
51. H. B. Cheadle to Military Intelligence Division, M.A. Barcelona Report No. 6949, "Statistics on Aerial Bombings and Sea Bombardments Against Catalonia," December 9, 1938, RG 165 M-1445, Roll #8, NARA.
52. Cortada, *Modern Warfare in Spain*, xxiii–xxv.

53. Thomas, *Spanish Civil War*, 863–64.
54. Esdaile, *Spanish Civil War*, 294–95.
55. For more details on the respective forces, see Beevor, *Battle for Spain*, 372–73; and Hooton, *Spain in Arms*, 231–33.
56. Thomas, *Spanish Civil War*, 869.
57. Proctor, *Hitler's Luftwaffe*, 239; Esdaile, *Spanish Civil War*, 298–99.
58. H. B. Cheadle to Military Intelligence Division, M.A. Barcelona Report No. 6972, "Foreign Nationalist Aviation," December 31, 1938, p. 3, RG 165 M-1445, Roll #8, NARA.
59. Salas Larrazábal, *Air War over Spain*, 290–91.
60. Esdaile, *Spanish Civil War*, 296.
61. Salas Larrazábal, *Air War over Spain*, 291; Thomas, *Spanish Civil War*, 870–73.
62. Esdaile, *Spanish Civil War*, 298.
63. Hooton, *Spain in Arms*, 237.
64. E. R. W. McCabe, Assistant Chief of Staff, G-2, to Chief of Staff, "The Situation in Barcelona," January 26, 1939, p. 2, RG 165 M-1445, Roll #8, NARA.
65. H. B Cheadle to Military Intelligence Division, M.A. Perpignan Report No. 6985, "The Military Situation," February 1, 1939, p. 9, RG 165 M-1445, Roll #8, NARA.
66. Beevor, *Battle for Spain*, 381.
67. Proctor, *Hitler's Luftwaffe*, 246–47.
68. Hooton, *Spain in Arms*, 235–37.
69. Hooton, *Spain in Arms*, 235.
70. Salas Larrazábal, *Air War over Spain*, 293–94.
71. Howson, *Aircraft of the Spanish Civil War*, 235.
72. Alpert, *Franco and the Condor Legion*, 191.
73. Salas Larrazábal, *Air War over Spain*, 302; Thomas, *Spanish Civil War*, 886.
74. See Esdaile, *Spanish Civil War*, 302; and Salas Larrazábal, *Air War over Spain*, 295–99.
75. Thomas, *Spanish Civil War*, 886, 891–92.
76. Cortada, "Casado López, Segismundo," 111–12.
77. Thomas, *Spanish Civil War*, 895–99.
78. Salas Larrazábal, *Air War over Spain*, 301.
79. Beevor, *Battle for Spain*, 392–94.
80. Thomas, *Spanish Civil War*, 912–13.
81. H. B. Cheadle to Military Intelligence Division, M.A. Spain Report No. 7007, "The Closing Chapter of the Spanish Civil War," April 3, 1939, p. 3, RG 165 M-1445, Roll #8, NARA.
82. Thomas, *Spanish Civil War*, 915.
83. Cheadle to Military Intelligence Division, M.A. Spain Report No. 7007, "Closing Chapter," 4.
84. Cheadle to Military Intelligence Division, M.A. Spain Report No. 7007, "Closing Chapter," 4.

CHAPTER 10. AFTER-ACTION REPORT

1. Shiner, "Heyday of the GHQ Air Force," 156, 162. Calculation of currency from 1939 to 2025 is from "Inflation Calculator," amortization.org, accessed April 11, 2025.
2. Nalty, "Reaction to the War in Europe," 172–74.
3. H. H. Arnold, Major General, Air Corps, Chief of the Air Corps, to the Secretary of War, Memorandum, July 30, 1940, RG 107 166-1200-B5, NARA.
4. E. C. Langmead, Major, Air Corps, to Chief of the Materiel Division, "Exhibit 'A' Summary Sheets of Topics of Conf. 7–2 & 3, 1940," July 8, 1940, pp. 17–17a, RG 107 A1–166–1200, NARA.
5. Arnold to Secretary of War, Memorandum, July 30, 1940.
6. Nalty, "Reaction to the War in Europe," 172, 179–81, 190.
7. Shiner, "Heyday of the GHQ Air Force," 157; Nalty, "Reaction to the War in Europe," 178.
8. Office of the Chief of the Air Corps to Robert Lovett, Assistant Secretary of War, "Memorandum," February 10, 1941, RG 107 A1–99–1, NARA.
9. Robert A. Lovett to Secretary of War, "Present Air Corps First Line Combat Strength," March 24, 1941, RG 107 A1–99–1, NARA.
10. H. H. Arnold, Commanding General, Army Air Forces, to Secretary of War, "Comparative Summary of Air Forces Strength as of July 1, 1939, and April 1, 1942," May 4, 1942, RG 107 A1–99–1, NARA.
11. Nalty, "Reaction to the War in Europe," 193–94.
12. H. H. Arnold, Major General, Air Corps, Chief of the Air Corps, to the Chief of Staff, "Coordination of Purchases of Airplanes by the U.S. Army and Navy and British Purchasing Commission—Conference for," August 5, 1940, RG 107 166–200-B4, NARA.
13. Robert Patterson, Assistant Secretary of War, to William Knudsen, The Advisory Commission to the Council of National Defense, "Revised Army Airframe Delivery Requirements," August 10, 1940, RG 107 166–200-A3, NARA.
14. Nalty, "Reaction to the War in Europe," 173, 194.
15. H. H. Arnold, Deputy Chief of Staff for Air to Secretary of War, "Diversion of Additional Heavy Bombers," October 16, 1941, RG 107 A1–99–2, NARA.
16. Albert J. Baumler to Edward Raley, March 29, 1938, pp. 866–67, IRISREF A1399, Frames 834–94, AFHRA.
17. Baumler to Raley, March 29, 1938, 868.
18. Baumler to Raley, March 29, 1938, 871.
19. Baumler to Raley, March 29, 1938, 877.
20. Kenney, "Airplane in Modern Warfare," 17–22, 36; quote on page 22.
21. C. E. Duncan, Major, Air Corps, to Assistant Secretary of War, "Chart #19581 AC," January 19, 1940, RG 107 205–961-A4/A5, NARA.
22. Robert A. Lovett to Secretary of War, "Present Air Corps First Line Combat Strength," March 24, 1941, RG 107 A1–99–1, NARA.

23. Townsend Griffiss, M.A. Valencia. Report No. 6471, "Special Report on Spanish Government Air Force," February 21, 1937, p. 21, IRISREF A2873, Frames 2264–287, AFHRA.
24. Duncan to Assistant Secretary of War, "Chart #19581 AC," January 19, 1940.
25. Miller, *Airlift Doctrine*, 21.
26. McFarland and Newton, "American Strategic Air Offensive against Germany," 216.
27. Proctor, *Hitler's Luftwaffe*, 256.
28. Salas Larrazábal, *Air War over Spain*, 304.
29. Yenne, *White Rose of Stalingrad*, 122.
30. Smith and Hall, *Five Down*, 301–2, 306. Smith and Hall are rightly skeptical of the determination of suicide (303–5). Edwards (*Airmen without Portfolio*, 105–6) presents a slightly different version of the crime scene.
31. Cortada, *Modern Warfare in Spain*, xxiii–xiv.
32. Thomas, *Spanish Civil War*, 921.
33. Proctor, "Kindelán Y Duany, Alfredo (1872–1962)," 283.
34. W. M. Smith, "Mercenary Eagles," 96–104; also Smith and Hall, *Five Down*, 311–12.
35. Proctor, *Hitler's Luftwaffe*, 261.
36. Corum, *Wolfram von Richthofen*, 3. The full Russian name of the VVS is *Voenno-Vozdushniye Sily* (Military Air Force).
37. "World War: CASUALTIES: Bruno's Last Flight," *Time*, August 18, 1941, https://content.time.com/time/magazine/article/0,9171,802107,00.html.
38. Harvey, "Soviet Air Force versus the Luftwaffe," 49.
39. Bolloten, *Spanish Civil War*, 312.
40. Beevor, *Battle for Spain*, 402–5.
41. Thomas, *Spanish Civil War*, 948–49.
42. Smith and Hall, *Five Down*, 308–9.
43. U.S. Congress, "Proceedings of Army Pearl Harbor Board," 1577–78.
44. U.S. Congress, "Pearl Harbor Board," 1579–81, 1591.
45. "Graduation Exercises of Tactical School," *Air Corps Newsletter* 22, no. 11 (June 1, 1939), accessed April 2, 2025, https://media.defense.gov/2011/Apr/21/2001330165/-1/-1/0/AFD-110421-046.pdf, 2 (at pp. 220–21 of PDF).
46. Henry Arnold, "General Arnold's Address Before Tactical School Graduates," *Air Corps Newsletter* (June 1, 1939), 3–4 (at pp. 222–24 of PDF).
47. Arnold, "General Arnold's Address," 4.
48. Arnold, "General Arnold's Address," 5.
49. Nalty, "Reaction to the War in Europe," 179.
50. H. H. Arnold, Lieutenant General, U.S.A., Commanding General, Army Air Forces, to E. S. Adams, Major General, President War Department Decorations Board, "Recommendation for Distinguished Service Medal," August 4, 1942, TGMR.

51. J. E. Daly, Adjutant General, to Townsend Griffiss, Major, Air Corps, Letter, May 9, 1941, TGMR.
52. I. B. Summers, Col, A.G.D., to Townsend Griffiss, Major, Air Corps, "Travel Orders," October 30, 1941, TGMR.
53. Arnold, H. H., to Joseph McNarney, Cablegram 96, Paraphrase, October 28, [1941], TGMR.
54. [Griffiss], Handwritten Notes, November 30, [1941], TGMR.
55. James Chaney to Townsend Griffiss, Paraphrase, November 19, 1941, TGMR.
56. Adjutant General to SPOBS, London, Telegram—"Promotion Griffiss," November 21, 1941, Document # 311.22x201, TGMR.
57. Townsend Griffiss to James Chaney, Paraphrase, November 25, 1941, TGMR.
58. [Townsend Griffiss], Report, January 3, [1942], TGMR, 1–3.
59. [Griffiss], Report, January 3, [1942], 3.
60. [Griffis], Report, January 3, [1942], 4–6.
61. [Griffiss], Report, January 3, [1942], 10.
62. [Griffiss], Report, January 3, [1942], 10.
63. Townsend Griffiss to James Chaney, SPOBS, London, Telegram, "Col. Griffiss Return," January 12, 1942, TGMR.
64. [Townsend Griffiss], Handwritten Notes, January 5–February 8, [1942], TGMR, 22.
65. [Townsend Griffiss], Typewritten Notes, January 24, 1942, TGMR, 2.
66. [Griffiss], Typewritten Notes, January 24, 1942, 2.
67. [Townsend Griffiss], Handwritten Notes, [February 1942], TGMR.
68. [Townsend Griffiss], Handwritten Notes, January 5–February 8, [1942], TGMR, 25. Bracketed text indicates uncertainty of the word.
69. Adler to H. H. Arnold, Cable No. 428, February 17, 1942, TGMR.
70. James Chaney to Adjutant General, Cablegram, No. 600, February 17, 1942, TGMR.
71. James Chaney to Adjutant General, Cablegram, No. 610, February 19, 1942, TGMR.
72. Fallers, Cairo, to G-2, War Department, Radiogram—Paraphrase, No. 849, February 23, 1942, TGMR.
73. James Chaney to Adjutant General, Cablegram, AC 4, March 9, 1942, TGMR.
74. James Chaney to H. H. Arnold, Draft, Outgoing Cablegram—"Particulars Col. Griffiss Death," March 17, 1942, TGMR.
75. "Copy of Finding of Court of Enquiry into the Loss of Liberator A.M. 918 (G-AGDR)", TGMR.
76. James Chaney to H. H. Arnold, Draft, Outgoing Cablegram—"Particulars Col. Griffiss Death," March 17, 1942.
77. James Chaney to Adjutant General, Cablegram, No. 600, February 17, 1942, TGMR.
78. Edward F. Witsell, Major General, the Adjutant General, to Mrs. Katherine H. W. Griffiss, Letter, May 28, 1947, TGMR.

79. E. S. Adams, Major General, U.S.A., President, War Dept Decorations Board to H. H. Arnold, Lieutenant General, U.S.A.A.F., "Recommendation for Distinguished Service Medal," July 18, 1942, TGMR.
80. H. H. Arnold, Lieutenant General, U.S.A., Commanding General, Army Air Forces, to E. S. Adams, Major General, President War Department Decorations Board, "Recommendation for Distinguished Service Medal," August 4, 1942, TGMR.

BIBLIOGRAPHY

ACRONYMS
AFHRA: Air Force Historical Research Agency, Maxwell Air Force Base, Alabama
MID: Military Intelligence Division
NARA: National Archives and Records Administration, College Park, Maryland
TGMR: Townsend Griffiss Military Records, National Archives, St. Louis, Missouri

NEWSPAPERS AND MAGAZINES
Air Corps Newsletter
Evening Star (Washington, D.C.)
Literary Digest
Military Times
New York Times
Newsweek
Princeton Union (Princeton, Minnesota)
Readers Digest
Scientific American
Time
U.S. Air Services

PRIMARY SOURCES
Adams, E. S., and H. H. Arnold. Correspondence. TGMR.
Adjutant General to SPOBS. London. Telegram—"Promotion Griffiss," November 21, 1941. Document # 311.22x201. TGMR.
Adler to H. H. Arnold. Cable No. 428. February 17, 1942. TGMR.
"Aerial Warfare in Spain." Translated from *Revue de l'Armée de l'Air* (February 1937). IRISREF A2817. Frames 1438–1449. AFHRA.
"Air Transport—Spain," 1938. IRISREF A1398. Frames 1011–1020. AFHRA.
Allied and Associated Powers. Treaty of Peace with Germany (Treaty of Versailles), June 28, 1919. Accessed May 21, 2023. census.gov.
Arnold, H. H. "Air Lessons from Current Wars." *U.S. Air Services* 23, no. 5 (May 1938): 17–18, 32.
Arnold, H. H., and Ira Eaker. *This Flying Game*. New York: Funk and Wagnalls, 1936.
Arnold, H. H., and Ira Eaker. *This Flying Game*. 2nd ed. New York: Funk and Wagnalls, 1938.

Arnold, H. H., to Assistant Secretary of War. "Air Corps Procurement Program and Procedures." July 8, 1940, RG 107 A1-166-1200. NARA. Copy.

Arnold, H. H., to Chief of Staff. "Coordination of Purchases of Airplanes by the U.S. Army and Navy and British Purchasing Commission—Conference for." August 5, 1940. RG 107 A1-166-1200. NARA. Copy.

Arnold, H. H., to Joseph McNarney. Cablegram 96. Paraphrase. October 28, [1941]. TGMR.

Arnold, H. H., to Secretary of War. Correspondence. RG 107 A1-99. NARA.

Arnold, H. H., to Secretary of War. Memorandum, July 30, 1940. RG 107 A1-166-1200. NARA. Copy.

Arnold, Henry H. *American Airpower Comes of Age: Gen Henry H. "Hap" Arnold's World War II Diaries.* Vol. 1. Edited by John W. Huston. Maxwell Air Force Base, AL: Air University Press, 2002.

"Aviation in Offensive Operations and Series of Comments Thereon," 1938. Translated from Russian. IRISREF A2873. Frames 358-400. AFHRA.

Baldwin, Stanley. "Address to House of Commons." *HC Debate*, November 10, 1932. Volume 270, cc525–641. UK Parliament: Hansard 1803–2005. http://hansard.millbanksystems.com/commons/1932/nov/10/international-affairs.

Baumler, Albert J., and E. W. Raley. Correspondence, 1938. IRISREF A1399. AFHRA.

Bevans, Charles I., comp. *Treaties and Other International Agreements of the United States of America, 1776–1949*. Vol. 2, *Multilateral, 1918–1930*. Washington, DC: Department of State Publication, 1969. https://tile.loc.gov/storage-services/service/ll/lltreaties/lltreaties-ustbv002/lltreaties-ustbv002.pdf.

Bolin, Luis. *Spain: The Vital Years*. Philadelphia: J. B. Lippincott, 1967.

Bowers, Claude, to Secretary of State. October 12, 1936. RG 165. Box 1544. 2610-S-50-009. NARA.

Bowers, Claude G. *My Mission to Spain*. New York: Simon and Schuster, 1954.

Bryan, G. H. "Artificial Flight." *Science Progress* 6, no. 5 (October 1897): 531–53. http://www.jstor.com/stable/43414675.

[Castro]. "Document of the General Cause of Valencia, on José Selles Ogino," September 25, 1942. C. 4,912,633: 49–51. *Documento de Cause General de Valencia*. 1389. Exp 9: page 48. National Historical Archive (Spain). https://www.solosequenosenada.com/misc/jose-selles-ogino/index.php.

Chaney, James. Handwritten Note. January 13, [1942]. TGMR.

Chaney, James, and Adjutant General. Correspondence. TGMR.

Chaney, James, to H. H. Arnold. Draft. Outgoing Cablegram—"Particulars Col. Griffiss Death." March 17, 1942. TGMR.

Cheadle, H. B., and MID. Correspondence. RG 165 M-1445. Roll #8. NARA.

Chennault, C. L. *The Role of Defensive Pursuit*. N.p.: N.p., 1933. Available online at Air University Library, https://www.airuniversity.af.edu/Library/.

Ciano, Galeazzo. *Ciano's Diplomatic Papers*. Edited by Malcom Muggeridge. Translated by Stuart Hood. Long Acre, London: Odhams Press Limited, 1948.

BIBLIOGRAPHY

"Copy of Finding of Court of Enquiry into the Loss of Liberator A.M. 918 (G-AGDR)." [March 1942]. TGMR.

Daly, J. E., to Townsend Griffiss. Letter, May 9, 1941. TGMR. National Archives. St. Louis, Missouri. Copy.

Dickinson, Derek D., and Edwin C. Parsons. "My Air Duel with Bruno Mussolini." *Readers Digest*, March 1939, 34–37.

Douhet, Giulio. *The Command of the Air*. Translated by Dino Ferrari. 1921. New York: Coward-McCann, 1942.

Duncan, C. E., to Assistant Secretary of War. "Chart #19581 AC." January 19, 1940. RG 107 A1-205–961. NARA.

Fallers, [unknown], to G-2. War Department. Radiogram—Paraphrase. No. 849. February 23, 1942. TGMR.

Finch, George A. "The United States and the Spanish Civil War." *American Journal of International Law* 31, no. 1 (1937): 74–81. https://doi.org/10.2307/2190716.

Fiske, Norman E. Correspondence. 1936. RG 165 M-1445. NARA.

Foreign Office, United Kingdom. *Further Correspondence Respecting Morocco*. Part 74, January to December 1936. Archives Direct. FO 413/85. https://www.archivesdirect.amdigital.co.uk.

Foreign Office, United Kingdom. *Further Correspondence Respecting Morocco*. Part 75, January to December 1937. Archives Direct. FO 413/85. https://www.archivesdirect.amdigital.co.uk.

Fuller, H. H. Correspondence, 1936–39. RG 165 M-1445. NARA.

Fuqua, Stephen O. Correspondence, 1935–38. RG 165 M-1445. NARA.

Graves, George M. "The Consul at Vigo (Graves) to the Secretary of State,". 852.2221 Dahl, Harold/10: Telegram, July 27, 1937. *Foreign Relations of the United States Diplomatic Papers, 1937, General. Volume I*, 529–31. U.S. Department of State, Office of the Historian.https://history.state.gov/historicaldocuments/frus1937v01/d500.

Griffiss, Townsend. "The Air Warfare in Spain and Its Effect upon the Air Rearmament of France," August 11, 1938. RG 165 M-1445. Roll #8. NARA. Copy.

Griffiss, Townsend. Correspondence. TGMR.

Griffiss, Townsend. Correspondence, 1936–38. RG 165 M-1445. NARA.

Griffiss, Townsend. Notes. TGMR.

Griffiss, Townsend. Reports. TGMR.

Griffiss, Townsend. *When You Go to Hawaii, You Will Need This Guide to the Islands*. Boston: Houghton Mifflin, 1930. https://hdl.handle.net/2027/miun.afj6725.0001.001.

Griffiss, Townsend, to Military Intelligence Division. M.A. Valencia Report No. 6471. "Special Report on Spanish Government Air Force," February 21, 1937. Call #248.501-79. IRISREF A2873. Frames 2264–287. AFHRA. Copy.

Griffiss, Townsend, to Military Intelligence Division. M.A. Valencia Report No. 6530. "Organizational Training, Tactics Deployed," April 25, 1937. IRISREF A2817. Frames 1425–1433. AFHRA.

Hemingway, Ernest. *The Complete Short Stories of Ernest Hemingway.* The Finca Vigía Edition. 1987. Reprint, New York: Scribner, 2003.
Hemingway, Ernest. *For Whom the Bell Tolls.* 1940. New York: Scribner, 2020.
Jaeneke, Erwin. "The Part Played by the Condor Legion in the Overthrow of Communist Hegemony in Spain." In *The German Air Force in the Spanish Civil War*, edited by Karl Drum, translated by Klamerth, 1–59. Newark, DE: Air Enterprise Publications, 1988.
Jellinek, Frank. *The Civil War in Spain.* London: Victor Gollancz, 1938.
Kenney, George. "The Airplane in Modern Warfare." *U.S. Air Services*, July 1938, 17–22, 36.
Knoblaugh, H. Edward. *Correspondent in Spain.* Camden, NJ: Sheed and Ward, 1937.
Kroner, Hayes A., to Assistant Chief of Staff, G-2. M.A. London Report No. 38607. "Eyewitness Information on Spanish War," March 9, 1937. RG 165 M-1445. Roll #7. NARA.
Langmead, E. C., to Chief of the Materiel Division. "Exhibit 'A' Summary Sheets of Topics of Conf. 7–2 & 3, 1940," July 8, 1940. RG 107 A1-166-1200. NARA. Copy.
Lee, Raymond E., to Military Intelligence Division. M.A. London Report No. 38512. "Employment of Troops in Domestic Disturbances," January 25, 1937. RG 165 M-1445. Roll #7. NARA.
"Lessons from the Spanish Civil War," Command and General Staff School, December 1, 1937. RG 165 M-1445, Roll #7. NARA.
Lilienthal, Otto. "Practical Experiments for the Development of Human Flight." *Scientific American* 74, no. 10 (March 7, 1896): 153–54. https://www.jstor.org/stable/10.2307/26116699.
Lincoln, F. H. Correspondence. RG 165. Box 1544. NARA.
Lincoln, F. H., to Assistant Chief of Staff. WFD. "Antiaircraft Artillery in Spain," March 12[?], 1937. RG 165 M-1445. Roll #7. NARA. Copy.
"List of Letter Contracts Approved by the Assistant Secretary of War," [September 11, 1940]. RG 107 A1166-1200. NARA.
Lovett, Robert A., to Secretary of War. Correspondence. RG 107 A1-99. NARA.
McCabe, E. R. W., to Chief of Staff. "The Situation in Barcelona," January 26, 1939, RG 165 M-1445, Roll #8, NARA. Copy.
Milne, M.B. "Trade Treaties and Capitulations in Morocco." *Journal of the British Institute of International Affairs* 5, no. 1 (January 1926): 32–43. https://www.jstor.org/stable/3014518
"Miscellaneous Documents concerning Spanish Civil War—Plans Division," IRISREF A1399. Call # 145.91-135MM. Frames 571–770. AFHRA.
"Miscellaneous Folder, in Personal Collection of Laurence S. Kuter," 1939. IRISREF A1844. Call # 168.7012-23. Frames 652–802. AFHRA.
Mitchell, William. *Winged Defense: The Development and Possibilities of Modern Air Power Economic and Military.* Edited by Donald R. McCoy. 1925. Port Washington, NY: Kennikat Press, 1971.

Morgan, John, to Claude Bowers. Telegram, October 15, 1936. RG 165. Box 1544. 2610-S-50-012-1. NARA.
Mumford, Lewis. *Technics and Civilization*. San Diego: Harcourt Brace, 1934.
Office of the Chief of the Air Corps, to Robert Lovett. Memorandum, February 10, 1941. RG 107 A1-99-1. NARA.
Office of the Chief of the Information Section of Anti-Aircraft Defense. "Extract from the Record of Enemy Aerial Activity Summarized in the Bulletin of Anti-Aircraft Defense," July 27, 1938. RG 165 M-1445, Roll #8. NARA.
O.N.I. Report No. 57. "Miscellaneous Documents concerning Spanish Civil War—Plans Division," August 31, 1936. Call #145.91-135MM. IRISREF A1399. Frames 685–86. AFHRA.
Orwell, George. *Homage to Catalonia*. New York: Harcourt, Brace and World, 1952.
Partridge, Earle E. Interview by Tom Sturm and Hugh N. Ahmann. April 23–25, 1974. Colorado Springs, CO. U.S. Air Force Oral History Program. K239.0512-729. Maxwell AFB, AL: Albert F. Simpson Historical Research Center, Air University.
Patterson, Robert, to William Knudsen. "Revised Army Airframe Delivery Requirements," August 10, 1940. RG 107 A1-166-1200. NARA. Copy.
Patton, George S., and John B. Coulter. Correspondence, 1936. RG 165 M-1445. Roll #7. NARA.
Phillips, Thomas R. "Preview of Armageddon." *Saturday Evening Post*, March 12, 1938, 12–13, 96–100. IRISREF 2756. IRISNUM 15609. Frames 38–47. AFHRA.
Phillips, William. "Acting Secretary of State to All Consulates in Spain," 852.00/2510a: Circular Telegram, Washington, August 7, 1936. *Foreign Relations of the United States Diplomatic Papers, 1936, Europe, Volume II*, 389. U.S. Department of State, Office of the Historian. https://history.state.gov/historicaldocuments/frus1936v02/d389.
Sawyer, E. O., to E. W. Raley. Letter regarding Spanish Airlift, October 25, 1937. IRISREF 1398. Call # 145.91-1350. Frame 1017. AFHRA.
Schultz, John W. N., to John H. Woodbery. Memorandum, May 19, 1939. RG 107 A1-205–961. NARA.
Smith, Truman, to Military Intelligence Division. M.A. Berlin Report No. 15,397. "Experiences with Modern Weapons," July 16, 1937. RG 165 M-1445. Roll #7. NARA.
"Spain—Civil War." 1938. IRISREF A1399. Call #145.91-135MM. Frames 571–770. AFHRA.
"The Spanish Situation—August 6, 1936." RG 165 M-1445. Roll #7. NARA.
"Spanish War—Extracts from Publications." 1937. IRISREF A1399. Frames 771–833. AFHRA.
Stimson, Henry L., Secretary of War, to President. Letter, May 6, 1941. RG 107 A1-99-2. NARA.
Strong, Anna Louise, *Spain in Arms: 1937*. New York: Henry Holt and Company. 1937.

Summers, I. B., to Townsend Griffiss. "Travel Orders," October 30, 1941. TGMR.
Sun Tzu. *The Art of War*. Translated by Lionel Giles. Edited by Dallas Galvin. 1910. New York: Barnes and Noble Classics, 2003.
Tangye, Nigel. "Spanish Follyday Lessons." *Aeroplane*, February 24, 1937. AFHRA. IRISREF A2756. Call # 248.211-23 Pt.1.
Tinker, F. G., Jr., and E. R. W. McCabe. Correspondence, 1938. RG 165. M-1445. Roll #8. NARA.
Tinker, F. G., Jr. *Some Still Live*. New York: Funk and Wagnalls, 1938.
"The Truth about Air Raids in Spain." IRISREF 2756. Frames 1456–1457. AFHRA.
U.S. Treasury Department, Bureau of Internal Revenue. *Statistics of Income for 1936, Part I: Compiled from Individual Income Tax Returns, Estates Tax Returns, and Gift Tax Returns*. Washington, DC, 1938. https://www.irs.gov/pub/irs-soi/36soireppt1ar.pdf.
U.S. War Department. Adjutant General's Office. *Army List and Directory*. April 20, 1936. Washington, DC: Government Printing Office, 1937. https://archive.org/details/armylistdirector1936unit/page/n1/mode/2up.
U.S. War Department. Adjutant General's Office. *Army List and Directory*. October 20, 1936. Washington, DC: Government Printing Office, 1937. https/archive.org/details/armylistdirecto1936unit_0.
U.S. War Department. Adjutant General's Office. *Army List and Directory*. October 20, 1937. Washington, DC: Government Printing Office, 1937. https://archive.org/details/armylistdirecto1937unit_0.
U.S. War Department. Adjutant General's Office. *Army List and Directory*. April 20, 1939. Washington, DC: Government Printing Office, 1939. https://archive.org/details/armylistdirecto1939unit_0/page/n1/mode/2up.
Veblen, Thorstein. *The Theory of the Leisure Class*. 1899. Project Gutenberg. ISO-8859-1. https://www.gutenberg.org/ebooks/833.
Waite, Sumner. Correspondence. RG 165 M-1445. Roll #7. NARA.
Wells, H. G. *The War of the Worlds*. 1898. N.p.: Aerie, 1987.
Wells, H. G. *The World Set Free*. 1913. N.p.: CreateSpace Publishing, 2014.
Westover, Oscar, to Townsend Griffiss. "Commendation," November 4, 1936. TGMR. Copy.
Witsell, Edward F., to Mrs. Katherine H. W. Griffiss. Letter, May 28, 1947. TGMR. Copy.
Wood, O. S., to M.A. London. "Military Information on Civil War in Spain," December 11, 1936. RG 165 M-1445. Roll #7. NARA. Copy.
Wright, Orville, and Wilbur Wright. "The Early History of the Airplane." In Wright, Wright, and Claxton, *Early Aviation*, 5–16.
Wright, Orville, Wilbur Wright, and William J. Claxton. *A History of Early Aviation*. St. Petersburg, FL: Red and Black Publishers, 2009.
Wright, Wilbur. "Some Aeronautical Experiments." In Wright, Wright, and Claxton, *Early Aviation*, 27–38.

SECONDARY SOURCES

Alpert, M. "The Clash of Spanish Armies: Contrasting Ways of War in Spain, 1936–1939." *War in History* 6, no. 3 (1999): 331–51.

Alpert, Michael. *Franco and the Condor Legion: The Spanish Civil War in the Air.* London: Bloomsbury Academic, 2019.

Angelucci, Enzo, ed. *The Rand McNally Encyclopedia of Military Aircraft: 1914–1980.* Chicago: Rand McNally and Company, 1981.

Angelucci, Enzo, ed. *The Rand McNally Encyclopedia of Military Aircraft: 1914 to the Present.* New York: Crescent Books, 1990.

Barfield, Norman. "The Age of the Flying Boat." In Jarrett, *Biplane to Monoplane*, 89–106.

Bartlett, John. *Bartlett's Familiar Quotations: A Collection of Passages, Phrases, and Proverbs Traced to Their Sources in Ancient and Modern Literature*, edited by Justin Kaplan, 16th ed. Boston: Little, Brown, 1992.

Baughen, Greg. *The Rise and Fall of the French Air Force: French Air Operations and Strategy 1900–1940.* Croydon, UK: Fonthill Media Limited, 2018.

Beevor, Antony. *The Battle for Spain.* Rev. ed. New York: Penguin Books, 2006.

Benton, Jeffrey C. *They Served Here: Thirty-Three Maxwell Men.* Maxwell Air Force Base, AL: Air University Press, 1999.

Berg, A. Scott. *Lindbergh.* New York: G. P. Putnam's Sons, 1998.

Biddle, Tami Davis. *Rhetoric and Reality in Air Warfare: The Evolution of British and American Ideas about Strategic Bombing, 1914–1945.* Princeton, NJ: Princeton University, 2004.

Bijker, Wiebe E., Thomas P. Hughes, and Trevor Pinch, eds. *The Social Construction of Technological Systems: New Directions in the Sociology and History of Technology.* Cambridge, MA: MIT Press, 2012.

Bolloten, Burnett. *The Spanish Civil War: Revolution and Counterrevolution.* Chapel Hill: University of North Carolina Press, 1991.

Bolloten, Burnett, and George Esenwein. "Negrín, Juan." In Cortada, *Historical Dictionary*, 360–62.

Bonilla, Diego Navarro, and Guillermo Vicente Cano. "Photographic Air Reconnaissance during the Spanish Civil War, 1936–1939: Doctrine and Operations." *War in History* 20, no. 3 (2013): 345–80.

Boyd, Carolyn P. "Hernández Saravia, Juan." In Cortada, *Historical Dictionary*, 256–257.

Boyne, Walter J. *The Influence of Air Power upon History.* New York: Giniger, 2003.

Bradley, Ken. *International Brigades in Spain 1936–1939.* Oxford, UK: Osprey Publishing, 1994.

Buckley, John. *Air Power in the Age of Total War.* Bloomington: Indiana University Press, 1999.

Budiansky, Stephen. *Air Power.* New York: Penguin Group 2005.

Bungay, Stephen. *The Most Dangerous Enemy: A History of the Battle of Britain*. London: Aurum Press, 2015.
Callihan, John C., ed. *Innovation and Achievement*. Wickliffe, KY: Westvaco Corporation, 1987.
Carr, Raymond. *Spain: 1808–1975*. 2nd ed. Oxford, UK: Clarendon Press, 1982.
Cavagnaro, Catherine. "Performance: The Perfect Aircraft (For the Mission): No Such Thing as 'No Compromises.'" AOPA Pilot, September 1, 2019. https://www.aopa.org/news-and-media/all-news/2019/september/pilot/performance-the-perfect-aircraft.
Chandler, David G. *Atlas of Military Strategy*. New York: Free Press, 1980.
Coffey, Thomas M. *Lion by the Tail*. New York: Viking Press, 1974.
Corn, Joseph J. *The Winged Gospel: America's Romance with Aviation*. Rev. ed. Baltimore, MD: Johns Hopkins University Press, 2002.
Corral, Pedro. "A Ukulele, a Torture Box and a Judo Black Belt: The Story of Republican Pilot José 'Chang' Sellés." *A Scribe's Quotations* (blog), August 7, 2020. https://pcorralcorral.blogspot.com/2020/08/un-ukelele-un-cajon-de-tortura-y-un.html.
Cortada, James W. "Casado López, Segismundo." In Cortada, *Historical Dictionary*, 111–12.
Cortada, James W. "Franco Y Bahamonde, Ramón (1896–1937)." In Cortada, *Historical Dictionary*, 226–27.
Cortada, James W., ed. *Historical Dictionary of the Spanish Civil War, 1936–1939*. Westport, CT: Greenwood Press, 1982.
Cortada, James W. *Modern Warfare in Spain: American Military Observations on the Spanish Civil War, 1936–1939*. Washington, DC: Potomac Books, 2012.
Corum, James S. "The Spanish Civil War: Lessons Learned and Not Learned by the Great Powers." *Journal of Military History* 62, no. 2 (April 1998): 313–34. https://www.jstor.org/stable/120719.
Corum, James S. *Wolfram von Richthofen: Master of the German Air War*. Lawrence: University Press of Kansas, 2008.
Courtwright, David T. *Sky as Frontier: Adventure, Aviation, and Empire*. College Station: Texas A&M University Press, 2005.
Edgerton, David. *The Shock of the Old: Technology and Global History since 1900*. Oxford, UK: Oxford University Press, 2007.
Edwards, John Carver. *Airmen without Portfolio: U.S. Mercenaries in Civil War Spain*. Westport, CT: Praeger, 1997.
Ennels, Jerome A., Sr., Robert B. Kane, and Silvano A. Wueschner. *Cradle of Airpower: An Illustrated History of Maxwell Air Force Base, 1918–2018*. Maxwell Air Force Base, AL: Air University Press, 2018.
Esdaile, Charles J. *The Spanish Civil War: A Military History*. Abingdon, Oxon, UK: Routledge, 2019.
Finney, Robert T. *History of the Air Corps Tactical School, 1920–1940*. 1955. Bolling Air Force Base, Washington, DC: Air Force History Support Office, 1998.

Fountain, James. "The Notion of Crusade in British and American Literary Responses to the Spanish Civil War." *Journal of Transatlantic Studies* 7, no. 2 (Summer 2009): 133–47.

Fritzsche, Peter. *A Nation of Fliers: German Aviation and the Popular Imagination.* Cambridge, MA: Harvard University Press, 1992.

Goss, Hilton P. "The Spanish Civil War: The First Phase, 1936–1937." In *Civilian Morale under Aerial Bombardment, 1914–1939*, 143–203. Montgomery, AL: Maxwell Air Force Base, 1948.

Graham, Helen. *The Spanish Civil War: A Very Short Introduction.* Oxford, UK: Oxford University Press, 2005. https://archive.org/details/helen-graham-the-spanish-civil-war-a-very-short-introduction-590/page/n7/mode/2up.

Graham, Loren R. *The Ghost of the Executed Engineer: Technology and the Fall of the Soviet Union.* Cambridge, MA: Harvard University Press, 1993.

Harvey, A. D. "The Soviet Air Force versus the Luftwaffe." *History Today* 52, no. 1 (2002): 48.

Hall, R. Cargill, ed. *Case Studies in Strategic Bombardment.* Washington, DC: Air Force History and Museums Program, 1998. https://www.govinfo.gov/app/details/GOVPUB-D301-PURL-LPS48359.

Hills, George. *Spain.* New York: Praeger, 1970.

Hines, Stephen, ed. *Webster's New Reference Library: A Handbook of Dictionaries.* Rev. ed. Nashville, TN: Thomas Nelson, 1989.

Hochschild, Adam. *Spain in Our Hearts.* Boston: Houghton Mifflin Harcourt, 2016.

Hooton, E. R. *Spain in Arms: A Military History of the Spanish Civil War, 1936–1939.* Havertown, PA: Casemate, 2019.

Hooton, Ted. "Military Aviation—the Slow Developer." In Jarrett, *Biplane to Monoplane*, 55–74.

Howson, Gerald. *Aircraft of the Spanish Civil War: 1936–39.* Washington, DC: Smithsonian Institute Press, 1990.

Howson, Gerald, *Arms for Spain: The Untold Story of the Spanish Civil War.* New York: St. Martin's Press, 1999.

Hurley, Alfred F., and William C. Heimdahl. "The Roots of U.S. Military Aviation." In Nalty, *Winged Shield*, 3–34.

Huston, John W., ed. *American Airpower Comes of Age: General Henry H. "Hap" Arnold's World War II Diaries.* Vol. 1. Maxwell Air Force Base, AL: Air University Press, 2008.

Irujo Ametzaga, Xabier. "Special Feature: The Nature and Rationale of the Gernika Bombing." *The Volunteer*, December 19, 2013. https://albavolunteer.org/2013/12/the-nature-and-military-rationale-of-the-bombing-of-gernika/.

Jackson, Gabriel. *Spanish Republic and the Civil War, 1931–1939.* 1965. 1972. Princeton, NJ: Princeton University Press, 2012. https://www.google.com/books/edition/Spanish_Republic_and_the_Civil_War_1931/vpOwwZWGtBcC?hl=en&gbpv=0.

Jackson-Schebetta, Lisa. "Companies to Keep: Air-Raid Dramas and International Ethical Responsibility in America, 1936–1939." *Alabama Review* 65, no. 3 (July 2012): 33–52.

Jacobs, W. A. "The British Strategic Air Offensive against Germany in World War II." In Hall, *Case Studies in Strategic Bombardment*, 91–182.

Jarrett, Philip, ed. *Biplane to Monoplane: Aircraft Development 1919–39*. London, UK: Putnam Aeronautical Books, 1997.

Johnston, Verle B. "Jarama, Battle of." In Cortada, *Historical Dictionary*, 276.

Joint Publication 1. *Doctrine of the Armed Forces of the United States*. March 25, 2013, incorporating Change 1. July 12, 2017. Washington, DC: Joint Chiefs of Staff, 2017.

Joint Publication 3-01. *Countering Air and Missile Threats*. April 21, 2017. Validated May 2, 2018. Washington, DC: Joint Chiefs of Staff, 2018.

Joint Publication 5-0. *Joint Planning*. June 16, 2017. Washington, DC: Joint Chiefs of Staff, 2017.

Juntunen, Kim M. "U.S. Army Attachés and the Spanish Civil War, 1936–1939: The Gathering of Technical and Tactical Intelligence." MA thesis, U.S. Military Academy, West Point, 1990.

Kelley, John M. *Claire Lee Chennault: Theorist and Campaign Planner*. Fort Leavenworth, KS: School of Advanced Military Studies, U.S. Army Command and General Staff College, 1993.

Kelly, Fred C. *The Wright Brothers*. New York: Harcourt, Brace, 1943.

Kerber, L. L. *Stalin's Aviation Gulag: A Memoir of Andrei Tupolev and the Purge Era*. Edited by Von Hardesty. Washington, DC: Smithsonian Institution Press, 1996.

Kinney, Jeremy R. *Airplanes: The Life Story of a Technology*. Baltimore, MD: Johns Hopkins University Press, 2008.

Lannon, Frances. *The Spanish Civil War: 1936–1939*. Oxford, UK: Osprey Publishing, 2002.

Lawrence, Mark. *The Spanish Civil Wars: A Comparative History of the First Carlist War and the Conflict of the 1930s*. London: Bloomsbury, 2017.

Licata, Elizabeth. "Cicero J. Hamlin's Descendants." Buffalo as an Architectural Museum, July/August 2000. http://buffaloah.com/h/hamln/hamlin2.html.

Lister, Enrique. *Nuestra guerra: Aportaciones para una historia de la guerra nactional revolucionaria del pueblo español, 1936–1939*. Paris: Éditions de la librairie du Globe, 1966.

Little, Douglas. "Red Scare, 1936: Anti-Bolshevism and the Origins of British Non-Intervention in the Spanish Civil War." *Journal of Contemporary History* 23, no. 2 (April 1988). https://www.jstor.org/stable/260850.

Logoluso, Alfredo. *Fiat CR.32 Aces of the Spanish Civil War*. Edited by Tony Holmes. Oxford, UK: Osprey Publishing, 2010.

Macklin, Graham D. "Major Hugh Pollard, M16, and the Spanish Civil War." *Historical Journal* 49, no. 1. (2006): 277–80. http://www.jstor.org/stable/4091748.

Marquis, Christopher G. "'¿Quién Sabe?' U.S. Airmen in the Spanish Civil War." Master's-level research paper. Auburn University, 2018.

Marquis, Christopher G. "American Aerial Perspectives: Observations on the Technological Development of Military Aviation during the Spanish Civil War, 1936–1939." MA thesis, Auburn University, 2020.

Maurer, Maurer. *Aviation in the U.S. Army, 1919–1939*. Washington, DC: Office of Air Force History, 1987. https://media.defense.gov/2010/Sep/23/2001330114/-1/-1/0/AFD-100923-007.pdf.

McCarthy, James P., and Drue L. DeBerry, eds. *The Air Force*. Andrews Air Force Base, MD: Hugh Lauter Levin Associates, 2002.

McCullough, David. *The Wright Brothers*. New York: Simon and Schuster, 2015.

McFarland, Stephen L., and Wesley Phillips Newton. "The American Strategic Air Offensive against Germany in World War II." In Hall, *Case Studies in Strategic Bombardment*, 183–252.

McNeill, William H. "The Industrialization of War." *Review of International Studies* 8, no. 3 (July 1982): 203–13. http://www.jstor.com/stable/20096953.

Meilinger, Phillip S. "Trenchard and 'Morale Bombing': The Evolution of Royal Air Force Doctrine before World War II." *Journal of Military History* 60, no. 2 (April 1996): 243–70. http://www.jstor.com/stable/2944407.

Mets, David R. "Army Roots." In McCarthy and DeBerry, *Air Force*, 10–29.

Miller, Charles E. *Airlift Doctrine*. Maxwell Air Force Base, AL: Air University Press, 1988.

Morris, Craig F. *The Origins of American Strategic Bombing Theory*. Edited by Paul J. Springer. Annapolis, MD: Naval Institute Press, 2017.

Mortensen, Daniel R. "The Air Service in the Great War." In Nalty, *Winged Shield*, 35–70.

Moy, Timothy. "Transforming Technology in Army Air Corps, 1920–1940." In *The Airplane in American Culture*, edited by Dominick A. Pisano, 299–332. Ann Arbor, MI: University of Michigan Press, 2003.

Mulvey, Stephen. "Townsend Griffiss, Forgotten Hero of World War II." *BBC News*, February 14, 2012. http://www.bbc.com/news/magazine-17011105.

Munson, Kenneth. "The Biplane's Fall from Favour." In Jarrett, *Biplane to Monoplane*, 11–28.

Murphy, Justin D., and Matthew A. McNiece. *Military Aircraft, 1919–1945: An Illustrated History of Their Impact*. Santa Barbara, CA: ABC-CLIO, 2009.

Murray, Williamson, and Allan R. Millett, eds. *Military Innovation in the Interwar Period*. Cambridge, UK: Cambridge University Press, 1996.

Nalty, Bernard C., "Reaction to the War in Europe." In Nalty, *Winged Shield*, 165–200.

Nalty, Bernard C., ed. *Winged Shield, Winged Sword: A History of the USAF*. Vol. 1: *1917–1950*. Washington, DC: Air Force History and Museums Program, 1997.

Navarro Bonilla, Diego, and Guillermo Vicente Cano. "Photographic Air Reconnaissance during the Spanish Civil War, 1936–1939: Doctrine and Operations." *War in History* 20, no. 3 (2013): 345–80. https://doi.org/10.1177/0968344513 483070.

Ottanelli, Fraser. "Anti-Fascism and the Shaping of National and Ethnic Identity: Italian American Volunteers in the Spanish Civil War." *Journal of American Ethnic History* 27, no. 1 (Fall 2007): 9–31.

Patterson, Michael Robert. "Stephen Ogden Fuqua, Major General, United States Army." Arlington National Cemetery. Accessed March 19, 2017. http://www.arl ingtoncemetery.net/sofuqua.htm.

Payne, Robert. *The Civil War in Spain: 1936–1939*. New York: G. P. Putnam's Sons, 1962.

Payne, Robert. *A Portrait of André Malraux*. Englewood Cliffs, NJ: Prentice-Hall, 1970.

Payne, Stanley. *Spain: A Unique History*. Madison: University of Wisconsin Press, 2008.

Payne, Stanley G., and Jesús Palacios. *Franco: A Personal and Political Biography*. Madison: University of Wisconsin Press, 2014.

Phillips, Richard T. "'A Picturesque but Hopeless Resistance': Rehe in 1933." *Modern Asian Studies* 42, no. 4 (July 2008): 733–50.

Preston, Paul. *Franco*. New York: Basic Books, 1994.

Preston, Paul. *The Spanish Civil War: Reaction, Revolution and Revenge*. Rev. ed. New York: W.W. Norton, 2007. https://books.google.com/books/about/The_Span ish_Civil_War.html?id=2vioVIdend4C.

Proctor, Raymond L. *Hitler's Luftwaffe in the Spanish Civil War*. Westport, CT: Greenwood Press, 1983.

Proctor, Raymond L. "Kindelán Y Duany, Alfredo (1872–1962)." In Cortada, *Historical Dictionary*, 283.

Quesada, Alejandro de. *The Spanish Civil War 1936–1939 (1): Nationalist Forces*. Oxford, UK: Osprey Publishing, 2014.

Quesada, Alejandro de. *The Spanish Civil War 1936–1939 (2): Republican Forces*. Oxford, UK: Osprey Publishing, 2015.

Renstrom, Arthur G. *A Bibliography Commemorating the One-Hundredth Anniversary of the First Powered Flight, December 17, 1903*. Washington, DC: NASA, 2002.

Rhodes, Richard. *Hell and Good Company: The Spanish Civil War and the World It Made*. New York: Simon and Schuster, 2015.

Ritchie, Sebastian. *RAF Small Wars and Insurgencies in the Middle East, 1919–1939*. [Cranwell, Lincolnshire, UK]: Royal Air Force, Centre for Air Power Studies , 2011.

Salas Larrazábal, Jesús. *Air War over Spain*. Translated by Margaret A. Kelley. London: Ian Allan, 1974.

Schatzberg, Eric. "Technik Comes to America: Changing Meanings of Technology before 1930." *Technology and Culture* 47, no. 3 (July 2006): 486–512. https://doi.org/10.1353/tech.2006.0201.

Sganga, Rodolfo, Paulo G. Tripodi, and Wray R. Johnson. "Douhet's Antagonist: Amedeo Mecozzi's Alternative Vision of Air Power." *Air Power History* 58, no. 2 (Summer 2011): 4–15. https://www.jstor.org/stable/10.2307/26276033.

Shiner, John F. "The Coming of the GHQ Air Force, 1925–1935." In Nalty, *Winged Shield*, 101–34.

Shiner, John F. "From Air Service to Air Corps: The Era of Billy Mitchell." In Nalty, *Winged Shield*, 71–100.

Shiner, John F. "The Heyday of the GHQ Air Force, 1935–1939." In Nalty, *Winged Shield*, 135–62.

Slessor, J. C. *Air Power and Armies*. 1936. Tuscaloosa, Alabama: University of Alabama, 2009.

Smith, Merritt Roe, and Leo Marx, eds. *Does Technology Drive History? The Dilemma of Technological Determinism*. Cambridge, MA: MIT Press 1995.

Smith, Richard K., and R. Cargill Hall. *Five Down, No Glory: Frank G. Tinker, Mercenary Ace in the Spanish Civil War*. Annapolis, MD: Naval Institute Press, 2011.

Smith, William Marion, Jr. "Mercenary Eagles: American Pilots Serving in Foreign Air Forces Prior to the United States Entry into the Second World War, 1936–1941." PhD diss., University of Arkansas, 1999.

Stinton, Darrol. "The Structural Revolution." In Jarrett, *Biplane to Monoplane*, 127–40.

Sullivan, Brian R. "Fascist Italy's Military Involvement in the Spanish Civil War." *Journal of Military History* 59, no. 4 (1995): 697–727. https://10.2307/2944499.

Thomas, Hugh. *The Spanish Civil War*. 3rd ed. New York: Harper and Row, 1986.

Tierney, Dominic. "Franklin D. Roosevelt and Covert Aid to the Loyalists in the Spanish Civil War, 1936–39." *Journal of Contemporary History* 39, no. 3 (2004): 299–313. http://www.jstor.org/stable/3180730.

U.S. Air Force. *Statistical Digest, Fiscal Year* 2008. https://www.afhistory.af.mil/Portals/64/Statistics/2008%20USAF%20Stat%20Digest.pdf?ver=2017-04-25-125736-453&timestamp=1493139462337.

U.S. Congress. "Proceedings of Army Pearl Harbor Board." In *Joint Committee on the Investigation of the Pearl Harbor Attack*. Washington, DC: United States Government Printing Office, 1946. https://www.govinfo.gov/app/details/CHRG-79jhrg79716p28.

Vincenti, Walter G. "The Retractable Airplane Landing Gear and the Northrop 'Anomaly': Variation-Selection and the Shaping of Technology." *Technology and Culture* 35, no. 1 (January 1994): 1–33. Accessed September 18, 2007. https://doi.org/10.2307/3106747.

Whitewood, Peter. *The Red Army and the Great Terror: Stalin's Purge of the Soviet Military*. Lawrence: University Press of Kansas, 2015.

Whiting, Kenneth R. *The Development of the Soviet Armed Forces, 1917–1966*. Maxwell Air Force Base, AL: Air University, 1966.

Winchester, Jim, ed. *Classic Military Aircraft: The World's Fighting Aircraft: 1914–1945*. London, UK: Amber Books, 2010.

Winchester, Jim. *Military Aircraft Visual Encyclopedia*. London, UK: Amber Books, 2022.

Woodman, Harry. "Armaments Development." In Jarrett, *Biplane to Monoplane*, 183–94.

Yenne, Bill. *The White Rose of Stalingrad: The Real-Life Adventure of Lidiya Vladimirovna Litvyak, the Highest Scoring Female Air Ace of All Time*. London: Bloomsbury Publishing, 2013. https://books.google.com/books?id=pZGqCw AAQBAJ&source=gbs_book_other_versions.

INDEX

Notes:
Page numbers in *italics* refer to illustrations.
The following unique abbreviations appear frequently in this index:
Nat. Spain: Nationalist Spain
Rep. Spain: Republican Spain
SCW: Spanish Civil War

Abraham Lincoln Battalion. *See* International Brigade, XV
Acosta, Bertrand, 106–7
aerial cannons, 94, 197–200, 233, 237
aerial photography, 92–93, 185, 233
Aeronáutica Naval (Spain), 38
aeronautical engineers, 190–94
Aguirre, José Antonio, 69, 127, 144
air basing, 142, 169, 230
Air Corps Act (1926), 22
Air Corps Tactical School (ACTS), 20, 22–23, 209, 245–46
air dominance: compared to air supremacy, 218; during operations, 68, 135, 162, 206, 222; impact on seapower, 143; lack of, 173
Air Force, Nationalists: 59, 81, 116, 156–57, 199, 202; air dominance of, 91, 94, 210; air superiority of, 218, 238; anti-shipping, 69, 153; bombing missions of, 66, 85, 132, 142; close air support by, 93; inventory of, 74, 115, 188; Kindelán command of, 55, 65, 241; operations of, 65, 68, 80, 88–89, 113, 136, 145–46, 147, 149, 160–61, 162–63, 173–74, 206–8, 219–22, 217, 223

Air Force, Republican Spain: 53, 68, 148, 154, 221–22; anti-shipping, 131; bombing missions of, 153; force size of, 206, 218; Hidalgo de Cisneros commander of, 67; inventory of, 197, 222; lacking airpower doctrine, 66, 114; losses of, 94, 217; operations of, 80, 83, 88–89, 97–99, 135, 145, 146–49, 160–61, 162–63, 173–74, 208–9, 219–22; opinions of: 107, 207; status of, 89–95; tactics of, 141, 153; Tinker's knowledge of, 122
Air Force, Soviet Red Army (VVS). *See* VVS
air forces, Spanish, 38–39
air mail controversy, 24–25
Air Ministry (Spain), 89, 92, 154
air observations, 20
Air Raid (MacLeish), 216
air routes, 247–48
air superiority, 14, 94, 208, 211; definition of, 217; importance to victory, 233, 239; in *Command of the Air*, 195; mission of, 13, 20; of Nationalists, 89, 136, 151, 217, 218, 221, 223, 238; of Republicans, 145; Slessor's advocacy of, 145
air supremacy, 91, 141, 217–18, 238
aircraft: Baumler's opinion of, 121; development of, 235; for Franco, 40; foreign support with, 51; France-to-Spain transport of, 52–53, 58, 66, 91, 107, 195; in combat operations, 43, 68, 70, 94, 95, 97–99, 135, 145, 152, 205, 206; in Northern Territory, 144; in Spanish air forces, 38;

303

Italian models of, 82; losses of, 153, 174; obsolescence of, 243; production of, 90, 138, 212; quality of, 89, 169–70, 237; quality versus quantity of, 140, 210; quantity of, 142–43, 218; reconnaissance missions of, 93; reinforcements of, 87, 132; SCW employment of, 235; Soviet promises of, 219; Soviet restrictions on, 92; Spanish purchase of, 44; specialization in, 234; streamlining of, 181; transport-style of, 236; U.S. Army adoption of, 182; U.S. inventory of, 228–29, 230, 246; U.S.S.R.-to-Spain transport of, 72; U.S.-to-Britain transport of, 231; U.S.-to-U.S.S.R. transport of, 247; variety of, 115, 179
aircraft type (Britain): DeHavilland DH-4, 11; DeHavilland DH.89 Dragon Rapide, 40–43, 46, 54, 62, 232; DeHavilland Puss Moth, 39; Hawker Hart, 47; Vickers Vildebeest, 47–49, 90, *187*, 197
aircraft type (France): Bloch MB.210, 92; Bloch-81 hospital, 52; Breguet XIV, 11; Breguet XIX, 38, 47, 65–66, 72, *75*, 90, 106; Dewoitine 371/372, 53–55, 60, 66, 92; Dewoitine 500, 197–98; Dewoitine 510, 198; LeO-20, 52; Loire 46 C1, *73*, 92, 195–96; Morane Saulnier-225, 52; Nieuport 11, 11; Potez 25, 52, 65, 195; Potez 29 hospital, 52; Potez 54 bomber class, 52–53, 66, 92, 195, 200; Potez 540, 53–54, *75*; Potez 542, 54; Spad XIII, 11
aircraft type (Germany): Arado Ar 95, 186, *187*; Arado Ar 196, 186; Dornier Do 11, 59; Dornier Do 17, 184, 207; Dornier Do 23, 59; Dornier Wal, 38, 45–46, 48, 50, 63, *187*; Fieseler Fi 156 Storch, 185; Fokker F.VIIa, 50, 63; Fokker F.VIIbs, 50, 63; Gotha G.IV, 9–10; Heinkel He 111, 128, 163, 183–84, 207, 237; Heinkel He 111B-2, 184, *190*, 200; Heinkel He 112, 120, 199; Heinkel He 45 Pavo, 173, 186; Heinkel He 51, 47, 55, 60, 66, *73*, 74, 80, 82, 88, 111, 115, 123, 128, 135, 173, 183–85, 195, 207, 237; Heinkel He 59, 200; Heinkel He 59B, *187*; Heinkel He 70 Rayo, 186; Junkers Ju 52, 56–60, *60*, 61, 63, 65, 68–69, 74, *75*, 80–81, 84, 88–89, 93, 99, 111, 114–15, 128, 135, 145–46, 175, 183–84, 194–96, 200, 237; Junkers Ju 86, 116, 183–84, 237; Junkers Ju 86D-1, *190*; Junkers Ju 87 Sturzkampfflug-zeug (Stuka), 161, *161*, *190*, 207; Messerschmitt Bf 109, 184–85, 219, 237; Messerschmitt Bf 109B, 119, 123, 128, 136, 163, 174, 183–85, *193*, 199, 207–9, 221, 224; Messerschmitt Bf 109D, 199–200; Messerschmitt Bf 109E, 184–85, 221–22; Messerschmitt Bf 109E-1, *193*
aircraft type (Italy): Breda Ba 65, 163; Cant Z 501 Gabbiano, *187*, 188; Cant Z 506B Airone, 186, *187*, 188; Caproni Ca 310 Libeccio, 189, *190*; Fiat BR.20 Cignona, 189, *190*, 200; Fiat CR.32 Chirri, 55, 60, 68, *73*, 74, 80, 82, 84, 87, 91, 96, 98, 111, 113–14, 120, 124–25, 128, 135, 147, 162–63, 173–74, 187, 189, 199, 207, 217, 220, 222–23, 240; Fiat CR.42 Falco, 189–90; Macchi MC 202 Folgore, 190; Romeo Ro 37, 89, 163; Savoia-Marchetti SM.62, 38, 46, 90, *187*; Savoia-Marchetti SM.79 Sparviero, 128, 131, 173, 187–89, *190*, 200; Savoia-Marchetti SM.81 Pipistrello, 54–55, 61–62, 69, 74, *75*, 81, 84, 131, 163, 165, 175, 187–89, 200
aircraft type (Soviet Union): Ilyushin Il-4, 194; Lavochkin LaGG-3, 194;

INDEX

Mikoyan-Gurevich MiG-3, 194; Petlyakov Pe.2, 194; Polikarpov I-15 Chato, 59, 72, *73*, 73, 80, 83, 87, 98–99, 110–11, 113, 115–16; 118, 135, 162–63, 173–74, 183, 192, 196, 198, 207–9, 219–22, 224, 237; Polikarpov I-152 Super Chato, *193*, 193, 205, 207; Polikarpov I-16 Mosca, 54, 55, 72, *73*, 73–74, 80, 83, 88–89, 98–99, 113, 115, 118, 121, 125, 163, 173, 183, 192, 198–99, 207–9, 217, 222, 234, 237–38, 243; Polikarpov I-16 Type 5 Mosca, 193–94; Polikarpov I-16 Type 10 Super Mosca, 173, *193*, 193–94, 205; Polikarpov R-5 Resantes, 83–84, 93, 116, 119–20; 192, *193*, 194, 238; R-Z Natacha, 192, *193*, 222, 238; Tupolev ANT-58, 194; Tupolev SB-2 Katiuska, 72, 74–75, *75*, 80, 93, 173, 192, 194, 200, 207, 217, 222; Tupolev TB-3; Yakovlev Yak-7, 194
aircraft type (Spain): CASA Breguet, *See* aircraft type (France); CASA-Vickers Vildebeest, *See* aircraft type (Britain); Nieuport Ni-H 52, 38, 46, 47–48, 55, 59, 66, 68, 72, *73*, 90, 92, 124, 196
aircraft type (U.S.): Bell P-39 Airacobra, 230, 235; Boeing B-17 Flying Fortress, 24, 214–15, 230; Boeing F4B, 73; Boeing P-12E, 47; Consolidated B-24 Liberator, 250–51; Curtiss C-46, 236; Curtiss F9C Sparrowhawk, 73; Curtiss Hawk II, 73; Curtiss JN-3, 10; Curtiss P-36 Hawk, 235; Curtiss P-40 Kittyhawk, 230, 235, 248–49; Douglas A-20 Havoc, 230; Douglas B-18, 245–46; Douglas B-23, 230; Douglas C-47, 236; Douglas C-53, 236; Douglas C-54, 236; Douglas DC-2, 49, 50, 63, 65; Douglas XB-18, 24; Lockheed P-38 Lightning, 235; Martin B-10, 23, 74–75; North American P-51 Mustang, 234–35; Republic P-47B, 235; Seversky P-35, 235

airlift: airpower function of 1, 240; discussion of, 158, 169; importance of, 233–34, 238–39, of Army of Africa, 56–61, 68, 70, 232; U.S. study of, 62–63

airpower: 182, 237; at Guadalajara, 98; communication for, 142; criticism of, 152; during Aragón Campaign, 162–63, foreign involvement, 118, history in Spain, 44–46, impact on morale, 141, importance of 1, 13, 100, 246; in Northern Campaign, 147, 149; in SCW, 50, 89–95, 232–40; Italian quality of, 82; lecture on, 154–58; Nationalist use of, 151; relevance to WWII, 1; Republicans squander, 144; Spanish consolidation of, 45; T. Phillips article on, 167; theories of, 13–22; U.S. build-up of, 228–31; use during WWI, 14

airpower advocates: 13, 22, 141, 168–69, 237, 239

airpower lessons: Arnold's speech on, 169; from SCW, 94, 139–43, 232–40, Griffiss's report on, 114, 142; lecture on, 154–58; Russian loss of, 194

airpower technology: determinism of, 179–80; expected advancement of, 13; Germany's priority of, 188, 238; importance of, 140; in Spain, 89; in SCW, 178–79, 182, 237–38; with radio, 92–93, 142, 216–17

airpower theorists, 13
Albacete, 88, 91, 93, 108, 202, 223
Alcalá de Henares, 95, 112, 114, 136
Alcalá Zamora, Niceto, 33
Alcazar (Toledo), 36, 41, 67–68, 95, 155
Alfa Romeo radial engines, 187, 188
Alfonsists, 145
Alfonso XIII (king), 33, 44
Alicante, 222

INDEX

Alksnis, Yakov, 165
Allison, Jim "Tex," 112
Almirante Cervera (Nat. Spain), 38
Almirante Valdés (Rep. Spain), 38
Alpert, Michael, 129, 181
American Neutrality Policy, 102–5
American Patrol, 110–11
Anarchists, 79, 129–30, 225–26
Andalusia: air battle in, 49, 65; air raid in, 68; division of, 36; Nationalist advances in, 67, 79, 232; Nationalist dominance of, 86; Republican advances in, 63
Andrews, Frank, 25
Anglo-Italian Treaty (1938), 164
Anschluss, 164–65, 170
antiaircraft artillery: defensive counterair by, 68, 84, 160–61, 163, 173, 205, 208; development of, 143, 201–02, 235, 238; Douhet skeptical of, 236; effectiveness of, 153, 158; Fuqua's experience with, 163–64; importance of, 212, 222; in Guadalajara battle, 95; in SCW, 178; inaccuracy of, 15; lack of, 131; Mitchell's opinion of, 18; Republican report of, 174; T. Phillips's advocacy of, 167
Antonov-Ovssenko, Vladimir, 70–71, 148
Aragón, 36, 145, 151
Aragón Campaign, 161–63, 165, 186, 239
Aranda, Antonio, 36, 147, 162, 171
Armée de l'Aire (France), 52, 53, 195, 210, 212
Army Air Corps, U.S., 20, 168, 214, 228; absorbed into USAAF, 230; acquisitions by, 24; air mail delivery by, 24–25; airpower views during SCW, 235; Baumler's standing with, 122; formation of, 22; growth of, 246; support to Britain, 231; technology of, 180; Tinker's training in, 109;

transport inventory of, 236; Westover chief of, 213
Army Air Force, U.S. (USAAF), 119, 230–31, 235–36, 252
Army Air Service, U.S., 11, 22
Army Corps, IV (Rep. Spain), 96
Army Corps, V (Rep. Spain), 205
Army Corps, XII (Rep. Spain), 205
Army of Africa (Nat. Spain): advances on Madrid, 68, 155; airlift of, 56–61, 70, 233; assaults Madrid 77; breaks out from Seville 63; joins rebellion, 37; relieves Alcazar, 67–68; requires transportation, 50; stationed in Morocco, 38; transport of, 51, 61
Army of the Center (Rep. Spain), 77, 224
Army of the Ebro (Rep. Spain), 205–6, 209
Army of the Levant (Rep. Spain), 158–59, 171
Army, Popular (Rep. Spain), 69, 146
Army, U.S., 9, 22–24, 182, 231
Arnold, Henry "Hap": *215*, 247; ACTS graduation speech, 245–46; agreement with Marshall, 229–30; aircraft production, 229; background of, 213–15; decoration endorsement, 252; receives news of Griffiss's death, 251; speech on airpower, 168–70, 235; USAAF build-up 231, 236
As de Bastos group (Italy), 220
Asensio, José, 77
assault aircraft. *See* ground attack aircraft
Assault Guards (Spain), 35, 37
assistant military attaché for air, 32, 89, 139
Assistant Secretary of Air, 22
Asturias, 67, 127, 144, 186; Council of, 147; Franco's suppression of, 42; López Ochoa's suppression of, 34; Nationalists conquer, 151; Republic

INDEX

of, 146; Republican control of, 36; revolt within, 33
Aviación del Tercio Extranjero (Italy), 55, 59, 82
Aviación Militar (Spain), 38, 40, 72
Aviazione Legionaria (Italy), 82, 98, 144, 149
Azaña, Manuel, 27, 69, 136, 221
Azuqueca Airfield (Campo X), 88–89, 99

Badajoz, 63, 65–66
Baker Board, 25–26
Balbo, Italo, 187
Balearic Islands, 45, 232
Baleares (Spain), 38
Balmes, Amadeo, 41
Barcelona, 34, 46, 71, 134, 162; Azaña moves to, 69; bombing campaign against, 165–66, 218; bombing impact upon, 212, 236; CAMPSA factory bombing, 174–75; fighting within 130, 225; Goded arrested in, 39, 232; government in 170, 217; government moves to, 158; Griffiss stationed in, 160; Nationalists capture 220; Republican control of, 36; spared direct assault, 171
Basque Country, 67, 186; defense of, 127–28; dissension within, 132; Nationalists conquer, 151; Republican control of, 36; vessels of, 38
Battle of Britain, 227–29, 230, 239
Baumler, Albert "Ajax", 110, 118, 245; air victory of, 113; background of, 108; correspondence with Raley, 120–22, 234; fate of, 124; illness of, 119–20; life after SCW, 244; opinion of SB-2; pilots I-16s, 198–99
Bay of Biscay, 127, 131
Bayo, Alberto, 66
Beard, Charles, 179
Bebb, William Henry Cecil, 40
Beevor, Antony, 134

Belchite (town), 145–46, 151, 162
Belchite, Battle of, 145–46, 149, 152, 156, 189
Bergonzoli, Annibale, 95, 99
Bernasconi, Mario, 149
Bertram, Otto, 41
Berzin, Jan Pavlovlich, 148
Bilbao, 154, 239; Iron Ring construction, 69, 127–28; Nationalists capture, 119, 132, 134, 144, 145; vulnerabilities of, 156
Blanche, Antonio, 99
Blue Division (Spain), 244
Blue Patrol (Nat. Spain), 88–89
Blum, Léon, 52–53, 148, 165, 170, 182
BMW engines, 59, 186
Bolín, Enrique, 62–63
Bolín, Luis, 40, 41, 50, 54, 62
bomber escort, 94, 140, 157, 208–9, 233–34, 238
bomber interception, 20, 23, 91, 94, 157–58, 233–34
bombs, proliferation of, 200
Bonomi, Ruggero, 55, 80
Bowers, Claude, 30, 39, 43–44, 52, 67, 78
Breda machine gun, 55, 199
Brihuega, 96–97, 99, 113
Brunete (town), 119, 135–36
Brunete, Battle of, 145, 156, 159; air operations during, 119–20, 135–36, 142, 149, 152; Bf 109s appear during, 136; Dahl shot down during, 123; diversion of troops to, 144; events of, 134–37; importance of, 138
Burgos, 185, 226

Cabanellas, Miguel, 46, 67
Cádiz, 47, 58, 197
Callihan, John C., 179
Calvo Sotelo, José, 35, 39, 42
Campeche (Soviet Union), 69
Campo X. *See* Azuqueca Airfield
CAMPSA, 174–75

Canarias (Spain), 38
Canary Islands, 43, 130; flight from, 83, 232; Franco stationed at, 40–42; funeral of Balmes, 41; Nationalist control of, 36
Cantabria, 127, 151
Cantière Riuntini dell'Adriatico (Cant), 188
Capronis, 61–62
Carabineros, 33, 37
Carlists, 37, 145
Carney, William B., 204
carpet bombing, 147
Cartagena, 38, 69, 71, 224, 226
Casa de Campo, 79
Casado, Segismundo, 136, 224–26
Casares Quiroga, Santiago, 37, 42, 158
Cascon, Manuel, 48
Castellón, 171
Castilian Corps (Nat. Spain), 170–71
Castillo, José, 35
Catalonia, 162, 189, 205; bombing of, 218; defensive capability of, 175; forces of, 138, 158; government located in, 170; Nationalist occupation of, 221–22; separatist uprising 33; separatists within, 130
Catalonian Offensive, 218–22
Caudillo, 68
Cenni, Giuseppe, 82
Central Aero-Hydrodynamics Institute (TsAGI), 191–92
Central Zone (Rep. Spain): 162, 205, 222; forces of, 158; internecine fighting within, 224–26; Nationalist campaign against 170; Negrin unpopular within, 221
Champlain, 120
Chaney, James, 246–249
Chautemps, Camille, 148
Cheadle, Henry R., 188, 218–21, 226
Chennault, Claire: ACTS assignment, 20–21; command in China, 244; controversy, 21–22; *Role of Defensive Pursuit*, 21; skeptic of strategic bombing, 13; vindicated by SCW, 240
Churchill, Winston, 14
Císcar (Rep. Spain), 148
Citizen Act (1907), 105
Civil Guards (Spain), 37
Clinical Hospital (Madrid), fighting in, 80
close air support: 13, 173, 211; Griffiss's report on, 93–94; importance of, 157, 239; in Guadalajara battle, 95; in Madrid operations, 100; in Northern Campaign, 127; in WWI, 14; role of biplanes in, 234; T. Phillips's advocacy of, 167
Combined Chiefs of Staff, 230
Comintern, 70–71
Command and General Staff College (CGSC), 22
Command and General Staff School (CGSS), 154, 167, 169, 236
command of the air (concept), 16, 19–20
Command of the Air (Douhet): 15, 18, 195, 237
Communists, 43, 129–30, 134, 224–26
Compañía Hispano-Marroquí de Transportes (HISMA), 57
Companys, Luis, 33
Condor Legion (Germany): 82, 173, 184, 240; bombing of Guernica, 118, 128; bombing operations of, 88; carpet bombing by, 147; establishment of, 70; fighting at Ebro, 208; final raid by, 222; force size at Ebro battle, 206; fratricide by, 161; in Northern Campaign, 144; sinks *Císcar*, 148; strafing retreating forces, 221; strikes at Málaga, 87; W. von Richthofen's service with, 82, 165, 219, 242
Constant, Samuel V., 32
Construcciones Aeronáutica S.A. (CASA), 47, 196–97

INDEX

Coolidge, Calvin, 22
Coppi, Giovanni, 95–97, 99
Córdoba, 49, 63, 66, 88
Corpo Truppe Volontarie (CTV) (Italy), 82, 95–99, 172, 219
Cortada, Roldán, 130
Cortes, 34–35, 66, 221
Corum, James S., 83, 128–29
Corunna Road Offensive, 83–84, 100
cost plus fixed fee (CPFF) contracts, 229
Cot, Pierre, 53, 181, 194
Counterair: as function of airpower, 1, 240; budgetary needs for, 212; defensive, 13, 94, 143; delay in, 157; distinguishable in SCW, 233; Douhet skeptical of, 236; in Levant Offensive, 173; in Madrid operations, 100; Mecozzi's advocacy of, 20; missing at Valencia, 131; offensive, 135, 154; role of aircraft types in, 234. *See also* bomber interception.
coup (1932), 33–34, 42
coup (1936), 42, 45; events of, 35–36; failure of, 39, 67, 126; navy battles during, 38
coup (Casadist), 224–26
Cuatro Vientos Airfield, 44, 49, 66
Cuse, Robert, 104–5

Dahl, Edith Rogers (Kaye), 110, 242
Dahl, Harold "Whitey": 109–10, 118; at Guadalajara, 113–14; imprisonment of, 123–24; life after SCW, 241–42; shot down, first time, 112; shot down, second time, 119, 135
Daimler-Benz engines, 184, 221
Daladier, Edouard, 175, 212
Dávila Arronda, Fidel, 132–34, 144, 147, 161, 219
Deutschland (Germany), 131, 143
Devers, Jacob, 246
Dickinson, Derek "Dick," 124–25
director general of aeronautics, 45

Division, 1st, "God wills it" (Dio lo vuole) (Italy), 95, 99
Division, 2nd, Black Flames (Fiamme nere) (Italy), 95–97, 99
Division, 3rd (Rep. Spain), 207
Division, 3rd, Black Feathers (Penne nere) (Italy), 95, 97–98
Division, 11th (Rep. Spain), 96–99, 135–36
Division, 12th (Rep. Spain), 95–97
Division, 14th (Rep. Spain), 96–97, 99
Division, 35th (Rep. Spain), 146
Doolittle, James "Jimmy," 26
Douhet, Giulio: 15, 19, 212; air force advocate, 16; *Command of the Air*, 15; command of the air (concept), 16; criticism of, 20, 155; death of, 15; influence of, 187; meeting with Mitchell, 18; skeptic of antiaircraft artillery, 201, 238; skeptic of bombing interception, 23; strategic bombing views, 13, 15, 189, 211; technological determinism of, 180–81; theory debated, 166–70; views tested in SCW, 85–86, 210, 236
Duralumin, 59
Durruti, Buenaventura, 79–80

Ebro, Battle of the: 172, 186, 194; conclusion of, 217; events of, 205–9; air operations in, 206–9; aftermath, 218–19
Eden, Anthony, 164
Edwards, John Carver, 106
El Valasco (Spain), 38
Elda, 223
Ely, Eugene, 9
embassy, U.S. (Barcelona), 220–21
embassy, U.S. (Madrid), 64, 78–79, 85
Engineers and the Price System (Veblen), 179
Esdaile, Charles, 170, 220
España (Nat. Spain), 38, 65, 131, 143

España squadron, 53
Estremadura, 36, 79, 89, 175, 232–33
Experiments in Aerodynamics (Langley), 3–4

Falange, 35, 37
Falco, José, 222
Fanjul, Joaquín, 49
Farman engines, 195
Fascists (Italian), 95–99
Fascists (Spanish). *See* Falange
Faymonville, Philip, 248–49
Fechet, James E., 23
Fernández, Antonio, 44
Fiat A radial engine, 189
Figueras, 221–22
Finch, George, 103
Findley, Earl, 167
firm fixed price (FFP) contracts, 229
First Aero Squadron, 10
Fiske, Norman, 56
Five Down, No Glory (Smith and Hall), 111
flight, 3–8
flying boats, 48
flying fortress, 53, 94
Flynn, Eddie, 44
Fokker, Anthony, 9
For Whom the Bell Tolls (Hemingway), 67, 241
Foulois, Benjamin, 10–11, 25–26
Franco Bahamonde, Francisco: 39, 63, 77, 129, *133*, 151, 155–56, 170, 182, 185; appointed Caudillo, 68; appointed Generalissimo, 67; as dictator, 243–44; benefitted from airpower, 232–33; communication with Casada, 224; commutes Dahl's execution, 124; consolidation of support, 51; crushes Asturian revolt, 33; declares victory, 226; directs airlift, 62; discretion of, 42; diverts forces to Aragón, 145; early life of, 41–42; flight to Morocco, 39–43, 50, 56, 83; friction with W. von Richthofen, 221; halts Madrid assault, 80; orders Levant offensive, 171; permits Guadalajara withdrawal, 99; promotes Kindelán, 241; reinforces Ebro front, 206; resentment toward Italy, 86; safe zone order by, 81, 237; support of Germany and Italy, 68, 70, 100, 149
Franco Bahamonde, Ramón, 45, 48, 188
Fuenterrabia, 43, 67
Fuentes de Ebro, 146, 152
Fuller, Horace: assessment of Brunete, 137; on antiaircraft defense, 201–2; on aviation, 136; on bombing assessment, 85; on *España*, 131; on heat ray, 202; on incendiary bombs, 200; on machine guns verses cannons, 198–99
Fuqua, Stephen O.: 28–29, 64–65, 158; appointed military attaché, 29–30; becomes columnist, 241; escape from Catalonia, 221; forms information center, 64; impact of reports, 154; on Barcelona bombing, 166, 236; on Calvo Sotelo's murder, 35; on CAMPSA factory bombing, 174–75; on combat claims, 173; on French aircraft; on López Ochoa's arrest, 34; on Madrid bombing, 85; on militias, 37, 126; ordered to Valencia, 78–79; retirement of, 218; visit to Ebro front, 207–9; visit to XV International Brigade, 152–53, 163–64; with Griffiss, 89
Futurismo, 181

Galatea (Britain), 226
Galera Macías, Emilio, 193
Galician Corps (Nat. Spain), 162, 171
Galland, Adolf, 135, 147, 165
Gamir, Mariano, 144, 146
Gandesa, 162–63, 205

INDEX

García LaCalle, Andrés, 88–89, 95, 110–11, 113, 165, 220
García Morato, Joaquin: 55, 207, 242; ace status of, 82; aerial victories of, 65–66, 68, 80; commands Blue Patrol, 88; death of, 240; praised by Sperrle, 147; presumed dead, 223; strafes Lukacs's car, 134
Garcia-Valiño, Rafael, 171–72, 206
Garibaldi Battalion (Italy), 97–98
Gavotti, Giulio, 9
General Headquarters, Air Force (GHQAF), 25–26, 122, 214, 230
George Washington Battalion. *See* International Brigade, XV
Getafe Airfield: bombed by Nationalists, 66; captured by Nationalists, 77, 80; CASA factory at, 47, 197; Republican control of, 46; support in early missions, 48–49
Gijón, 144–9, 156
Gil Robles, José María, 45–46
Giral, José, 37, 53, 64, 71, 221
Gnome-Rhône engine, 73, 195
Goded, Manuel, 39, 67, 232
gold, 71–72, 138
Gomez Trejo, Francisco. *See* Tinker, Frank G.
González, Valentin (pseud. El Campesino), 96, 98, 204
Goriev, Vladimir, 148
government, Spanish Republican. *See* Republicans, Spanish
government, U.S., 63, 102–5
Graves, George M., 123–4
Great Aerodrome, 4
Great Terror (or Great Purge), 191. *See also* Stalin, Josef
Great War. *See* World War I
Griffiss, Katherine H.W., 251
Griffiss, Townsend: 30–32, *32*, 144, 158; "Air Warfare in Spain", 209–13; advising Bowers's relocation, 43–44;

airpower lessons of, 233–234; April 1937 report, 114–19; as special Army observer, 246; assistant military attaché, 30, 32; commended by Westover, 32; death of, 250–51; departure from Spain, 209; graduation from ACTS, 245; implicated by Dahl, 123; in Valencia, 85; mission to locate Bowers, 43; mission to U.S.S.R., 247–49; on air activity, 153–54; on airpower lessons, 139–43; on Bilbao defense, 132; on bombing precision, 237; on *España* sinking, 131; on French aircraft, 52–53; on Guadalajara, 98; on heat ray, 202; on I-16; on Ju 52s; on Ju 86s; on Loire 46s; on machine guns verses cannons, 198–99; on Spanish airpower, 46, 72; on Teruel air operations, 160; ranking of fighters, 54; recommended for decoration, 252; special report, 89–95, 236; *When You Go to Hawaii, You Will Need This Guide to the Islands*, 32
ground attack aircraft, 20, 83, 93, 167, 238
GRU (Soviet Union), 71, 83
Guadalajara (city), 47, 95–97, 99
Guadalajara, Battle of: aftermath of, 100, 125–27; close air support after, 211; events of, 95–99, 132, 136; importance of airpower, 156; importance of basing, 142; Vickers Vildebeests at, 197
Guernica: 158, 237; bombing of, 118, 128–29, 149, 184; foundation of Basque republic, 69; incendiary bombs at, 200, 238
Guernica (Picasso), 129, 216
Guerra di rapido corso, 96
Guerrero, Miguel, 49

Hall, Elbert J., 11
heat ray, 93, 202–3

Hemingway, Ernest, 67, 112–13, 120, 241
Henke, Alfred, 56–58
Hernández Saravia, Juan, 158, 171, 219
Herrán, García de la, 49
Herrick, Myron, 12
Hidalgo de Cisneros, Ignacio, 67, 90–91, 114, 154, 219, 224
Hindenburg (Germany), 183
Hispano-Suiza, 44, 47, 196–97
Hispano-Suiza engine, 44, 47, 125
Hitler, Adolf: 108, 215; allied with Mussolini, 244; authorizes combat, 61; Nationalist appeal to, 50, 56–57; oversees aerial rearmament, 183; secures Munich Agreement, 209; support to Nationalists, 51, 70
Hitler's Luftwaffe and the Spanish Civil War (Proctor), 199–200
Homage to Catalonia (Orwell), 134
Hooton, E.R., 84, 127–28, 137, 144, 220
Hoover, Herbert, 29, 103–4
Hornet engine, 121
Hotel Florida, 112, 242
Howell Commission, 21, 26
Howson, Gerald: defense of Polikarpov, 73; on Bf 109, 185, 199; on He-111, 184; on Loire 46C-1, 196; on Potez 54, 53; on SM.81, 55; on Vickers Vildebeests, 197
Huesca, Battle of, 134
Hull, Cordell, 78

Ibarra Palace, 97–98
Ibárruri, Dolores (pseud. La Pasionaria), 101, 224–25
incendiary bombs, 128, 131, 178, 200–1, 233, 238
independent air force: 22, 45, 141; ACTS support of, 22; Arnold and Marshall postpone, 230; Mitchell's support of, 16, 213; of Britain, 13
Industrial Party (Soviet Union), 190–91

Infantry Division, 2nd (Rep. Spain), 87
Infiesto, 147
Innovation and Achievement (Callihan), 179
insurgents. *See* Nationalists
interdiction, 1, 13–14, 20, 96, 240
International Brigade, XI, 79, 83–84, 96–98
International Brigade, XII, 79, 84, 96
International Brigade, XV: 87, 102, 136, 152, 162–63
International Brigades: 113, 134, 152–53; arrive in Spain, 69; at Corunna Road, 84; at Guadalajara, 96–97; at Jarama, 87; dismissed from service, 217; force estimate of, 138
International Tank Regiment, 146
Iron Ring: 156, 172; bombing of, 149, 239; construction of, 69, 127–28; Nationalists break through, 132
Irujo Ametzaga, Xabier, 129
Irun, 43, 63, 67
Isotta-Franchini Asso V-engine, 188
Italo-Ethiopian War, 54, 62, 104, 139, 235

Jackson-Schebetta, Lisa, 216–17
Jaime I (Rep. Spain), 38, 61
Jarama, Battle of: aftermath of, 100; air operations during, 88–89, 115; events of, 87–89; LaCalle Squadron during, 111–12; recovery from, 95, 97
Jean Weems (Britain), 153
Jerrold, Douglas, 40
Joint Army-Navy Technical Board, 11
joint operations, 82
Junkers Jumo engines, 183–84
Junkers, Hugo, 59, 182
Jurado, Enrique, 96, 136

Kemeny, Mata Zalka (pseud. General Lukacs), 134, 136
Kenney, George, 235–36

INDEX

Kerber, L.L., 191–92
Kill Devil Hill, 6
Kindelán, Alfredo, 44, 55, 165, 241
Kitty Hawk, NC, 5–7
Knoblaugh, Edward, 65, 72, 79, 81, 124, 237
Koch, Charles "Tiny," 108, 113
Koenig, Theodore, 32
Komosomol (Soviet Union), 69
Kosokov Squadron, 111, 113, 118
Kuibyshev, U.S.S.R., 246–50

La Corse (France), 153
La Cucaracha group (Italy), 219
LaCalle Squadron, 88–89, 95, 111–14
LaCalle, Andrés García. *See* García LaCalle, Andrés
LaCalle, Victor, 95–97
Lafayette Escadrille, 10, 105
Lahm, Frank, 8
Langley, Samuel P., 3–4
Largo Caballero, Francisco: 84, 132; appoints Prieto, 66; becomes commander-in-chief, 69; becomes prime minister, 64; orders Madrid evacuation, 77; orders transfer of gold, 71; resigns as prime minister, 130
Las Palmas, 40–42, 50, 56
Layton, Edwin, 244
Lee, Raymond, 86, 201
legionnaires. *See* Spanish Foreign Legion
Leider, Ben, 110–12
Lend Lease Act, 231
Levant Offensive, 171–74, 202
Lewis gun, 48, 55
Liaison Task Force (Nat. Spain), 171–72
Libertad (Rep. Spain), 38
Liberty Engine, 11
Lilienthal, Otto, 4–5
Lincoln, F.H. 78, 201
Lindbergh, Charles, 11–12, 25
Líneas Aéreas Postales Españolas (LAPE), 40

Líster, Enrique: at Jarama, 87; command of 11th Division, 96–99, 135–36; command of V Army Corps, 205; during Catalonia defense, 220; during Levant Offensive, 204; on Fuentes de Ebro, 146
Literary Digest, 139
Littorio Division (Italy), 95, 99
Llano de la Encomienda, Francisco, 127, 144
Llop, Tomás Roig, 220
Locarno Treaties, 182–83
Logoluso, Alfredo, 124–25
Lopatin, Vseyelod (pseud. General Montenegro), 176
López Ochoa, Eduardo, 34
Lord, Frederick Ives, 107
Los Alcázares, 46
Lovett, Robert, 230
Lufthansa, 41, 56–57, 186
Luftwaffe: airlift mission, 56–58; as force of intimidation, 215; fighter aircraft of, 82; in Battle of Britain, 228; Mölders as general of, 242; prioritized over navy, 186; reinstatement of, 183

MAC 34 machine guns, 196
machine guns, small-caliber, 197–200
MacKenzie-Papinau Battalion. *See* International Brigade, XV
Macklin, Graham D., 40
MacLeish, Archibald, 216
Madrid: 34, 36, 39, 44, 46, 84, 88–89, 96, 136, 162, 197, 228; after defense of, 100–1, 152; air defense of, 72, 92–93, 111; antiaircraft defense of, 201; armed militias in, 37; at risk of occupation, 63; attempted encirclement of, 87; bombing effect upon, 85–86, 155–57, 167–68; bombing of, 108; Casada seizes power in, 244–25; casualties during war, 138; defense of,

77, 81, 87, 126; entrenchments near, 141; first air attack on, 66, Fuqua departs, 79, interior lines at, 147; Malraux's arrival in, 53; mercenaries visit, 112–13; murders in, 35; Nationalist advance toward, 63, 67–69, 71, 218, 222, 232–33; Nationalist plans for, 39, 94–95; Nationalists capture, 226; Nationalists diverted from, 145; Republican base, 38; safe zone within, 237; telephone high-rise in, 117; under siege, 134
Madrid Reinforced Division (Nat. Spain), 83
Madrid, Battle of, 79–81, 82, 100
Maestrazgo Corps (Nat. Spain), 206
Magic Fire, Operation (Unternehmen Feuerzauber), 57, 169
Maginot Line, 127
Majorca. *See* Mallorca
Málaga, 36, 49, 86–87, 95, 134
Mallorca: 66, 166, 188; Nationalist seizure of, 39, 232; rebellion on, 36; Republican invasion of, 64
Malraux, André, 53
Manises Airfield, 196, 202
Mantelli, Adriano, 82
March to the Sea. *See* Aragón Campaign
Markov, Dmitriy Sergeyevich, 192
Marshall, George, 229–30
Martínez Barrio, Diego, 37, 221
Matthews, Herbert, 112, 204–5
Maxwell Field, 245–46
McCabe, E.R.W., 123
McNarney, Joseph, 247
Mecozzi, Amadeo, 13, 20, 189, 240
Melilla, Morocco, 35, 41–42
Méndez Núñez (Rep. Spain), 38
Menéndez, Leopoldo, 171
Meneses Field, 93
Mera, Cipriano, 96–97, 99
mercenaries, U.S., 102, 105–7, 112–13, 119–23

Mérida, 63, 65–66
Merriman, Robert, 152, 163
MG-15 machine gun, 59, 161, 185
MG-17 machine gun, 161
Miaja, José: 77–78; command at Brunete, 135; defense of Guadalajara, 96; defense of Madrid, 77, 84, 87, 100; escapes by plane, 226; joins National Council of Defense, 225; opposes surrender, 223; visits LaCalle Squadron, 113–14
Michela, Joseph, 248
Miguel de Cervantes (Rep. Spain), 38
Mikulin engine, 192
Milch, Erhard, 58
Militär Wochenblatt, 201
military attaché: 30, 45, 123, 154, 212; bombing reports from, 85–86; Cheadle's appointment as, 188, 218; Fuqua's appointment as 29; Fuqua's responsibility as, 78; Griffiss's record as, 252; in Britain, 201; in Germany, 200; in U.S.S.R., 248; observations from SCW, 233–34; orders to, 81
Military Intelligence Division (MID), U.S. Department of War, 30, 62, 85, 93, 210, 218
militias, 37, 68–69
Millán Astray, José, 42
Ministry of Air (Spain), 45
Minorca, 36, 223
Mitchell, William "Billy": *11*, 16–18; air force advocacy, 16; court-martial of, 17; death of, 26; Howell Commission testimony of, 26; in St. Mihiel offensive, 11, 16; post–WWI service of, 17; strategic bombing advocacy, 13; *Winged Defense*, 18
Mola, Emilio: 67, 77; advances on San Sebastián, 63; commands Madrid assault, 76; commands Northern campaign, 127; death of, 132, 232; plans for 1936 coup, 35, 39

Mölders, Werner, 165, 174, 208–9, 239, 242
Monasterio, José, 160
Montalbán, 160, 162
Montegnacco, Bruno, 82
morale bombing. *See* strategic bombing
Morato, Gómez, 42
Moreau, Rudolph Freiherr von, 57
Morgan, John, 79
Moroccan Corps (Nat. Spain), 162, 205–6, 219
Morocco, 36–37, 41–42, 50, 57, 61, 232
Morrow Board, 22
Moscardó, Jose, 36, 95–96, 98–99
Moy, Timothy, 23
Moyell, K.A., 175
Munich Agreement, 209, 215, 225, 227
Muñoz Grandes, Agustín, 147
Mussolini, Benito (Il Duce): 156, 182, 244; at Bruno's funeral, 243; building Italian airpower, 187; Nationalists appeal to, 50, 62; support to Nationalists, 51, 70, 97, 108
Mussolini, Bruno, 124–5, 243

"Night before Battle" (Hemingway), 112–13
Nadashkevich, Aleksandr Vasil'yevich, 191
Nalty, Bernard, 180
Nanetti, Nino, 97, 132, 136
Nathan, George, 136
National Council of Defense (Rep. Spain), 224–25
National Defense Act (1916), 10
National Defense Council, 229
Nationalists: 39, *49*, *100*, 122, 125, 134, 154, 155–56, *159*, *176*, *225*; airpower critical to, 232–33; communication with Casada, 224; court-martial of Dahl, 242; defense of Guernica raid, 129; Ebro casualties, 217; force size of, 138; increasing air dominance of, 150; Italian intervention for, 55; lack of aircraft industry, 197; notice of Soviet presence, 69; operations of, 43–44, 63, 66–67, 70–71, 76–77, 79–80, 83–84, 86–89, 93–99, 100–1, 112, 119–20, 126–27, 132, 135–36, 144–46; 158, 159–63, 165, 204–9, 217–19, 223; Patriarca's service with, 124; reach the sea, 164; recognized by Britain and France, 224; relief of the Alcazar, 67–68; reorganization of, 82; results of Northern Campaign, 148, 151; superior reconnaissance of, 185; support of Germany and Italy, 51, 68; supporters of, 64; ultimate victory of, 226; united under Franco, 51; victory expected, 137, 165, 170, 222
Naval Academy, U.S., 109, 120
Navarra (Nat. Spain), 38
Navarro Bonilla, Diego, and Guillermo Vicente Cano, 185
Navy, Nationalists, 59
Navy, Spanish, 37–38
Navy, Spanish Republican, 38, 50, 58–59, 224, 233
Navy, U.S., 23–24, 73, 109, 231
Negrín, Juan: 130–31, 182; escapes to France, 221; flees Spain, 224–25; hoping to persist, 171, 177, 223–24; transfer of gold: 71
Neutrality Act, 103
Neutrality Act (1935), 104
Neutrality Act (1937), 105
New York Times: on censorship, 36; on coup, 27; on Fuqua appointment, 28; on one-year anniversary of SCW, 137–39; on two-year anniversary of SCW, 204–5; on *War of the Worlds* reaction, 216; on Wright Flyer, 8
Newsweek, 101, 241
night bombing, 88, 238
Nin, Andrés, 134

NKVD (Soviet Union), 134, 149, 190, 196
nonintervention, 91, 103, 105
Non-Intervention Committee, 131–32, 175–76
Non-Intervention Treaty, 53, 61, 70, 164
Norden bombsights, 23–24
Northern Campaign: 156–57, 186, 222; beginning of, 127–30; casualties of, 148; Mola's death during, 232; Republican failures during, 151
Northern Front, 127
Northern Territory: campaign for, 125, 153; critical loss of, 149; defense of, 69, 134–35, 144; pivot to, 100, 126–27
Northern Zone. *See* Catalonia
Núñez de Prado, Miguel, 46

"Operations" (RAF document), 14
Office of Chief of the Air Corps, 61, 94, 121–22
Office of Naval Intelligence (ONI), 65, 122
OGPU (Soviet Union), 190–91
Omaha, 221
Operation X (Soviet Union), 71
Orgaz, Luis, 41, 56, 83
Orwell, George, 134
Osipenko, Polina, 240
Ostfriesland (Germany), 17
Oued Mellah (France), 153

"Planes Debunked," 139
"Preview to Armageddon" (Phillips), 167
Palchinsky, Peter, 190–91
Parachutists, 80, 117–18, 143, 233
parasol style (monoplane), 48
Parsons, Edward C., 125
Partido Obrero de Unificación Marxista (POUM), 130–31, 134, 149
Partridge, Earl E., 108
Patriarca, Vincent, 124–25

Patterson, Robert, 231
Pavlov, Dmitri (pseud. General Pablo), 84–97
Peñaroya, Battle of. *See* Pozoblanco, Battle of
Peninsula, Spanish: 48–50, 51, 177; air bases on, 90; airlift to, 56, 70, 232–33; Army of Africa on, 63; Nationalist air superiority on, 151; rebellion on, 36; Republican advantage on, 37–38; sea convoy to, 59; Soviet interest in, 150
Perpignan, France, 52–53, 221
Pershing, John J., 10
Petlyakov, Vladimir Mikhaylovich, 192
Phillips, Thomas R., 167
Phillips, William, 104
Picasso, Pablo, 129, 216
Plocher, Hermann, 165
Plus Ultra (Spain), 45, 48, 188
Polikarpov, Nikolai, 72–73, 83, 182, 191
Pollard, Hugh, 40, 43
Popular Front (Spain), 34, 42–43, 45, 53, 158
Power and Armies (Slessor), 19
Pozas, Sebastián, 77
Pozoblanco, Battle of, 223
Prada, Adolfo, 146–48
Prieto, Indalecio: 72, 124; appointment of, 66; appoints Hidalgo de Cisneros, 67; leads Republicans in exile, 241; orders *Císcar* departure, 148; reinforces Basque Country, 132; resigns, 165
Primo de Rivera, Miguel, 35, 45
Proctor, Raymond, 41, 58–59, 129, 174, 199, 206
Puente Bahamonde, Ricardo de la, 42
PV-1 machine guns, 198

Queipo de Llano, Gonzalo, 62–63, 67

"Rebels Smash On as Spain Observes War Anniversary," 204

"Royal Air Force War Manual," 14
Raab, Antonius, 196
radar, 203
Raley, Edward, 61–62, 74–75, 120–23, 234, 244
Reader's Digest, 125
rebels. *See* Nationalists
reconnaissance, 1, 238, 249
Regia Aeronautica (Italy), 20, 187–89
Regulares: ambushed, 137; Asturian suppression by, 33; joins rebellion, 37; Madrid assault by, 77, 79–80; on the peninsula, 67; transport to peninsula, 50
Republican Brigade, 65th (Rep. Spain), 96
Republican Northern Army (Rep. Spain), 95–96
Republicans, Spanish: *49*, 51, 63, *100*, 107, 124–25, 130, 155–56, *159*, *176*, 193, *225*; antiaircraft capabilities, 175, 201; casualties of, 148, 217; changes in government, 232; defense of Madrid, 80; demoralization, 134, 165; dismiss of International Brigades, 217; find Nationalists orders 79; force size of, 138; foreign support of, 51, 53–54; government flees to Valencia, 76–78; government in Barcelona, 158, 166, 170; government in exile, 241; heat ray experiments of, 93; interception of Nationalist messages, 154; loss of Málaga, 86–87; modernizing airpower, 89; morale within, 204–5; operations of, 63–64, 66–67, 83–84, 87–89, 95–99, 113–14, 119–20, 126–27, 134–37, 145, 147, 151, 159–63, 171–72, 176–77, 185, 206–9, 220–23; risk of defeat, 68, 70, 94, 122, 170, 218–19; Soviet influence in, 92, 149, 196; split by Casadist coup, 224–25; stability of, 85; Stalin's support of, 70–71; transfer of gold reserves, 71–72; ultimate defeat, 226; wary of Franco, 41
Requetés. *See* Carlists
Reserve Army (Rep. Spain), 171
Richthofen, Wolfram von, 82–83, 128–29, 165, 219, 221, 242–43
Rif War, 42, 44
Río Alfambra, 160, 171
Río Ebro, 145, 162, 172, 205–6, 208
Río Henares, 95–96, 98
Río Jarama, 87–88
Río Llobregat, 220
Río Manzanares, 79
Roatta, Mario, 82, 86, 95, 98–99
Rohstoffe und Waren Einkaufsgesellschaft (ROWAK), 57
Rojo, Vincente, 223
Role of Defensive Pursuit (Chennault), 21
Romerales Quinto, Manuel, 35–36
Ronda, 67
Roosevelt, Franklin D., 24, 104–5, 215, 228–29
Roosevelt, Theodore, 7
Rosenberg, Marcel, 71
Rossi, Silvio, 95, 99
Royal Air Force (RAF) (Britain), 13–14, 228, 239, 251

Salamanca, 67, 70, 99
Salas Larrazábal, Ángel, 68, 80, 165, 174
Salas Larrazábal, Jesús, 48, 55, 134–35, 146, 173–74
Salvador, Julio, 66, 207
San Javier air-sea base, 46, 48, 87
San Sebastián, 43–44, 63, 65, 67
Sánchez Barcaiztegui (Rep. Spain), 38
Sania Ramel Airfield, 42
Sanjurjo, José: 39, 67; coup attempt, 33–34; death of, 39, 132, 232; exiled, 34
Santander, 127, 144–45, 156
Sanz Sáinz, Augustin, 108
Saragossa, 46, 145–46, 152–53

Saturday Evening Post, 122, 167
Sawyer, E.O., Jr., 62–63
Scanlon, Martin, 32
Scientific American, 5
Selfridge, Thomas, 9, 240
Selles, José "Chang," 110, 112–14, 118–19
Serov, Anatoli, 135, 240, 242
sesquiplanes, 47
Seville: 34, 46, 57, 70; base for offensive, 63; Hispano-Suiza factory at, 197; Queipo de Llano control of, 62; Sanjurjo's occupation of, 33; transport destination, 50
Seville, Duke of, 86
Shenandoah, 17
ShKAS machine guns, 198–99
Shvetsov radial engine, 193
Signal Corps, U.S., 8, 20
Skarbov, A., 192
Slater, Hugh, 163–64
Slessor, John, 13, 19, 240
Smith, Merritt Roe, 179
Smith, Richard K., and R. Cargill Hall, 111, 120
Smith, Truman, 200–1
Smushkevich, Yakov (pseud General Douglas), 95–96, 196, 243
Social Construction of Technological Systems (Bijker, et al), 180
social constructionism, 180–81
Socialists (Spain), 130
Solchaga, José, 127, 147, 172
Some Still Live (Tinker), 108, 122
Soría Division (Nat. Spain), 95–96, 98–99
Soviet Central Design Bureau (TsKB), 72–73
Spain, 45, *49*, 75, 81, *100*, *159*, *176*, *225*; air operations in, 61, 65, 83, 166; airpower in, 44, 94; foreign troops in, 69, 176–77; French support of, 53, 91, 195, 202; Griffiss appointed to, 89; history of, 33, 44; impacted by civil war, 148, 160; lack of industry, 139; Nationalist plans for, 39; Nationalists conquer, 224–26; political climate, 35, 41, 130; Tinker's proposal for, 122; U.S. mercenaries in, 119–29, 234; under Franco, 39, 227, 243–44
Spain in Arms (Hooton), 220
Spanish Air Force. *See* Air Force, Republican Spain; Air Force, Nationalists
Spanish Civil War, 2, 39, 61, 137, 182, 204; airlift during, 56; airpower in, 1, 89–95, 168–69, 186, 200, 215, 232–40; CGSS lecture on, 154–58; fates of participants of, 240–44; foreign intervention in, 57, 63; Griffiss's knowledge of, 210, 213, 252; Guernica's significance to, 129; Hemingway's writings about, 112–13, 241; lessons of, 194, 212; start of, 27; strategic bombing during 1, 139; technology tested in, 180–81, 216–17; U.S. mercenaries in, 102, 122, 124; unique character of, 168, 185
Spanish Civil War, The (Esdaile), 220
Spanish Civil War, The (Thomas). *See* Thomas, Hugh
Spanish Foreign Legion: assaults Madrid, 77, 79–80; establishment of, 42; joins rebellion, 36–37; led by Franco, 67; suppresses Asturian revolt, 33; transport of, 50
Spanish Navy. *See* Navy Nationalists; Navy, Spanish; Navy, Spanish Republican
Spanish-American Squadron. *See* LaCalle Squadron
Spanish-American War, 41
Special Staff W (German), 57, 71
Sperrle, Hugo von, 70, 83, 147, 149
Sperry S-1 bombsight, 24
Spirit of St. Louis, 12
St. Mihiel Offensive, 11, 16, 29

Stalin, Josef, 130, 182, 240; purges of: 148–49, 165, 176–77, 190–91, 238, 243; support for Republic, 51, 69–71, 219
Stari Bolshevik (Soviet Union), 69
Stashevsky, Artur, 71, 148
State, U.S. Department of, 78, 104–5, 122–23, 242
Stern, Moishe (pseud. Kléber), 83
Stimson, Henry, 103, 231
Straits of Gibraltar: aerial combat over, 49; airlift across, 57–58, 62; convoy across, 233; patrolled by Republican Navy, 38, 50, 59
strategic bombing, 13–14, 19, 187, 189; belief and skepticism of, 13; critique of, 20–21; in *Command of the Air* (Douhet), 195; in SCW, 1, 139, 210–12, 237; not tested in Spain, 239; support for, 14, 19, 22; theory debated, 166–70; U.S. priority of, 230
Sullivan, Brian R., 188–89
Swierczewski, Karol (pseud. Walter), 146

Tablada Airfield, 57
tactics, 115–16, 140–2
Tagueña, Manuel, 205, 207, 209
tail-spinning, 5
tanks/tankettes: 138, 219; Ansaldo tankettes: 68, 95; in Northern Territory, 144; operations of, 84, 87, 97–99, 135, 145–46, 205; T-26 tanks, 72
Tarazona, Francisco, 174, 222
Tarragona, 88, 175, 220
Task Force, 1 (Nat. Spain), 127
Taylor, Charles, 6
technological determinism, 179–81
technology, history of, 178–82
Teruel (town), 154, 158–60, 172
Teruel, Battle of: 159–61, 164, 171, 186; air superiority in, 239; antiaircraft defense in, 202; government demoralized by: 165

Tetuán, Morocco, 39, 42, 60
Thaelmann Battalion, 84, 97
Theory of the Leisure Class (Veblen), 179
Thomas, Hugh: on force size estimates, 37; on Franco, 42; on Northern Campaign, 149; on Prieto, 66–67; on Romerales Quinto, 35; on violence after elections, 34
Time, 28, 216
Tinker, Frank G., 74, 99, 108–10, 124, 234; as "Francisco Gomez Trejo", 109; assigned to Kosokov squadron, 118; combat experience of, 111–12, 119, 135; death of, 240–41; earns first victory, 113; leaves Spain, 120; on I-15s, 73; on I-16 machine guns, 198–99; on Miaja, 113–14; on Nieuports, 47–48; on other mercenaries, 106; *Some Still Live*, 108, 122; visits Madrid, 112
Toledo, 67–68, 95
Tomás, Belarmino, 146–47
Torrijos, 67–68
Tourist Group Union (Reisegesellschaft Union) (Germany), 58
Trenchard, Hugh, 13–16
Trijueque, 96–98, 113
TsKB-29, 191
Tukhachevsky, Mikhail, 148
Tupolev, Andrei Nikolayevich, 182, 191–92
Turia Corps (Nat. Spain), 172

U.S. Air Services, 139, 167–68, 235–36
Unión Militar Española (UME) (Spain), 77
unity of command, 68, 127
unity of effort, 232
University City (Madrid), 79–80
Uritsky, Semon R., 71
Usaramo (Germany), 58

Valdés, Luis, 135
Valencia: 34, 86, 93, 124, 132, 158, 162, 196, 202; air battle over, 174;

antiaircraft defense of, 202; Baumler hospitalized in, 120; bombing impact upon, 211–12; bombing of, 131, 175, 239; fly-over parade at, 92; government flees to, 76–78; government in, 101, 148; Griffiss assigned to, 85, 89, 94, 131, 153–54; mercenaries sent to, 107; Nationalist objective, 170–72, 219, 222; Nationalists capture, 226; Republican control of, 36; Selles's life in, 119; threatened by capture, 204
Valencia Road, 87, 112
Valle, Giuseppe, 189
Varela, José, 67, 79, 83, 170–71
Vázquez Sagastizábal, Manuel, 223
Veblen, Thorstein, 179
Vega, Etelvino, 205
Versailles Treaty, 182–83
Vesna, Operation, 191
Vickers machine gun, 47–48, 196
Villa, Francisco "Pancho," 10
Vinaròs, 162, 164
Vincent, Jesse, 11
Vita (Spain), 241
Volkmann, Helmuth, 149
VVS (Soviet Union), 243

Waite, Sumner, 85, 107
War Department (Spain), 45
War of the Worlds (broadcast) (Welles), 215–17
War of the Worlds (novel) (Wells), 216
War, U.S. Department of, 32, 167, 229, 251; contract with Langley, 4; orders Fuqua to Valencia, 78; plan for air inventory, 169–70; Tinker contacts, 122–23; utilized Griffiss's reports, 252
Way, Charles, 202–3
Welles, Orson, 216
Wells, H.G. 216

Wendelin, Eric, 79, 124
Westover, Oscar "Tubby," 32, 213
When You Go to Hawaii, You Will Need This Guide to the Islands (Griffiss), 32
White, Thomas, 32
Wilberg, Helmuth, 57
Williams, Samuel Rily, 64
Wilson, Woodrow, 10
Wing, 1st, 213
Winged Defense (Mitchell), 18
Winged Shield, Winged Sword (Nalty), 180
wing-warping, 5
Wood, Edward Frederick Lindley (Lord Halifax), 164
Wood, O.S., 81
Woodman, Harry, 197
World War I (WWI): 19, 59, 82, 110, 146 149, 172, 197, 218; air tactics of, 93; airpower during, 9–10, 13; antiaircraft artillery during, 201; comparison with SCW, 233; consequences of, 182; departure from U.S. policy, 103; Lafayette Escadrille in, 105; Spanish neutrality during, 44; U.S. entry into, 10
World War II (WWII): 153, 227–28, 235; airpower in, 1, 14, 186; SCW relevance to, 238–44
Wright Brothers, 4–8, 9, 182
Wright Cyclone engine, 23, 73, 74, 193
Wright Flyer, 8–9, 44, 240
Wright, Orville, 4, 6, 8–9, 16, 240
Wright, Wilbur, 4–6, 44

Xylinder, Rudolf, 200–1
XYZ Line, 172, 174, 176, 205, 226

Yagüe, Juan, 63, 66, 67
Yashukin, Mikhail, 135

ABOUT THE AUTHOR

Christopher G. Marquis is a retired U.S. Air Force officer. He received an MA in history from Auburn University. He works as a contract administrator for Northrop Grumman. Marquis lives in West Melbourne, Florida, with his wife and five children.

The Naval Institute Press is the book-publishing arm of the U.S. Naval Institute, a private, nonprofit, membership society for sea service professionals and others who share an interest in naval and maritime affairs. Established in 1873 at the U.S. Naval Academy in Annapolis, Maryland, where its offices remain today, the Naval Institute has members worldwide.

Members of the Naval Institute support the education programs of the society and receive the influential monthly magazine *Proceedings* or the colorful bimonthly magazine *Naval History* and discounts on fine nautical prints and on ship and aircraft photos. They also have access to the transcripts of the Institute's Oral History Program and get discounted admission to any of the Institute-sponsored seminars offered around the country.

The Naval Institute's book-publishing program, begun in 1898 with basic guides to naval practices, has broadened its scope to include books of more general interest. Now the Naval Institute Press publishes about seventy titles each year, ranging from how-to books on boating and navigation to battle histories, biographies, ship and aircraft guides, and novels. Institute members receive significant discounts on the Press' more than eight hundred books in print.

Full-time students are eligible for special half-price membership rates. Life memberships are also available.

For more information about Naval Institute Press books that are currently available, visit www.usni.org/press/books. To learn about joining the U.S. Naval Institute, please write to:

Member Services
U.S. Naval Institute
291 Wood Road
Annapolis, MD 21402-5034
Telephone: (800) 233-8764
Fax: (410) 571-1703
Web address: www.usni.org

www.ingramcontent.com/pod-product-compliance
Lightning Source LLC
Jackson TN
JSHW020221081025
92228JS00001B/2